MONEY
POSSESSIONS
A N D
ETERNITY

RANDY C. ALCORN

Tyndale House
Publishers, Inc.
Wheaton, Illinois

Front cover photo © Craig Aurness/WEST LIGHT

All Scripture references, unless otherwise
noted, are from *The Holy Bible,* New International Version, copyright 1973, 1978, 1984 by
the International Bible Society. Used by per-
mission of Zondervan Bible Publishers.

Library of Congress Catalog Card Number 89-50622
ISBN 0-8423-8731-5
Copyright 1989 by Randy C. Alcorn
All rights reserved
Printed in the United States of America

02   01   00
12   11   10   9   8

To my precious daughters,
Karina Elizabeth Alcorn
and
Angela Marie Alcorn
with the prayer and expectation
that your dreams will not be the fleeting dreams
of a materialistic culture,
but the eternal dreams
of the Risen Christ

CONTENTS

PREFACE

PART FOUR
HANDLING OUR MONEY
AND POSSESSIONS

PREFACE

The man of pseudo faith will fight for his verbal creed but refuse flatly to allow himself to get into a predicament where his future must depend upon that creed being true. He always provides himself with secondary ways of escape so he will have a way out if the roof caves in. What we need very badly these days is a company of Christians who are prepared to trust God as completely now as they know they must do at the last day.
A. W. Tozer

This book trespasses on enemy territory. It invades the turf of a powerful adversary, attempting to cross a war zone laced with mines. It seeks to recover strategic territory that rightly belongs to the true King.

Satan is the Lord of Materialism. "Mammon" is but an alias of the Prince of Darkness, who has vested interests in whether or not we understand and obey Christ's commands concerning our money and possessions. The Enemy will not give ground without a fight. Because of the spiritual warfare that surrounds this great subject of money and possessions, if this book is to be read with eternal benefit, it must be read with prayer. Our use of money and possessions is a decisive statement of our eternal values. What we do with our money loudly affirms which kingdom we belong to. Whenever we give of our resources to further God's kingdom, we cast a ballot for Christ and against Satan, for heaven and against hell. Whenever we use them selfishly and indifferently we do the opposite.

The key to a right use of money and possessions is a right perspective—an *eternal* perspective. Each of our lives is positioned like a bow, drawn across the strings of a cosmic violin, producing vibrations that resound for all eternity. The slightest action of the bow produces a sound, a sound that is never lost. What I do today has tremendous bearing on eternity. Indeed, it is the stuff of which eternity is made. The everyday choices I make regarding money and possessions are of eternal consequence.

The game becomes more serious only as the stakes are raised—or when we begin to realize how high they actually are. Large segments of modern evangelicalism have succumbed to the heresy that this present life may be lived selfishly and disobediently without serious effects on the eternal state. Never have so many Christians believed the lie that our money and possessions are ours to do with as we please. Never have so many thought that as long as we affirm with our lips a certain doctrinal statement, we may live our lives in indifference to human need and divine command, and all will turn out well in the end.

There is something in this book to offend everyone. Some of it offends me, and I wrote it. Please understand that it is not my intention to insult or irritate anyone. Any offenses are simply the by-product of trying to be faithful to the principles of Scripture—which have an annoying tendency to take issue with the way we prefer to think and live.

I have undoubtedly erred in some of my conclusions. I ask the reader to examine carefully the hundreds of Scripture passages cited to discern where those errors may be. We can shine a flashlight on a sundial at night and make it tell any time we want. Only the sun tells the true time. The flashlight is the changing and fleeting opinions of men, the sun the eternal Word of God.

God's Word is grain; man's is straw. His Word is the fire that consumes and the hammer that breaks (Jer. 23:28-29). This book should be judged not in the light of prevailing opinion, but in the light of God's Word. A. W. Tozer used to say, "Listen to no man who has not listened to God." To the degree that my words do not match up to the Scriptures, they are utterly worthless. To the degree that they stand up under the scrutiny of God's Word, they should be taken seriously.

In a time of uncertainty and misplaced values in ancient Israel, we are told there were two hundred "men of Issachar, who understood the times and knew what Israel should do" (1 Chron. 12:32). These men are said to have had "all their relatives under their command." My prayer is that this book would be used of God to develop and assist such people. In the midst of material confusion, self-centeredness, and eroded values, may God raise up an army of those who understand the times and know what the people of God should do with their money and possessions. Like the men of Issachar, may we lead our families and our churches in adopting these values and living lives that will count for eternity.

I want to express my deepest thanks to some special people who significantly influenced this book. First, Wendell Hawley, Ken Petersen, and Wightman Weese of Tyndale House, for their enthusiasm, kindness, and valuable assistance; Rod Morris, for years ago encouraging me to write on this subject; Larry Gadbaugh, for offering helpful suggestions on early drafts of this manuscript; Bruce Wilkinson, for his excellent insights on eternal rewards that helped strengthen chapters eight and nine.

Special thanks is due my wonderful wife, Nanci, my loyal partner in the adventure of living and giving. I also want to acknowledge our close friends, Alan and Theda Hlavka, Ron and Kathy Norquist, and Don and Pat Maxwell. These three couples have encouraged us with their love for Christ and their desire to glorify him with their money and possessions.

Finally, I offer my heartfelt thanks to my beloved Savior, Jesus Christ. He is the Audience of One, whose opinion of this book—and everything else—is the only one that ultimately matters.

PART I

THE CHALLENGE OF MONEY AND POSSESSIONS

CHAPTER 1

MONEY: WHY IS IT SO IMPORTANT TO GOD?

He who has God and everything has no more than he who has God alone. C. S. Lewis

Jesus Christ said more about money than about any other single thing because, when it comes to a man's real nature, money is of first importance. Money is an exact index to a man's true character. All through Scripture there is an intimate correlation between the development of a man's character and how he handles his money. Richard Halverson

Were I the Bible's editor, I would cut out much of what it says about money and possessions. Anyone can see it devotes a disproportionate amount of space to a subject of secondary importance. When it comes to money and possessions, the Bible is sometimes redundant, often extreme, and occasionally shocking. It turns many readers away, and, worse yet, tries to interfere with our lives and leaves us feeling guilty. Or, to avoid guilt feelings, it forces us to invent fancy interpretations so we can get around its plain meanings.

As it stands, these large portions of Scripture have little appeal to sophisticated people (such as us) in an advanced culture (such as ours). In fact, if the Bible were written today and was judged by what it says about money and possessions, it would never get into print. Even if it did, it would be mercilessly censured by its reviewers and never see a second printing.

And after all, we come to the Bible for comfort—not for a lecture on finances. If we want to know about money, we can go to the newspaper's business section, subscribe to the *Wall Street Journal* or read one of the finance magazines, *Fortune, Forbes,* or *Money.* Scripture should concern itself with the spiritual and heavenly. Money is physical and earthly. The Bible is religious; money is secular. Let God talk about love and grace and brotherhood, thank you. Let the rest of us talk about money and possessions.

For serious Christians some hard questions are in order here. How *could* the Bible's Author and Editor justify devoting twice as many verses to money than to faith and prayer combined? And how could Jesus say more about money than both heaven and hell? Didn't he know what was really important?

Some years ago, I planned a three-week sermon series on money. I began by compiling just a cross section of biblical passages on the subject. I spent weeks on it. Every passage led to another, and to another, and another. By the time I was done, I had before me a full-fledged book, a book from within a Book. This book had a staggering amount to say about money, how we are to view it, and what we are to do with it. If ever I became convinced that God cares a great deal about our money—a great deal more than most of us imagine—it was then.

I shook my head as I realized the three messages I had allotted to money could explore no more than a thimbleful of a vast ocean of truth. The sheer enormity of Scripture's teaching on this subject screams for our attention. And the haunting and immensely important question is, why? Why does God give us all this instruction on money and possessions? What is the point? With so much to be said, so much he could tell us that we really need and want to know, why did the Savior of the world spend a full 15 percent of his recorded words on this one subject? Why did he say more about how we are to view and handle money and possessions than about any other single thing? Why?

MONEY AND CONVERSION

The enigma deepens when we look at how closely Jesus linked money to salvation itself. When Zaccheus said he would give half his money to the poor and pay back four times over those he had cheated, Jesus did not merely say, "Good idea." He said, "Today salvation has come to this house" (Luke 19:9). This is amazing. Jesus judged the reality of this man's salvation based on his willingness, no, his cheerful *eagerness* to part with his money for the glory of God and the good of others.

Then there is the flip side of Zaccheus—the rich young ruler (Matt. 19:16-30; Luke 18:18-30). This earnest, decent, hardworking, young urban professional asked Jesus what good thing he could do to get eternal life. Jesus recited God's commandments, which the man said he had kept. Then the Lord delivered his bottom line: "Go, sell your possessions and give to the poor, and you will have treasure in heaven. Then come, follow me."

Were Jesus our student in a modern evangelism training seminar, we would raise our eyebrows, take him aside, and correct both his methodology and his theology. We would certainly handle the situation differently! First, we would probably commend the rich young ruler for his interest in spiritual things. Then we might tell him, "Just believe, that's all; ask God into your life—you don't really have to *do* anything."

When he said, "OK, I believe" (which he no doubt would have, since it had cost nothing), we would walk away duly impressed with our catch.

Think how blessed we would feel, knowing that God's kingdom was greatly enhanced by the conversion of this well-known influential wealthy man! Soon there would be articles and books all about him, and he would be on TV and radio talk shows. He would be put on boards, speak at rallies, and receive invitations to share his testimony in churches and

17

conferences all over the country, quite possibly making him into a *very* rich young ruler.

But bereft of our knowledge of how to close a conversion, Jesus struck a low blow that cost him a valuable convert: "Sell your possessions, give to the poor and follow me." That this was the wrong thing to say we might surmise by the results: "When the young man heard this, he went away sad, because he had great wealth."

After losing this potential follower, a man so sincere that he was grieved to turn away from Christ, Jesus explained to the disciples how hard it is for a rich man to enter the kingdom of God. Harder in fact than for a camel to go through a needle's eye (which, contrary to some modern interpretations, was no easier then than it is now). This statement left the disciples "greatly astonished" (Matt. 19:23-25). They simply did not understand the barrier wealth presents to genuine spiritual birth and growth. Neither, apparently, do we.

Notice that Jesus didn't tell the young man, "Give 10 percent to the poor." Neither did he say, "Set up a trust fund, keep the principal intact, and give the interest to the poor." The young man would have gladly done either of those. Jesus stopped him dead in his tracks by telling him to give up *everything* and follow him.

As we will see in a later chapter, Jesus did not and does not call all his disciples to liquidate their possessions, give away all their money, and pull up stakes to become traveling missionaries. But Jesus knew that *money* was the rich young man's god. He also knew that no man can enthrone the true God unless in the process he chooses to dethrone his other gods. If Christ is not Lord over a person's money and possessions, then he is simply not that person's Lord. Just as Jesus gauged Zaccheus's true spiritual condition by his willingness to part with his money, so he gauged the rich young ruler's true spiritual condition by his unwillingness to part with his money.

The principle is timeless—there is a powerful relationship between a person's true spiritual condition and his attitude and actions concerning money and possessions.

Zaccheus and the rich young ruler are not isolated cases. When his audience asked John the Baptist what they should do to bear the fruit of repentance, first he told them to share their clothes and food with the poor. Then he told the tax collectors not to collect and pocket extra money. And finally he told the soldiers not to extort money and to be content with their wages (Luke 3:7-14). In all three cases, the conclusive proof of a spiritual change was an altered perspective on the handling of money and possessions.

The reality of the spiritual conversions of the Ephesian occultists was demonstrated by their willingness to burn their magic books, worth the vast sum of 50,000 days' wages (Acts 19:18-20). And the extent of the first Christians' transformation was most clearly evidenced in their willingness to surrender their money and possessions to meet each others' needs (Acts 2:44-45; 4:32-35).

To liquidate and disperse cheerfully the assets one had spent a lifetime accumulating was no more natural then than now. And that is the whole point. Conversion and the filling of the Holy Spirit were supernatural experiences that produced supernatural responses. While there was still the private ownership of property, the joyful giving and sharing of this property became the new "norm" of supernatural living.

If a first-century Christian were to visit us today and gauge *our* spiritual condition by our attitudes and actions regarding money and possessions, to what conclusions would he come?

A POOR WOMAN AND A RICH MAN

Just for a few moments, play the role of financial counselor. Today you have two appointments, first with an elderly woman and then a middle-aged man.

The woman's husband died six years ago. She has this to say: "I'm down to my last two dollars. I have no more money, the cupboards are bare, and this two dollars is all I have to live on. Yet I feel like I should put the whole two dollars in the church offering. What do you think?"

What *do* you think? What would you tell her? (Don't read on till you think about it.) Perhaps you would say something like this: "That's very generous of you, dear, but remember that God gave you common sense and wants you to take care of yourself. He knows you have to eat. And he knows your heart, that you *want* to give. I'm sure God would have you keep that two dollars and buy some food for tomorrow. He wants your needs to be met, and you can't expect him just to send down food from heaven if you give up the little money he's already provided, now can you? After all, God wants us to do the sensible and responsible thing."

Your next appointment is with a successful, hard-working, middle-aged farmer whose crop production has been excellent the last several years. He tells you, "I'm planning on tearing down my old barns to build bigger ones so I can store up crops and goods and have plenty saved up for the future. Then I can take it easy, retire early, maybe do some traveling and have a good time. What do you think?"

What's your answer? Maybe something like this:

"Sounds good to me! You've worked hard; the Lord's blessed you with good crops. It's your business, your crops, and your money. If you can save up enough to take care of yourself the rest of your life, by all means go for it. I wish I were in a position to do the same!"

Doesn't our advice to this poor widow and this rich man seem reasonable enough? Would you say anything differently? What would *God* say? In this case we need not speculate—Scripture tells us exactly what he says.

In Mark 12 we meet a poor widow. She put in the temple offering box two tiny copper coins, worth a fraction of a penny. This was the only money she had. Jesus called his disciples together to teach them a lesson from the woman. Did he question the wisdom of her actions? Did he say she should have been more sensible than to surrender her only remaining resources? No, he gave her an unqualified commendation for her choice: "I tell you the truth, this poor widow has put more into the treasury than all the others. They all gave out of their wealth; but she, out of her poverty, put in everything—all she had to live on."

Jesus regarded the woman as wise. He set her up as a model for his disciples to follow. He enshrined her example in the Word of God that all believers in future generations might emulate her faith, commitment, and sacrificial generosity.

In Luke 12 we meet a rich man. We are not told that he gained his wealth dishonestly, that he exploited others, or that he was irreligious. More than likely, he attended synagogue weekly, visited the temple three times a year, tithed, and prayed, as most Jews did. He has every appearance of a man who worked diligently to build his business. Now, like any good businessman, he wanted to expand that business by building bigger barns. His purpose was to accumulate enough wealth to retire early, enjoy himself, and have a good time. Sounds like the American dream, doesn't it?

So what did God have to say to this man? "You fool! This very night your life will be demanded from you. Then who will get what you have prepared for yourself?"

Jesus added, "This is how it will be with anyone who stores up things for himself but is not rich toward God" (Luke 12:21).

By our standards, both outside *and* inside the church, the widow's actions seem unwise, the rich man's wise. But God, who knows the hearts of both and sees through the eyes of eternity, elevates the poor woman as eternally wise and the rich man as eternally foolish.

If this surprising evaluation does nothing else, it should certainly capture our attention, for it shows that our standards of wisdom about money are not only radically different from God's but diametrically opposed to them.

If we take these passages seriously, realizing they were written for us today, we must ask ourselves some probing questions. Who is more frequently featured in Christian magazines and talk shows—poor widows or rich fools? Who receives the most respect and attention in Christian organizations? Who is most highly esteemed in churches? Who serves on our boards and determines our direction? Does the church have a scarcity of poor widows and a surplus of rich fools? If so, does this explain the moral and spiritual erosion so evident in the Christian community?

THE STORY MONEY TELLS

A study of Zaccheus, the rich young ruler, the poor widow, the rich fool, and many other biblical passages raises many questions but answers many more. We come to understand that our perspective on and handling of money is a litmus test of our true character. It is an index of our spiritual life. Our stewardship of money tells a deep and consequential story. It forms our biography. In a sense, how we relate to money and possessions is the story of our lives.

If this is true of all men in all ages, does it not have special application to us who live in a time and place of unparalleled affluence? To us who live in a society where almost the entire populace enjoys daily comforts and conveniences that King Solomon never dreamed of? Where even the poverty level exceeds the average standard of living of virtually every other society in human history, past or present?

Take a man or woman who works from age twenty-five to sixty-five and makes $15,000 a year. We will not consider the value of benefits provided, interest earned, pay raises, or other possible sources of income, such as inheritance or Social Security. Even without all these extras, in his lifetime this person of modest income by our standards will handle well over half a million dollars. He will manage a fortune. And if Scripture is true, and men must give an account of their lives to God (Rom. 14:12; 2 Cor. 5:10), then one day this man must answer these questions: Where did it all go? What did I spend it on? What has been accomplished for eternity through my use of all this wealth?

In the account of the poor widow, Mark wrote, "Jesus sat down opposite the place where the offerings were put and watched the crowd putting their money into the temple treasury" (Mark 12:41). Notice we are not told, "Jesus happened to see . . ." No, it seems he deliberately *watched* to observe what people were giving.

Picture the scene. How close was Jesus to the offering box? Close enough to see that some people put in large amounts. Close enough even to see two tiny coins in a shriveled old hand and to identify them as copper (Mark 12:41-42).

Jesus was interested enough in who was giving what to make an immediate object lesson to the disciples about the true nature of trusting God as demonstrated in sacrificial financial giving (Mark 12:43-44).

If we stop to think about it, this passage makes all of us who suppose that what we do with our money is our business and only our business feel terribly uncomfortable. On the contrary, it is painfully apparent that it is *God's* business—that God makes it his business. He does not apologize for watching with intense interest what we do with the money he has entrusted to us. If we use our imaginations, we might even peer into the invisible realm to see him gathering some of his subjects together this very moment. Perhaps you can hear him using *your* handling of finances as an object lesson.

The question is, what kind of lesson?

GETTING CLOSE TO HOME

Does the incessant call to put Christ before all, deny ourselves, take up our cross and follow him (Matt. 10:38; Mark 8:34; Luke 14:27) have some bearing on us today? Can we indeed put Christ before all, deny ourselves, take up our crosses and follow him, with no apparent effect on what we do with our money and possessions?

What are we to think of all the current teaching on money and possessions that emphasizes what *doesn't* apply to us? We are assured by confident voices that the Old Testament practice of tithing doesn't apply to us, that the New Testament practice of sacrificial giving by liquidating assets and giving to the poor doesn't apply to us, that the biblical prohibitions of interest and the restriction of debt don't apply to us, that the commands not to hoard and stockpile assets don't apply to us and so on and so on. At some point we must ask, "Then what in the world *does* apply to us?"

Sometimes more is to be learned from the passages of Scripture we avoid or skim over than those we underline or post on our refrigerator. The Bible contains an arsenal of such verses on the subject of money and possessions, and they just keep firing away at us. No wonder C. S. Lewis called God "The Transcendental Interferer." He has this annoying habit of stepping into our lives even when we have pulled in the welcome mat and bolted the door. God can throw a great party but he also knows how to ruin one.

The more we allow ourselves to grapple with these unsettling passages, the more we are pierced. Jesus wounds us with his words about money. Then, just when we think we will heal, we run into another passage, and Christ reaches out from it and picks the scab. Our only options, it seems, are to let him wound and pick at us until he accomplishes what he wishes, *or* to avoid his words and his gaze and his presence altogether by staying away from his Word. The latter option is easier in the short run. But no true disciple can really be content with it.

By now some readers are long gone and others who remain are uncomfortable. I must admit that I share your discomfort. You may even be thinking, "I'd rather not deal with these issues; I'm content doing what I'm doing." But are you *really* content? Are any of us who know Christ, who have his Spirit within, really content when we haven't fully considered his words? When we haven't completely opened ourselves to what he has for us? Comfortable, perhaps. Complacent, certainly. But not content.

I, for one, hate to live with that nagging feeling deep inside that when Jesus called people to follow him he had more in mind than I'm experiencing. I don't want to miss out on what he has for me. If he has really touched your life, I don't think you do either.

The fear of dealing with what God expects me to do with my money is exceeded by the fear of not dealing with it. I don't want to stand before him one day and try to give an answer for how I could call myself a disciple without ever coming to grips with the issue of money and possessions. Even a cursory reading of the New Testament shows this issue to be right at the heart of discipleship.

I might feel a little better trying to squirm out of responsibility for some minor or obscure teaching of Scripture. "I just didn't understand it, Lord. It was unclear. You really didn't give us much to go on." But I can't help but feel that if I plead ignorance in this area of money and possessions, God is liable to say to me, "I spent a large part of the Bible teaching you about money and possessions—what more would you have wanted me to say than what I said? Was your problem that these passages were unclear . . . or that they were *too* clear?"

Yet, for all these sobering implications, I must quickly add that for me the process of discovering God's will about money and possessions, rather than being burdensome, has been tremendously liberating. My own growth and enlightenment in financial stewardship has closely paralleled my overall spiritual growth. In fact, it has *propelled* it. I have learned more about faith, trust, grace, commitment, God's provision and other basics of the Christian life in this area than in any other.

I have also learned why Paul said, "God loves a cheerful giver," and I have found that a cheerful giver loves God, and loves him more deeply each time he gives. To me, one of the few experiences comparable to the joy of leading someone to Christ is the joy of making wise and generous choices with my money and possessions. Both are supreme acts of worship. Both are what we were made for.

I write this book not as a critic or crusader but as an excited learner. I feel like a child who has found a wonderful trail hidden in the woods—a trail that countless others have blazed, but one which seems to the child to be as new and fresh as if it had never before existed. Such a child is invariably anxious for others to join him in a great adventure. The exhilaration of this adventure is impossible to describe. It can only be experienced. Those readers who have already begun the journey will readily understand what I am saying.

My hope is that even if you have come to this book as a spectator, you will leave it a participant. I pray that you will join a multitude of God's people, past and present, in not just talking about but living out the grace of Jesus Christ in the realm of money and possessions.

WHAT THIS BOOK IS ABOUT

As you have probably discerned already, I am not a financial counselor by profession, and this is not a typical book on money.

I am a pastor. My background is not in economics, investments, or accounting. My background is in biblical studies, theology, teaching, and counseling. I am writing this book because the Bible, my interactions with others, and my personal experience all speak with one voice in affirming something profound and revolutionary. They substantiate what the greatest Theologian, Teacher, and Counselor knew only too well—that the issue of money and possessions lies at the very heart of the Christian life.

How we view our money and possessions is of the utmost importance. What we do with our money will (and I choose these words deliberately) influence the very course of eternity.

To understand the truth about money and possessions, to

understand life at all, we simply must understand the true nature of earth and heaven. We must clearly behold these two kingdoms with their two kings, two citizenries, and two treasuries. If we don't see this we are destined, at best, to a superficial or even token religious experience. If we *do* see, the door is unlocked to the exhilarating realm of Christian discipleship, where "following Christ" is not a comforting but meaningless buzzword, but an electrifying, life-changing reality.

This book won't tell you how to achieve all your financial goals. But it *will* provide the light in which your financial goals should be set. It will lay the foundation on which they should be built. And it will set forth the principles that should govern your efforts to achieve those goals.

I must confess, I'm a little leery of the endless number of books that tell us how to accomplish our financial goals. Such advice is valuable only if those goals are right goals, only if they are biblically based and Christ-centered. Much financial counsel, from secular and sometimes even Christian sources, serves the same purpose as instruction on how to maneuver a canoe that is heading toward a waterfall. It is important not just to know how to get a canoe down the river but to know where that river is taking you.

Before we learn the fine art of building a sturdy boat or the skill of staying in the boat as we head down the rapids, we would do well to make certain that our desired destination is really downstream rather than upstream. For if it is upstream, we would do better to get off the river altogether, forget the boat, and plot our course by land. It may be a harder trip, but then isn't arriving at the right destination the whole point of the trip in the first place?

I believe most of what we talk about today concerning finances is on the very fringes, light years from the core of the whole issue. We focus on things that belong at the tail end of stewardship discussions, not the beginning. We can't get up on the roof and install the gutters or television antenna before we lay the foundation and start the framing. We must realize that many of the things our society considers at the heart of financial planning today (insurance, the stock market, and retirement, for instance) literally did not exist in Jesus' world. Indeed, they do not exist through much of the world even today. This doesn't mean they are wrong, of course—only that they are secondary.

A friend who edits a Christian magazine in Kenya told me that though the Bible has a great deal to say to his readers, most financial material coming from America, Christian as well as secular, is irrelevant to them. Because so much of our economic structure is exclusive to our isolated segment of twentieth-century Western civilization, we can talk all day about what we consider the great financial issues without ever touching upon what the Bible considers the great financial issues.

As a pastor, teacher, and counselor, my interactions with others—as well as my observations of my own tendencies—have convinced me that in the Christian community today there is more blindness, rationalization, and unclear thinking about money than anything else.

"Do not conform any longer to the pattern of this world, but be transformed by the renewing of your mind" (Rom. 12:2). If we wish to think about money and possessions as the world thinks, we need do absolutely nothing. Conformity is as natural as swimming downstream. But if we wish to think about money and possessions as *God* does, it is quite a different matter. The transformation required for such a thing simply can't be gained from the *Wall Street Journal* or *USA Today*. The one exclusive source that will give us God's perspective on money is his revealed Word.

Bookshelves and magazine racks are filled with advice on how to make, spend, and invest our money. I believe we need to set these guides aside, some of them permanently, but all of them long enough to blow the dust off the Bible. It is the one book worthy of the title a popular financial counselor has given his own: *The Only Investment Guide You'll Ever Need*.

To build that foundation we referred to, we need to understand what money really is (it is more than coins and currency), to whom it belongs, how God views it, and its potential use for the two different kingdoms. That is what this book is about.

You may be surprised to find that several chapters don't deal exclusively with money but with the larger issue of what eternity holds for us and how that in turn relates to our money. I believe this is the primary missing ingredient in most Christian books on finances. When we look at money only as money, and not in light of its impact on all eternity, we walk away with a cloudy and shortsighted vision resulting in cloudy and shortsighted financial decisions and life-styles.

This is why the central focus of this book is not on insurance as much as assurance, not securities but Security, not trusts but Trust, not principal but Principles, not real estate but Real Estate. You will not find in these pages "net worth" calculations, but you will see how God measures your life's worth on another basis. You will not learn here about the dangers of our enemy, inflation, but instead the tactics of a much truer Enemy of financial stewardship.

You won't find in this book advice about tax planning, where to put your IRA, or whether to buy term insurance or whole life. There is a place for such issues—at this point I should say there *may* be a place for them—but only after a close and careful look at what God has to say about money.

In these pages you won't find budget sheets, expenditure lists, a blueprint for a food cellar, or telephone numbers to place an order for gold bullion. But you *will* find many practical things that relate directly to biblical principles. These include such varied areas as transferring ownership to God, choosing a strategic life-style, evaluating ministry fund-raising techniques, and examining the Christian's role in multilevel sales.

You will find an analysis of religious materialism and the scandals it is creating, and the Christian prosperity doctrine, the health and wealth gospel that has been so widely adopted. We will ask the question of whether capitalism is more or less Christian than socialism, what Scripture says about private property, how we can really help the poor and reach the lost with our money, whether tithing is for us today, and how much and to whom the Bible calls us to give.

We will see what the Bible says about lending and borrowing, and explore the alarming philosophy that often underlies our going into debt. We will look at the implications of credit card use for the Christian and mortgage debts for churches. We will address true contentment and how to keep needs in focus in an economy based on wants. We will see how advertising preys upon greed and contributes to much of our material confusion. And we will uncover some of the most persistent spending myths that allow us to rationalize poor financial stewardship.

We will discuss the importance of wise counsel, whether it is right to have certain kinds of insurance, and if it is appropriate for Christians to risk money in investments. We will examine the difference between Scripture's injunctions to save and its warnings against stockpiling. We will also look at the stewardship of our money and possessions at death—what should we leave to our children and what shouldn't we? And speaking of our children, how can we raise them to see things as instruments of eternity's values rather than substitutes for them? What practical steps can we parents take to raise wise and generous financial stewards, rather than grabby materialists? All along, we will try to examine these things under the bright sun of our eternal futures, not the fading penlight of the present.

In our pursuit of the biblical truth about money, we will repeatedly come back to the practicalities of the present. But hopefully we will come back armed with solidly forged convictions that will help us take the tough steps of true discipleship and experience its incomparable and *eternal* rewards.

CONCLUSION

As we move together through the exciting issues ahead of us, may we determine not to be rich fools disguised as disciples. Instead, may we commit ourselves to developing the heart of the poor widow, learning to put boldly all our resources at God's disposal, as he has put all his resources at ours.

May we learn together in these pages the truth Martin Luther recognized when he said that for each of us there must be not only the conversion of the heart and mind but also the conversion of the purse.

CHAPTER 2

THE WEAKNESS OF ASCETICISM

If silver and gold are things evil in themselves, then those who keep away from them deserve to be praised. But if they are good creatures of God, which we can use both for the needs of our neighbor and for the glory of God, is not a person silly, yes, even unthankful to God, if he refrains from them as if they were evil?
Martin Luther

Away, then, with that inhuman philosophy which, while conceding only a necessary use of creatures, not only malignantly deprives us of the lawful fruit of God's beneficence but cannot be practiced unless it robs a man of all his senses and degrades him to a block. John Calvin

At times I crave an audible voice from heaven telling me exactly what I'm supposed to do with my money and possessions. Do

31

you know the feeling? Philip Yancey perfectly expresses my own dilemma when it comes to money:

> Many Christians have one issue that haunts them and never falls silent: for some, it involves sexual identity; for others, a permanent battle against doubt. For me, the issue is money. It hangs over me, keeping me off balance, restless, uncomfortable, nervous.
>
> I feel pulled in opposite directions over the money issue. Sometimes I want to sell all that I own, join a Christian commune, and live out my days in intentional poverty. At other times, I want to rid myself of guilt and enjoy the fruits of our nation's prosperity. Mostly, I wish I did not have to think about money at all. But I must somehow come to terms with the Bible's very strong statements about money.[1]

God gives us principles in his Word, principles that will change our thinking and our lives if we believe them. Yet we are still left with a lot of latitude, which raises a lot of questions. In light of global needs and the tendency to be distracted from the things of God, what should I possess? Should I own a house? A car? Two cars? If so, what kind of house or car? Is it all right to own a nice suit? Can I own one, but not two or three? How many pairs of shoes is too many? Is it all right to golf once in a while but too extravagant to belong to a club? Can I go out for dinner? If so, where and how often? Should I take a vacation that costs two hundred dollars but not one that costs two thousand? How can I be sure I'm pleasing God in my financial decisions?

Materialism is money-centered and thing-centered rather than God-centered, and has no place in the Christian life. But is there an opposite extreme? Can the pendulum swing away from materialism and go too far the other direction? I believe the answer is yes. That other extreme is asceticism. Asceticism is a way of thinking that sees money and things as evil. To the ascetic, the less you own, the more spiritual you are. If something isn't strictly essential, you shouldn't have it.

Materialism and asceticism are rooted in equally wrong views of money and possessions. In subsequent chapters, we will take a close look at materialism, including materialism in the church.

In this chapter we will consider the question of whether money is evil or good, then examine asceticism in light of history and Scripture.

UNDERSTANDING THE NATURE OF MONEY

If we are to understand our proper relationship to money, we must first understand what money really is.

Money is more than just metal disks or colored paper. It is a tool that simplifies trade. The farmer needs lumber more than beef, milk, and eggs, of which he has plenty. The lumberman needs beef, milk, and eggs more than one of his many stacks of boards. By trading their goods, both get what they want, and both walk away happy.

But money is a tool that can expedite such a trade and widen its circles to include others. Rather than trading two pigs for a plough and three sacks of grain, one man can give another the agreed-upon worth of the two pigs in the form of money. This saves time and energy—who wants to carry pigs and ploughs around everywhere he goes?

God encouraged the people of Israel to take advantage of money's convenience. He told them that if their place of worship was too far from their homes, they should exchange the tithes of their crops and livestock for silver, then convert it back to the goods of their choice once they arrived (Deut. 14:24-26).

Money allows much more flexibility than a direct exchange of goods. If I get fifty dollars for my pigs, I can use the money to buy the exact plough I want, two sacks of grain instead of three, or whatever I prefer and can afford. Instead of grain, I can buy coffee, a saddle, a lamp, or some books.

Money, then, is one person's promise of goods or services, which he grants in return for actual goods or services. In a sense, money is no more than a universally recognized IOU. Realizing its convenience, people consent to participate in an economic system in which money is the transferable object that makes it all possible. Of course, it is only the widespread participation of others in this same system that gives meaning to money. Without the mutual agreement that money means something, money means nothing.

Since money has no inherent value, but only ascribed value, money is not wealth. It merely symbolizes wealth. You can't eat money and you can't plough a field with it. You can use that $100 bill to light a cigar or wad up your gum but that is about it. Practically speaking, gold is much less valuable than some other metals. In and of itself, it is little more than a pretty paperweight or doorstop. Gold and coins and currency are only worth something in a society where other people have agreed to attach a certain value to them. That they do so is proven by their willingness to give goods and services in exchange for them.

Money is no more nor less than a pledge of assets, a means of payment, a medium of exchange, or an instrument of trade. It seems obvious, then, that there is no inherent good or evil about money—any more than there is inherent good or evil about the plough, pig, saddle, or sack of grain money represents. Seen in this light, money is neither moral nor immoral, but amoral. Puritan William Ames put it this way: "Riches . . . are morally neither good nor bad, but things indifferent which men may use either well or ill."[2]

THE TWO FACES OF MONEY

Money clearly has social and economic advantages and can be used for the betterment of people. As a plough is used for the good of honest labor, and a sack of grain used for the good of feeding a family, so money, which simply represents their value, can be used for good. If my neighbor's barn burns down, out of compassion I may give him grain. Or I may sell the grain and give him money instead to use as he wishes, perhaps to buy meat, lumber, or tools, which he may need more than grain. The grain and the money amount to the same thing, except that the money can be used for other goods besides grain.

Christian compassion can accomplish great good through the giving of grain or lumber or tools *or* the giving of money to alleviate suffering and meet needs. Money can be used to feed, clothe, and provide shelter for the homeless. It can provide for missionaries or build houses of worship. In this sense, money may appear to be good. But this is not really the case, for it is the *giver* who is doing good. People are moral or immoral, things are amoral. The money is an instrument of good, not good itself.

34

Money is no more responsible for the doing of good than a word processor is responsible for writing a book, or a baseball bat for hitting a home run.

On the other hand, money can be used to buy a slave, or a whip to be used on a slave. Money can be the motive for which a poor widow's land is foreclosed. Money can purchase sexual favors, bribe a judge, buy or sell cocaine. But note that in each case the evil resides in men, not in money, just as in the other cases the good resides in men, not in money.

Water is a gift of God, and used properly it gives life. But out of control, it may flood and drown and destroy. Fire is a gift of God. But out of control, it may bring horrible destruction and painful death. The greater a thing's potential for good when used rightly, the greater its potential for evil when used wrongly. So it is with money.

If this were a morally neutral world, we would expect money to be used in a morally neutral way. But the world is *not* neutral—it is sinful. And this is where the problem with money really lies. In a sinful world, money naturally becomes more than a neutral means of barter. It becomes an instrument of power. Power in the hands of sinful people is perverted into oppression. Money becomes an object of desire and worship, a false god. Sinful people, rejecting a God they do not wish to serve, serve themselves with the god of money. They ascribe to money the attributes of omnipotence and sovereignty. Money means control. I serve it, and in turn it serves me. "Money talks," while truth is bound and gagged.

Though there is nothing wrong with money, there is something desperately wrong with devotion to money: "People who want to get rich fall into temptation and a trap and into many foolish and harmful desires that plunge men into ruin and destruction. For the love of money is a root of all kinds of evil" (1 Tim. 6:9-10).

Given all the error, deception, and abuse that relates to money, Richard Foster argued forcefully that money is not neutral after all, but that it is "a 'power' that is demonic in character."[3] This appears to be an overstatement that leads logically to asceticism or even dualism (more about this later). Still, it is certainly true that money can be used for demonic purposes, and often is.

It is fair to conclude that if money can be used for either good or evil, and the one using it is more evil than good, it will most often be used for evil. But the problem is not the depravity of money. It is the depravity of man. Just as a useful shovel or hammer or fireplace poker becomes a murder weapon in the hands of a murderer, so useful money is a tool of evil in the hands of the evil—and so it will be until evil is no more.

USING MONEY FOR GOOD PURPOSES

Jesus said to his disciples, "I tell you, use worldly wealth to gain friends for yourselves, so that when it is gone, you will be welcomed into eternal dwellings" (Luke 16:9).

We will deal with the exact meaning of these words later, but for now the point is simply that Jesus tells us to do something good with "worldly wealth" (literally, "the mammon of unrighteousness"). It is as if he were saying, "Take this thing which is commonly used for evil and *you* use it for good. Look at this worn currency, smell in it the foul purposes for which it was used—perhaps to buy drugs or sex or injustice. It may have once been stolen, perhaps even killed for. But now that it is in *your* hands, use it wisely and well; use it for eternal purposes."

Jesus clearly said that we can and should use money for good purposes, both for this life and the next. As human hearts can be redeemed by Christ, in a sense, so can money. In the hands of the redeemed, under the Lordship of the Redeemer, money can serve redemptive purposes.

But lest we begin to think that money is not dangerous, Jesus said, "No servant can serve two masters. Either he will hate the one and love the other, or he will be devoted to the one and despise the other. You cannot serve both God and Money" (Luke 16:13).

While money is neutral, Money is not. Once we allow money lordship over our lives, it becomes Money. It jealously dethrones all else.

Now we come full circle, back to the issue of whether money is good or bad. Do you see the delicate balance of this whole passage? We are told, almost in the same breath, "Money (the mammon of unrighteousness) tends to be tainted and lends itself to abuse." "Money can be used for great and eternal good, and

God will reward you if you use it that way," and "Money can pull your heart away from God and become your Lord." The point is that money makes a good servant to those who have the right master, but it makes a terrible master itself.

To regard money as evil and thereby useless for purposes of righteousness is foolish and will end in poor stewardship. To regard it as good and therefore be undiscerning about its potential for spiritual disaster is equally foolish and will result in equally poor stewardship. Use it, Jesus said, but don't serve it.

The goal, then, is not that money be put to death, but that it be trained and handled with discipline, as a lion we are seeking to tame.

Money may be temporarily under my control. But I must always regard it as a wild beast, with power to turn on me and others if I drop my guard. Money must not call the shots. I may have plenty of money to buy a new car, but that is not the point, for I will not serve money. I serve God, so I will buy the car *only* if I sense his direction to do so.

Likewise, if I feel God's leading to go to the mission field or help a brother in need, I do not say, "No, there's no money, so I can't." That also would be serving money. God is my master, and money is at his disposal. I must first discern not what money says, but what God says. Money may be a factor, but it is never *the* factor. God, not money, is sovereign. Money—whether by presence or absence—must never rule my life.

Money is neither a disease nor a cure. It is what it is, nothing less and nothing more. Money may be well used or poorly used. But either way, how we use money is always of critical importance to our spiritual lives. It has lasting impact on two worlds, this one *and* the next.

TWO RESPONSES TO MONEY AND POSSESSIONS

There are, then, two equally incorrect beliefs about money. First, that it is automatically and always evil. Second, that it is automatically and always good. Both have the dubious advantage of all such unbalanced positions—they require no wisdom or discernment. Unfortunately, they also result in excesses that undermine rather than further kingdom purposes.

As stated earlier, the two extreme philosophies and life-styles that stem from these two incorrect beliefs about money are *asceticism* and *materialism*. Martin Luther compared humanity to a drunkard who falls off his horse to the right, only to get back on and fall off to the left. In the matter of money and possessions, asceticism is falling off the horse one way, materialism the other.

Before going further, I should clarify my use of the terms asceticism and ascetic. Others, including Eugene Peterson[4] and Dallas Willard[5], use these words in a positive way, linking them to the biblical spiritual disciplines, including meditation, prayer, and fasting. I fully agree with their emphasis on these spiritual disciplines and believe that the church desperately needs to revive them. What I am calling asceticism, following the term's most popular usage, is extreme, false, or dualistic asceticism. I will show what I mean by *ascetic,* and it is this meaning that is important, not the term itself, which can be legitimately used in a positive sense.

An ascetic, using our definition of the term, practices strict self-denial, depriving himself of all but the essential basics of the material world. Often asceticism is rooted in the philosophy of dualism. Dualism, championed by Plato among others, sees the spiritual, invisible world as good but the physical, visible world as evil.

It is easy to see why a dualist who values things spiritual and is consistent with his beliefs would be an ascetic. By avoiding physical pleasures and conveniences, he thinks he is avoiding sin. Ascetics in church history have denied themselves of nearly every possession and pleasure. St. Francis of Assisi objected to friars having books besides the Scriptures, since they were unnecessary. In contrast, Paul valued not only his Scriptures but also his other books and asked them to be brought to him in prison (2 Tim. 4:13). Francis taught that money should be shunned as the Devil himself. He and his disciples refused even to touch money. They glorified poverty and saw begging for food as a virtue, even a way of finding merit with God.

Many ascetics in church history refrained from marriage, and some who did marry even abstained from sexual relations with their spouses, believing that abstinence made them more spiritual. Others, misunderstanding Christ's words in Matthew 5:29-30 and 19:12, actually emasculated themselves to avoid the supposed evils of sex. Some literally beat their bodies; others spent most of their lives at the top of towers, seeking to avoid the defilements of the world.

SCRIPTURE AND ASCETICISM

The entire fabric of Old Testament teaching and Hebrew thought argues against dualism and, by inference and example, against extreme asceticism. There are not two gods, a god of the spiritual and a god of the physical. There is one God who is God of both. The same God created the spiritual *and* the physical worlds, and he created both for us to enjoy.

Except perhaps for one small sect, the Essenes, the Jews did not labor under the notion that the physical world was bad and that God was not in it. On the contrary, they saw material things as from the hand of God, a Father's loving supply for his children. Every time the earth produced, they saw God at work. He was the Lord of harvest, the Lord of life. As his grateful children, they celebrated national feasts to recognize and rejoice in his material provision (Deut. 16:15). These feasts were parties. By God's command a portion of the holy tithes were set aside to underwrite them (Deut. 14:22-27). The Israelites worshiped, fellowshiped, celebrated, and in the process—frivolous as it may sound—had a great deal of fun.

Similarly, the Jews saw sex as God's gift, to be shunned outside of marriage but thoroughly enjoyed within it (Prov. 5:18-19). The rabbi-turned-apostle Paul not only had to command the materialistic Corinthians to avoid immorality, but charge the ascetics in the church to stop overreacting to the problem of immorality by withholding themselves from sexual relations with their spouses (1 Cor. 7:3-5). Satan is the master of extremes, and he cares little which side of the horse we fall off. He cares only that we don't stay in the saddle.

Scripture portrays the material and the spiritual not as an either-or but a both-and proposition. The material must not take precedence over the spiritual. Nonetheless it is a necessary, legitimate, and rightly enjoyable part of our existence in this God-created material world.

Tim Hansel addressed the ascetic Christian's misreading of Scripture:

Irony of ironies, his commitment to Jesus Christ has become a prison rather than a blessing. So blinded by religious observations and reservations, he fails to see the festivity that was so central in the life of Jesus. He forgets that Jesus, despite the sad world he inhabited, was the prime host and the prime guest of the party. Jesus let himself be doused with perfume. He attended to wedding wine and wedding garments. The Bible is full of merriment. The feast outruns the fast. It is crammed with spitted kids and lambs and fatted calves, grapes, pomegranates, olives, dates, milk, and honey.[6]

In his first letter to Timothy, Paul warned his pastor friend that there will be those who "abandon the faith and follow deceiving spirits and things taught by demons" (1 Tim. 4:1). Those responsible for these teachings are described as "hypocritical liars, whose consciences have been seared as with a hot iron" (4:2). Paul issued a "wanted poster" on these theological criminals, and here is how he described them:

> They forbid people to marry and order them to abstain from certain foods, which God created to be received with thanksgiving by those who believe and who know the truth. For everything God created is good, and nothing is to be rejected if it is received with thanksgiving, because it is consecrated by the word of God and prayer. (1 Tim. 4:3-5)

The phrase "everything God created is good" is the theological death knell for asceticism. Every thing is fair game to have and enjoy *unless* it violates the commands of God's Word, such as, "Do not steal" or "Do not commit adultery," and as long as it is participated in thankfully and prayerfully.

A BRIGHTER SIDE TO ASCETICISM

It would be wrong, however, to cast all ascetics in the same light. Richard Foster shows us the other side of some of these ascetics in his book *Freedom of Simplicity*.[7] Some were godly people, deeply devoted to the Lord. They were not all the sour shriveled crab apples we envision, faces gaunt and drawn and uncracked by smile, lips and ears never violated by laughter. On the contrary, St. Francis and his band were filled with the love of life. They bubbled with humor and humanity, singing merrily as they went about their simple tasks. While some ascetics were morose and regarded pleasure a sin, as do some today, others delighted all the more in what they had, little as it was. They enjoyed scraps of bread and cups of cold water as feasts.

It is hard to know what to think of saints who retreated to the desert to meet God when those of us who retreat to the desert today won't go without suntan oil and golf clubs. In fact, it is difficult for Westerners to imagine a good time without corks popping and bands playing or—in Christian circles—fried chicken, punch, coffee, cookies, and doughnuts. But some of these followers of Christ found more joy in their simple celebrations of life than we do with all our modern conveniences and pleasures.

While their theology was sometimes bent and their path may not be for us, we should be careful not to dismiss the lessons to be learned by the ascetics who walked before us in church history. We, after all, have our own bent theology, and the path of materialism has surely led even more into darkness than the path of asceticism.

THE MODEL OF MOTHER THERESA

We need not go back centuries to see those who have lived ascetic lives. Mother Theresa of Calcutta and the sisters of her order, the Missionaries of Charity, are well known for their work. Through their vow of poverty, they have sought to identify with the poor, homeless, diseased, and dying people to whom they minister. I have seen their work firsthand and commend them for it. They are an example to all of us of what it means to serve.

Yet, with all the respect due Mother Theresa and her coworkers—and it is considerable—we could be misled by the view of material things they appear to take. I am not discussing their actual beliefs, only what their actions seem to suggest. For instance, in a sensitive and moving documentary about her life and work, Mother Theresa is shown instructing others to downgrade a modest facility donated to the mission. She directs them to remove the carpet and hot water hook-up that are already in place. The carpet is torn out, then thrown onto the streets below. There is no indication that it was sold and the proceeds distributed to the poor. The point seems only to be that because they *could* do without the carpet, therefore they *should* do without it, even if no one else would benefit through their sacrifice.

This selfless gesture may appear to be spiritual precisely because of its selflessness. But does it really square with the biblical teaching on material things? Could not the readily available hot water have been immensely helpful in caring for the many sick people in the facility? By choosing to forgo what was already provided, the workers would then have to either do without the benefits of hot water or take the time, effort, and expense to heat the water on stoves. Or, if they had no stoves, with fire fueled by wood. Likewise, couldn't the carpet have helped keep the building warm and brought some level of comfort to the suffering? Of what harm was the carpet in the building? Of what good was it once thrown out on the streets?

Are all things convenient and modern automatically wrong? If carpet and hot water are to be avoided, why do the Missionaries of Charity use medicines to care for the sick? Why does Mother Theresa ride in trucks and fly in airplanes? If technology is undesirable, why do many of the sisters in the order wear glasses? Surely they could get along without them, just as the facility could get along without hot water and carpet.

My point is not to criticize—who am I to criticize such devotion and sacrifice?—only to point out the necessary inconsistency of asceticism. Ultimately, every form of asceticism is selective and somewhat arbitrary. If material things and pleasures are bad or unspiritual or undesirable, we can always eat a little less, wear a little less, and get along with a little less sleep. If material things are bad, consistency would demand that to be untainted one must not eat, drink, or wear anything. Since the body itself is material, both masochism and suicide are logical extensions of pure asceticism. Without daily compromising his position, a true ascetic's lifespan would be short indeed.

Even John the Baptist wore clothes and sandals and ate his locusts and honey. And wasn't honey a bit indulgent—couldn't locusts have sustained him? The Amish, who refuse to use electricity, nevertheless use gas engines, pulleys, wheels, and other technologies that were once as modern as electricity is now. Is a lamp lighted by oil more spiritual than a lamp lighted by electricity? Is either less spiritual than a candle, a match, or no light at all?

THE INADEQUACIES OF ASCETICISM

The Reformers, including Luther, rejected the inherent virtues of asceticism taught by the Catholic church. The Puritans, who are often but wrongly viewed as ascetics, made statements such as this: "These earthly things are the good gifts of God, which no man can simply condemn, without injury to God's disposing hand and providence, who hath ordained them for natural life." Another maintained, "Riches are consistent with godliness, and the more a man hath, the more advantage he hath to do good with it, if God give him an heart to it." Puritan William Ames rejected the monks' vow of poverty as "madness, a superstitious and wicked presumption, being that they sell this poverty for a work of perfection . . . which will much prevail for satisfaction and merit before God."[8]

These are some of the perspectives we must bring to asceticism to identify its errors and dangers:

1. *Poverty is not piety.* Nowhere in Scripture is poverty considered inherently virtuous. God cares for the poor; yes, but this is out of his compassion—not their merit. It is just as erroneous to think poverty is a sign of spirituality as to think wealth is. "The Lord sends poverty and wealth; he humbles and he exalts" (1 Sam. 2:7). In fact, the scriptural ideal is specifically stated to be neither wealth nor poverty but something in between (Prov. 30:8-9).

Wealth brings its attractions to sin, but so does poverty. Richard Baxter stated, "Poverty also hath its temptations. . . . For even the poor may be undone by the love of that wealth and plenty which they never get: and they may perish for over-loving the world, that never yet prospered in the world."[9]

2. *Spirituality is a matter of the heart, not the material circumstances.* A materialist can have little and still be a

materialist, just as an alcoholic doesn't need a bottle to be an alcoholic. An ascetic may trust in his self-denial and not know Christ. He may be as proud of his lack of things as a rich man may be of his things. The man who owns little may not pray at all; the man with much may pray earnestly.

We must be careful not to stereotype sainthood and judge righteousness by outward appearances. Hearing the word "saint," our minds must not be so narrow as to only envision St. Francis living in austerity. They must be broad enough to include C. S. Lewis debating an issue with Oxford colleagues as he smoked his pipe and drank his ale, or R. G. LeTourneau daydreaming the design of his next earth-moving machine. Saints come in many different trappings. We err when we draw too many conclusions from the trappings themselves.

3. *Asceticism can be an attempt to win favor with God or man*. It is one thing to wish to please God but quite another to try to earn one's standing before him through self-denial. The ascetic life-style can be a bid to impress both God and other people with our spirituality. Christ condemned the Pharisees for trying to impress the audiences of heaven and earth with their public self-denial of giving, prayer, and fasting (Matt. 6:1-18). Impure motives can drive ascetics as strongly as materialists.

Many ascetics choose to suffer in order to cope with their feelings of guilt. This may be guilt for their own sins or guilt because others have lived in poverty while they have not. But we must realize that only divinely ordained and therefore *purposeful* suffering, not suffering per se, is godly. God is glorified through suffering brought upon us because of our faithfulness to Christ, not that which we bring upon ourselves in an attempt to prove ourselves faithful. He is glorified by outwardly focused self-denial for the good of others, not inwardly focused self-deprivation for the good of ourselves, such as trying to remove our guilt feelings. He is looking for those willing to be made martyrs for his purposes, not those eager to be made martyrs for their own purposes.

The sacramental view of suffering puts God in my debt, for which he blesses me with salvation, or saves others through my suffering rather than through Christ's. Neither suffering in general nor poverty in particular has inherent merit or atoning powers. Satan, fallen angels, and unredeemed men will suffer in

44

hell for eternity, but their suffering will have no atoning properties whatsoever. God may use our suffering to extend his grace and build our faith, and in that sense to purify us, but not to atone for our guilt.

The Roman Catholic concept of purgatory subtly infiltrates the thinking of many Christian ascetics. But ultimately, self-inflicted punishment is as prideful and self-righteous as it is biblically unfounded. What an inflated opinion of myself I must have to believe *my* suffering can remove my guilt before an all-Holy God. Only Christ's suffering had redemptive value. God calls me to accept the atonement, not to repeat it.

4. *Asceticism can lead to unfair condemnation of others who choose a different path.* One's own standard of living can become a yardstick by which to measure others. I may see others as unspiritual if they own a house and I don't, or if their house is bigger than mine or their car is newer than mine, or their clothes are nicer than mine. Often asceticism's very attempt to deny the flesh becomes just another way of feeding and parading the flesh. We are to pursue God, not sainthood, or the appearance of sainthood, for its own sake.

5. *Modern conveniences can free up time to pursue spiritual aims, as well as enhance ministry to others.* In biblical times almost the whole day might be devoted to the earning of money and the preparing of meals. Cannot a microwave oven or a dishwasher be a blessing of God to free time for focused prayer, hospitality, and a variety of ministries in the home, neighborhood, community, and church?

Can we not assume that Jesus used the best affordable tools in his carpentry, or do we imagine him cutting wood with his bare hands? If he were living in this society, wouldn't our Lord take advantage of the current technology in his trade? Would he hesitate to travel in a car any more than he did a boat? Would he avoid using a microphone if using one would facilitate his ministry to the crowds?

6. *It would be disastrous if every believer dropped out of society's mainstream and abandoned capital production.* Who would support the Mother Theresas in their work? Who would provide the medical advances that their ministries utilize, make the glasses they wear, or build the trucks or repair the planes? St. Francis and his band often begged for food. They wouldn't touch

money, but someone had to make money to care for them. The generation of capital is necessary, not unspiritual. It is inconsistent to secularize those who produce material goods and spiritualize those who do not but nevertheless depend on those who do.

It is one thing to live simply and devote large portions of my income to help the needy. It is quite another to disdain the generating of income, withdraw from the "system" as if the economics of human trade were inherently wrong, and end up contributing to rather than helping alleviate the problem of poverty.

7. *Many forms of asceticism are not conducive to evangelism.* If we all adopted the monastic practice of retreating from society to escape materialistic temptations, how could people in all walks of life be reached with the gospel? (Mother Theresa is in the thick of society, but many ascetics withdraw.)

Paul makes clear that part of our calling in this world is to rub shoulders with non-Christians, regardless of their sins and life-styles. We must be actively involved in their lives, and therefore present in their world (1 Cor. 5:9-10). We must, as Jesus said, not be of the world but at the same time we must remain in it (John 17:15-16).

There is much good in regularly retreating from the world. But the purpose should be to draw near to God and then come back to this troubled materialistic society and reach out to those troubled materialists for whom Christ died. We must all battle materialism. But the hardest, most critical, and most rewarding battle is not for those who withdraw from society but for those who remain in its midst.

8. *Asceticism doesn't deliver what it promises.* Many expect to find peace, purity, and personal holiness in the ascetic life-style. Yet Paul not only warned against the inaccurate assumptions underlying asceticism and the abuses it fosters (1 Tim. 4:1-5), but about the fact that it simply does not accomplish its purpose: "Such regulations indeed have an appearance of wisdom, with their self-imposed worship, their false humility and their harsh treatment of the body, but they lack any value in restraining sensual indulgence" (Col. 2:23). Union with Christ, not self-deprivation, is the foundation of holiness (Col. 3:1-17).

History confirms that withdrawing from society does not

eliminate or necessarily even curb the sin nature. "The monastic orders, however, did not really escape from the problem of a Christian attitude toward the handling of wealth. The members of these orders did not own property as individuals. But the orders entered at once into the field of creating and accumulating wealth. In many cases the monks in their group relationships fell into all of the sins of avarice which had formerly characterized individuals who were dominated by covetousness."[10]

9. *Our Lord lived simply, but was not an ascetic.* In fact, Jesus was condemned for going so far as to party with gluttons and drunkards (Matt. 11:19; Luke 7:34). He not only drank wine, he made wine for a wedding celebration (John 2:1-11). He trafficked with equal ease among the poor, such as John the Baptist and Bartimaeus, and the wealthy, such as Mary, Martha, Lazarus, Nicodemus, Zaccheus, and Joseph of Arimathea (Matt. 27:57-61; John 19:38-42). Jesus accepted material support from wealthy women (Luke 8:2-3). While others criticized the waste, Christ gratefully accepted the extravagant anointing of his body (Matt. 26:6-12; Luke 7:36-50; John 12:1-8).

Christ's birth drew poor shepherds and rich kings. His death drew a poor thief and a rich man who gave a tomb for his burial. His life drew many of both poor and rich. Poverty and wealth both bowed their knee before the Messiah, and he was pleased to accept both into his kingdom.

QUESTIONS TO CONSIDER

Is it possible that we may learn from the ascetics without choosing their path? Can we follow the example of many Christians of the past and present who were not ascetics but chose a far more simple and uncluttered life-style than ours? Might we elect to give up enough things to detach ourselves from the things we have, yet hold onto enough to use for the welfare of ourselves and others?

Can we do what Jesus commanded us to—use money, but not serve it? Can we discover what it means to invest money for eternal purposes? Is it possible to live in a materialistic culture without being tainted by materialism?

These are some of the challenges and opportunities money

and possessions thrust upon all of us who would follow a clear-thinking, simple-living Galilean, who was and is the Son of God.

We have explored the way of asceticism and seen that though it has a certain appeal, it also has many flaws and dangers. In the following chapters we will take a closer look at materialism, that other unbalanced alternative that has silently but powerfully assumed control of countless lives, not only outside the church but inside it.

NOTES

1. Philip Yancey, *Money* (Portland: Multnomah Press, 1985), 3.
2. Quoted by Leland Ryken, *Worldly Saints* (Grand Rapids: Zondervan, 1986), 63.
3. Richard Foster, *Money, Sex, and Power* (San Francisco: Harper and Row, 1985), 24-25.
4. Eugene Peterson, *Working the Angles* (Grand Rapids: Eerdmans, 1987), 9-10.
5. Dallas Willard, *The Spirit of the Disciplines* (San Francisco: Harper and Row, 1988).
6. Tim Hansel, *When I Relax I Feel Guilty* (Elgin, Ill: David C. Cook,1981), 43.
7. Richard Foster, *Freedom of Simplicity* (San Francisco: Harper and Row, 1981), 52-73.
8. Ryken, 58, 61, 70.
9. Ryken, 61.
10. Holmes Rolston, *Stewardship in the New Testament Church* (Richmond, Va: John Knox Press, 1950), 129-30.

CHAPTER 3
THE NATURE OF MATERIALISM

For over a hundred years, a large part of the American people has imagined that the virtual meaning of life lies in the acquisition of ever-increasing status, income, and authority. Robert Bella

The lust for affluence in contemporary society has become psychotic; it has completely lost touch with reality. Richard Foster

The comic strip "Cathy" depicts an interesting dialogue between a young man and woman. Pointing to each item as they refer to it, first one, then the other says, "Safari clothes that will never be near a jungle. Aerobic footwear that will never set foot in an aerobics class. Deep-sea dive watch that will never get damp. Keys to a four-wheel-drive vehicle that will never experience a hill. Architectural magazines we don't read filled with pictures of furniture we don't like. Financial strategy software keyed to a checkbook that's lost somewhere under a computer no one knows how to work. Art poster from an exhibit we never went to of an artist we never heard of." Finally, with blank stares, one says, "Abstract materialism has arrived," to which the other rejoins, "We've moved past the things we want and need and are buying those things that have nothing to do with our lives."

The bumper stickers, which rival the comics for their value as a thermometer of current attitudes, also reflect a hint of irony and cynicism in the midst of this materialistic society—"I owe, I owe, so off to work I go"; "He who dies with the most toys wins"; "Every body needs to believe in something—I believe I'll have another beer."

Have you taken a close look at America lately? When we are not buying lottery tickets or watching big winnings on game shows, one of our favorite national pastimes is wandering through shopping malls just to see what else we can want or buy. Our "shop till you drop" society has produced the "Home Shopping Network" and its spin-offs, displaying products on television to be purchased just by making a phone call. Today's couch potato materialist doesn't have to fight through the mall or even pick up a catalog. His next possession is only a phone number and a credit card away.

A STUDY IN MATERIALISM

In February 1955, *Fortune* magazine interviewed a large sampling of twenty-five-year-olds starting out in business. The study portrayed them as dedicated to family and community service. Twenty-five years later, in 1980, *Fortune* repeated the same exercise with a new crop of twenty-fives, but this time the results were strikingly different. The following extracts are worth quoting at length because they capture so well the spirit of modern Western materialism. Speaking of the twenty-five-year-olds she interviewed, Gwen Kinkead said:

> They believe that business offers the fastest means of gratifying their frankly materialistic requirements.

50

Deferred success, the traditional basis of the work ethic, holds little appeal. They expect to enjoy immediately a relatively high level of material comfort. Terry Michel, a management trainee at Connecticut General Life Insurance Company, echoes the consensus: "I like to spend money. I didn't feel like giving up any luxuries. I grew up with lots of land, private school, horses, dogs, a car at sixteen."

To a stranger from another generation, they sometimes seem a grabby bunch.

It seems that, almost unprincipled, this class flaunts its ambitions. Why bother with goals, they ask, if you don't shoot for the top?

Worries about marketability have turned this group into congenital scale-watchers who tote up their chances of promotion, weigh their salaries against the going market rate, and never, never do anything that won't enhance their records.

The women in the group are generally hell-bent to climb the tallest corporate peaks.

Dwight Billingsly, a utilities consultant in a Washington, D.C., firm, strikes a common chord: "I plan to set up my own business, be independent, report to no one," he says. "Though I have more money now than I ever thought possible, I'd like all the money in the world, and to own a major-league baseball or football team."

The Good Life is defined as being free to follow their impulses, and above all, never worrying about money.

They are unabashed materialists who crave the latest labor-saving and electronic hardware, along with frequent entertainment and travel.

Scarcely any twenty-fives have children at present. Most of those who doubt they will ever be parents say they can't spare the time. Explains Edward Beam, a planning officer at Chicago Northern Trust Company, "I love kids, but I don't want any. I'm too selfish to give what's necessary to raise them properly. Eventually, I'd resent their taking me away from my interests, just as I'd be upset that I wasn't devoting enough attention to them."

Some already view owning a home (and having two incomes to cover the mortgage) as more desirable than having children. Later the choice may be between having children and an even higher standard of living—or greater job mobility.

One woman in the group stated she expected to have a family in five years or so, "once we're financially secure enough to afford good child care so I can continue to work." She adds, "We want to make sure my career is well-established, that we have all the material things we want, that our bills are caught up so we don't fight over what little money we'll have to raise a family on. With our life-style, we can't afford good child care and all the things we like."

Few devote time to public service or volunteer work or express concerns about social problems. Organized religion, favored by the 1955 group as a social and family adhesive, appears too proscriptive or irrelevant to today's secular twenty-fives. The majority call themselves agnostic or privately spiritual.[1]

THE ORIGIN OF MATERIALISM

Materialism did not begin in the later twentieth century, or even with the industrial revolution, or the rise of modern Western capitalism. One look at the treasures of King Tut should convince us of this! Furthermore, it is a problem not restricted to the wealthy—no one has ever needed money to be a materialist. Those who have much may be consumed by what they have; those who have little may be consumed by what they don't have. Materialism is a matter of the heart.

Materialism was rampant in Christ's time and place, but it did not begin there either. It began in a garden where the first man and woman chose to follow their appetites rather than the command of God, seeking fulfillment in the one thing God told them was forbidden (Gen. 3). A. W. Tozer described the ongoing results of their sin and ours:

> Before the Lord God made man upon the earth He first prepared for him a world of useful and pleasant things for his sustenance and delight. In the Genesis account of the

52

creation these are called simply "things." They were made for man's use, but they were meant always to be external to the man and subservient to him. In the deep heart of the man was a shrine where none but God was worthy to come. Within him was God; without, a thousand gifts which God had showered upon him.

But sin has introduced complications and has made those very gifts of God a potential source of ruin to the soul.

Our woes began when God was forced out of His central shrine and things were allowed to enter. Within the human heart things have taken over. Men have now by nature no peace within their hearts, for God is crowned there no longer, but there in the moral dusk stubborn and aggressive usurpers fight among themselves for first place on the throne. This is not a mere metaphor, but an accurate analysis of our real spiritual trouble. There is within the human heart a tough, fibrous root of fallen life whose nature is to possess, always to possess. It covets things with a deep and fierce passion. The pronouns *my* and *mine* look innocent enough in print, but their constant and universal use is significant. They express the real nature of the old Adamic man better than a thousand volumes of theology could do. They are verbal symptoms of our deep disease. The roots of our hearts have grown down into things, and we dare not pull up one rootlet lest we die. Things have become necessary to us, a development never originally intended. God's gifts now take the place of God, and the whole course of nature is upset by the monstrous substitution.[2]

WHAT IS MATERIALISM?

Webster's *New Collegiate Dictionary* defines materialism as "a theory that physical matter is the only or fundamental reality and that all being and processes and phenomena can be explained as manifestations or results of matter." The dictionary adds two other definitions flowing from the first: "A doctrine that the only or the highest values or objectives lie in material well-being and in the furtherance of material progress"; "a preoccupation with or stress upon material rather than intellectual or spiritual things."

Materialism begins with what we believe. Not merely what we *say* we believe, not our doctrinal statement, but the philosophy of life we actually live by. Hence, while any true Christian would deny belief in the philosophical underpinnings of materialism (he couldn't be a Christian if he didn't), he may nonetheless be preoccupied with material rather than spiritual things and therefore in fact be a practicing materialist.

A pure materialist has no room at all for the spiritual realm. A practicing materialist may say whatever he wishes about the spiritual realm. He may go to church every week, he may serve communion or preach, but if he centers his life around the accumulation of things, he is therefore, despite his most heated denials, a materialist.

As the first man and woman valued what they considered appealing over what God said was right, so the materialist attaches the wrong price tags to the things of this world as compared to the things of God. Of course, one need not actually buy or own an item to overvalue it. A materialist may be rich or poor, own much or own little, be a miser or a spendthrift. Materialism usually surfaces in one's life-style, but it is first and foremost a matter of the heart.

(The far-reaching moral and social implications of materialism are developed in appendix A, "Materialism, Man and Morality.")

WARNINGS FROM THE WORD

Materialism fills the pages of Scripture. Achan's lust for money and possessions brought death to himself, his family, and dozens of men in battle (Josh. 7). The prophet Balaam would have cursed God's people for Balak's payment (Num. 22:4-35). Delilah betrayed Samson to the Philistines for a fee (Judg. 16). Solomon's lust for more and more wealth led him to disobey flagrantly the prohibitions of God's law concerning the accumulation of large amounts of horses, gold, silver, and wives (Deut. 17:16-17). To gain wealth, Gehazi lied to Naaman and then to Elisha, for which he was afflicted with leprosy (2 Kings 5:20-27). Ananias and Sapphira withheld money they said was given to the Lord and were struck dead for it (Acts 5:1-11). In the ultimate act of treachery, the materialist Judas asked the chief priests, "What are you willing to give me if I hand him over to you?" then betrayed the Son of God for thirty pieces of silver (Matt. 26:14-16, 47-50; 27:3-10).

Jesus Christ sounded a sober warning against materialism in any form and in any age: "Watch out! Be on your guard against all kinds of greed; a man's life does not consist in the abundance of his possessions" (Luke 12:15).

Jesus warned against "all kinds of greed," suggesting that this enemy comes in many forms, some obvious but others dangerously subtle. It is not the well-marked land mines that cost soldiers their legs, or lives, but the well-disguised ones.

Greed surfaces in possessiveness and covetousness. Possessiveness relates to what we have, covetousness to what we want. To be possessive is to be selfish and unsharing with what we own. To covet is to long for and to be preoccupied with having what God has not given us. It is the passion to possess what is not ours to have.

Greed is not a harmless pastime but a serious offense against God. Just as the lustful man is an adulterer (Matt. 5:28) and the hateful man a murderer (1 John 3:15), so the greedy man is an idolater (Col. 3:5).

Greed, or Money-worship, is a violation of the first and most fundamental of the Ten Commandments: "I am the Lord your God. . . . You shall have no other gods before me" (Exod. 20:2-3). The last of the commandments is the warning against covetousness (Exod. 20:17). In between is the command not to steal, and stealing is of course the product of greed. The ten great laws of God, written in stone, from beginning through middle to end contain strict prohibitions of materialism.

Warnings against materialism pervade Scripture. Greed is considered the source of almost every destructive force imaginable, including war (James 4:1-3). The lust for money and things is considered the root of a thousand social evils, the most basic of which is apostasy, turning away from the true God (1 Tim. 6:10).

There are communist materialists just as there are capitalist

55

materialists, Republican materialists and Democrat materialists, materialists in management and in labor, both secular and religious, both rich and poor materialists. Greed transcends all economic philosophies, social systems, political parties, religions, and financial situations. It is part of the basic sin condition.

What will happen to the affluent person or society that does not reverse its materialism? Basic physics gives us the answer. The greater the mass the greater the hold that mass exerts. This explains why the largest planets are capable of holding so many satellites in orbit. Similarly, the more things we own—the greater their total mass—the more they grip us, hold us, set us in orbit around them. Finally, like a black hole, a gargantuan cosmic vacuum cleaner, they mercilessly suck us into themselves, until we become indistinguishable from the things, surrendering our humanity—and thereby our society—to the inhuman gods we have idolized.

This is the final end of materialism.

THE STUPIDITY OF MATERIALISM
No matter how much we may dislike the word "materialism," it perfectly describes the predominant mind-set of our society. But we must understand that materialism is not just wrong. It is stupid. It was this stupidity Jesus was getting at when he asked his profit-conscious audience, "What good will it be for a man if he gains the whole world, yet forfeits his soul? Or what can a man give in exchange for his soul?" (Matt. 16:26).

The parable of the rich fool portrays just that, a fool, not an ingenious entrepreneur or a successful businessman (Luke 12:16-21). A fool is one who either does not recognize the truth or chooses to ignore it. The rich fool of the parable thought he was captain of his fate. He made his plans without taking into account God's plans. He failed to come to grips with three fundamental facts—the mortality of the present life, the eternality of the future life, and the fact that the future life is being forged by the present life.

The rich fool was a materialist. He acted irrationally, as if he could escape death or at least delay it indefinitely. He neglected to number his days and thereby gain a heart of wisdom (Ps. 90:12).

Scripture describes men as "like grass" and our achievements as "the flowers of the field." The grass withers and the flowers fall—in the eyes of eternity this earthly life comes and goes in the blink of an eye (Isa. 40:6-8). "But man, despite his riches, does not endure; he is like the beasts that perish" (Ps. 49:12). "Man is a mere phantom as he goes to and fro: He bustles about, but only in vain; he heaps up wealth, not knowing who will get it" (Ps. 39:6).

A Greek philosopher once said, "All men think it is only the other man who is mortal." The way we scurry about accumulating things is testimony to our unspoken doctrine that we are exceptions to the law of death.

The rich fool was not "rich toward God"; that is, he did not earn and spend and give his money in a God-centered but in a self-centered way. He hoarded and stockpiled money and possessions rather than freely releasing them to serve God and meet human needs. He was too self-sufficient to seek God in prayer, too independent to ask God's counsel on how much to keep and how much to give, too preoccupied with the business of "success" to open his heart in love to meet the needs of those around him. Though he probably believed there was a God, the rich fool was a fool precisely because he lived as if there were no God (Ps. 14:1).

His Talmud said, "Man is born with his fist clenched but dies with his hands wide open." His Scriptures said, "Naked a man comes from his mother's womb, and as he comes, so he departs. He takes nothing from his labor that he can carry in his hand" (Eccles. 5:15). But the rich fool was too busy being successful to notice.

When one of the wealthiest men in history, John D. Rockefeller, died, his accountant was asked, "How much did John D. leave?"

The accountant's reply was classic: "He left all of it."

"You can't take it with you." Or as someone has put it, "You'll never see a hearse pulling a U-Haul."

Perhaps we need to read the obituaries to remind ourselves how short our time here is. Perhaps we need to visit the local junkyard to remind ourselves where all these things we work for and chase after will one day end. The wise man thinks ahead. The foolish man acts as if there were no eternal tomorrow.

THE DOCTRINE OF REVERSAL

When we read Luke 16:19-31, we are confronted with the unpleasant story of another rich man and a poor man named Lazarus. The rich man dressed well, lived in luxury, and was apparently healthy. Lazarus was a beggar, diseased and dirty, "longing to eat what fell from the rich man's table" (Luke 16:21). If asked, "Who would you rather be, the rich man or Lazarus?" everyone, church-goer or not, at this point in the story would surely respond, "The rich man, of course."

Keep in mind that, as in the case of the rich fool of Luke 12, we are not told this rich man was dishonest or irreligious or that he was any better or worse in character than most other rich men or poor men. We do not even know that he despised poor Lazarus. We only know that he ignored him, that he lived his own life as if the poor man didn't exist, and that he did not use his wealth to care for him.

The story goes on. Both men die; Lazarus goes to heaven, the rich man to hell. When the rich man begs Abraham from across the gulf to send Lazarus to relieve his suffering, Abraham replies, "Son, remember that in your lifetime you received your good things, while Lazarus received bad things, but now he is comforted here and you are in agony" (Luke 16:25).

And *now* who would we rather be, the rich man or Lazarus? Now, of course, we would like to switch places. But that is Abraham's point—after death, it is too late to switch.

This parable represents a strong and often overlooked New Testament teaching which, for lack of a better term, I'll call "the doctrine of reversal." Simply put, it teaches that in eternity many of us will find ourselves in opposite conditions from our current situation on earth.

This is an obvious point in the parable we have just discussed. In this life, the rich man "lived in luxury every day," while Lazarus begged at his gate, living in misery. At the moment of death their situations reversed—the rich man was in hell's torment, and the poor man in heaven's comfort.

It would be both simplistic and theologically inaccurate to conclude heaven is earned by poverty and hell is earned by wealth. But this parable is not isolated—it corroborates a host of Christ's other teachings as well as those of the apostles.

In the song she composed in anticipation of Christ's birth, Mary said, "He has filled the hungry with good things but has sent the rich away empty" (Luke 1:53).

"Blessed are the poor," and "Woe to the rich," Jesus said, precisely because their status will one day be reversed (Luke 6:20-25). The poor in spirit, those who mourn, are meek, who hunger and thirst for righteousness and are persecuted will be relieved and fulfilled and have great reward in heaven (Matt. 5:3-12). Those praised in this world will not be highly regarded in the next, and vice versa (Matt. 6:1-4, 16-18). Those exalted in this life will often be humbled in the next; those humbled here will be exalted there (Matt. 23:12).

Those poor in this world will often be rich in the next; those rich in this world will often be poor in the next (James 1:9-12). The poor are reassured that the hoarding and oppressing rich will one day be punished and the honest poor will be relieved (James 5:1-6). The voice from heaven says of materialistic Babylon, "Give her as much torture and grief as the glory and luxury she gave herself" (Rev. 18:7).

Some of these passages may present us with theological difficulties, but all of them clearly intend to remind us that temporal sacrifices will pay off in eternity and temporal indulgences will cost in eternity.

These are the kinds of verses that gave endless encouragement to the Christian slaves and should have served warning to the plantation owners who profited from their slavery. The reversal doctrine is inevitably comforting to the poor and weak, and threatening to the rich and powerful. But it is nonetheless a consistent teaching of the New Testament—one which once again confirms that materialism is not only wrong but terribly stupid. Conversely, giving and caring and sharing and trusting God are not only right, but smart.

Someday this upside down world will be turned right side up, and nothing in all eternity will turn it back again. If we are wise, we will spend our brief lives on earth positioning ourselves for the turn.

RECOGNIZING MATERIALISM

After one of our church's missionaries was home for a month, he said, "I've been overwhelmed with the dominance of materialism in this country." When another missionary was leaving after a year's furlough, we asked him, "What struck you the most in the time you were home with us?" His matter-of-fact reply was sobering—"What struck me the most was how people use their houses to make statements to each other; their houses aren't just places to keep warm and dry, but showcases to display their wealth and impress each other."

Both these men were from other cultures. The sad thing is that if either had stayed another year or two, he might no longer have noticed. Like the frog that boiled to death by degrees, we tend to gradually acclimate to our materialism, becoming desensitized to it, and finally regarding it as the norm rather than an aberration.

The hardest part of dealing with our materialism is that it has become so much a part of us. Like people who have lived in darkness for years, we have been removed from the light so long we do not know how dark it really is. Many of us have never known what it is *not* to be materialistic. It is normal, the only way we know. This is why we need so desperately to read the Scriptures, to grapple with these issues, bring them to God in prayer, discuss them with our brothers and sisters, and look for and learn from those rare models of nonmaterialistic living in our Christian communities.

I'm convinced that if we were to gain God's perspective, even for a moment, and were to look at the way we go through life accumulating and hoarding and displaying things, we would have the same feelings of horror and pity that any sane person has when he views people in a mental asylum endlessly beating their heads against the wall.

CONCLUSION

For years, among Christians, the argument against materialism has been, "Materialism is wrong." Materialism *is* wrong, but, since this line of argument has been generally ineffective, perhaps it is time for a new approach—"Materialism is stupid; in fact, materialism is insane."

Promising fulfillment in money and things and lands and houses and cars and clothes and boats and campers and hot-tubs and world-travel, materialism has left us bound and gagged, pathetically thinking what the drug addict thinks, that our only hope is getting more of the same. All the while the voice of God, so hard to hear through the clatter of our things, tells us that even if materialism *did* bring happiness in this life—which it clearly does not—it leaves us woefully unprepared for the next.

NOTES
1. Gwen Kinkead, "On a Fast Track to the Good Life," *Fortune* 7 April 1980: 74-84.
2. A. W. Tozer, *The Pursuit of God* (Harrisburg, Penn: Christian Publications, 1958) 21-22.

CHAPTER 4

THE DANGERS OF MATERIALISM

The soul is a spiritual thing, riches are of an earthly extract, and how can these fill a spiritual substance? How man does thirst after the world, but, alas, it falls short of his expectation. It cannot fill the hiatus and longing of his soul. Thomas Watson

The poorest man I know is the man who has nothing but money. John D. Rockefeller

Surrounded by wealthy socialites, a beautiful young woman sat at a dinner party on a luxury boat. To her surprise, a millionaire sitting near her passed her a note asking, "Would you go to bed with me tonight for ten thousand dollars?"

Blushing, the woman paused for a moment, then wrote back, "Yes."

A few minutes later the two left the party. When they were

alone the man asked the woman, "Would you go to bed with me for *ten* dollars?"

Outraged, she challenged him, "What kind of woman do you think I am?"

Matter-of-factly he replied, "Oh, we've already determined what kind of woman you are. Now we're just trying to find your price."

IDOLATRY AND ADULTERY

Satan works under the assumption that every person has a price. Often, unfortunately, he is right. Many people are willing to surrender themselves and their principles to whatever god will bring them the greatest short-term profit.

The Old Testament portrays Israel as a bride who has turned into a prostitute, abandoning her rightful husband, God, and selling herself to the highest bidder. The prophets develop this metaphor to embarrassing extents (Isa. 57:3-9; Jer. 3:1-10; Ezek. 16:1-48). The nauseating descriptions depict God's hurt and horror at the spiritual adultery of his people. The sin of idolatry is a wanton betrayal of a husband who loves us enough to die for us.

The New Testament tells us that greed "is idolatry" (Col. 3:5). Idolatry is worshiping and serving as god anything other than the true God. In his book *Idols For Destruction,* Herbert Schlossberg considers the idolatrous nature of materialism:

> The common expression that describes such a value system as "the pursuit of the almighty dollar" is soundly based in the recognition that the exaltation of possessions to the level of ultimacy is the end of a religious quest, one that seeks and ascribes ultimate meaning. Like all idolatries, it finds ultimate meaning in an aspect of the creation rather than in the Creator. And like all idolatries it finds outlet in destructive pathologies that wreck human lives.[1]

Scripture alludes to these destructive pathologies:

> People who want to get rich fall into temptation and a trap and into many foolish and harmful desires that plunge men

into ruin and destruction. For the love of money is a root of all kinds of evil. Some people, eager for money, have wandered from the faith and pierced themselves with many griefs. (1 Tim. 6:9-10)

Jesus said the rich are at a spiritual disadvantage (Matt. 19:23-24). The problem, of course, is not that God doesn't love the rich. The problem is that the rich don't love God. They simply have too much else to love already.

This is why Jesus didn't say it is "wrong" to serve God and money, or it is "difficult" to serve God and money, but that it is simply impossible to serve God and Money (Matt. 6:24). Why? For the same reason a woman cannot have two husbands. When we carry on a love affair with the world we are committing spiritual adultery. We place God in the role of the jilted husband. He loves us still and longs for our return but will not allow us in his intimate chambers when we are prostituting ourselves to another. God will not be a half-husband. He will not be comforted by the fact that we call him "Savior" when we refuse to follow him as Lord.

Materialism is the two things God hates most—idolatry and adultery. The magnitude of God's abhorrence for materialism and its antichrist nature is demonstrated in the final great act preparatory to the return of Christ—the once and for all destruction of the secularistic, materialistic system of this world, called "Babylon the Great." It is said of this Babylon, "The kings of the earth committed adultery with her, and the merchants of the earth grew rich from her excessive luxuries." A voice from heaven pleads with God's people—a voice that we would do well to listen to today:

> Come out of her, my people, so that you will not share in her sins, so that you will not receive any of her plagues; for her sins are piled up to heaven, and God has remembered her crimes. Give back to her as she has given; pay her back double for what she has done. Mix her a double portion from her own cup. Give her as much torture and grief as the glory and luxury she gave herself. (Rev. 18:4-7)

The merchants who gained their wealth from this corrupt

materialistic philosophy will say, "Woe! Woe, O great city, dressed in fine linen, purple and scarlet, and glittering with gold, precious stones and pearls! In one hour such great wealth has been brought to ruin!" (Rev. 18:16-17).

Ultimately, all heaven is to rejoice at the destruction of materialism's stronghold: "Rejoice over her, O heaven! Rejoice, saints and apostles and prophets! God has judged her for the way she treated you" (Rev. 18:19).

God's hatred for materialism is rooted in its idolatrous and adulterous nature. But materialism brings with it countless other dangers to the individual, family, church, and society. The rest of this chapter identifies and develops some of these dangers.

MATERIALISM PREVENTS OR DESTROYS THE SPIRITUAL LIFE

Jesus rebuked the Christians of Laodicea because while they thought they were rich, due to their material wealth, they were actually desperately poor in the things of God (Rev. 3:17-18). Materialism blinds us to our own spiritual poverty. Puritan Richard Baxter said, "When men prosper in the world, their minds are lifted up with their estates, and they can hardly believe that they are so ill, while they feel themselves so well."[2]

The theologian Augustine said, "Thou hast made us for Thyself, O God, and the heart of man is restless until it finds its rest in Thee." The philosopher Pascal added, "There is within every man a God-shaped emptiness that only he can fill." Materialism is a fruitless attempt to find meaning by those who have not found meaning in the only place it can be found—God. Materialism is not only evil; it is tragic and pathetic:

> Has a nation ever changed its gods? (Yet they are not gods at all.) But my people have exchanged their Glory for worthless idols. Be appalled at this, O heavens, and shudder with great horror," declares the Lord. "My people have committed two sins: They have forsaken me, the spring of living water, and have dug their own cisterns, broken cisterns that cannot hold water. (Jer. 2:11-13)

Imagine people dying of thirst, frantically trying to dig

cisterns, but finding that they cannot hold water. In their final desperate attempts to quench their thirst, maddened by the scorching sun, they shovel sand into their mouths, choking and retching as death comes upon them. Imagine that all the while, just a stone's throw away, there is a sparkling spring of cold fresh water, pure and life-giving. This is the picture God paints through Jeremiah. Every attempt to find life in anyone or anything but God is vain. Materialism is a dead-end street.

MATERIALISM DENIES THE LIABILITIES OF WEALTH

The disadvantages of material prosperity never occur to the materialist. Prosperity is the whole point of living—what drawbacks could it possibly have?

The following are extracts from an insightful letter John Steinbeck wrote to Adlai Stevenson, recorded in the *Washington Post* January 28, 1960: "A strange species we are. We can stand anything God and nature can throw at us save only plenty. If I wanted to destroy a nation, I would give it too much, and I would have it on its knees, miserable, greedy, sick."[3]

A leader of the persecuted church in Romania who has spent considerable time in the West as well once told a group of us, "In my experience, 95 percent of the believers who face the test of persecution pass it, while 95 percent who face the test of prosperity fail it."

This was precisely Thomas Carlyle's point when he said, "Adversity is hard on a man, but for one man who can stand prosperity, there are a hundred that will stand adversity." Hosea put it this way: "When I fed them, they were satisfied; when they were satisfied, they became proud; then they forgot me" (Hos. 13:6).

One of life's great ironies is that the poor and humble man who walks with God is rewarded with prosperity, gradually turns his attention away from his Lord, then finally becomes the proud rich man who comes under God's judgment. Some have wondered why God is still blessing many of the Western nations with wealth despite our departure from our godly heritage. Perhaps the "blessing" is no longer a blessing at all but a curse in disguise. The greatest blessing would be that which would return us to following our God—and our wealth is certainly not doing that.

A good argument can be made from Scripture that the possession of riches is almost always a spiritual liability (Mark 10:23-25). If Jesus was serious when he said how hard it is for a rich man to enter God's kingdom, and I see no evidence that he was joking, and if being part of the kingdom of heaven is the highest blessing a man can have, then how can we assume that having riches is always a blessing of God? Was God blessing the rich fool or the rich man who neglected Lazarus or the wealthy and wicked kings of Israel and Babylon and Assyria?

God first sent the quail as a loving provision for the children of Israel. But after they had grumbled and complained, he said he would send quail again, "until it comes out of your nostrils and you loathe it" (Num. 11:18-20). Material prosperity can begin as a blessing of God, but it can become a curse.

Given the statements and examples of Scripture, and the testimony of human history, if God was going to curse a man, what more effective means could he use than to heap wealth on him?

MATERIALISM BRINGS
UNHAPPINESS AND ANXIETY

The average person's life consists of an endless string of materialistic "If onlys." If only I could get a raise; if only I could get a better-paying job; if only I could buy a new car; if only I could get that boat, country cottage, dress, rifle, toy, set of tools, *then* I would be happy. Life is wasted in the endless pursuit of that which, even if attained, will never bring fulfillment.

In *The Lion, the Witch and the Wardrobe* C. S. Lewis told of the boy Edmund who sampled the Witch's turkish delight, then sacrificed all that is good to get more of it—only to find that the more he gorged himself on it, the sicker and less satisfied he became. We fail to realize that the bait of wealth hides the hook of addiction and slavery.

Who is it we want to be like? The rich? The string of broken families and broken lives among the rich should tell us something. Note, for instance, the pitiful life of Howard Hughes

68

who, with all his money and power, became a miserable, crazed, and pathetic creature. Consider the testimonies of five other extremely wealthy men:

John D. Rockefeller: "I have made many millions, but they have brought me no happiness."

W. H. Vanderbilt: "The care of $200,000,000 is enough to kill anyone. There is no pleasure in it."

John Jacob Astor: "I am the most miserable man on earth."

Henry Ford: "I was happier when doing a mechanic's job."

Andrew Carnegie: "Millionaires seldom smile."[4]

Dr. Aaron Beck and his associates did a ten-year study of patients hospitalized with suicidal intentions. He published the results in *The American Journal of Psychiatry*. One of the fifteen major risk factors contributing to a suicidal frame of mind was listed simply as "Financial Resources." The terse commentary was "Risk increases with resources."[5]

This conclusion is well-illustrated in the number of suicides and breakdowns that commonly occur during large drops in the stock market and other financial downturns. It is also demonstrated in the epidemic levels of high blood pressure and hypertension among the most "successful" professionals.

Similarly, I once took a test designed to predict a person's lifespan, barring accidents. It was based on statistical probabilities and included instructions to add so many years if I exercised regularly, subtract so many years if I smoked, etc. One statement was particularly striking: "Subtract two years from your life if your family income is over $40,000 a year."

The uncertainty and insecurity of material things makes materialism the mother of anxiety. This is why Christ's discourse on earthly and heavenly treasures is immediately followed by his admonitions not to worry about material things (Matt. 6:25-34). People lay up treasures on earth rather than in heaven not only because of greed and covetousness and selfishness, but because of fear, insecurity, and anxiety. Yet putting our hope in earthly treasures does nothing but multiply anxiety, precisely because they are so uncertain.

The man with his primary investments in the stock market will have his hopes rise and fall with the stock market. The man whose greatest riches are in banks will be destroyed when the banks fail, as will the farmer whose greatest asset is his crops when his crops fail. In contrast, the man whose hope is in God will be devastated only if God fails—which is an impossibility. Any man who has the rug pulled out from under him was standing on the wrong rug. To set our heart on earthly riches is not only to deprive God of glory, others of help, and ourselves of reward, but to destine ourselves to perpetual insecurity.

Paul said the rich should not "put their hope in wealth, which is so uncertain," but in God "who richly provides" (1 Tim. 6:17). Solomon made a profound observation when he noted, "The sleep of the laborer is sweet, whether he eats little or much, but the abundance of a rich man permits him no sleep" (Eccles. 5:12). The more we have the more we have to worry about.

MATERIALISM ENDS IN ULTIMATE FUTILITY

In the most powerful exposé of materialism ever written, Solomon recounted his attempts to find meaning in pleasures, laughter, alcohol, foolishness, building projects, and the pursuit of personal interests, as well as amassing slaves, gold and silver, singers, and a huge harem to fulfill his sexual desires (Eccles. 2:1-11). He achieved the ultimate in material success and international fame living by this philosophy: "I denied myself nothing my eyes desired, and refused my heart no pleasure." And what was Solomon's conclusion as he looked back over this remarkable life that people today dream of emulating? "Yet when I surveyed all that my hands had done and what I had toiled to achieve, everything was meaningless, a chasing after the wind; nothing was gained under the sun."

The best things in life are free, as available to the poor as the rich, and often more easily accessed by the poor. "Come, all you who are thirsty, come to the waters; and you who have no money, come, buy and eat! Come, buy wine and milk without money and without cost" (Isa. 55:1). "Whoever is thirsty, let him come; and whoever wishes, let him take the free gift of the water of life" (Rev. 22:17). The only thing worth buying cannot be bought with human resources. God's Son bought us our salvation, and he freely gives himself to all who seek him. Money cannot buy salvation, and it cannot buy rescue from judgment—"wealth is worthless in the day of wrath" (Prov. 11:4). As Tertullian put it in A.D. 200, "Nothing that is God's is obtainable by money."

John Piper helped us envision the final irony of materialism:

> Picture 269 people entering eternity in a plane crash in the Sea of Japan. Before the crash there is a noted politician, a millionaire corporate executive, a playboy and his play-mate, a missionary kid on the way back from visiting grandparents. After the crash they stand before God utterly stripped of MasterCards, checkbooks, credit lines, image clothes, how-to-succeed books, and Hilton reservations. Here are the politician, the executive, the playboy, and the missionary kid, all on level ground with nothing, ab-solutely nothing in their hands, possessing only what they brought in their hearts. How absurd and tragic the lover of money will seem on that day—like a man who spends his whole life collecting train tickets and in the end is so weighed down by the collection he misses the last train.[6]

MATERIALISM LEADS TO PRIDE AND ELITISM

According to Scripture, God has given us our intelligence (Dan. 2:21), our abilities (Rom. 12:6), and our capacity to earn money (Deut. 8:18).

The Bible is full of references to and examples of the fact that our tendency in prosperity is to believe that we deserve the credit for what we have and to grow proud and thankless (Deut. 6:1-15; 31:20; 32:15-18; 2 Chron. 26:6-16; Ps. 49:6; 52:7; Prov. 30:8-9; Hos. 13:4-6). Paul asked the prideful Christians of Corinth, "For who makes you different from anyone else? What do you have that you did not receive? And if you did receive it, why do you boast as though you did not?" (1 Cor. 4:7). Paul told Timothy, "Command those who are rich in this present world not to be arrogant" (1 Tim. 6:17).

Why have faith in God when you have faith in yourself? Why

trust God when you have all your bases covered? Why pray when you have everything under control? Why ask for your daily bread when you own the bakery? Self-sufficiency is the great enemy of faith and prayer, which are the heartbeat of the Christian life. We pride ourselves on our "financial independence," but where would we be without God, from whom our every breath is a gift?

One of the ugliest manifestations of pride is elitism, a shared sense of superiority over others held by a privileged class of people. Elitism is at the heart of racism, nationalism, and denominationalism. It is sometimes the driving force behind private clubs, restaurants, hotels, schools, fraternities, certain churches, and countless other sites and affiliations.

While waiting in a doctor's office, I browsed through a beautiful magazine that described itself as "a magazine like no other, intended for an elite group of subscribers." It then said, "In order to maintain the high quality of our magazine we must limit its printing. We cannot accept more than 100,000 subscribers."

Why would accepting more subscribers lower the quality of the magazine, since the next 100,000 copies would be printed and mailed exactly like the first? The idea, of course, is elitism. It is a matter of pure snob appeal. I am one of the privileged who receives this magazine, and you are not. Whether anyone reads the magazine is debatable, but it makes a statement, and besides, it looks great on a coffee table, and for what it costs it should!

Beyond the obvious ego-massage of such an approach, there is a critical danger in elitism. Jesus came to die for every person of every social and economic level, and Paul reminded the proud Corinthians that the church is made up of the dregs of this world (1 Cor. 1:26-31). But elitism boosts our egos by making us think we are somehow more worthy than others. Few things are more repugnant to the Lord than the tendency of the rich to despise the poor (Job 12:5). Yet our clubs and social circles, sometimes even our churches, foster this very attitude.

MATERIALISM PROMOTES INJUSTICE AND EXPLOITATION

Money is power. Power is not intrinsically evil, of course, but it *is* intrinsically dangerous. Only an all-good God can afford to be all-powerful, for he uses his power to redeem the poor in spirit, and bring them justice. Among sinful human beings, the old adage is correct, as an endless string of despots have gone out of their way to prove—"power corrupts and absolute power corrupts absolutely."

James condemned the rich, making an almost universal assumption that anyone who is rich practices injustice to the poor and will come under God's judgment for it (James 5:1-6). The Old Testament prophets spoke out so consistently against the oppression of the poor by the rich that they give the distinct impression that a righteous rich man is a very rare phenomenon indeed (Isa. 10:1-3; Jer. 5:27-28; 15:13; Hos. 12:8; Amos 5:11, 24; Mic. 6:12).

The rich man will usually be a materialistic man. The materialistic man will always be an unjust man. The wealthier the man, the greater his opportunity for injustice. The wealthy man is no more inherently sinful than the poor—he simply has more means and opportunity to subsidize, expand, and impose his sins upon others.

In Philippi, Paul was permitted to preach the gospel openly, until he cast out the future-predicting demon from the suffering slave girl, who "earned a great deal of money for her owners by fortune-telling" (Acts 16:16). The girl was freed from a horrible burden, but they did not care about her. The bottom line was that they lost their meal ticket—their gravy train had been derailed. "When the owners of the slave girl realized that their hope of making money was gone, they seized Paul and Silas and dragged them into the marketplace to face the authorities" (Acts 16:19).

Before we self-righteously decry this unconscionable exploitation, we should not forget what a short time ago it was that slavery was a common practice in America. We should also not forget that slavery was abolished in the North before the South not because of the superior morality of Northerners but the simple fact that slavery was largely unprofitable in the North, while it was very profitable in the plantations and cotton fields of the South. Had it been equally profitable in both parts of the nation, and we must realize this to our shame, slavery might still exist in this country.

But we need not go back 140 years to find notorious examples of exploitation. Consider today's profit-based abortion business, which is lucrative for the abortionist and financially advantageous to the parents (executioners), who do not wish to interrupt their careers, jeopardize their house and car payments, or dissipate their income on an intruder. It is a tragic fact that many abortions are procured not only by single mothers but by married couples for financial reasons.

Consider also the industries of alcohol, drugs, pornography (including but not limited to child pornography), prostitution, sensationalist tabloids, and, to a degree, television and motion-pictures, none of which hesitate to exploit human beings for financial gain.

While I personally believe in the legitimacy of a strong military defense, it is also apparent that certain companies have profited immensely by the production of weapons, that these companies welcome wars anywhere in the world in order to turn a profit, and are willing to produce and sell weapons indiscriminately at the cost of human lives.

Perhaps the most obvious example of the exploitation of people for financial gain in America is the tobacco corporations. For thirty-five years they have defended their multibillion-dollar industry in the face of incontrovertible evidence that millions of people suffer terrible disease and death because of cigarette smoking. The tenacity with which the tobacco industry hires lobbyists and propagandists to juggle and explain away the research and statistics and defend the indefensible, at the cost of untold human suffering, is a clear sacrifice of moral principle on the altar of the almighty dollar. Whether or not the leaders in this industry attend church and tithe of their incomes is not particularly relevant—the fact remains that they embody materialism, with its elevation of financial profit over human welfare, in its clearest form.

MATERIALISM FOSTERS IMMORALITY AND THE DETERIORATION OF THE FAMILY

"Motives having to do with money or sex account for 99 percent of the crimes committed in the United States, but those with money as their object outpoint sexual offenses by a ratio of four to one."[7]

Materialism underlies the vast majority of illegal activities in this country. Yet most forms of materialism are perfectly legal, and many enjoy the highest status, evoking the admiration and envy of society.

Commonly, those who enjoy prosperity, power, and privilege also indulge in sexual immorality. Prosperous King David, spoiled by getting everything he wanted, did not deny himself one more possession—another man's wife (2 Sam. 11).

Surveys confirm a strong moral decline in people who are used to having what they want materially:

> Among both men and women the incidence of marital infidelity rises in conjunction with an increase in income. Of the married men earning $20,000 a year, only 31 percent conduct extracurricular love affairs; of the men earning more than $60,000, 70 percent.[8]

Of course, the point is not the income itself but the life-style it usually underwrites. A Christian can make a million dollars a year, give generously, live modestly, and avoid much of the added temptation to immorality. In light of such statistics, we should not be surprised by the frequency of immorality among Christians, even Christian leaders, who live in wealth. After all, those who gorge their material appetites are not likely to curb their sexual ones.

A look at the people who occupy our attention through the media tells us something of the inseparability of materialism and sexual immorality in our society:

> Much can be determined about a nation's ideals and future welfare by the character of its models. Who are the most admired people in America? Spiritual leaders, civil leaders, altruistic social reformers? Hardly.
>
> The heroes and idols of America are actors and actresses, jet-setters and yacht owners, entertainers and rock stars. With a glass of wine or a joint in one hand and somebody else's mate in the other, they prance, jiggle, curse, and swindle their way into the hearts of Americans. Our homage to such celebrities tells us as much about us—and our probable destiny—as it does them.[9]

We must not overlook the contribution of marital infidelity to the widespread breakdown of the family. A consequence of adultery is often divorce, and the consequences of divorce in the lives of the children of our churches and communities and nation are inestimable. Even when adultery does not result in divorce, it destroys the fabric of marriage and prevents the home from being a climate of faithfulness and a moral sanctuary from the corruption of the world. Anything that contributes to an increase in immorality, as materialism clearly does, directly contributes to the breakdown of families and the consequent deterioration of society.

John Piper is on target again when he points out the emptiness of materialism and the immorality it fosters:

> Who do you think has the deepest, most satisfying joy in life, the man who pays $140 for a fortieth-floor suite downtown and spends his evening in the half-lit, smoke-filled lounge impressing strange women with ten-dollar cocktails, or the man who chooses the Motel 6 by a vacant lot of sunflowers and spends his evening watching the sunset and writing a love letter to his wife?[10]

The same principle that links wealth to sexual immorality links it to almost any temptation. A famous athlete was recently asked why he turned to drugs. His answer was simple: "Because I had so much money I didn't know what to do with it." His money, while not sinful itself, provided him greater temptation and opportunity to sin.

MATERIALISM DISTRACTS US FROM OUR CENTRAL PURPOSE

When Jesus described the various kinds of people who respond to the gospel, he stated that some seed "fell among thorns, which grew up and choked the plants" (Matt. 13:7). He later explained to the disciples, "The one who received the seed that fell among the thorns is the man who hears the word, but the worries of this life and the deceitfulness of wealth choke it, making it unfruitful" (Matt. 13:22). Notice once more the clear relationship between wealth and worry. For the first nine years my wife and I lived in our present house, we had an ugly old orange carpet, and we were never concerned about what happened to it. Finally it wore through to the floor and we replaced it. The first day we got our new carpet, there was an accident that burnt a hole in it. Any day previous to that one we wouldn't have cared. But now our emotional energy was poured into regret and anxiety about the carpet.

It takes time to hover over our things, and that time must come from elsewhere—for instance, from time spent cultivating intimacy with God, from time spent in his Word and prayer, time spent visiting and ministering to the needy, and time spent developing relationships with people who need Christ. Every item I add to my possessions is one more thing to think about, talk about, clean, repair, display, rearrange, and replace when it goes bad.

I buy a television, but that is just the beginning. I hook up an antenna, I subscribe to a cable service, I buy a VCR, I rent movies, I get a recliner to watch my programs in comfort. This all costs money, but it also takes immense amounts of time, energy, and attention.

Acquiring a possession may also push me into redefining my priorities and make me unavailable for ministry. For instance, if I buy a boat, the problem is not just the money. I must now justify my purchase by *using* the boat, which may mean frequent weekends away from church, making me unavailable to teach a Sunday school class or work in the nursery or lead a small group or . . . Of course, the problem is not the boat, but me; yet the bottom line is the same. As Jesus said in the parable, worries and wealth can choke me, making me unfruitful.

Suppose I buy some rental property. First there is the big down payment, then monthly payments that may go on the rest of my life. There are bills to pay, taxes that always go up, repairs that have to be made. The financial drain is substantial, but the drain on my mental energy and my time may be even greater. There is the hassle of finding the right renters, the anxiety that they may mistreat the home, the concerns when their payments are late, the worry about possible vandalism and weather damage, the compulsion to drive by just to make sure everything is all right.

Then, every few years I have to go in, clean up the place, and start over looking for the right renters. And when I hear there is an expressway that may go through the area and reduce the property value, suddenly I am circulating petitions and attending meetings to persuade the city council to build it near someone else's property, not mine. Remember, all this is in addition to the ongoing concerns related to the home I actually live in! I'm certainly not suggesting it is wrong for a Christian to own rental property. But the practical question is a fair one—do I own this property, or does it own me?

What is true of rental property is true to lesser or greater degrees of everything we own. What I am pointing out is simply a law of life—the tyranny of things. And the central issue is not the things themselves, but the depletion of the resources of time, energy, enthusiasm, and money that could have been invested in the kingdom of God. The key question is not the general, "Should a Christian own this or that," but the specific, "Does God want *me* to own this or that in light of the drain on my resources it will create?"

I must ask myself if in this particular case the benefits for God's kingdom outweigh the liabilities ownership always brings. Will this commitment of my resources, which are God's resources, contribute to or detract from my devotion to and service for my Lord? The answer to these questions may be different for two different believers. But in every case the questions should be asked before the decisions are made.

Like the circus plate spinner who runs frantically from one plate to the next, quickly spinning each again lest it fall and crash, many of us center our lives around things and concerns and activities that demand our constant attention and thereby draw attention away from what God has called us to be and do.

Paul told Timothy, "No one serving as a soldier gets involved in civilian affairs—he wants to please his commanding officer" (2 Tim. 2:4). Notice that Paul did not say civilian concerns are wrong, just that they are distracting. The believer lives to please his Commander. He recognizes that involvement in peripheral things is bound to tap resources that need to be wholly devoted to the overriding cause, the spiritual battle for the kingdom of God. If one is to be a true soldier, not just show up for an occasional weekend drill, he must avoid not only the entanglements of sin but the entanglements in "legitimate things" that result in preoccupation with the peripheral. Everything we accumulate is one more thing that can potentially take our attention away from God.

In the parable of the great banquet, Jesus described the invitations that went out to three men (Luke 14:16-24). One said he had to go look at his newly bought field. Another just got married and didn't have the time. Still another just bought five yoke of oxen and was anxious to try them out. The master is angry at these excuses, and he orders his servants, "Go out quickly into the streets and alleys of the town and bring in the poor, the crippled, the blind and the lame." Speaking of those originally invited, who were preoccupied with other concerns, Jesus said, "I tell you, not one of those men who were invited will get a taste of my banquet."

The most striking thing about this parable is that there was nothing wrong with what any of the three men were involved with. They didn't stay away from the banquet because they were busy stealing or committing adultery. They stayed away because they had more pressing concerns—one a new wife, the others, new possessions. But for "good" reasons or bad, the bottom line is the same—they were so preoccupied with their new treasures that they said no to the banquet-giver and missed the banquet.

For what good and legitimate and compelling reasons are *you* saying no to God? Are there possessions and pressing concerns which are causing *you* to miss the banquet?

CONCLUSION

The ultimate tragedy of materialism is illustrated in the true story of two miners in the Klondike gold rush. After striking a large deposit of gold, they were so excited about unearthing more and more gold each day that they neglected to store up provisions for the winter. Then the first blizzard came. Nearly frozen, one of them wrote a note explaining their foolishness, then lay down to die, having come to his senses too late. Months later a prospecting party discovered the note and their frozen bodies, lying on top of a huge pile of gold.

79

Obsessed with their treasure, these miners had not taken into account that the fair weather would not last and the winter was coming. Hypnotized by their wealth, they failed to prepare for the imminent future. The gold that seemed such a blessing proved to be a curse.

Dazzled by his riches and the prospect of having more, the materialist lives out his life on earth as if this were all there is, failing to prepare for the long life ahead. One day, sooner than he thinks, he will find out he was wrong. In that day he will discover that all the wealth in the world can do nothing for him. But then it will be too late.

We who are alive need to make that discovery now—while it is still not too late for us.

NOTES
1. Herbert Schlossberg, *Idols for Destruction* (Nashville, Tenn.: Nelson, 1983), 88-89.
2. Leland Ryken, *Worldly Saints* (Grand Rapids, Mich.: Zondervan Publishing House, 1986), 62.
3. Quoted by Richard Halverson, *Perspective* 24 June 1987.
4. Quoted by Bruce Wilkinson in his "Walk Thru Rewards" seminar and notebook (Atlanta, Ga.: Walk Thru the Bible Ministries).
5. Beck, Aaron, *The American Journal of Psychiatry,* May 1985.
6. John Piper, *Desiring God* (Portland, Oreg.: Multnomah Press, 1987), 156.
7. David E. Neff, "Drunk on Money," *Christianity Today* 8 April 1988: 15.
8. Neff, 15.
9. Randy C. Alcorn, *Christians in the Wake of the Sexual Revolution* (Portland, Oreg.: Multnomah Press, 1985), 153-54.
10. Piper, 157.

CHAPTER 5

MATERIALISM IN THE CHURCH

Experience shows that it is an easy thing in the midst of worldly business to lose the life and power of religion, that nothing thereof should be left but only the external form, as it were the carcass or shell, worldliness having eaten out the kernel, and having consumed the very soul and life of godliness. Richard Mather

We always pay dearly for chasing after what is cheap. Aleksandr Solzhenitsyn

"God loves you and has a wonderful plan for your bank account." So reads the bold caption of an advertisement in a Christian magazine.

Another ad in several Christian magazines features an expensively dressed man, standing in front of a beautiful home, leaning against a brand new, shiny automobile. The text of the ad tells the reader how he too can become wealthy in his spare time through the Christian ministry opportunity the ad presents.

One Christian author and speaker offers to answer the question, "Who is the Antichrist?" for anyone who will send him $25. The same man will tell you how to earn $10,000 a month (allowing about eight weeks to reach that level of income) in a Christian multilevel marketing plan. All you have to do is send him $10 to find out what it is.

When it comes to materialism, what ought to be a fixed gulf between the world and the church is often no more than a tiny washed-out trench. It is increasingly difficult to tell where the world ends and the church begins.

Religion is capable of baptizing every evil in the world and making it appear to be spiritual. Religious materialism, even when doused in the most spiritual fragrances, is still materialism.

RELIGIOUS MATERIALISM IN SCRIPTURE AND HISTORY

The father of "Christian" materialism was Simon (Acts 8:18-21). When he saw the power of the Holy Spirit he saw dollar signs. He wanted to bottle the Holy Spirit and sell it for his own gain. If Simon were with us today—take a closer look; he is—he would undoubtedly be merchandising the Spirit on radio, television, and every high visibility medium imaginable.

Once Simon began to lose followers to Philip, he was willing to buy into the Christian faith, since it looked like a promising venture. Though he appeared at first to be a genuine convert, Simon's attitude toward God and money gave him away. The Apostle responded to his proposition saying, "You thought you could obtain the gift of God with money," and rebuked him: "Your money perish with you!" The message was clear—God is not selling anything, and he himself is not for sale.

Unfortunately, a thousand Simons infiltrate the church in every age. In the early sixteenth century, Pope Leo X raised funds by selling the forgiveness of sins in the form of "indulgences." For a fee set by the church, a person could supposedly deliver a deceased loved one from purgatory—or even pay against his own future sins. In order to literally buy from the pope the office of archbishop of Mainz, Albert of Brandenburg borrowed a huge sum of money from the bank and, with Leo's authorization, began to sell indulgences in Germany in order to repay the debt.

Albert's chief salesman was Johann Tetzel, who traveled from town to town selling forgiveness as if it were a sack of potatoes or a pair of shoes. Tetzel's catchy chant went like this: "As soon as the coin in the coffer rings, the soul from Purgatory springs." When Tetzel brought his act to Wittenberg, a German priest named Martin Luther was outraged and responded by writing his ninety-five theses, which he nailed to the Wittenberg Church door on October 31, 1517. This marked the beginning of the Protestant Reformation, with its return to the authority of the Scriptures and the doctrine of salvation by faith. And all because one man stood up to oppose the swelling tide of religious materialism.

RELIGIOUS MATERIALISM TODAY

In the last ten years, an amazing array of novelties and trinkets has flooded the religious market, joining the Scripture wall hangings and knickknacks that have been around for decades. We now have our own Jesus jewelry, anointing oil key chains, Scripture tea, Scripture cookies, Scripture soap, Bible belt buckles, prayer and praise pots, Christian dolls, including a Barbie look-alike, and even a soft plastic toy called "Scapegoat" on which Christians can physically take out their frustrations. These things aren't necessarily wrong—they simply reflect our perceived need to replace secular things with religious things.

Each day the mailboxes of a million Christians are full of pleas for money. I have received letters from Christian organizations labeled "personal" and "confidential" that are posted as bulk mail, meaning that at least hundreds and probably thousands and tens of thousands received the same "confidential" letter, asking them each "personally" to send their "essential" gift to keep this "vital" ministry afloat.

Knowing that many people don't even bother opening most of these requests for money, some religious organizations no longer identify themselves on the envelope. Others have begun packaging their mailings to look like they are checks, notifications of sweepstakes winnings, or important notices from the IRS—anything just to get the recipient to open the letter. "The end justifies the means" is the life verse of some religious fund-raisers.

One evangelist wrote requesting the amount of $27 from everyone on his mailing list. He promised to pray over all their letters accompanying their checks as if he were selling his prayers as well as God's answers. He said the $27 had to be in his hand by a certain date and promised to tell any givers the real secret of why the Lord chose that odd amount of $27.

To those who sent in their $27, he responded by asking for a special offering of $48 to pay his television bills. We can only guess how much more money he requested from those who sent in the $48. The same evangelist promised that for $100 he would embroider the giver's name on his pillowcase.

One woman was thrilled to receive a "personal" letter from a Christian leader, indicating that her face was brought to his mind in a vision. God then told him to write to her personally to ask for money. He didn't mention the thousands of others "personally" called up by the computer and sent the identical letter. Believing the letter was written only to her and that God had to be in all this, she sent him money. He did not explain how, having seen her face in the vision, he managed to come up with her name and address.

Some Christian radio and television ministries sell their booklets and blessings at $25 a whack. Others send out holy water, talismans, sacred crosses, and healing handkerchiefs touched by their evangelists. Within a six-month period, one evangelist sent everyone on his mailing list a packet of water from the Sea of Galilee, a "holy cloth" dipped in water from the Jordan river, two coins from Jerusalem, and "communion grape juice from the Holy Land." He also sent them all a plastic coated mustard seed, telling them to carry it with them wherever they go because it will "cause you to be blessed in everything you undertake."

Enclosing a prayer cloth with a picture of Jesus, the same evangelist asked the recipients to cut off the bottom of the cloth (on the dotted line) and send it back with an offering, promising he would touch their cloth with his own hands and pray for them

84

individually. Some mailings from other "ministries" even imply a promise to secure in prayer the salvation of one's loved ones if a certain amount of money is sent (shades of Tetzel!).

One evangelist writes, "The Lord told me to cut up seventy of my neckties that I've worn in my miracle crusades, and send the cloths to 300 of my closest friends." In another letter he claims he needs $300,000 more to make it through the month, and says he is personally going to borrow $100 to give to his ministry and suggests his supporters do the same. Another mailing comes from the man's mother, who says what a fine boy he really is, explaining why everyone should send him money. Still another tactic, used by more than one organization, is the letter saying, "Satan is attacking our ministry through the postal system, and our mailings are apparently being stolen. We must know if you've received this mailing. Please notify us by sending back the enclosed envelope with your offering."

Materialism shows itself in other ways besides money. Theological liberalism, for instance, is a man-centered system that denies eternal realities. The "good news" is that somehow a God without holiness helps a man without sin by a Christ without a cross. God is not taken seriously but is simply used to promote a human agenda. The fact that this agenda may include some benevolent causes doesn't eliminate its exclusive focus on the present life and its therefore materialistic bent. Denying the heart and soul of the gospel, liberalism's attempts to help the world without addressing its ultimate spiritual problem have the same effect as rearranging the furniture on the Titanic.

MATERIALISM AND THE CHRISTIAN LEADER

Anyone with a few hundred dollars can print a brochure, a letterhead, and some business cards, and suddenly be a "ministry." Before long they buy a mailing list from another Christian ministry, and they are on their way, accountable to no one but themselves, and free to tap and dissipate the resources of the Christian community. Attributing their success to the Holy Spirit, often their real power comes from their mailing lists and the gifts of sincere but gullible people.

Some big name Christian celebrities fly around the country

charging a minimum of thousands of dollars for each speaking engagement or musical performance. With egos even bigger than their bank accounts, they are respected most by those who know them least, and least by those who know them best. Many of those on the speaking and singing circuits are fine men and women of God, but some are sadly lacking in character and integrity. They foist themselves upon an undiscerning Christian community with nothing to commend them but an ability to speak or perform, a busy schedule, a book they wrote, a tape they recorded, and words of recommendation from people who don't even know them. When will we learn that talent and notoriety are neither indicators of nor substitutes for character?

In some circles, pastors routinely have mail order and honorary "doctorate degrees" hanging on their walls and delight in being addressed as "Doctor." I recently saw a catalog of an unaccredited seminary where the faculty members average four doctorates each.

Some pastors play the numbers game of grossly exaggerating their church attendance to impress their colleagues, denominations, and communities. Others hang huge pictures of themselves in the church foyer and put their names in large bold print on every piece of literature printed by the church.

One fundamentalist magazine advertised an upcoming rally in the South. The woman bringing the most visitors, the magazine promises, will be crowned queen. Along with her ten runner-up "princesses," she will have her picture taken with a well-known evangelical preacher. Another well-known preacher was recently available after a speaking engagement to shake hands with anyone willing to pay $100 to his ministry. This blatant appeal to ego and its elevation of God's servants as celebrities is just one more form of religious materialism.

How many senior pastors have been pedestaled, fawned over, and spoken of as if the church belonged to them, not Christ? How many large church pastors are given periodic "love offerings," though their salaries are already five times higher than the youth pastor's? Is it any wonder these men begin to believe they are something special, that they grow arrogant and often fall into immorality and disgrace?

Satan is the master of extremes. He is delighted when pastors are underpaid and underappreciated and just as delighted when they are overpaid and overappreciated. For the Devil's tastes, let pastors be crucified or let them be worshipped. When he cringes, and I say this as a pastor, is when we are given the respect we are due and the accountability we need, no more and no less.

One Christian leader tells of a pastor who offered him $1,000 just to come meet with his board and share some biblical principles. When he declined, saying he needed to be spending more time with his family, the pastor replied, "OK, we'll pay you $2,000." After he declined again and the ante was upped to $3,000, this leader made clear he didn't appreciate someone trying to buy him away from his family.

How often does the same thing happen when pulpit committees, especially from large churches, approach a potential pastor? He may say, "Thanks for asking, but I've prayed about it and I believe God would have me stay in my present ministry." But the next thing that happens is the pulpit committee comes back with a better offer, with perhaps an additional $10,000 in salary and promises of a new car and other benefits. Since this is using money in an attempt to persuade a man to violate his stated conviction, what can it be called but bribery? Does the fact that it happens among God's people make it any better—or in reality does it make it worse?

The Lord decried the fact that priests and prophets alike were corrupted by money (Mic. 3:11). Peter reminded church leaders that they were to be characterized by an eagerness to serve, not a greed for money (1 Pet. 5:2). Paul insisted that no lover of money was qualified to be a church leader (1 Tim. 3:3). In A.D. 400 Jerome warned the church, "Shun, as you would the plague, a cleric who from being poor has become wealthy, or who, from being nobody has become a celebrity."[1]

We can thank God that he has countless faithful servants in the ministry, some even in radio and television and other highly visible ministries. But their job is made much more difficult by the religious materialists who cast a shadow on their profession and raise doubts about their credibility.

In recent years several Christian organizations have been called to account for their financial improprieties and unreported, or exaggerated, revenues. This is particularly disturbing when we consider that it was for their deliberately inaccurate account of their financial transactions that God performed the first disciplinary act in church history—striking dead Ananias and Sapphira (Acts 5:1-11). While God may be exercising patience in his response to us today, for which we should be thankful, lest large segments of the church drop dead, we should not be lulled into thinking his disposition has changed toward our need for financial integrity.

MULTILEVEL MATERIALISM
While most of this book is directed to the individual, the family, and the church, many of the illustrations in this chapter deal with Christian ministries and organizations. This is because the materialism of individuals and families and churches naturally surfaces in and lends support to materialism on the larger and more visible scale. But we must be careful not to divorce some of these notorious examples from the very seeds in our own lives from which they arise. The purpose is not to point an accusing finger at others but to understand the presence and manifestations of our own materialism with a view toward changing our own thinking and behavior.

Multilevel marketing businesses provide an example of how large organizations can both reflect and foster materialism in the lives of individuals, families, and churches. Hundreds of thousands of Christians have at one time or another been part of multilevel sales organizations, some of which explicitly claim to be Christian.

I am about to tread on difficult and sensitive territory, and more than a few toes in the process, so some initial clarifications are in order. First, I am not referring to "pyramid schemes" based on the multilevel chain-letter approach where others are enlisted to send in their money for the hope of rising to the top and receiving huge profits. While there is a pyramid element to some multilevel sales companies, pyramids per se are illegal, while legitimate multilevel sales organizations are not.

I want to clarify that a number of multilevel sales organizations, both Christian and secular, do in fact offer good products at a fair price. Furthermore, there is nothing at all wrong with selling products or making a profit. Every Christian needs to work for a living, and sales is a legitimate and respectable profession.

Finally, I recognize that many good Christians are only nominally involved in multilevel sales and do not aggressively recruit others. Furthermore, some of those who *are* heavily involved are nevertheless not guilty of the kinds of attitudes and actions I will address. However, I urge such people to read on with an open mind—for they may be unconsciously or indirectly contributing to some very serious problems.

Countless people over the years have told me the same story, with varying degrees of hurt or anger, and I have experienced it enough times myself to know that it really happens. They are warmly approached by a fellow Christian who appears to be genuinely interested in them. Typically, he or she works into the conversation his involvement with this line of cleaning products or vitamins or cosmetics, then moves to his pitch. Or, he calls and says, "I have a tremendous money-making opportunity to share with you and want you to come over to discuss it," but refuses to disclose what he has in mind. In several cases I know of, the caller has actually lied rather than reveal his true purpose.

A number of times I have received "the call" from an old fellow-alumnus from Bible college or seminary or some other Christian I have met along the way. First, he asks about me and my family, saying pleasant and flattering things, then finally he moves to his real reason for calling. When I politely say "no" to his proposition, sometimes he will not accept a "no" and I must get firmer. Then all his interest for me and my family is suddenly transferred to the next person on his contact list, which basically consists of every person he has ever met whose name he can remember.

With inspiration from silver-tongued success speakers, positive-thinking gurus, pop psychologists, and pop theologians, whose repertoire of Scripture verses is limited to the prosperity passages, some multilevel sales organizations are so materialistically oriented and money-driven as to make even a secularist blush. Of course, interspersed with the promise of luxury cars and trips around the world are spirit-soothing reminders that the Christian will be able to give more to God and others than ever before. The most effective appeals to the flesh are made under the guise of the Spirit.

The distinctive of multilevel sales is that people are not just potential customers but potential distributors who come "under" their recruiter, who from that point forward makes a percentage of their profits as well as his own. Not only is every occasion a potential sales pitch and every person a potential sale, but in this system every person is a potential salesman, making money for me. In such a system, people naturally become hot items—objects, not subjects. Their personal welfare may be a concern, but it is not *the* concern. No matter how much I deny it, my interest in them is primarily utilitarian—my concern is what they can do for me. If it is really them I'm concerned about, I must ask how interested in them I was before they became part of the blueprint for my own prosperity.

A man and his wife were invited to dinner by two close friends who had recently become involved in a multilevel sales company. Before dinner was served, the man noticed out of the corner of his eye that his host had deliberately tipped over the gravy bowl, spilling it onto the tablecloth. Saying something like "clumsy me," he marched into the kitchen, then reappeared with a bottle of cleaning fluid and proceeded to demonstrate its amazing ability to get gravy stains out of tablecloths. He then went straight into a sales pitch for his multilevel sales organization and its wonderful products, which sell themselves. The other couple was deeply hurt and shaken by this deception and manipulation, and that was not only the end of the evening but the end of a long and valued friendship.

The victimized man in the above story told me, "It's no problem if someone asks me to buy something—I can just say yes or no. But when people set you up like that, and especially a good Christian friend . . . something is really wrong."

Something *is* really wrong. This is the same exploitative and manipulative approach, the same method of using people that we identified in the previous chapter as one of the prime characteristics of materialism. Sadly, it is far more common in the Christian community than any of us would like to believe. And it is not just in multilevel sales.

A woman and her family visited our church one Sunday, got hold of our church directory, and, we found out later, immediately started calling people straight down the list, offering her services with a particular multilevel sales company. When she called my wife, this woman shared how much she enjoyed our church and that her family had already decided ours would be their new church home. After some more pleasantries, she then tried to sell her particular product. When my wife politely said she wasn't interested, the woman's previously sweet tone noticeably changed and she asked if there were others in the church already selling her product. When my wife said "Yes," there was a quiet "Oh," and the conversation ended. So did the relationship with our church—they did not come back even one more Sunday, presumably moving on to "greener pastures" at a church with less sales competition and more profit potential.

Because an up-front and to-the-point approach may be quickly dismissed, the more covert sales approach is often adopted. Unfortunately, it lends itself to ulterior motives, and people are targeted rather than cared for and related to in honesty. Strategies are developed to effectively persuade people to overcome their resistance—including the strategy of keeping them in the dark to get them to a meeting they would otherwise never attend, as well as showing profit scenarios that one in a thousand achieve, rather than showing what an average person really makes.

Instead of openly relating as brothers and sisters in Christ, people come with hidden agendas and unspoken purposes, calculating how to produce a desired response. Others begin to catch on to this, and the result is a loss of credibility. People sense what is too often true—they are being viewed as potential profits rather than human beings. They are the object of a recruitment strategy that borders on headhunting. How many of us, due to our past experiences with such people, now instinctively ask, sometimes unfairly, "Why is he being so nice to me? What's his angle? What's he leading up to?" That we should have to ask such questions out in society is sad enough. That we should have to ask them inside the church is tragic.

It is particularly regrettable when pastors and lay leaders are involved in multilevel marketing and use their contacts with people as a platform for their personal financial profits. When the pastor or lay leader calls or knocks on the door, people don't know whether he is there to minister or to make contact with a potential customer or recruit. In some cases the caller himself may not really know. This is a conflict of interests that can undermine the integrity of an entire ministry.

How does the multilevel marketing phenomenon work out in the life of the church? Sometimes, no doubt, it works out fine. But sometimes it produces fanatics whose "ministry" is their day and night devotion to their sales and recruitment, who use but are of no use to the body of Christ. Sometimes it produces people who seem capable of thinking and talking about nothing other than their lucrative business and how they will soon be able to quit their other job, buy their dream home, and retire in paradise. Sometimes it produces people who use church social gatherings and home Bible studies to share their "testimonies" of how this company or this product has transformed their lives. Sometimes it even produces people who move from church to church to get more customers, who exaggerate or downright lie about their profits, and who go into debt to pursue materialistic life-styles as proof of their success and God's blessing—the "fake it till you make it" approach.

Deep involvement in multilevel sales changes people, and often not for the best. Some end up fueling the greed of their brothers and sisters in Christ, tampering with their priorities, and encouraging them to pursue a path of materialism. Some go so far as to restrict their friendships to those who work under them or over them or buy their products or are useful to them in some other way. Some become evangelists who spread tapes and literature far and wide, anxious to pass on "the good news" of their wonderful organization and money-making opportunity, while they may not have shared the true "Good News" for years. Sometimes, in fact, their "gospels" get hopelessly confused. Most of us can only handle one gospel—when there are two we end up sharing the one that is most to our immediate advantage.

Besides the well-known larger multilevel sales organizations, there are numerous smaller ones and many others that have come and gone through the years. Some garages are still filled five years later with products that were supposed to "sell themselves." But why do multilevel sales plans manage to thrive in the Christian community in the first place? The answer is that the church is an ideal climate for such a system because there is already an established level of trust ("He's a good church-goer and my brother in Christ") and a well-established network of people—also known as contacts—who are already linked by having something important in common (Christ and the church).

While there is nothing wrong with a businessman having customers from his own church—indeed, such a thing is natural and healthy when it develops on its own—it is another thing for him to go out and actively recruit them. When we do that, something ugly starts to happen to us and to our view of others. We begin using the body of Christ to further our own purposes for financial gain. And those who see no danger in this are, in their very failure to see it, living proof of how dangerous it really is.

MODERN MONEY CHANGERS AND
AN ANGRY CARPENTER

Religion was turned into big business by the money changers, who made their profits exchanging currency and selling "convenience" animals for sacrifice in the temple. Apparently, they charged an excessive price and probably engaged in loud haggling that destroyed the climate of worship (John 2:13-17). Jesus was outraged that people would see the community of saints as an opportunity to earn a quick profit and make a place of worship part of a scheme for personal gain. After driving out with a whip the salesmen and their animals, scattering the coins and overturning the money tables, the strong-armed carpenter from Galilee nailed the frightened materialists to the wall with words that could, no doubt, be heard in the streets: "Get these out of here! How dare you turn my Father's house into a market!"

Is Christ any less outraged by materialism in the church today? Are we less deserving of his wrath than those two thousand years ago? Will God hesitate to turn the whip on us any more than he did on them?

In 1987 and 1988 the public gained an unprecedented and disturbing look at the inner workings of three of the major Christian television ministries. What happened has much to teach us—and may well represent the whip of the outraged Son of God disciplining and purging the modern Christian community for our materialism.

Before moving further into an area that will offend still more readers, let me once again make an initial clarification. In each of the three well-known scandals I am about to refer to, I personally believe the Christian leaders involved were originally sincere and honestly devoted to the Lord. In fact, the same may be true of them presently. But that does not take away from the force of what happened to them nor the seriousness of the wrong thinking that characterized their lives and ministries. On the contrary, their sincerity is what is most alarming. There are wolves in sheep's clothing, but there are also terribly misguided sheep, some of whom take on the role of shepherds. They may not devour the flock and be done with it, as a wolf might do. Instead, they may lead it astray, all the while adding new sheep to their flocks daily. I have no personal vendetta against these people or their organizations. While in this chapter and the next I have deliberately not mentioned specific names in my illustrations, in this particular case the names are so well known, and the publicity so far-reaching, that to withhold names would be pointless.

For years the PTL network, headed by Jim and Tammy Faye Bakker, had maintained a superficial and wealth-oriented emphasis, replete with heavy makeup, large flashy jewelry, expensive clothes, and frequent mention of trips to exotic places. The Bakkers had their lavish homes, limousines, and endless other "fringe benefits" from their viewer's ministry contributions, including a heated and air-conditioned dog house and chandeliers in their walk-in closets. Yet all the while they made frequent pleas, sometimes in tears, for people to "please send more money for our ministry."

The words were evangelical, but the life-style and values were Hollywood—a baptized Hollywood dressed in a Sunday suit, but Hollywood nonetheless. Many observers could not help but believe that beneath the surface of this ego-feeding opulence and showiness was a serious spiritual and moral erosion just waiting to be revealed. It *was* revealed, as most will remember, and the details do not need to be dredged up here. It is sufficient to say that the story involved adultery, payoffs, addictions, power struggles, and opulence even beyond what was imagined.

All this is the very stuff of which soap operas are made, but this time the soap opera was sponsored and funded by the evangelical community, which was pouring $100 million a year into the PTL network, not including revenues from the Heritage Theme Park, "a Christian Disneyland," and Tammy Faye's books and records.

Meanwhile, television evangelist Oral Roberts stepped into the show. Roberts defended the Bakkers, telling the Christian public to "send more money than ever to PTL" and rebuking a third television evangelist for supposedly plotting a takeover of PTL. (It is interesting to note that when Oral Roberts came on television to defend Jim Bakker, a thunderstorm suddenly cut off the telecast. One couldn't help but wonder if God was trying to get a word in edgewise.)

The man who revealed Jim Bakker's exploits to Assembly of God officials was well-known televangelist Jimmy Swaggart. This was significant for several reasons, including the fact that a year earlier Swaggart had similarly exposed prominent New Orleans pastor and televangelist Martin Gorman, who admitted to one adulterous affair but filed a lawsuit against Swaggart for accusing him of still other immoral relationships (this became an important factor later in the story). Swaggart, accused of trying to eliminate his television competitors and take over the PTL empire, publicly decried Bakker's perversions and stated, "Jim Bakker is a cancer on the body of Christ."

By this time a fourth televangelist, Jerry Falwell, had been asked to lead PTL peacefully from chaos to stability. Despite his sincere efforts to do so, he became the center of further controversy, especially when he publicly revealed Jim Bakker's sexual encounters in specific detail. The secular media, dubbing this "The Holy Wars," gleefully reported the daily casualties.

Only days before his questionable intervention in this scandal, Oral Roberts had received a 1.3 million dollar gift from a millionaire dog-racer (his fortune made in the same gambling arena that Roberts publicly opposed for years). This strange benefactor then stated to the press that Roberts "needs psychiatric help."

The "life-saving" 1.3 million dollars from the dog-racer climaxed what might be the most bizarre fund-raising attempt in television history, which is no small claim. Oral Roberts had publicly announced that God had told him he would take his life unless by a certain date he could raise $8 million for a medical scholarship program.

The implications of this fund-raising scenario were far-reaching. As a world without Christ looked on, God was cast in the role of a ruthless money-loving gangland figure, who was holding Roberts for ransom and threatening to kill him if someone didn't cough up the ransom money. A Celestial Loanshark, God the Father (or the Godfather?) was portrayed as even more capricious and vindictive than the Mafia, since Oral Roberts, presumably, was not a double-crossing weasel or a sniveling welsher, but one of God's faithful "boys," one of his own gang!

The only thing that can be said for this fund-raising technique is that, unfortunately, it worked. And that is the scariest thing of all; for in a materialistic system, if it "works," that is if it makes money, then it is right. Morality, if there is any such thing to the materialist, is simply a function of economics.

Unfortunately, the Oral Roberts story did not end there. Less than a year later he called off the medical scholarship program he had been ready to die for. Apparently, either God or Oral had changed his mind, and neither alternative spoke highly of either party. After the bad publicity this generated, Oral—or was it God?—changed his mind once again and said God had called 80,000 followers to give $100 each to raise the $8 million *per year* the program requires. Finances got so bad, in fact, that Roberts had to sell his $3.25 million Beverly Hills mansion.

Meanwhile, after receiving some anonymous tips, former pastor and televangelist Martin Gorman, still outraged at Swaggart for exposing his adultery, reputedly hired a private detective to follow Swaggart. Swaggart, whose castigation of Jim Bakker's perversions was still fresh in the public mind, was then confronted with pictures of himself with a prostitute. Swaggart confessed that he had paid her to perform pornographic acts, and that he had an obsession with pornography going back to his childhood. In an issue that sold out in five days, one prostitute posed for *Penthouse* and recounted her raunchy involvements with Swaggart. Seeming to express genuine repentance, yet defying his denomination's attempts at discipline, Swaggart was back to his television ministry only three months later. Oral Roberts assured the public that he had healed Swaggart of his lust problem over the phone.

By this time it was hard to tell the difference between ministries and miniseries. In one nine-month period, the whole country and a good share of the entire world had come to believe that of the televangelists whose names they knew, three were greedy sexual perverts, and a fourth was not playing with a full deck. One other, Falwell, had been unfairly linked with the whole mess. Judging by the radical decrease in financial gifts all around, the public wasn't so sure of the remaining televangelists either!

One sociologist, quoted in *Newsweek,* stated, "What you have seen here is the natural rise and fall of unchecked power."[2] He could just as easily have said "unchecked materialism."

To those who understand the ingredients, such scandals were predictable, if not inevitable, long before they surfaced. The combination of human depravity and the staggering financial proportions and lack of accountability of these ministries spelled nothing but temptation and could produce nothing but disaster.

ARE WE TO BLAME TOO?

The problem is not that "media ministries are bad." Christian publishing is a media ministry, and without it this book wouldn't be in your hands. In fact, you wouldn't even have a Bible. There are many fine ministries in television and radio as well. In no way do I intend to lump them all together or to throw out the good with the bad. I also recognize that there are many sincere Christians even in those organizations rocked by scandal and, from direct conversations with some of them, I also know that there are serious efforts being made to build from a new foundation and correct the structural, moral, and spiritual weaknesses that produced or allowed so many of the problems in the first place.

But a fundamental question remains. Of the most obviously shallow, superficial, egocentric and materialistic "ministries," many of which are still in business, we must ask, "Why did the Christian community support them in the first place? And why do we continue to support them?"

Part of the answer may be that there are many non-Christian contributors trying to "buy into" salvation as a businessman might buy into a real estate deal. But surely the majority are at least professing Christians. And this forces us to a sobering conclusion—namely that it is not that these people up front are superficial and materialistic and we are not, but that we are superficial and materialistic and they are giving us precisely what we want. Except when they embarrass us by falling into sexual immorality, though ironically moral failure is one of the many natural results of the very life-styles we make possible and even encourage with our donations.

If their supporters did not like what they are doing, their ministries would cease to exist because the money would dry up. Is the truth of the matter that their values are the mirror image of our own? Is the truth that in our own way, given our own financial means, we are just as materialistic, just as ego-centered, just as shallow and superficial, and sometimes even as immoral as they?

The indictment is not just on them but on the undiscerning ones who support them. People should have long ago seen through these organizations and invested their money and time and prayers instead in the innumerable faithful servants of God on the local and national and international scenes that elevate Christ's name rather than their own.

"But I don't support these scandalous ministries and I never did." Scripture doesn't let us off so easily. There is one body of Christ, and we are all members of it. I cannot separate myself from the rest of the evangelical church in my country. Her successes are mine, and so are her failures. I must ask, how is my life resisting the materialism of the church rather than contributing to it? How am I providing a model that is a clear alternative to the materialism that has so undermined the integrity of the Christian community?

Because we allow—at best—and endorse—at worst—a false or superficial form of the Faith, people without Christ judge the church by the three-ring circus that makes the front page and walk away with one of two responses. They feel worse: "Obviously these Christians don't have the answer, and I was hoping they did because I really need an answer." Or they feel better, saying, "Just as I suspected, they're all a bunch of hypocrites anyway, and I should feel fine because I'm as good as they are, or better." Either way, the church's folly is the world's loss—and, worst of all, shame is brought to the sacred name of Christ.

Of course, the truth is that the only thing worth counterfeiting is that which is in the first place valuable. People make counterfeit currency and jewels, not counterfeit bottle caps or garbage. Since the truth of the gospel is priceless, we should expect it to be continuously counterfeited. Bank employees are taught to identify counterfeit bills not primarily by studying counterfeits but by handling the real thing. If you are not acquainted with the original, you can easily be deceived by an imitation. But once you are familiar with the genuine article, you will be able to spot a counterfeit.

No matter how many counterfeit bills someone runs across, he should never conclude, "There's no such thing as real money." What the world needs is the genuine gospel, lived and proclaimed by a genuine church. Then it will dismiss the counterfeits for what they are rather than concluding that because there are so many counterfeits there must not be a true gospel.

HOW DID WE GET HERE?

Is the church, in its treatment of money and possessions, really any different than the world? We have our philanthropists, to be sure, but so does the world. We have charities and relief funds, but so does the world.

Why does the Christian community in the Western world bear so little resemblance to the church described in the early chapters of Acts? It is not that we have said nothing about the subject of money and possessions. On the contrary, innumerable Christian financial teachers, writers, investment counselors, and seminar leaders have ridden in on the wake of our national prosperity in recent years. But what have most of them brought us? While some take pains to be biblical, many simply parrot their secular colleagues. Other than beginning and ending with prayer and sprinkling in some Bible verses, there is no fundamental difference. They reinforce people's already materialistic attitudes and life-styles. They suggest a variety of profitable plans in which people can hoard and stockpile the bulk of their resources. In short, to borrow a term from Jesus, some (by no means all) are helping people to be the most successful "rich fools" they can be.

Not wanting to come across as negative—the unpardonable sin of our day—or to spoil the party for ourselves or others, we have failed to take materialism as a serious threat to godliness. We have rationalized and justified our lust for money and possessions. But we have not been content to leave it there—we have actually baptized our materialism, couched it in religious terms, and affirmed it as God's plan for our lives. This is prosperity theology, the gospel of health and wealth, and the subject of our next chapter.

Meanwhile, a sobering question remains, one that will not go away and one that every Christian must ask in light of his own values and life-style: Can a materialistic world ever be won to Christ by a materialistic church?

NOTES
1. "Quick Quotes on Money," *Christian History Magazine* (Worcester, Penn.: Christian History Institute, 1987), 7: 2, 4.
2. Larry Martz, "TV Preachers On the Rocks," *Newsweek* 11 July 1988: 26.

CHAPTER 6

PROSPERITY THEOLOGY: THE GOSPEL OF WEALTH

Religion begat prosperity and the daughter devoured the mother.
Cotton Mather

The figure of the Crucified invalidates all thought that takes success for its standards. Dietrich Bonhoeffer

"God doesn't want his children driving Volkswagens; he wants them driving Cadillacs. God wants only the best for his kids!" So says a popular radio preacher.

A television evangelist begs his audience, including widows living on Social Security, to send in their dollars, lest his program be canceled. Implied is the message that God doesn't want the program canceled. Next to him, tears washing her mascara down her cheeks, is his wife, whose bracelets and rings and necklaces cost more than many viewers make in a year. When criticized for living in opulence from funds supporters send for his ministry, this same man stands before the press and defends his life-style as "a commandment from Christ."

An elderly couple receive a packet of "Holy Bible Anointing Oil." The accompanying letter says, "It is God's will for you to feel good in your body and have plenty of money." The recipients are to put their finger in the oil and make a cross on their foreheads. Then they are told to anoint their checkbooks, after which the minister of God writing the letter says, "Now, write out the largest check you can, and send it to me. I need your help."

A mailing from another evangelist says, "I feel led of the Lord, [Brother/Sister—inserted by computer] [first name—inserted by computer], to write personally to you there in [city name inserted by computer] and send you the enclosed red cloth that I have anointed with oil. If you need healing in your body, pin this red cloth inside your clothing next to the place that needs healing. If you have a financial need, carry this cloth in your billfold." Another mailing promises healing from touching the enclosed cloth—"God spoke to me that he will use this anointed Easter Cross Prayer Cloth just like he used Paul's in Acts 19:11-12."

Still another "man of God" stands before his audiences and rebukes the "spirit of poverty," assuring them of material prosperity. He sends a Christmas letter concerning "the urgent need you have to get into true biblical prosperity as the wise men did. The money they brought literally met the financial needs of Mary, Joseph, and the child in that desperate hour." By wisely sending money to this evangelist in *his* desperate hour, according to the letter, one may expect to become materially prosperous just like the wise men were.

These are but a few manifestations of a large and vocal segment of American evangelicalism that subscribes to what is called "prosperity theology," or the "health and wealth gospel." Once again, the problem is not just "out there," but "in here." The Christian ministries mentioned above thrive only because they have willing supporters, eager to get their share of the prosperity pie. This chapter does not simply apply to some extreme and offbeat Christian leaders. It applies to the attitudes and life-styles of millions of mainstream Christians who, to varying degrees, have bought into prosperity theology.

THE OLD TESTAMENT AND PROSPERITY

What makes every heresy dangerous is its element of truth. Truth serves to bootleg in the lie. Without a sugarcoating of truth, the lie would never be swallowed.

The element of truth that makes prosperity theology credible is that some Old Testament teaching does in fact link material prosperity with God's blessing. Because he approved of them, God gave material wealth to Abraham (Gen. 13:1-7), Isaac (Gen. 26:12-14), Jacob (Gen. 30:43), Joseph (Gen. 39:2-6), Solomon (1 Kings 3:13), and Job (Job 42:10-17). God also promised the people of Israel that he would reward them materially for faithful financial giving (Deut. 15:10; Prov. 3:9-10; 11:25; Mal. 3:8-12).

God promised the Israelites he would reward their obedience in the form of children, crops, livestock, and victory over enemies (Deut. 28:1-13). These thirteen verses are immediately followed by fifty-four more describing in detail the curses that will come upon them if they don't obey God—including diseases, heat and drought, military defeat, boils, tumors, madness, and blindness. Note that this teaching is double-edged: prosperity for obedience, adversity for disobedience.

However, the Old Testament also warns against the dangers of wealth—especially that we may forget the Lord and attribute our wealth to our own strength, ingenuity, or righteousness (Deut. 8:7-18). Furthermore, it recognizes clear and frequent exceptions to the prosperity-adversity doctrine, especially noting that the wicked often prosper as much or more than the righteous. The psalmist said, "I have seen a wicked and ruthless man flourishing like a green tree in its native soil" (Ps. 37:35). "For I envied the arrogant when I saw the prosperity of the wicked. . . . This is what the wicked are like—always carefree, they increase in wealth" (Ps. 73:3, 12). Solomon saw "a righteous man perishing in his righteousness, and a wicked man living long in his wickedness" (Eccles. 7:15). Jeremiah, a righteous man who lived in constant adversity, framed the question this way: "You are always righteous, O Lord, when I bring a case before you. Yet I would speak with you about your justice: Why does the way of the wicked prosper? Why do all the faithless live at ease?" (Jer. 12:1).

This is a critical issue for believers in any age. Is material wealth or achievement or fame or victory or success an indication of God's reward or approval of men? If so, then he is an evil God, for history is full of successful madmen and prosperous despots. During their rise to power and the height of their regimes, surrounded by material wealth, was God on the side of Hitler and other butchers of history? Is God also on the side of wealthy cultists, dishonest business executives, immoral rock stars, and ruthless loan sharks?

If wealth is a dependable sign of God's approval, and lack of wealth his disapproval, then Jesus and Paul were on his blacklist, and the Mafia is the apple of his eye.

CHRIST AND PROSPERITY

Many Jews in Old and New Testament times appear to have believed in a direct cause-and-effect relationship between righteousness and prosperity on the one hand, and sin and adversity on the other. Health and wealth meant God approved; sickness and poverty meant he did not. Job's "comforters" thought there must be hidden sin in his life to account for his loss of prosperity, but they were wrong. God approved of Job, yet he allowed him to lose everything.

The well-to-do Pharisees lived and breathed prosperity theology and relished labeling everyone beneath their social caste as "sinners" (Luke 15:1-2; John 9:34). Christ's disciples betrayed their own belief in the prosperity doctrine when they asked, "Rabbi, who sinned, this man or his parents, that he was born blind?" (John 9:2). Jesus responded by saying their presupposition was entirely wrong: "Neither this man nor his parents sinned, but this happened so that the work of God might be displayed in his life" (John 9:3). In other words, God had a higher purpose for this man's adversity that simply didn't fit in the neat little boxes of, "Do good and you'll be well off" and "Do bad and you won't be."

Note also their response when Christ told his disciples, "It is hard for a rich man to enter the kingdom of heaven," and "It is easier for a camel to go through the eye of a needle than for a rich man to enter the kingdom of God" (Matt. 19:23-24). "When the disciples heard this, they were greatly astonished and asked, "Who then can be saved?" (19:25).

Why the great astonishment? Because they were accustomed to thinking of wealth as a sign of God's approval. So if the wealthy, of whom God obviously approves—why else would he make them wealthy?—would have a hard time going to heaven, how could the poor—of whom God obviously disapproves—ever make it? They had not yet grasped the significance of their own Lord's life-style, for the same one whose Father said of him, "This is my beloved Son in whom I am well pleased," was also the Son of Man who did not have a place to lay his head and owned nothing but a robe and sandals.

Jesus said of his Father in heaven, "He causes his sun to rise on the evil and the good, and sends rain on the righteous and the unrighteous" (Matt. 5:45). In other words, God extends his common grace to all. The air breathed by every man, sinner or saint, is God's gift, regardless of the man's morality. Christ's words suggest that what we call prosperity is often no more than incidental—the evil man may have good soil and a large crop, the good man poor soil and a small crop. The evil man may live a long life, suffer little, and prosper much, while the righteous man may have his life cut short, may live it in pain, and may be materially poor. All this will, of course, be radically reversed in the life to come.

But the New Testament goes one step farther. It demonstrates not only that the righteous may suffer despite their righteousness, but will often suffer precisely *because* of their righteousness—"Everyone who wants to live a godly life in Christ Jesus will be persecuted" (2 Tim. 3:12). The early Christians consistently suffered for their faith and were assured that "your brothers throughout the world are undergoing the same kind of sufferings" (1 Pet. 5:9). A materialistic world system does not look with favor upon a true disciple of Christ, as the Lord himself told his disciples (John 15:18-20).

These should be disturbing thoughts for any of us whose goal is to be hailed a success by the standards of this world. If we fit in so well with the world, is it because we are living by the world's standards and not our Lord's?

LIVE LIKE THE KING'S KID?

There is a great irony to the popular saying in health and wealth circles, "Live like a king's kid." *The* "King's kid" was Jesus, who lived a life exactly the opposite of what is meant by the phrase today, a life without material abundance. The King we serve is stripped down for battle. He will don the royal robes of victory at the end of the age, and so shall his faithful servants with him, but this is now the age for battle garb, not regalia.

And how, after all, did the King send his "kid" into this world? Born in lowly Bethlehem, raised in corrupt and despised Nazareth, part of a pious but poor family that offered two doves because they could not afford a lamb (Lev. 12:6-8; Luke 2:24). Christ wandered the countryside dependent on others to open their homes, for he had none of his own. "Live like a king's kid." Whatever king's kid the prosperity proponents are speaking of, it obviously isn't Jesus.

Prosperity theology sees as our model the ascended heavenly Lord rather than the descended earthly Servant. But Jesus warned his disciples not to follow a lordship model, but his own servant model (Mark 10:42-45). In *this* life we are to share in his cross—in the *next* life we will share in his crown (2 Tim. 2:12).

In verses you will never see embroidered or framed or even posted on refrigerators, the King promised persecution, betrayal, flogging, and the opportunity to be dragged before courts and tried for our faith (Matt. 10:16-20). He warned, "In this world you will have trouble" (John 16:33), and said, "Any of you who does not give up everything he has cannot be my disciple" (Luke 14:33).

Not the stuff of which prosperity mailers and sermons are made.

PAUL AND PROSPERITY

Other than the life and teachings of Christ, the most powerful refutation of prosperity theology is the life and writings of the greatest theologian in church history, the Apostle Paul. As the health gospel tries to experience the full redemption of the body in this life, so the wealth gospel tries to experience heaven's rewards on earth. Since these are two inseparable sides of the prosperity coin, we will look at Paul's life in terms of both health and wealth, as well as other trappings of success.

Raised a Pharisee, and therefore a believer in prosperity theology, Paul was one of those who could not believe Jesus was Messiah due to Jesus' obvious lack of success. God's disapproval of the man Jesus was surely self-evident in his questionable parentage, his disreputable place of upbringing, his lack of formal education, his poverty, and, above all, his shameful death. But once Paul bowed his stubborn knee to the Carpenter from Galilee, he also turned his back forever on his old prosperity theology.

In the letter to the Philippians, written from a prison—not a plush office or the Rome Hilton—Paul said, "It has been granted to you on behalf of Christ not only to believe on him, but also to suffer for him" (1:29). He then depicted Christ as the suffering Servant, whose ultimate prosperity came after his life on this earth, not during it (2:5-11). Indeed, had Jesus laid claim to prosperity in this life, there would have been no crucifixion, no atonement, no gospel, and no hope for any of us.

In Philippians 3, Paul talked about his credentials of success, his diplomas and awards. These he once highly valued, but later said, "Whatever was to my profit I now consider loss for the sake of Christ. What is more, I consider everything a loss compared to the surpassing greatness of knowing Christ Jesus my Lord, for whose sake I have lost all things. I consider them rubbish, that I may gain Christ" (Phil. 3:7-8).

As a result of following Christ, Paul lost all things. What little money and things might pass through his hands he also considered a loss. The translators are too kind to us, for Paul actually did not call his credentials and possessions "rubbish," but rather "dung"—manure or excrement. That is how he views all the things he once valued, when he stacks them up against Christ.

In another letter, Paul described his daily adversity, his persecution for Christ, and his nearness to death (2 Cor. 4:7-12). Two chapters later he refers to his troubles, hardships, distresses, beatings, imprisonments, riots, sleepless nights, and hunger, as well as the experience of nearly dying, and being sorrowful and poor (2 Cor. 6:3-10).

Perhaps the most graphic portrayal of Paul's difficult life was later in the same letter:

> I have worked much harder, been in prison more frequently, been flogged more severely, and been exposed to death again and again. Five times I received from the Jews the forty lashes minus one. Three times I was beaten with rods, once I was stoned, three times I was shipwrecked, I spent a night and a day in the open sea, I have been constantly on the move. I have been in danger from rivers, in danger from bandits, in danger from my own countrymen, in danger from Gentiles; in danger in the city, in danger in the country, in danger at sea; and in danger from false brothers. I have labored and toiled and have often gone without sleep; I have known hunger and thirst and have often gone without food; I have been cold and naked. Besides everything else, I face daily the pressure of my concern for all the churches. Who is weak, and I do not feel weak? Who is led into sin, and I do not inwardly burn? (2 Cor. 11:23-29)

Paul seemed to be making a strong case for what we could call "adversity theology," or the "sickness and poverty gospel." I sometimes wonder if in his dreams the apostle ever heard a faint chorus of voices from the far future saying, "Paul, you don't have to live like this—why don't you trust God and live like a king's kid?"

The truth is, Paul *did* hear some of these same voices in his own day. In fact, in his first letter to the Corinthians, Paul had to defend himself against the "super-apostles," those well-off ministers who berated him because he was not experiencing their wealth and prestige (1 Cor. 4:8-13). He said to them, "Already you have all you want! Already you have become rich! You have become kings" (v. 8). He said, "We are weak, but you are strong! You are honored, we are dishonored!" (v. 10). Paul faced off with these prosperity preachers, pointing out that they had jumped the gun on reigning with Christ by living as kings rather than as servants in this world. Paul's point was clear—don't try to reign prematurely!

Looking again at 2 Corinthians, we see that Paul explained that God had given him some spiritual privileges, including special revelations. Then he said:

> To keep me from being conceited . . . there was given me a thorn in the flesh, a messenger of Satan, to torment me. Three times I pleaded with the Lord to take it away from me. But he said to me, "My grace is sufficient for you, for my power is made perfect in weakness." Therefore I will boast all the more gladly about my weaknesses, so that Christ's power may rest on me. That is why, for Christ's sake, I delight in weaknesses, in insults, in hardships, in persecutions, in difficulties. For when I am weak, then I am strong. (2 Cor. 12:7-10)

Paul indicated that, first of all, God had a definite purpose in his illness or disability. We don't know what the disease was, but among other things it apparently caused his deteriorating eyesight. His affliction, Paul said, was "given" to him in order to keep him from being conceited.

Second, God had a specific purpose for not removing the disease—to teach Paul that his grace alone was sufficient. Paul was not to trust in his own strength but in God's. His disease was a day-by-day reminder of his need to trust in the Lord rather than his own gifts, accomplishments, or privileged position.

Instead of assuming God wants us healthy, we need to realize that he may accomplish higher purposes through our sickness rather than our health. We may pray for health and pray for healing when we are sick, which is exactly what Paul did. But notice that he prayed only three times. When God chose not to heal him, he did not "name it and claim it" and demand that God heal him. Instead, he acknowledged God's spiritual purpose in his adversity.

Today's health and wealth preachers bypass the rest of this passage and say, "Look, Paul called this disease a 'messenger of Satan.' It's from the devil, not God. The devil wants us sick, but God wants us well." Paul called the ailment a messenger of Satan, to be sure. But God is bigger than all beings and sovereign over all wills, and Satan is just one more agent he can use to accomplish his own purpose. After all, whose purpose and plan is the passage talking about? It was not Satan, but *God* whom Paul saw as the ultimate giver of the disease, for Satan would never give anyone something to keep him from being conceited. And it was not Satan but God who refused to remove the disease despite Paul's pleadings.

If you have prayed for healing and not received it, take heart—you are in good company! Not only was Paul not healed, but he had to leave Trophimus in Miletus because of sickness (2 Tim. 4:20), and his beloved friend Epaphroditus was gravely ill as well (Phil. 2:25-30). His son in the faith, Timothy, had frequent stomach disorders, concerning which Paul didn't tell him to "claim healing" but to drink a little wine for medicinal purposes (1 Tim. 5:23). Those who claim "anyone with enough faith can be healed" apparently have more faith than the Apostle Paul.

Paul, like many of God's servants in the early church, was neither healthy nor wealthy, and it is clear that God did not intend for him to be healthy or wealthy. Of course, Paul is now enjoying perfect health and wealth for all eternity, but when he was on this earth, it was God's higher plan that for much of his life he not have either.

When Paul was taken in chains from his filthy Roman dungeon and beheaded at the order of the opulent madman Nero, two representatives of humanity faced off, one of the best and one of the worst. One lived for prosperity on earth and one did not. One now lives in prosperity in heaven, the other does not. We remember both men for what they truly were, which is why we name our sons "Paul" and our dogs "Nero."

Leland Ryken offers this summary of the Puritans' perspectives on these very issues:

> In the first place, the Puritans disagreed that godliness is a guarantee of success. Thomas Watson went so far as to say that "true godliness is usually attended with persecution. . . . The saints have no charter of exemption from trials. . . . Their piety will not shield them from sufferings."
>
> If godliness is not a guarantee of success, then the converse is also true: success is not a sign of godliness. This is how the Puritans understood the matter. John

Cotton stated that a Christian "equally bears good and evil successes as God shall dispense them to him." Samuel Willard wrote, "As riches are not evidences of God's love, so neither is poverty of his anger or hatred." Samuel Heiron said that just as many of God's "beloved servants do feel the smart of poverty, so even the most wicked . . . have a large portion in this life."[1]

THE NEW TESTAMENT UNDERSTANDING OF WEALTH

How then can we explain the apparent contradiction between the words and life-styles of Christ and the apostles, on the one hand, and the Old Testament prosperity passages on the other? The answer lies in the fundamental differences between the Old and New Covenants, which we will explore in chapter 11, "The Steward's Pilgrim Mentality." For now, it is sufficient to point out that the New Testament reflects a major change in its understanding of true wealth.

In the New Testament the Greek word *ploutos* is used six times for material riches put to evil purposes (Matt. 13:22; Mark 4:19; Luke 8:14; 1 Tim. 6:17; James 5:2; Rev. 18:17). Yet the same word is used eleven times in the positive sense, every one of which refers to *spiritual,* not material, riches (Rom. 11:33; Eph. 1:18; Phil. 4:19; Col. 1:27).

The New Testament Christian believes in true and eternal spiritual riches. In fact, once he experiences those riches in a deep and personal way, he finds them to be of such a profoundly satisfying nature that he can never again elevate earthly and material riches to the place of importance they once held.

DIDN'T CHRIST PROMISE PROSPERITY IN THIS LIFE?

The most popular New Testament prooftext for prosperity theology is in two parallel accounts that come on the heels of Christ's disciples pointing out they had left all to follow him: "I tell you the truth," Jesus replied, "no one who has left home or

111

brothers or sisters or mother or father or children or fields for me and the gospel will fail to receive a hundred times as much in this present age (homes, brothers, sisters, mothers, children and fields—and with them, persecutions) and in the age to come, eternal life" (Mark 10:29-30).

"I tell you the truth," Jesus said to them, "no one who has left home or wife or brothers or parents or children for the sake of the kingdom of God will fail to receive many times as much in this age and, in the age to come, eternal life." (Luke 18:29-30) In a letter to supporters, one famous evangelist, referring to the Mark 10 passage, said, "To my knowledge, God's people have never received their one hundred fold return. It's been there in God's Reward System, but never understood or received—until now!" The point seemed to be that, thanks to this man and his fellow prosperity preachers, the people of God can now tap into what Jesus intended from the beginning—that all his followers would be materially prosperous in this life.

But is this really what Jesus meant? Three responses are in order.

First, no matter what Jesus was saying in these passages, it surely does not contradict the whole tenor of the New Testament, which demonstrates by direct teaching and repeated example that followers of Christ will often, indeed will *usually* not be materially wealthy in this life. This was undeniably true of the apostles, who were the very ones Jesus was speaking to.

Second, almost none of those who claim the benefits of this passage have ever actually fulfilled the conditions of the promise in the first place. Unlike the apostles to whom Jesus was speaking, they have never given up all their material goods nor left their families to follow Christ.

Third, the phrase "in this present age" does indeed refer to this world, but a critical question remains—in what exact sense does it mean we are to receive "many times" or "a hundred times" as much in terms of home, wife, brothers, sisters, parents, children, and fields?

Notice that the only components of a material nature are "fields" and possibly "homes." Yet even the word for home (oikia) may mean not the house itself but the household, or inhabitants of the house—that is, the family (Matt. 12:25; John 4:53; 1 Cor. 16:15).

But even if Christ referred to a physical house, is he really promising that all believers who give up the roof over their head will literally own many other houses in this life? Clearly not, since everything we know of the apostles he was speaking to, from biblical and extrabiblical history and tradition, clearly demonstrates they were not men of material means. To put it in terms that the health and wealth proponents understand, none of the apostles owned a Jerusalem condo, a ranch house in suburban Bethany, a cabin in the mountains at Carmel, or a summer beach house near Caesarea. And if the "hundredfold" blessing was a literal promise of houses, those receiving it would have to own a hundred houses, not just a half dozen, as well as a hundred fields.

Furthermore, if Jesus literally meant the faithful believer would own large numbers of homes or fields, did he then also mean that he would have large numbers of wives (a hundred to be exact) and that by some miracle others would become his literal parents? Of course not!

What Christ was saying was that the follower of Christ, in leaving what is his, becomes part of the larger family of faith, where relationships are deep and meaningful and possessions are freely shared. Everywhere the apostles went they would find "homes" that were theirs for as long as they wished to stay, "wives" who would care for them, converse with them, and prepare them meals from the harvest of the "fields" freely shared with them. They would have "brothers" and "sisters" to fellowship with, "parents" to give them wisdom and guidance and love, and "children" who would learn at their feet, and whom they would guide into Christlikeness. This same rich reservoir of relationships and possessions is available today to all who follow their Lord.

Paul had no permanent home (though his prison cells nearly qualified), no fields, no wife, no literal children, but he proudly called Timothy and the Thessalonians and others his beloved children. After describing his lack of health and wealth, Paul demonstrated the real meaning of Luke 18 by describing himself as "having nothing, yet possessing everything" (2 Cor. 6:10).

This is not to suggest that no New Testament principles related to God's blessing apply in a literal material way. Jesus said, "Give, and it will be given to you. A good measure, pressed

113

down, shaken together and running over, will be poured into your lap. For with the measure you use, it will be measured to you" (Luke 6:38).

Both Scripture and experience demonstrate God's frequent material blessing upon those who generously share what he has entrusted to them. In refuting the excesses of prosperity theology, I do not want to minimize the fact that God is a giver by nature, that he loves to give to his children, that he rewards our generosity, and that often that reward may include financial and material blessings. (We will take a closer look at this in chapter 13, "Giving: Reciprocating God's Grace.")

WHY DOES GOD PROSPER US?

As long as it is clear that the evil may prosper and the righteous may not, I have no argument with anyone who says God sometimes or even often chooses to prosper his people in material ways. But the great question is, "For what purpose does he prosper us?" Once he has blessed us financially, what does he expect us to do with this abundance?

The health and wealth preachers imply we may do whatever we please with God's provision. We may buy our beautiful homes and cars and take our dream vacations and live in wealth and prosperity as long as we give God the credit for it all. Whether God *wants* the credit for some of these life-styles is another question. Indeed, not only *may* we do these things, some prosperity preachers go so far as to say God expects us to, or even commands us to, in order that we would not be "bad witnesses" by appearing to be poor! By this standard, Jesus and Paul were the worst of witnesses. Their words are only a slight variation on Christ's: "By this shall all men know that you are my disciples, that you have lots of money and fabulous possessions."

In the context of financial giving Paul said, "And God is able to make all grace abound to you, so that in all things at all times, having everything that you need [not *want*], you will abound in every good work" (2 Cor. 9:8). In other words, Paul said that God provides us with abundance precisely so we can give it to others to meet their needs.

He further said that the God who "supplies seed to the sower" will "increase your store of seed" (9:10). But why does God give seed to the sower—so he can hoard it or eat the seed himself? No, so he can *scatter* it, spread it out so it can produce life and bear fruit among others. "You will be made rich in every way so that you can be generous on every occasion, and through us your generosity will result in thanksgiving to God" (9:11). Not just "made rich" but "made rich so that we may be generous on every occasion." Paul made this point in the previous chapter of the same letter:

> Our desire is not that others might be relieved while you are hard pressed, but that there might be equality. At the present time your plenty will supply what they need, so that in turn their plenty will supply what you need. Then there will be equality. (2 Cor. 8:13-14)

God has richly blessed us financially not that we would show ourselves to be his children by living above the standards of others, but so that we could show ourselves to be his children by coming down a few rungs on the ladder of affluence, in order to bring others up a few rungs—"that there might be equality." Not government-dictated equality, not equality superimposed by socialism, not that forced artificial equality that robs giving of its beauty, but spontaneous from-the-heart equality. God could have distributed goods equally in the first place, but he wants to rely on his people to do it in his name. He wants us to be the conduit whereby he meets the needs of others for whom he not only cares, but cared enough to die.

John Piper thoughtfully identified the purpose of God's abundant provision:

> God is not glorified when we keep for ourselves (no matter how thankfully) what we ought to be using to alleviate the misery of unevangelized, uneducated, unmedicated, and unfed millions. The evidence that many professing Christians have been deceived by this doctrine is how little they give and how much they own. God *has* prospered them. And by an almost irresistible law of consumer culture (baptized by a doctrine of health, wealth, and

prosperity) they have bought bigger (and more) houses, newer (and more) cars, fancier (and more) clothes, better (and more) meat, and all manner of trinkets and gadgets and containers and devices and equipment to make life more fun. They will object: Does not the Old Testament promise that God will prosper his people? Indeed! God increases our yield, so that by giving we can prove our yield is not our god. God does not prosper a man's business so he can move from a Ford to a Cadillac. God prospers a business so that 17,000 unreached peoples can be reached with the gospel. He prospers the business so that 12 percent of the world's population can move a step back from the precipice of starvation.[2]

GOD THE GREAT GENIE

Teaching the "seed faith" and "hundredfold return" principles, one pastor triumphantly told of a woman in his large church whose still-new car was about to be repossessed. As an act of faith, claiming God's "promise" of a hundredfold return, she put $20 in the offering. Sure enough, the next day she received $2,000 in the mail and was able to catch up on her payments, keep her car, and even have some extra spending money.

This is a nice enough testimony, but it raises some questions. Did it occur to the woman (or the pastor) that perhaps she should not have gone into debt in the first place, that her beautiful car might be a luxury God didn't approve of, or that God might want her to give up her car and invest the $2,000 in his kingdom (and not expect a check in the mail for $200,000 just for doing so)? It apparently did not occur to either one (nor, unfortunately, to most of the congregation) that many unrighteous people also received checks in the mail that day, while many more righteous than the woman (or the pastor) did not.

Prosperity teaching raises the very question Satan asked of God: "Does Job fear God for nothing?" (Job 1:9) Though Job's faith was genuine, it is clear that many people today are less interested in God himself than the fringe benefits he supposedly offers. The world comes to a prosperous church with mixed motives. Sir Robert L'Estrange observed, "He that serves God for money will serve the Devil for better wages."[3]

The basic problem with the health-and-wealth gospel, as well as most other forms of religious materialism, is that it is man-centered rather than God-centered. When approached from the prosperity posture, prayer degenerates into coercion, where we "name it and claim it," and keep on pulling his leash till God comes through. This kind of persistence is not the kind Jesus encouraged, but an attempt to arm-twist the Almighty into increasing comforts and underwriting life-styles concerning which we have not bothered to consult him in the first place.

"Faith" becomes a crowbar to break down the door of God's reluctance, rather than a humble and subservient attempt to give thanks and discern and lay hold of his willingness. It seems never to occur to us that when we claim the blood of Christ, believing God will (God *must*) take away this illness or handicap or financial hardship, that we may be asking him to remove the very things he has put into our lives to conform us to the image of Christ and to make us more usable vessels for his purposes.

But such talk is nonsense to us, for we have predetermined that our will is God's. Consequently, we treat God as an object, a tool, a means to an end—the end we in our pseudosovereignty have arbitrarily decreed to be best. God's blessing on financial giving is turned into a money-back guarantee whereby he is obligated to do precisely what we want him to, like the Florida man who heard the pastor say that if he gave a hundred dollars God would give him a thousand back—the thousand never came, so he brought a lawsuit against the church.

In prosperity theology, God is seen as a great no-lose lottery in the sky, a cosmic slot machine in which you put in a coin and pull the lever, then stick out your hat and catch the winnings while your "casino buddies" (in this case, fellow Christians) whoop and holler (or say "Amen") and wait their turn in line.

In this sort of system, God's only reason for existing is to give us what we want. If we had no needs, God would probably just disappear—after all, what purpose would he have anymore? With this kind of slick (and sick) theology, prayer ceases to be sacred. Instead of a means to give him glory and draw strength for the battle, prayer degenerates into an endless "wish list" to take before our Santa God.

To the religious materialist, the health and wealth Christian, God is little more than a wish granter. We call him "Master" but

117

it is *we* who are the masters—he is but the genie. Instead of rubbing a lamp, we quote a verse or say "Praise the Lord" three times, and presto, change-o, alakazam, the smoky God with the funny hat and big biceps is indebted to act out the script we have written for him. Consider God's role in relation to us in these words of a prominent preacher of prosperity: "Put God to work for you and maximize your potential in our divinely ordered capitalist system."[4]

WHO'S WORKING FOR WHOM?

Our pragmatic use of God demonstrates a clear lack of interest in God himself. After all, who cares what the genie is like? Genies serve one purpose—to grant us our wishes and make us prosperous and happy. Instead of the great subject of our faith, God is for many of us merely an object. This attitude explains the glut of sermons, books, articles, seminars, and conversations about us and the dearth of those about God. Content and fulfilled just that he can be at our service, or so we think, our genie is introduced and dismissed at our convenience. "You can go now, God—I'll call you back when I think of something else I want."

The Bible shows us a very different picture of God, a picture in which he is central, his glory is the focal point of the universe, and his sovereign purpose entitles him to do what he wills, whether or not that includes our particular whims and wishes.

When righteous Job lost everything that was his, even his own sons and daughters, he fell to the ground and worshiped, saying, "The Lord gave and the Lord has taken away; may the name of the Lord be praised." We are told, "In all this, Job did not sin by charging God with wrongdoing" (Job 1:21-22).

In contrast to Job, disciples of the prosperity doctrine conclude, when they lose their health and wealth, that they must have committed some unknown sin. If they can only find and confess it, they will get their health and wealth back. The only other alternative, and many come to this conclusion as well, is that God's promises are not true, that God is undependable, and that he has forsaken them. This was the posture of Job's wife: "Curse God and die." Job's response was a simple question that exposes the shallowness of prosperity theology: "Shall we accept good from God and not trouble?" (Job 2:9-10).

PROSPERITY AND PROVINCIALISM

I have thought a lot about prosperity theology. I thought about it as I walked through the streets of Cairo's Garbage Village, shaking the grimy hands of the Christians who live there in abject poverty. I thought about it when I worshiped alongside faithful believers on a rough backless bench in a dirt-floor church in Kenya. I thought about it again when I sat in a dim room with pastors behind the Iron Curtain. And I thought about it once more as I was flown across my own country, put up in a plush hotel room, and picked up in a limousine to take me to a Christian television studio for a twenty-minute interview.

I have thought about prosperity theology and about God long enough to know what I think God thinks of it.

While justified by isolated prooftexts of Scripture, prosperity theology as we see it today is really just the product of the materialism and success psychology that dominates the industrialized nations. The health-and-wealth gospel will thrive in North America, western Europe, Korea, Japan, and other economically progressive places. But where does it fit in Bangladesh, Ethiopia, Cambodia, or Romania? It is the product of our place and time, a reflection not of the Bible but our own materialism and self-preoccupation.

In California, a sharp-looking businessman stands up at a luncheon to give his testimony: "Before I knew Christ, I had nothing. My business was in bankruptcy, my health was ruined, I'd lost the respect of the community, and I'd almost lost my family. Then I accepted Christ as my Savior and Lord. He took me out of bankruptcy and now my business has tripled its profits in the last three years. My blood pressure has dropped to normal, and I feel better than I've felt in years. And, best of all, my wife and children have come back, and we're a family again. God is good—Praise the Lord!"

In China, an old and disheveled former university professor gives his testimony: "Before I met Christ, I had everything. I made a large salary, lived in a nice house, enjoyed good health, was highly respected for my credentials and profession, and had a good marriage and beautiful children. Then I accepted Christ as my Savior and Lord. As a result, I lost my post at the university, lost my beautiful house and car, and spent five years in prison. Now I work for a subsistence wage at a factory, and I live in pain from my neck that was broken in prison. My wife rejected me because of my conversion. She took my children away and I haven't seen her or them for ten years. But God is good, and I praise him for his faithfulness."

Both men are sincere Christians. One gives thanks because of what he has gained. The other gives thanks in spite of what he has lost.

Material blessings and restored families are definitely worth being thankful for, and the brother in China would be grateful to have them again (indeed, he gives heartfelt thanks each day for the little he has). And while the brother in California is certainly right to give thanks, he and the rest of us must be careful to sort out how much of what he has experienced is part of the gospel and how much is not. For any gospel that is more true in California than in China is not the true gospel.

And whether it be proclaimed by an angel from heaven or a television evangelist or a local church pastor or a fund-raising letter, Scripture makes clear what our response must be to any gospel other than the true one (Gal. 1:6-9).

NOTES

1. Leland Ryken, *Worldly Saints* (Grand Rapids, Mich.: Zondervan, 1986), 60.
2. John Piper, *Desiring God* (Portland, Oreg.: Multnomah Press, 1987), 163-64.
3. "Quick Quotes on Money," *Christian History Magazine* (Worcester, Penn.: Christian History Institute, 1987), 7:2, 4.
4. Ibid.

PART II

SEEING MONEY AND POSSESSIONS IN ETERNITY'S LIGHT

CHAPTER 7

TWO TREASURIES, TWO PERSPECTIVES, TWO MASTERS

I have held many things in my hands and I have lost them all. But whatever I have placed in God's hands, that I still possess. Martin Luther

He is no fool who gives what he cannot keep to gain what he cannot lose. Jim Elliot

In the greatest sermon ever preached, Jesus masterfully defined the believer's proper relationship to money and possessions:

> Do not store up for yourselves treasures on earth, where moth and rust destroy, and where thieves break in and steal. But store up for yourselves treasures in heaven,

123

where moth and rust do not destroy, and where thieves do not break in and steal. For where your treasure is, there your heart will be also.

The eye is the lamp of the body. If your eyes are good, your whole body will be full of light. But if your eyes are bad, your whole body will be full of darkness. If then the light within you is darkness, how great is that darkness!

No one can serve two masters. Either he will hate the one and love the other, or he will be devoted to the one and despise the other. You cannot serve both God and Money. (Matt. 6:19-24)

Jesus always has two kingdoms in mind. He spoke here of the two treasuries, two perspectives, and two masters of those two kingdoms.

Each couplet presents two options and demands one choice. There is a default choice if "no choice" is made. In a world gone wrong, unless the right choice is deliberately made and tenaciously clung to, the wrong choice will be implemented. In that case, as if on automatic pilot, people will inevitably spend their lives investing in the wrong treasury, adopting the wrong perspective, and serving the wrong master.

TWO TREASURIES

Jesus didn't say we can lay up treasures both in earth and heaven. He didn't say we are to lay up treasures in heaven *in addition to* those on earth, but *instead of* them. No matter how much or how little material wealth a person has (and everyone has some), he must be careful not to "treasure" it. He should be grateful for it, he is free to enjoy it, but he must not ascribe to it worth beyond its due.

A. W. Tozer suggested we may discover what our treasure is by answering four basic questions:

What do we value most? What would we most hate to lose? What do our thoughts turn to most frequently when we are free to think of what we will? And finally, what affords us the greatest pleasure?[1]

Based on these four questions, what is *your* treasure?

When money is spent on heavenly treasure, it is of eternal value. When spent on earthly treasure—unless with a view toward heavenly treasure—money is only of temporary value. Moths destroy fabric, rust destroys "precious" metals, and thieves can steal almost anything. Jesus could have gone on—fires consume, floods destroy, governments seize, enemies attack, investments go sour. No earthly treasure is safe.

Aggressive Investing. We must realize Jesus didn't tell us we are wrong in wanting to lay up treasures. On the contrary, he commanded us to lay up treasures. He was simply saying, "Stop laying them up in the wrong place, and start laying them up in the right place."

Christ's primary argument against amassing material wealth was not that it was bad, but simply that it was a poor investment. Material things just won't stand the test of time. And even if they did, even if they escaped moths and rust and thieves, they cannot stand the test of eternity.

When we think of missionaries, we often visualize simple people with no aspirations for treasures or greatness. This may sometimes be so, yet following Christ's own words, a godly missionary might passionately desire treasures.

John Wesley said, "I value all things only by the price they shall gain in eternity." Similarly, David Livingston stated, "I place no value on anything I possess, except in relation to the kingdom of God." God's kingdom was the reference point for these men. They saw all else in light of the kingdom. They were compelled to live as they did not because they treasured *no things,* but because they treasured the *right things.*

We often miss something in missionary martyr Jim Elliot's famous words, "He is no fool who gives what he cannot keep to gain what he cannot lose." We focus on his willingness to sacrifice and serve, and so we should, but we overlook his passion for personal gain. Without question, Jim Elliot was looking for profit. What separated him from the common Christian was not that he didn't want treasure, but that he wanted *real* treasure. He was not satisfied with treasure that would be lost. He was content only with treasure that would last.

We must understand that Christ's basic position on wealth is not that it should be rejected but that it should be pursued. It is an understatement to say God does not object to an investment mentality. According to Jesus, God *has* an investment mentality. Our Creator and Savior agrees wholeheartedly with us—"Wealth is worth seeking." There is just one difference, and that is the difference in our answer to the question "What *is* true wealth?"

Discovering True Wealth. Jesus vividly described what it is like when we discover true wealth: "The kingdom of heaven is like treasure hidden in a field. When a man found it, he hid it again, and then in his joy went and sold all he had and bought that field" (Matt. 13:44).

Now this man, like almost all of us, was probably quite attached to his possessions. Yet, having seen the value of this great treasure in the field, he sold "all he had" to obtain it. Did the sacrifice pain him? Did he have doubts and regrets? Absolutely not! "In his joy" he sold all to obtain the treasure. Why? It was a simple question of relative value. Until he found the treasure, all his possessions seemed valuable. But compared to the dazzling beauty and incalculable worth of what he had discovered, everything he had owned and treasured to that point seemed worthless. "The pearl of great price," the parable immediately following this one, teaches the same lesson.

John White said this about the man in the parable who gives up everything for this one great treasure:

> The choice he faces lies between his worthless bits and pieces and the field with buried treasure. There is nothing *noble* about his sacrifice. There would, on the other hand, be something incredibly stupid about not making it. Anyone but a fool would do exactly as the man did. Everyone will envy him his good fortune and commend him not on his spiritual character but on his common sense.[2]

Of course, the great Treasure is Christ himself. To gain Christ—this was what made everything else seem comparatively worthless to Paul (Phil. 3:7-11). But part of gaining Christ was the prospect of eternal reward, symbolizing Christ's stamp of approval on his faithful service while on earth. This prospect of eternal reward from his Master's hand was Paul's consuming motivation throughout his life (1 Cor. 9:24-27), and his greatest anticipation at his death (2 Tim. 4:6-8).

What does it mean to lay up treasure in heaven instead of on earth? It means that Christ offers us the incredible opportunity to trade earthly goods and currency for eternal kingdom rewards. By putting our money and possessions in his treasury, we assure ourselves of eternal rewards beyond our comprehension.

Consider the implications of this offer. We can trade temporal possessions that we cannot keep anyway to gain eternal possessions that we cannot lose. This is like a child given a chance to trade bubble gum for a new bicycle, or a man offered ownership of the Coca-Cola company in exchange for a sack of bottle caps. Only a fool would pass up the opportunity.

What we keep we will lose. What we give and share and do in Christ's name will ultimately come back to us in heaven, in a far better and permanent form.

This perspective, if truly grasped, inevitably fosters an investment mentality. For instance, with $10,000 I may be able to buy a new car. With the same $10,000 I could support ten Nigerian or Indian missionary families full-time for an entire year. If I have an investment mentality, I ask myself, "What's the better investment for eternity?"

Of course, it *may* be God's will for me to buy a car, and a car used for his purposes can also be an investment in the kingdom. But I must be careful not to rationalize. A $1,000 used car or no car at all may serve his kingdom purposes equally well or far better—and allow me to make an investment in heaven that will never get scratched, dented, stolen, totaled, or have to be traded in for a new model.

A Safe Place for Your Money. Note that in Matthew 6 the laying up of heavenly treasures, not the renunciation of earthly treasures, is the central focus. We are to avoid laying up treasures on earth not as an end in itself, but as part of a life strategy to lay up treasures in heaven. A man may give up all his earthly treasures without ever investing in heavenly treasures. Jesus is not looking for ascetics, but eternally-wise investors of their money and possessions.

Where is the safest place to put your money? Jesus stated that ultimately there is only *one* safe place to put our money and that is in the kingdom of God. He said, in essence, "You can't take it with you," then quickly added a life-changing corollary: "But you can send it on ahead." By wisely and generously using our earthly resources, which will mean forgoing many earthly treasures, we can lay up treasures in heaven.

Returning to the question posed earlier, "What is *your* treasure? Is it your house? Car? Boat? Library? Gun collection? Is your treasure in art, coins, or gold? Is it in savings, a retirement program, insurance policies, annuities, real estate, or commodities? Is your treasure five hundred shares of AT&T or IBM?" Some people may have some of these without them being their treasure. But for most of us the very having of them presents a constant temptation that they will become our treasures.

Paul told the rich in this world that they may, through their generosity and good deeds, "lay up treasure for themselves as a firm foundation for the coming age" (1 Tim. 6:18-19). Christians throughout the ages have taken these passages literally and have been far less serious about earthly treasures and far more serious about heavenly treasures than we are. John Bunyan wrote his classic *Pilgrim's Progress* from an English prison cell to which he was condemned for unlicensed preaching of the gospel. This is how he interpreted the words of Christ and Paul:

> Whatever good thing you do for Him, if done according to the Word, is laid up for you as treasure in chests and coffers, to be brought out to be rewarded before both men and angels, to your eternal comfort.[3]

Imagine for a moment that you are alive at the very end of the Civil War. You are living in the South, but your home is really in the North. While in the South you have accumulated a good amount of Confederate currency. Suppose you also know for a fact that the North is going to win the war and that the end could come at any time. What will you do with all of your Confederate money?

If you were smart, there is only one answer to the question. You would cash in your Confederate currency for U.S. currency—the only money that will have value once the war is over. You would keep only enough Confederate currency to meet your basic needs for that short period until the war was over and the money would be worthless.

The believer has inside knowledge of an eventual major change in the worldwide social and economic situation. The currency of this world—its money, possessions, fashions, and whims—will be worthless at our death or Christ's return, both of which are imminent. This knowledge should radically affect our investment strategy. For us to accumulate vast earthly treasures in the face of the inevitable future is equivalent to stockpiling Confederate money despite our awareness of its eventual worthlessness. To do so is to betray a basic ignorance of or unbelief in the Scriptures.

Kingdom currency, backed by the eternal treasury, is the only medium of exchange recognized by the Son of God, whose government will last forever. The currency of his kingdom is our present faithful service and sacrificial use of our resources for him. The payoff in eternity will be "a sure foundation," consisting of treasures beyond our wildest dreams.

In the investment world there are experts and advisors known as "market timers." When they read the signs that the stock market is about to take a downward turn, they recommend switching funds immediately into more dependable or consistent investments, such as money markets or certificates of deposit. In Matthew 6, Jesus functioned as the foremost investment advisor, the ultimate expert in the economies of earth and heaven. His strategy was simple, requiring no background in economics to understand it. He told us to, once and for all, switch investment vehicles. He said to transfer our funds from *earth,* which is volatile and ready to take a permanent dive, to *heaven,* which is totally dependable, insured by God himself, and is coming soon to forever replace the economy of earth.

Where Is Your Heart? Christ's words were direct and profound: "Where your treasure is, there your heart will be also." What we do with our possessions is a sure indicator of what is in our hearts. Jesus was, in effect, saying to us, "Show me your checkbook and your VISA statement and your receipts for cash expenditures and I'll tell you where your heart is." What we do with our money does not lie. It is a bold statement to God of what we truly value.

But what we do with our money is more than an indicator of where our heart is. According to Jesus, it is a *determiner* of where our heart is. This is an amazing and exciting prospect. If I want my heart to be in one particular place and not in another, then I need to put my money in that place and not in the other.

Do you wish you had a great heart for missions like other people you know? You can, according to Jesus. Put your money into missions and your heart will follow. Do you want a heart for the poor? Then give your money to the poor. Do you want your heart to be in your church? Give your money to the church. Your heart will never be where your money isn't. It will be where your money is. If most of your money is in General Motors, your house, or your hobby, where is your heart going to be?

"My heart isn't in the things of God." Is it because your treasure isn't in the things of God? Put your resources, your assets, your money and possessions, your time and talents and energies into the things of God, and that is where your heart will be.

TWO PERSPECTIVES

After dealing with the two treasuries, Jesus spoke of two perspectives: "The eye is the lamp of the body. If your eyes are good, your whole body will be full of light. But if your eyes are bad, your whole body will be full of darkness."

Physical vision here is a metaphor of spiritual vision or perspective. By perspective I mean the way in which, and the clarity with which, we look at all of life. The unbeliever looks at life as a brief interval that begins at birth and ends at death. In looking to the future he looks no further than his own life span, if even that. His vision is restricted to the horizons of this world.

Like a myopic horse with blinders on, the man without Christ can see neither far nor wide. His vision is pitifully short and narrow. Bereft of eternal perspective, he is bound to take all the wrong turns and come to all the wrong conclusions. He will think, "If this life is all there is, why deny myself any pleasure or possessions?" Given his premise, why should he come to any other conclusion? People live for a higher purpose only when they have the vision to see a higher purpose.

Believers are people of an entirely different perspective. Our theology tells us that this life is the preface—not the book, the preliminaries—not the main event, the tune-up—not the concert. It is the testing period that will determine much of the composition of that eternal life for which we were born again.

The believer's view of reality is fundamentally different than the nonbeliever's. We live differently because we *see* differently. We look at the same raw data, are aware of the same facts, witness the same current events, but interpret them and relate to them in radically different ways. We eat the same food, exchange the same currency, but live according to two different purposes. These purposes are based squarely on two different perspectives of reality—one that looks at life in the short run and the other that looks at life in the long run.

When our eyes are set on eternity, the news that someone has come to know the Savior means a great deal more than the news of a salary raise or the prospect of getting a video camera. Of course, the salary raise and the video camera can both be used for the kingdom of God. But the point is that neither in themselves is ultimately important, while new birth *is* in itself ultimately important. It affects the destiny of a precious being for all eternity.

The Christian who accumulates great lands and houses and bank accounts to the exclusion of investing in eternity was not depicted by Jesus in his sermon as unrighteous, greedy, or selfish, though he may well be any or all of these. Rather, he was depicted as short-sighted or blind. Unwise is too weak a word—he is stupid, stupid on the grandest scale, as stupid as the rich fool of Luke 12. As stupid in fact as the man who found the treasure in the field would have been to hold on to his paltry possessions instead of giving them up for what was truly valuable.

The man with good eyes, with eternal perspective, is smart and perceptive and accurate in his appraisal. He is eternally wise like the poor widow of Mark 12. His vision corrected, he now sees life through the eyes of eternity. Unlike his fellows, he stares through the haze and peers beyond the horizons of this world to another, in which the prevailing experience will be largely and eternally different than it is now.

Momentary Sacrifice, Eternal Gain.   The people of God in past times pleased and obeyed him out of their perspective on the short duration of the present life compared to eternity (Heb. 10:34; 11:13-16).

Peter began his first letter by encouraging Christians to find joy in their trials by focusing not on the trial that will go on only "a little while," but on their heavenly inheritance that will never perish (1 Pet. 1:4-9; 5:10). Paul adopted the same perspective: "I consider that our present sufferings are not worth comparing with the glory that will be revealed in us" (Rom. 8:18). Notice the reference to "glory" is not the glory of Christ that will be revealed *to* us, but one that will be revealed *in* us. This corresponds to Paul's statement elsewhere: "For our light and momentary troubles are achieving for us an eternal glory that far outweighs them all" (2 Cor. 4:17).

Note the contrasts: "light" with what will "far outweigh," "momentary" with "eternal," and "troubles" with "glory." All this adds up to perspective. Paul said, "View the present in light of the future; see time in light of eternity; look beyond sacrifice to reward; bear the cross in anticipation of the crown." If we will do this—and we certainly can—it will radically alter the way we look at money, possessions, and life itself. And in changing our perspective, it will transform our behavior.

Paul spoke not of a glory achieved for Christ but "for us." Likewise, Jesus did not say, "Lay up for *God* treasures in heaven" but "Lay up for *yourselves* treasures in heaven" (Matt. 6:19-21). Of course, Christ will be glorified as the sole object of worship in heaven, but Scripture teaches that we will not only behold his glory but somehow participate in it.

This is the perspective of delayed gratification. It gives the believer one more incentive to do what the Philippian Christians did in giving to Paul's missionary work—to withdraw funds from one's earthly account currently in order to have them credited to his heavenly account (Phil. 4:17).

Suppose you dislike split pea soup but I was to tell you, "Eat split pea soup for a week and I'll provide you and your family with all the groceries you need for the rest of your lives." Wouldn't this promise change your perspective on eating split pea soup? You still might not like it, though even that could change. But you would gladly do it in light of the promised rewards. Soldiers and athletes and farmers all know that short-term sacrifices are justifiable in light of their long-term benefits (2 Tim. 2:3-6). This is precisely the case for those who view eternity in proper perspective.

The Most High Yields. Financial planners have a hard time convincing people to look down the road instead of just focusing on today, this week, or this year. "Don't think this year," they will tell you. "Think thirty years from now." Then they will share ways to prepare for thirty years from now by planning here, budgeting there, saving so much a month, contributing to an IRA, investing in this mutual fund or that real estate partnership.

It is only slightly less shortsighted to think thirty years down the road than to think thirty days. The wise man does indeed think thirty years ahead, but far more—he thinks an *eternity* ahead. He thinks not just to his retirement years, not merely to the end of his earthly life, but far beyond. We should not just say, "Think thirty years ahead," but "Think thirty million years ahead." But, of course, that isn't nearly long enough, and the measures of time become irrelevant anyway, so let us simply say, "Think an eternity ahead."

Financial counselors point out the difference between investing the same yearly amounts in an Individual Retirement Account starting at age twenty-five on the one hand, and at age forty on the other. At retirement the bottom line difference is hundreds of thousands of dollars. Good insight for the Christian who starts laying up for eternity—the sooner you get started the more you will have awaiting you.

A financial counselor will tell you, "You can't go back at age sixty-five and snap your fingers to compensate for forty years of poor planning." But what is far more important is that you can't reach the end of your life, snap your fingers, and compensate for a lifetime of poor planning to meet God. The rich fool is proof of that.

God's eternal prospectus bears a careful look in light of its guaranteed rate of interest. Jesus promises an ultimate return of a hundred times, a 10,000 percent rate of interest (Matt. 19:29). No certificate of deposit can begin to match that.

Let me assume the role of "eternal financial counselor" and offer this advice: choose your investments carefully; compare their rates of interest; consider their ultimate trustworthiness; and especially compare how they will be working for you a few million years from now.

If the nonbeliever sees with what Jesus called the "bad eye," the Christian's view of finances will be, *must be,* radically different than his. True, we may participate in some of the same earthly investments, our strategies may appear to overlap at times, and occasionally our short-term goals will be similar. But our long-term goals and purposes will be, must be, fundamentally different. As Christians we must not take our cue from the world but from the Word.

TWO MASTERS

Having spoken first of two treasuries, then of two perspectives, Jesus spoke finally of two masters. He said that while we might *have* both God and money, we cannot *serve* both God and Money.

I might have two jobs, three sisters, or five friends, but only one spouse. Some relationships by their very nature are exclusive. The most basic of these is our relationship with God. There is a throne in each life only big enough for one. Christ may be on that throne, or Money may be on that throne, but they cannot *both* be on that throne.

Mammon is a false god. It is Antichrist in the true meaning of the word. The Greek preposition *anti-* does not fundamentally mean "against" but "instead of." Hence, Antichrist is not just "one who is against Christ" but "one who is a substitute for Christ."

When he named it Mammon, Christ personified money to portray its danger. Mammon is an alternative messiah.

The four chapters that follow develop in more detail the concepts of eternity and eternal rewards. While it is a subject almost never dealt with in books on money and possessions, I believe it provides the essential perspective that allows us to see our money and possessions the way God sees them—through the eyes of eternity. Once we gain the perspective of eternity, we will eagerly follow our Lord's command to devote our short lives on earth to the pursuit of eternal treasure.

CONCLUSION

There are two treasuries, two perspectives, and two masters. Are you investing in the right treasury? Are you adopting the right perspective? Are you serving the right master?

Jesus gave us a choice—a life wasted in the pursuit of wealth on earth, or a life invested in the pursuit of wealth in heaven. Every heartbeat brings us one moment closer to eternity. The person whose treasure is on earth is always headed *away from* his treasure. The person whose treasure is in heaven is always headed *toward* his treasure. Whoever is headed away from his treasure has reason to despair. Whoever is headed toward his treasure has reason to rejoice.

Where is *your* treasure? Are you heading toward it or away from it? Do you have reason to despair or reason to rejoice?

NOTES
1. A. W. Tozer, "The Transmutation of Wealth," *Born After Midnight* (Harrisburg, Penn.: Christian Publications, Inc., 1959), 106.
2. John White, *The Cost of Commitment* (Downers Grove, Ill.: InterVarsity Press, 1976), 47.
3. Quoted by Bruce Wilkinson in the "Walk Thru Eternal Rewards" seminar notebook (Atlanta, Ga.: Walk Thru the Bible Ministries).

CHAPTER 8

THE STEWARD'S ETERNAL DESTINY

It ought to be the business of every day to prepare for our last day. Matthew Henry

He who provides for this life but takes no care for eternity is wise for a moment but a fool forever. John Tillotson

There is an old story of a slave who traveled with his master to Baghdad. Early one morning, milling through the marketplace, the slave sees Death in human form. Death gives him a threatening look, and the slave recoils in terror, convinced that Death intends to take him that day.

The slave runs to his master and says, "Master, help me. I have seen Death, and his threatening look tells me he intends to take my life this very day. I must escape him. Please let me leave

137

now and flee on my camel so that by tonight I can reach Samarra, where Death cannot find me."

His master agrees, and the terrified servant is off to ride like the wind for the fifteen-hour journey to Samarra.

A few hours later, the master himself sees Death among the throngs in Baghdad. He boldly approaches Death and asks him, "Why did you give my servant a threatening look today?"

"That was not a threatening look," Death replies. "That was a look of surprise. You see, I was amazed to see your servant today in Baghdad, for I have an appointment with him tonight in Samarra."

While some of the imagery is questionable, the basic moral of the story is on target. The time of our death is unknown. The way of our death is unpredictable. But the fact of our death is inescapable. The statistics are unwavering—of those who are born, 100 percent die. We may spend our lives running from death and denying death, but that will not stop death from coming at its appointed time.

Not talking about death won't postpone it a moment. Talking about death won't bring it a moment sooner. But it *will* give us opportunity to be better prepared for what surely lies ahead. And if life's greatest certainty is death, then wouldn't it be foolish not to be prepared for what lies beyond this life? Any life that leaves us unprepared for death is a foolish life. Matthew Henry put it this way: "It ought to be the business of every day to prepare for our last day."

Now, what does this have to do with our attitude toward money and possessions? It has *everything* to do with it. For this present life is but a brief moment in eternity. And the real question about how we view our money and possessions is not a question of the immediate but of the eternal. Without a doubt, the single greatest contributor to our inability to see money and possessions in their true light is our persistent failure to see our present lives through the lens of eternity.

THE LOST SENSE OF THE ETERNAL

A startling thing has happened among Western Christians. Many of us habitually think and act as if there is no eternity—or as if what we do in this present life has no bearing on eternity.

How many sermons about heaven or hell have most of us heard lately? How many gospel booklets even mention the words *heaven* or *hell*? Look carefully—you may be surprised. The trend is to focus not on our eternal future but our present circumstances. Yet Scripture states the reality of our eternal future should dominate and determine the character of our present life, right down to the words we speak and the actions we take (James 2:12; 2 Pet. 3:11-12).

In those rare times when we do seriously consider the afterlife, it seems strange, dreamlike, so otherworldly as to be unreal. So we come back to "reality"—our present lives and plans and possessions that we can see, hear, touch, feel, and taste. Things are real. *Now* is real. So we return quickly to the pressing business of the day, that which is immediately relevant, those all-important matters of the present. These might include what is happening in Hollywood or on Wall Street or in Washington or London, or what new self-help technique can make us beautiful or happy, or how we can decorate our house, or what kind of car we want to buy, or where we can get a low-interest loan.

Our devotion to the newspaper and neglect of the Bible is the ultimate testimony to our interest in the short-range over the long-range. We fail to ask how expensive clothes, cruises, face lifts, breast implants, and liposuctions will serve eternal purposes. Such questions are fit for dusty theologians and pious old ladies, perhaps, but not for us—which would be true enough if only dusty theologians and pious old ladies died, met their Maker, and spent eternity somewhere.

Being oblivious to eternity leaves us experts in the trivial, and novices in the significant. We can name that tune, name that starting line-up, name that actor's movie debut, name that country's leading export, and detail the differences between computer models or types of four-wheel drives. None of this is wrong, of course, but it is certainly revealing when we consider that most Christians, let alone the general public, do not even have an accurate picture of what the Bible says will happen to us after we die. We major in the momentary and minor in the momentous.

What does God have to say about our lives here? He says this life is so brief that we are like grass that grows up in the morning and wilts in the afternoon (Isa. 40:6-8). Our life here is but "mist that appears for a little while and then vanishes" (James 4:14).

When a good friend discovered she had only a short time to live, she told me of her radical changes in perspective. "The most striking thing that's happened," she said, "is that I find myself totally uninterested in all the conversations about material things. Things used to matter to me, but now I find my thoughts are never on possessions, but always on Christ and people. I consider it a privilege that I can live each day, knowing I will die soon. What a difference it makes!"

David likewise sought to gain God's perspective in light of the brevity of life:

> Show me, O Lord, my life's end and the number of my days; let me know how fleeting is my life. You have made my days a mere handbreadth; the span of my years is as nothing before you. Each man's life is but a breath. Man is a mere phantom as he goes to and fro; He bustles about, but only in vain; he heaps up wealth, not knowing who will get it. But now, Lord, what do I look for? My hope is in you. (Ps. 39:4-7)

Because this life is so brief, we might easily conclude it is also inconsequential. Indeed, from a human perspective it is inconsequential—all but a few lives are like a pebble dropped in a pond. They create ripples but for a moment, tiny ripples that smooth out, then are gone forever. A look at abandoned tombstones with names no one remembers is a stark reminder of our eventual anonymity in this world. What do you know about your great-grandfather? What will your great-grandchildren know about you?

Our brief stay here may indeed seem unimportant, but nothing could be further from the truth. For the Bible tells us that while men may not remember or care what our lives here have been, God remembers perfectly and cares very much. So much that the door of eternity swings on the hinges of our present lives on earth.

The Bible tells us it is this life that lays the foundation upon which eternal life is built. Eternity will hold for us what this life has invested in it.

No wonder Scripture makes clear that the one central business of this life is to prepare for the next!

THE LONG TOMORROW: WHAT LIES AHEAD?

As no piece of a puzzle can be truly understood apart from its greater context in the full puzzle, so our present lives—including what we should do with all our money and possessions—cannot be understood apart from the greater context of eternity. In the rest of the chapter, I would like to paint the backdrop of what A. W. Tozer called "the long tomorrow," against which the question of money—and all questions of life and stewardship—must be properly viewed.

Some of us have heard enough prophetic teaching to know a few facts about the tribulation and Antichrist, but are vague about our *personal* eternal future. The only certainty seems to be that if we know Christ as Savior we will be in heaven with the Lord. We might easily say, "Well, knowing I'll be in heaven is good enough for me." Apparently, however, it *isn't* good enough for God, because the fact is that his Word tells us very specifically about other dimensions of our personal futures. And most readers will find them quite different than what they have supposed.

DEATH AND JUDGMENT

We spoke already of the next item on our eternal agenda—death. "Man is destined to die once, and after that to face judgment" (Heb. 9:27). The old saying, "Nothing is certain but death and taxes," is half true—there *are* tax evaders, but there are no death evaders. Of course, those alive at the return of Christ may not technically die, but the result is the same—their earthly lives will be abruptly over, and they will move immediately to the afterlife.

Hebrews 9:27 continues our written-in-stone itinerary—man is destined to die "and after this comes judgment." This judgment is for *all* men, not some. Whether we go to Christ in death or he comes to us in his return, either way, we face judgment. This doctrine is as old as the church itself. The statement, "Christ will come again to judge the living and the

141

dead," found its way into the Apostles' Creed (A.D. 250), the Nicene Creed (A.D. 325) and the Athanasian Creed (A.D. 400).

GOD THE JUDGE

There seems to be built into every person, society, and religion some sense of accountability, a basic belief that good deserves reward and evil deserves punishment, and that somehow both will get what they deserve. God has written his moral law on human hearts (Rom. 2:12-16). This appears to include an inborn sense that one day we will be judged in light of that law.

Scripture confirms this inbred human expectation of judgment. It says that God will judge everyone (Acts 17:31), and he will judge fairly (Gen. 18:25). Specifically, he will judge us according to our deeds: "I the Lord search the heart and examine the mind, to reward a man according to his conduct, according to what his deeds deserve" (Jer. 17:10).

"Does not he who weighs the heart perceive it? Does not he who guards your life know it? Will he not repay each person according to what he has done?" (Prov. 24:12).

"They will be paid back for the harm they have done" (2 Pet. 2:13).

All men should live each day with this awesome awareness: "But they will have to give an account to him who is ready to judge the living and the dead" (1 Pet. 4:5).

God will judge us with total knowledge: "Nothing in all creation is hidden from God's sight. Everything is uncovered and laid bare before him to whom we must give account" (Heb. 4:13). Because his knowledge is total, his judgment is comprehensive and detailed—"Men will have to give account on the day of judgment for every careless word they have spoken" (Matt. 12:36). His judgment extends to what is hidden to men: "For God will bring every deed into judgment, including every hidden thing, whether it is good or bad" (Eccles. 12:14). He even knows the motives of men's hearts and judges us in that light (1 Cor. 4:5).

Because we are all sinners and the wages of sin is death, an all-holy God in his love for us judged Jesus for our sins (Isa. 53:9-10). By accepting Christ's atonement for our sins we may escape the everlasting punishment due us (Rom. 6:23; 2 Cor.

5:21). God's justice was satisfied, but only at the cost of his own blood. To purchase our redemption, Jesus experienced for us an eternity of hell in a few hours on the cross. Bonhoeffer was so right: grace is free, but it is not cheap.

THE UNBELIEVER'S JUDGMENT IN HELL

Hell is a place of punishment designed for Satan and the fallen angels (Matt. 25:41-46; Rev. 20:10). However, it will also be inhabited by those who do not accept God's gift of redemption in Christ (Rev. 20:12-15). Hell is an actual place, clearly and graphically spoken of by Jesus (Matt. 10:28; 13:40-42; Mark 9:43-44). Hell is as literal as heaven (Ps. 11:4-6) and as eternal as heaven (Matt. 25:46). Hell is a horrible place of suffering and everlasting destruction (Matt. 13:41-42; 2 Thess. 1:9). In hell people are fully conscious and retain all their capacities and desires with no hope for any fulfillment for all eternity (Luke 16:22-31).

Hell is indescribably dreadful, and if the Bible is to be trusted, it is undeniably real. God so desperately wants us *not* to go to hell that he paid the ultimate price so that we would not have to go. Nevertheless, apart from trusting Christ for salvation, any person's eternal future will be spent in hell.

Because God is fair, hell will not be the same for everyone. The severity of punishment will vary with the amount of truth known and the nature and number of the sins committed. This concept is foreign to most Christians, but is clearly taught in Scripture (Matt. 11:20-24; Luke 20:45-47, Rom. 2:3-5). There should be no consolation in this, however, for the least hellish part of hell will still be hell—eternal exclusion from the presence of God and the soothing light of his grace.

THE BELIEVER'S JUDGMENT IN HEAVEN

What awaits the believer after death? We all know the answer—heaven. Heaven is a real place in which we will worship God (Rev. 5:11-13), serve God (Rev. 7:15) and reign with God (Rev. 22:5). It is a place of great pleasure, characterized by magnificent beauty, including streets of gold and buildings of pearls, emeralds, and other precious stones

143

(Rev. 21:19-21). We will live, celebrate, eat, and drink in heaven (Luke 22:29-30; Rev. 19:9).

Heaven will be a wonderful place. But what we seldom consider is that at the entry point to heaven Scripture plainly tells us there is a judgment of believers that will determine for all eternity our place or status in heaven.

The Bible teaches two eternal judgments of the two types of people raised from the dead—a judgment of unbelievers and a judgment of believers (John 5:28-29). All true believers will pass the judgment of their faith in Christ. All unbelievers will fail the judgment of faith at the Great White Throne, since their names are not written in the Book of Life (Rev. 20:11-15).

But faith is not the only thing judged. Scripture repeatedly states *all* men, not just unbelievers, will be judged for their works (Prov. 24:12; Eccles. 12:14). The unbeliever's judgment of works comes at the Great White Throne (Rev. 20:12). The believer will not be condemned at the Great White Throne, but nonetheless he still faces a judgment of works himself, at what is called the "Judgment Seat of Christ."

The Lord's evaluation of the seven churches in Revelation 2 and 3 makes clear that he is watching us, evaluating us. He is "keeping score." As an instructor gives grades to his students, so Christ gives grades to the churches. To Christians Jesus says, "I am he who searches hearts and minds, and I will repay each of you according to your deeds" (Rev. 2:23).

Scripture teaches with unmistakable clarity that all believers in Christ will give an account of their lives to their Lord (Rom. 14:10-12). We will be judged by him according to our works, both good and bad (2 Cor. 5:10). The result of this will be the gain or loss of eternal rewards (1 Cor. 3:12-15; 2 Cor. 5:9-10; Rom. 14:10-12). God's Word treats this judgment with great sobriety. It does not portray it as a meaningless formality or a going-through-the-motions before we get on to the real business of heavenly bliss. Rather, Scripture presents it as a monumental event in which things of eternal significance are brought to light and things of eternal consequence are put into effect.

> If any man builds on this foundation [the foundation of Christ] using gold, silver, costly stones, wood, hay or straw, his work will be shown for what it is, because the

Day will bring it to light. It will be revealed with fire, and the fire will test the quality of each man's work. If what he has built survives, he will receive his reward. If it is burned up, he will suffer loss; he himself will be saved, but only as one escaping through the flames. (1 Cor. 3:12-15)

Our works are simply what we have done with our resources—time, energy, talents, money, possessions. The fire of God's holiness will reveal the quality of these works, the eternal significance of what we have done with our God-given assets. The fate of the works will be determined by their nature. If they are made of the right stuff (gold, silver, costly stones), they will withstand and be purified by the fire. But no matter how nice our works of wood, hay, and straw have been made to look in the display case of this world, they will not withstand the incendiary gaze of God's Son in the next.

"For we must all appear before the judgment seat of Christ, that each one may receive what is due him for the things done while in the body, whether good or bad" (2 Cor. 5:10).

"Whether good or bad" in the above verse is perhaps the most disturbing phrase for believers in the entire New Testament. It is so disturbing, in fact, that I have found any honest attempts to deal with it are met with tremendous resistance. Equally disturbing is the direct statement to Christians that not only will they receive reward from Christ for their good works, but, "Anyone who does wrong will be repaid for his wrong, and there is no favoritism" (Col. 3:25). If Christ has paid the price for our sin, if we confess and receive forgiveness of our sins, then what can this mean?

Our sins *are* totally forgiven when we come to Christ, and we stand justified in him. Nevertheless, Scripture speaks about a coming judgment, a judgment of our works, not our sins. When we commit sins or omit doing righteous acts we should have done, we are not doing what we could do to lay up precious stones on the foundation of Christ. Therefore, these sins contribute directly to the believer's "suffering loss." Through this loss of reward, the believer is considered to be receiving his "due" for his works "whether good or bad." So, what we do as believers, both good and bad, will have effects for eternity.

In light of this, the author of Hebrews said, "Therefore, since we are surrounded by such a great cloud of witnesses, let us throw off everything that hinders and the sin that so easily entangles, and let us run with perseverance the race marked out for us" (Heb. 12:1). Sin entangles our feet, puts us out of the competition, and results in losing both the race and the prize.

We must quickly remind ourselves that God is for us, not against us (Rom. 8:31). He has not only assured us that we won't face the Great White Throne Judgment, he also wants us to be commended at the Judgment Seat of Christ. He doesn't want the works of our lifetime to go up in smoke. He wants us to have eternal rewards—and he has given us every resource in Christ to live the godly life that will result in those eternal rewards (2 Pet. 1:3).

DOES GOD REALLY CARE ABOUT OUR WORKS?

The five-hundred-year-old play *Everyman* is a picture of all persons. As Everyman faces Death, he looks among his friends for a companion. One friend would accompany him on the journey through death to final judgment. His name was "Good Deeds."

Some of us may balk at such a picture. Yet it is explicitly biblical: "Then I heard a voice from heaven say, 'Write: Blessed are the dead who die in the Lord from now on.' 'Yes,' says the Spirit, 'they will rest from their labor, for their deeds will follow them'" (Rev. 14:13).

In Revelation 19:7-8 we are told "the wedding of the Lamb has come, and his bride has made herself ready. Fine linen, bright and clean, was given her to wear. (Fine linen stands for the righteous acts of the saints.)"

This passage offers several surprises. We might have expected to be told that Christ makes the bride ready, rather than she herself. We could also have expected that the fine linen would stand for the righteousness of Christ, or perhaps the righteous faith of the saints. But what we are told is that it stands for the righteous *acts* or *works* or *deeds* of the saints. If we will indeed be clothed according to our works for Christ, some of us may suffer from acute exposure!

Somewhere we have gotten the erroneous idea that "works" is a dirty word in God's sight. This is not the case at all. While he condemns works done to earn salvation, and works done to impress others, our Lord enthusiastically commends works done for the right reasons. In an often quoted passage, immediately after saying our salvation is "not by works," Paul added: "For we are God's workmanship, created in Christ Jesus to do good works, which God prepared in advance for us to do" (Eph. 2:8-10).

God created us to do good works. He has a lifetime of good works for each of us to do. Many of these works he intends to do with our money and possessions. And he will reward us according to whether or not we do them. Indeed, Scripture ties God's reward-giving to his very character: "God is not unjust; he will not forget your work and the love you have shown him as you have helped his people and continue to help them" (Heb. 6:10). The verses that follow in Hebrews 6 tell us that if we are to inherit God's promised blessings we must not become lazy but diligent in our God-given works.

Good works are essential to the Christian life, as James repeatedly stated (James 2:17-18, 22, 24, 26). "Who is wise and understanding among you? Let him show it by his good life, by deeds done in the humility that comes from wisdom" (James 3:13).

We know that Christ will say to some (but not all) believers, "Well done, good and faithful servant" (Matt. 25:21). It is significant that he will not say, "Well said," or "Well believed," but "Well *done*." In the account of the sheep and goats, where the "Well done" is spoken, that which separates the sheep from the goats is what they *did and did not do* with their time and money and possessions.

Peter said, "If you *do* these things [then] you will never fall, and you will receive a rich welcome into the eternal kingdom of our Lord and Savior Jesus Christ" (2 Pet. 1:10-11). What a powerful encouragement to the godly saint who has sacrificed in this life to prepare for the next! In heaven there waits for him a great welcoming committee and a hearty "Well done." But this is not automatic for believers—the conditional "if, then" makes it clear that if we do not do what Peter prescribed, then we will not receive this rich welcome when we enter heaven.

Where we spend eternity, whether heaven or hell, will be determined by our faith. Our further station in either place will be determined by our works. John Bunyan, ever motivated by this reality, said, "Consider, to provoke you to good works, that you shall have from God, when you come to glory, a reward for everything you do for him on earth."

A SECOND CHANCE?

My God-given resources of time, talents, money, and possessions have immense potential. They are the lever, positioned on the fulcrum of this life, that moves the mountains of eternity.

As evangelicals, we reject the doctrine of a second chance for unbelievers. We emphatically affirm, and rightly so, that there is no opportunity to come to Christ after death. But we must be equally aware that after death there is no second chance for believers either. There is no further opportunity for us to walk by faith and serve our Lord in this fallen world. As there is no second chance beyond this earth for the unbeliever to believe right, so there is no second chance for the disobedient Christian to live right.

This life ends at death. We can't do it over again. There is no retaking the course of life on this earth once we've failed it. There's no improving a "D" to an "A," no rescheduling of the final exams. There are no strings to pull, no going over the professor's head. Death is the final deadline, for which there is no extension.

A basketball game is over at the final buzzer. No shots taken thereafter count. Likewise, when the trumpet sounds Christ's return, time will be gone. It will simultaneously be the beginning of eternity and the end of that which determines eternity's composition. At that time, if we have failed to use our money, possessions, time, and energies for eternity, then we have failed—period.

It is not so simple as saying, "We'll be in heaven and that's all that matters." On the contrary, Paul spoke of loss of reward as a great and terrible loss. The fact that we are still saved is only a clarification, not a consolation—"if it is burned up, he will suffer loss; he himself will be saved, but only as one escaping through the flames" (1 Cor. 3:15). The receiving of reward from Christ is an unspeakable gain with eternal implications. The loss of reward is a terrible loss with equally eternal implications. How dare we say that being in heaven is all that matters to us, when so much else matters to God?

The bottom line of all this is that what we do in this life is of eternal importance. This begins with our choice to follow Christ, but it does not end there. You and I will never have another chance to move the hand of God through prayer to heal a hurting soul, to share Christ with one who can be saved from hell, to give a cup of water to the thirsty, to invest money to help the helpless, to rescue the unborn from murder, to further God's kingdom, to share our homes and our clothes and our love with the poor and needy.

What you do with your money and possessions and all your other resources in this life is the last chapter of your autobiography. This book you have written with the pen of faith and the ink of works will go unedited, into eternity, to be seen and read as is by the angels, the redeemed, and God himself. When we see today in light of the long tomorrow the little choices become tremendously important. Whether I read my Bible today, pray, go to church, share my faith, and give my money is of eternal consequence, not only for other souls, but for my own.

Those who have dabbled in photography understand the effect of the "fixer." In developing a photograph, the negatives are immersed in several different solutions. The developing solution parallels this life. As long as the photograph is in the developer it is subject to change. But when it is dropped in the fixer or "stop bath," it is permanently fixed. The photograph is now done. What you see is what you get. So it will be when we enter eternity—the lives we lived on earth will be fixed as is, never to be altered or revised.

Scripture simply does not teach what most of us seem to assume—that heaven will transform each of us into equal beings with equal possessions and equal responsibilities and equal capacities. It does not say our previous lives will be of no eternal significance. It says exactly the opposite.

Beyond the new heavens and new earth—which themselves are populated and structured according to what has been done in this life—there is no record of change. We might hope that what happens at the judgment seat will be of only temporary concern to the Judge, and that all of the disobedience and missed opportunities will just "blow over" and none of it will ever make any difference. But will God make all souls equal in heaven and thereby consider as equally valid a life of selfishness and indifference to others' needs as compared to a life spent on its knees praying and feeding the hungry and sharing the gospel? The Bible clearly tells us "No."

Donald Gray Barnhouse put it this way:

> Let us live, then, in the light of eternity. If we do not, we are weighting the scales against our eternal welfare. We must understand that "whatsoever a man soweth" must be taken in its widest meaning, and that every thought and intent of the heart will come under the scrutiny of the Lord at His coming. We can be sure that at the Judgment Seat of Christ there will be a marked difference between the Christian who has lived his life before the Lord, clearly discerning what was for the glory of God, and another Christian who was saved in a rescue mission at the tag end of a depraved and vicious life, or a nominal Christian saved on his deathbed after a life of self-pride, self-righteousness, self-love, and self-sufficiency. All will be in heaven, but the differences will be eternal. We may be sure that the consequences of our character will survive the grave and that we shall face those consequences at the Judgment Seat of Christ.[1]

If we really believed that our works in this life, what we do with all of our resources, will have an irreversible effect on eternity . . . then surely we would live differently!

CONCLUSION

We have been given fair warning that there lies ahead for each of us, at the end of the term, a final examination. It will be administered by the fairest yet strictest Headmaster in the universe. How seriously we take this clear teaching of Scripture is demonstrated by how seriously we are preparing for that day.

When we took courses in college, we asked others about the teacher: "What are his tests like? Does he take attendance? Is he a hard grader? What does he expect in your papers?" If I'm to do well in the course, I must know what the instructor expects of me. We must study the course syllabus, God's Word, to find out the answers to these questions. And when we find out, we should be careful to plot our lives accordingly—in light of the long tomorrow.

While visiting a missionary in Greece, the two of us spent a day in ancient Corinth. For an hour we sat on the same judgment seat Paul stood before in Acts 18, which he used to help the Corinthian Christians visualize Christ's future judgment of the believer. Together we read Scriptures that speak of that day when we will stand before the Lord's judgment seat and give an account for what we have done with all he has given us. We discussed the implications and prayed that when that day comes he might find us faithful and say to us, "Well done." Yet we prayed knowing that it is we, by virtue of our hourly and daily choices, who will determine what transpires on that day. It was one of the most sobering hours of my life.

Alfred Nobel was a Swedish chemist who made his fortune by inventing dynamite and other powerful explosives, which were bought by governments to produce weapons. When Nobel's brother died, one newspaper accidentally printed Alfred's obituary instead. He was described as a man who became rich from enabling people to kill each other in unprecedented quantities. Shaken from this assessment, Nobel resolved to use his fortune to reward accomplishments that benefited humanity, including what we now know as the Nobel Peace Prize.

Nobel had a rare opportunity—to look at the assessment of his life at its end, but to still be alive and have opportunity to change that assessment.

Let us put ourselves in Nobel's place. Let us read our own obituary, not as written by uninformed or biased men, but as an onlooking angel might write it from heaven's point of view. Look at it carefully. Then let us use the rest of our lives to edit that obituary into what we really want it to be.

Martin Luther said that on his calendar there were only two days: "today" and "that Day." May we make in eternity's light our moment-to-moment choices of what to do with our money and possessions. May we invest all that we are and have today in light of *that* Day.

NOTES
1. Quoted by Bruce Wilkinson in the "Walk Thru Eternal Rewards" seminar notebook (Atlanta, Ga.: Walk Thru the Bible Ministries).

CHAPTER 9

THE STEWARD'S ETERNAL REWARDS

It is my happiness that I have served Him who never fails to reward His servants to the full extent of His promise. John Calvin

Whatever good thing you do for Him, if done according to the Word, is laid up for you as treasure in chests and coffers, to be brought out to be rewarded before both men and angels, to your eternal comfort. John Bunyan

Two men owned farms side by side. One was a bitter atheist, the other a devout Christian. Constantly annoyed at the Christian for his trust in God, one winter the atheist said to him, "Let's plant our crops as usual this spring, each the same number of acres. You pray to your God, and I'll curse him. Then come October, let's just see who has the bigger crop."

153

When October came the atheist was delighted because his crop was larger. "See, you fool," he taunted, "what do you have to say for your God now?"

"My God," replied the other farmer, "doesn't settle all his accounts in October."

A CLOSER LOOK AT REWARDS

A day of judgment is coming upon all men, and God promises great reward for those who have served him faithfully (Rev. 11:18). He will reward every loyal servant for the spiritual labor done in this life—"at that time each will receive his praise from God" (1 Cor. 4:5).

God rewards generously, promising a return of "a hundred times" (Matt. 19:29). This is essentially a promise of infinite return—a return far out of proportion to the amount originally invested.

We earn rewards in a variety of ways. These include doing good works (Eph. 6:8; Rom. 2:6, 10), denying ourselves (Matt. 16:24-27), and treating others kindly even when they take advantage of us (Luke 6:35).

Rewards are promised to those who endure difficult circumstances out of their trust in God (Heb. 10:34-36) and to those who persevere under persecution for their faith (Luke 6:22-23). A life of godliness (2 Pet. 3:11-14) and compassionate obedience (Matt. 25:20-21) will be richly rewarded by our Lord. When we extend hospitality and give a meal to those too poor or incapacitated to pay us back, Christ promised us, "You will be blessed. Although they cannot repay you, you will be repaid at the resurrection of the righteous" (Luke 14:14).

Paul reminded us there is a "proper time" for the harvest—"Let us not become weary in doing good, for at the proper time we will reap a harvest if we do not give up" (Gal. 6:9). The believer's compensation, like that of the unbeliever, is usually deferred. "God doesn't settle all his accounts in October."

THE REWARD OF RULERSHIP

God promises to grant faithful believers positions of authority over others in the future kingdom. Believers will reign with

Christ over the world (Rev. 20:6), and will even rule over angels (1 Cor. 6:3). One parable tells us certain believers will be put "in charge of many things" (Matt. 25:21-23). On another occasion, Christ spoke of granting some of his followers rulership over a specific number of cities—five cities for one believer, eleven for another, and none for a third, in proportion to their faithful service (Luke 19:17-24).

It is apparent from most of these passages that while all believers will be with Christ, not all will reign with him, at least not with equal responsibility and authority. Conditions for reigning are clearly stated in several passages, including this: "If we endure, we shall also reign with him" (2 Tim. 2:12). Christ promised to persevering believers, "To him who overcomes, I will give the right to sit with me on my throne" (Rev. 3:21). Similarly he stated: "To him who overcomes and does my will to the end, I will give authority over the nations . . . just as I have received authority from my Father. I will also give him the morning star" (Rev. 2:26-28).

It is intriguing that in the immediate context of rewarding rulership to faithful believers, Jesus spoke of giving them "the morning star." This was the common name for the planet Venus. The reference may be only figurative, but is it possible that Christ has in mind his servants reigning not only over this world but others?

CROWNS AS REWARDS

Crowns are a common symbol of ruling power in Scripture, though it is possible they symbolize other forms of reward as well. Five crowns are specifically mentioned as rewards granted to believers:

1. The Crown of Life—given for faithfulness to Christ in persecution or martyrdom (James 1:12; Rev. 2:10).

2. The Incorruptible Crown—given for determination, discipline, and victory in the Christian life (1 Cor. 9:24-25).

3. The Crown of Rejoicing—given for pouring oneself into others in evangelism and discipleship (1 Thess. 2:19; Phil. 4:1).

4. The Crown of Glory—given for faithfully representing Christ in a position of spiritual leadership (1 Pet. 5:1-4). (Note that a prerequisite is "not greedy for money but eager to

155

serve"—a Christian leader's preoccupation with money or possessions can forfeit this reward.)

5. The Crown of Righteousness—given for joyfully purifying and readying yourself to meet Christ at his return (2 Tim. 4:6-8).

There is nothing in this list that suggests it is exhaustive. There may be innumerable crowns and types of crowns, and rewards unrelated to crowns. What they all have in common is that they are graciously given by the Lord Jesus, and earned through the faithful efforts of the believer.

These crowns ultimately bring glory to Christ as they are laid before his feet (Rev. 4:10). This latter passage demonstrates our rewards are given not merely for our recognition but for God's eternal glory. Though God's glory is the highest and ultimate reason for any course of action, Scripture sees no contradiction between God's eternal glory and our eternal good. On the contrary, glorifying God will result in our greatest eternal good. Likewise, pursuing our eternal good, as he commands us to do, will always glorify God. False humility that says "I want no reward" effectively means "I want nothing to lay at Christ's feet to bring him glory."

We are to guard our crowns carefully (Rev. 3:11). Why is this necessary? Because we can be disqualified from earning them (1 Cor. 9:27), we can lose them (1 Cor. 3:15), or have them taken from us (Matt. 25:28-29). We seek our rewards from men, thereby forfeiting them from God (Matt. 6:5-6). John warned, "Watch out that you do not lose what you have worked for, but that you may be rewarded fully" (2 John 8). We can not only fail to receive rewards, but apparently we can also forfeit rewards already in our account.

ETERNAL DIFFERENCES IN HEAVEN?

Not all Christians will hear the master say, "Well done, good and faithful servant" (Matt. 25:23). Not all of us will have treasure in heaven (Matt. 6:19-21). Not all of us will have the same position of authority in heaven (Luke 19:17, 19, 26). We will have differing levels of reward in heaven (1 Cor. 3:12-15). And there is no suggestion that, once given or withheld, either our rewards or our loss thereof are anything other than eternal and irrevocable in nature.

Scripture suggests that some Christians will be ashamed at

Christ's coming (1 John 2:28). While it seems incomprehensible that such shame should continue into the heavenly state, the doctrine of eternal rewards has a very sobering implication. The tangible results of those who have faithfully served Christ in this life and those who haven't will be evident for all eternity. They will be embodied in eternal possessions and positions that will differ obviously and significantly from person to person.

Scripture is explicitly clear that there is a payback in eternity according to what is done in time and that there will be differences in reward in heaven (Prov. 24:11-12; Matt. 19:27-30; Luke 14:12-14). In other words, to put it in terms we may find shocking, our experiences in heaven will not be the same for all of us.

We saw in the last chapter that hell will be terrible for all, but depending on their works in this life it will be more terrible for some than others (Matt. 11:20-24; Luke 20:45-47). Does it not also follow that while all people's experience in heaven will be wonderful, depending on their works in this life it will be more wonderful for some than others?

How could this be possible? Perhaps it is a matter of differing capacity. Two jars can both be full, but the one with greater capacity contains more. Likewise, all of us will be full of joy in heaven, but some may have more joy because their capacity for joy will be larger, having been stretched through their trust in God in this life. John Bunyan understood this to be true: "He who is most in the bosom of God, and who so acts for Him here, he is the man who will be best able to enjoy most of God in the kingdom of heaven."

No matter how we attempt to explain it, no matter how incompatible it seems with what most of us have supposed, it is simply a fact that the consistent doctrine of differing rewards and differing positions in heaven adds up to different experiences in heaven. These eternal experiences are presently being forged in the crucible of *this* life. What I do in this life with my money and possessions will significantly affect my eternal experience in heaven.

UNDERSTANDING SALVATION AND REWARDS

Whenever we speak of rewards, particularly because we speak of them so rarely, it is easy to confuse God's work and man's.

We may thereby mistakenly believe that heaven is a person's reward for doing good things. This is absolutely *not* the case. Our presence in heaven is in no sense a reward for human works, but a gift freely given by God in response to faith (Rom. 6:23; Eph. 2:8-9; Titus 3:5).

This chart may help distinguish the difference between regeneration and rewards:

REGENERATION	REWARDS
Past (1 John 3:2)	Future (Rev. 22:12)
Free (Eph. 2:8-9)	Earned (1 Cor. 3:8)
Can't be lost (John 10:28-29)	Can be lost (2 John 8)
Same for all Christians (Rom. 3:22)	Differ between Christians (1 Cor. 3:12-15)
For those who believe (John 3:16)	For those who work (1 Cor. 9:27)

The following chart shows how rewards relate to the larger context of the believer's life:

JUDGMENT	TIME	RELATIONSHIP	SCRIPTURE
Condemnation to New life	Past (Regeneration)	As a Sinner	2 Cor. 5:21; Rom. 6:1-23
Discipline or Rewards	Present (Sanctification)	As a Son	Heb. 12:5-11; James 1:2-4
Loss or Rewards	Future (Glorification)	As a Steward	1 Cor. 3:10-15; 2 Cor. 5:10

As a sinner, I was under condemnation for my sin until I accepted the provision of Christ, who took this condemnation on himself. At that point I was moved from condemnation to regeneration and new life.

As a son, I presently make choices that are either righteous or sinful. When they are sinful, my Father disciplines me for my own good in order to make me more holy and fruitful. His discipline is intended to turn me back to the path of righteousness. When I make right choices, I experience the immediate reward of God's approval and a variety of short-term benefits, as well as store up reward for myself in eternity. Of course, I may also forfeit certain temporal benefits—perhaps even my life—through my righteous choices. Eternal reward is guaranteed, whereas temporal reward, at least in its outward forms, is not.

As a steward or servant, my works will someday be evaluated by my Master, and he will reward me according to my works. The works worthy of reward are those done with faithfulness (1 Cor. 4:2) and right motives (1 Cor. 4:5), which only he is qualified to judge. To the degree that my life on earth has not been characterized by good works, or to the degree these works have been done unfaithfully and with improper motives, I will lose or forfeit my reward (1 Cor. 3:12-15).

Salvation, then, is a matter of God's work for man. In contrast, rewards are a matter of man's work for God. When it comes to salvation, man's work for God is no substitute for God's work for man. God saves us for Christ's work, not ours. Likewise, when it comes to rewards, God's work for man is no substitute for man's work for God. God rewards us for our work, not Christ's. (Of course, this doesn't mean we work in our own strength to earn rewards. Ultimately even our reward-earning works are empowered by the Holy Spirit—note the integration of God's work and man's in Paul's statement in Colossians 1:29: "To this end I labor, struggling with all his energy, which so powerfully works in me.")

Let me be sure this is perfectly clear. Christ paid the eternal price (hell) for all of our sins once for all (Heb. 10:12-18). If we have trusted him for that provision, we will *not* pay the eternal price; that is, we will not go to hell. He has fully forgiven our sins and we are completely secure in the love of Christ (Ps. 103:8-18; Rom. 8:31-39). Our salvation is sure, and we will *not* undergo the judgment of condemnation (John 5:24; Rom. 8:1).

But while the question of the forgiveness of our sins has every bearing on our eternal destination, it has no bearing on our eternal rewards. The Bible teaches not only forgiveness of sins, but consequences of our choices and actions that apply despite forgiveness. Forgiveness means God eliminates eternal condemnation. But it does not mean that our actions in this life have no consequences on earth—a forgiven person can still get AIDS or the death penalty. Neither does it mean they have no consequences in eternity—a forgiven person can still lose his reward and forfeit an eternal position of responsibility he could have had.

With our salvation, the work was Christ's. With our rewards, the work must be ours. We trust in Christ, lean on him, and draw upon him for power, but we must do the work if we are to receive the reward. As our forefathers put it, "We must bear the cross if we are to wear the crown."

Belief (trust, faith) determines our eternal destination, where we will be. Behavior determines our eternal rewards, what we will have. Works *do not* affect our redemption. Works *do* affect our reward. Just as there are eternal consequences to our faith, so there are eternal consequences to our works.

THE STEWARD'S MOTIVATIONS

"Why should I follow Scripture's teaching on money and possessions when it is so much fun to have all the nice things I want and do whatever I please with my money? I'm a Christian, and I know I'm going to heaven anyway, so why get radical about the whole thing? Why not have the best of both worlds, this one *and* the next?" Though few of us are honest enough to use such language, it accurately reflects a prevailing attitude in the Christian community.

The missing ingredient in many Christian lives today is motivation. Given our assumption (based either on erroneous instruction or lack of teaching) that what we do in this life won't have consequences for eternity, it is no wonder we are unmotivated to follow God's directions regarding money and possessions and just about everything else. When it comes right down to it, what difference will it make whether we do or don't? According to the prevailing theology, everything comes out in the wash, so it won't make any difference at all. But according to the Bible it will make a tremendous difference! The doctrine of eternal rewards for our obedience is the neglected key to unlocking our motivation.[1]

Moses was a motivated man. He "regarded disgrace for the name of Christ as of greater value than the treasures of Egypt, because he was looking ahead to his reward" (Heb. 11:26). He chose short-term disgrace, motivated by long-term reward.

Paul ran his race with his eyes on the prize, which motivated him to run hard and long. He strove not to get a crown of leaves that would rot, but "to get a crown that will last forever" (1 Cor. 9:24-25). Paul was unashamedly motivated by the prospect of eternal reward, and he acknowledged it freely and frequently (2 Cor. 4:16-18; 5:9-10; 2 Tim. 4:7-8). He likewise encouraged all believers to be motivated by rewards (Gal. 6:9-10; 1 Tim. 6:17-19; 2 Tim. 2:5, 12). Slaves, for instance, were to obey their masters in order to receive eternal reward (Eph. 6:5-9; Col. 3:22-25).

Another model of motivation by reward is Christ himself. He endured the cross "for the joy set before him" (Heb. 12:2). He humbled himself knowing that he would ultimately be exalted (Phil. 2:9).

Jesus said, "Whenever you give a feast, invite the poor, the crippled, the lame and the blind, and you will be blessed, because they cannot pay you back, for it will be paid back to you in the resurrection of the just" (Luke 14:13-14). Christ appealed not only to our compassion but to our eternal self-interests—if we do this compassionate act that goes unrewarded in this life, he will personally pay us back in the next life. What a tremendous source of motivation this can be when we feel our labors are unappreciated by others!

"Love your enemies, and do good, expecting nothing in return; and your reward will be great, and you will be sons of the Most High" (Luke 6:35). Once again, Christ sought to motivate us to good works by the promise of rewards.

Despite every statement to the contrary, the prospect of rewards is a proper motivation for the Christian's obedience—including the generous sharing of our money and possessions (Matt. 6:19-21). If we maintain it is wrong for the believer to be motivated by rewards, then we bring a serious accusation against Christ. We are effectively saying he is tempting us to sin every time he offers rewards for obedience. Since God does not tempt his children, it is clear that whatever he lays before us as a motivation to our behavior is pure and legitimate. It is not wrong for us to be motivated by the prospect of reward. Indeed, something is wrong if we are not motivated by reward. (Most of us use rewards to motivate our children—why are we surprised that God uses rewards to motivate his?)

THE POWER OF INCENTIVES

Businessmen work in a world of incentives. So do housewives and school children and every human being regardless of age, nationality, and economic circumstance. Every effective manager, every qualified leader knows the importance of incentives. These incentives are tangible motivators, and may be personal, social, spiritual, physical, or financial in nature. Unfortunately, too many of us consider incentives to be "secular" or "unspiritual."

The truth is that God made us the way we are, and that by his very design all of us need incentives to motivate us to do our jobs and do them well.

Love for people is an incentive to certain actions, as is the fear of punishment and the hope of reward. Every major choice involves a major consequence. And Scripture is brimming with the promises and warnings of this consequence for this choice, this punishment for this sin, this reward for this act of obedience. Some of these are short-term or temporal incentives (Prov. 3:9-10; Mal. 3:10-12), some are long-term or eternal incentives (Luke 12:32-33; Matt. 6:20), and still others involve both temporal and eternal incentives (Mark 10:29-30).

Of course, reward is not our only motivation. We should be motivated to serve God by our gratitude (Heb. 12:28). We should be motivated by our ambition "to be pleasing to him" (2 Cor. 5:9). But we must realize these motives are not in scriptural conflict with the motive of reward. The same Bible that calls upon us to obey God out of our love for him as Father and Redeemer (Deut. 7:9; 11:1; 30:20), also calls upon us to obey out of our fear of him as Creator and Judge (Gen. 2:17; Deut. 28:58-67; Heb. 10:30-31), and out of our hope in him as Rewarder of those who serve him (Deut. 28:2-9; Heb. 11:6). Each of these is legitimate, and each compliments the other. Sometimes we need the combined persuasiveness of all these incentives to do what is pleasing to the Lord.

My children love me, and sometimes this is a sufficient incentive for them to be obedient. But other times it isn't enough. Fortunately, they also fear me, in the best sense. They know I will punish wrongdoing. And they also know I am very pleased when they do the right thing. They know I will reward them for doing right, always with my words of approval, and sometimes in tangible ways.

Hopefully, we will evangelize people out of our love for God. If that isn't enough, our love for men should motivate us. But Scripture tells us we should also be motivated to evangelize out of our *fear* of God. We will stand before the judgment seat and be recompensed for our works, Paul said, "Since we know the fear of God, we try to persuade men" (2 Cor. 5:9-11). Love is one motivator, fear another. Either should suffice, but the two work together admirably.

The beauty of these complementary motivations is that there is an ultimate harmony in the moral universe. What is in God's best interests is also in others' best interests and in my best interests as well (not necessarily immediately but always ultimately). What is good is not good for God but bad for me, or bad for my neighbor but good for me. What is good is good for all. Every time I obey God, I am doing what is ultimately best for all. Every time I disobey him, I am doing what is ultimately worst for all. The Master and steward are both pleased when the steward does well, and both displeased when he does not.

The prospect of being praised by others is a strong motivator and reinforcer of our behavior. The child is motivated by the hope of being praised by his parents. Why not the child of God? The prospect of hearing my Father say to me, "Well done" should be tremendously motivating. The Pharisees "loved praise from men rather than praise from God" (John 12:43). Their problem wasn't that they were motivated by praise, but that they were content with praise from the wrong source—men, rather than God.

How should we respond to adversity for the sake of Christ? The Lord told us, "Rejoice in that day and leap for joy." *Why* should we leap for joy? "Because great is your reward in heaven" (Luke 6:23).

The believer who knows God's Word knows its promise of reward for obedience. There is a sense in which he operates by the philosophy, "Find out how the system works and get on the good side of it." God has set up a system that rewards obedience and punishes disobedience, that rewards others-centered sacrifice and punishes self-centered indulgence. What is right is also smart, because it will be rewarded. What is wrong is also stupid, because it will be punished. This is the system as God has made it. This system, not personal preference or what everyone else does, should be the Christian's basic frame of reference in deciding what to do with his money and possessions.

PLEASURE, POSSESSIONS, AND POWER

God has created each of us with certain desires that correspond to and make possible certain motivations. Specifically, each of us has built-in desires for pleasure, possessions, and power. At first this may sound unbiblical, for we have come to think of these things as temptations, not motivators.

Satan does indeed tempt us on each of these levels. The desire for pleasure can degenerate into hedonism, desire for possessions into materialism, and desire for power into egotism. We might relate the desire for pleasure to the lust of the flesh, the desire for possessions to the lust of the eyes, and the desire for power to the pride of life (1 John 2:16, KJV).

Satan approached Christ on all three of these levels during his wilderness temptation. He tempted him to make bread for the *pleasure* of eating, to worship Satan for the *possession* of all the world's kingdoms, and to cast himself from the temple for the *power* of commanding angelic intervention (Luke 4:1-13).

So if the desires for pleasure, possessions, and power make us vulnerable to temptation, how can they be used for good? How can they properly motivate us? We must understand that these things can only be appealed to in the first place because they have been built into us. They are part of the way God made us and intends us to be. The draw to pleasure, possessions, and power cannot be rooted in our sin nature, for a study of the first temptation demonstrates that Satan appealed to these desires in Adam and Eve *before* they were sinful (Gen. 3:1-7).

Christ had no sin nature. Satan knew this, but nevertheless appealed to him on these same three grounds—pleasure, possessions, and power. Why? Because Christ was human, and to be human is to have desires for these things. We want pleasure, possessions, and power not because we are sinful but because we are human.

But if this argument is unconvincing, there is a clincher—God himself appeals to each of these desires in us. He offers us the reward of *power* in his eternal kingdom (Matt. 20:20-28; Luke 12:42-44; 19:15-19), *possessions* in his eternal kingdom (Matt. 6:19-21; 19:16-22, 27-30), and *pleasures* in his eternal kingdom (Ps. 16:11).

God appeals to our natures as people, but *never* to our natures as sinners. Hence power, possessions, and pleasures are legitimate desires that he as our Creator has instilled in us, and by which he can motivate us to obedience. By them, also, the evil one can motivate us to disobedience.

HOW TO GAIN ETERNAL PLEASURE, POSSESSIONS, AND POWER

The way of the world and the temptation of the Devil is to try to gain each of these three things in the present world. The way of the Lord is to gain them in the future not by clinging to them in the present, but by *forgoing* them in the present. It is at this point that prosperity theology is so badly mistaken.

Consider the threefold disciplines of fasting, giving, and prayer, which are developed by Christ in Matthew 6:1-18. Fasting is denying the pleasure of eating to gain pleasure in God. Giving is denying the possession of riches to gain possessions from God. Prayer is denying one's own power to gain power from God. Eating, owning, and ruling are not bad—but in these three spiritual disciplines they are temporarily abstained from to accomplish a higher kingdom purpose.

For centuries, monastic orders have tried to tie into this concept through their vow of chastity (forgoing pleasure), vow of poverty (forgoing possessions) and vow of obedience (forgoing the power of living life one's own way).

But take notice of what we often overlook. One need not forgo power because he hates power. He may forgo it because he wants power in another world. Jesus told his disciples they could become great in the next world by being a servant in this one (Mark 10:42-44). Likewise, one does not forgo possessions here because he hates possessions, but because he wants them in another world. Jesus told his disciples they could become rich in the next world by giving up riches in this one (Matt. 6:19-21). It is not a matter of no gratification, but *delayed* gratification. It is

165

forgoing present temporal gratification to achieve future eternal gratification.

This is not self-denial for its own sake, but purposeful or strategic self-denial for God's glory and our own ultimate good. The key to all this, of course, is faith, the very faith described and exemplified in the Book of Hebrews (11:8-16). For it is faith that brings one to forgo something in this life out of belief that it—or a higher form of it—will be his in the next.

This is difficult to understand, partly because our sin nature has so badly tainted pleasures, possessions, and power in this world. But in eternity we will be able to handle these things because we will be pure and without sin. As our sinless Lord handles them properly, so we will be able to handle them properly.

What believers in prosperity theology do not realize is that when we fail to limit our seeking of pleasures, possessions, and power in *this* world, where we are yet sinful, the result will be disaster. Look closely at the scandals that have rocked Christian organizations in recent years, several of which we dealt with in chapter 5. The lives of the two most prominent fallen evangelists consisted of three basic elements in extensive measure: power, possessions, and pleasures. Both men rose to tremendous power over people, amassed a great deal of possessions, then indulged in many pleasures, which ultimately included sexual immorality. Like most of us, these men in their sinful human natures were simply incapable of handling in this life such vast portions of power, possessions, and pleasures.

CAN APPEAL TO OUR DESIRES REALLY BE SPIRITUAL?

God created us with certain desires, made us to be motivated by rewards that appeal to those desires, and calls us to action on the basis of promised rewards. As we have seen, the Scriptures are full of exhortations to act in certain ways to gain certain rewards. Yet somehow there persists among many Christians a belief that desire for power, possession, and pleasure in the next life is crass, and to pursue rewards is selfish, mercenary, and non-Christian. Three godly Englishmen of three different centuries offer us a very different perspective, and an explicitly biblical one.

John Bunyan, the seventeenth-century tinker imprisoned for preaching the gospel, stated:

> The rewards are such as should make us leap to think on, and that we should remember with exceeding joy, and never think that it is contrary to the Christian faith to rejoice and be glad for them.[2]

William Wilberforce, through his tireless efforts in Parliament, in the early nineteenth century finally succeeded in abolishing England's slave trade. He devoted most of his fortune to the cause of Christ. This was his perspective on our God-given desires: "Christianity proposes not to extinguish our natural desires. It promises to bring the desires under just control and direct them to their true object."[3]

C. S. Lewis, Oxford and Cambridge professor in the middle twentieth century, wrote prolifically on the Christian faith and developed a unique hearing on two continents. He diverted most of his royalties to charitable causes and individual needs, living simply and thinking often of that world beyond:

> The faint, far-off results of those energies which God's creative rapture implanted in matter when He made the worlds are what we now call physical pleasures; and even thus filtered, they are too much for our present management. What would it be to taste at the fountainhead that stream of which even these lower reaches prove so intoxicating? Yet that, I believe, is what lies before us. The whole man is to drink joy from the fountain of joy.[4]

> The New Testament has lots to say about self-denial, but not about self-denial as an end in itself. We are told to deny ourselves and to take up our crosses in order that we may follow Christ; and nearly every description of what we shall ultimately find if we do so contains an appeal to desire. If there lurks in most modern minds the notion that to desire our own good and earnestly to hope for the enjoyment of it is a bad thing, I submit that this notion has

crept in from Kant and the Stoics and is no part of the Christian faith. Indeed, if we consider the unblushing promises of rewards promised in the Gospels, it would seem that our Lord finds our desires not too strong, but too weak. We are half-hearted creatures, fooling about with drink and sex and ambition when infinite joy is offered us, like an ignorant child who wants to go on making mud pies in a slum because he cannot imagine what is meant by the offer of a holiday at the sea. We are far too easily pleased.[5]

We must realize once and for all that the seeking of reward and the fulfilling of desires is not anti-Christian. What *is* anti-Christian is the self-centeredness that is unconcerned about God and one's neighbor, and the preoccupation with the immediate fulfilling of desires that distracts us from finding our ultimate fulfillment in Christ.

The person who gives his life and his money and possessions to earn rewards from his God—the greatest of which is the resounding "Well done"—is one whose deepest thirsts will be eternally quenched by the Great Maker and Fulfiller of Desire.

With such a prospect available to us, devoting our lives to the "mud pies" of the power, possessions, and pleasures of this world is indeed to be far too easily pleased.

CONCLUSION

Writing in 1649 Richard Baxter said:

> If there be so certain and glorious a rest for the saints, why is there no more industrious seeking after it? One would think, if a man did but once hear of such unspeakable glory to be obtained, and believed what he heard to be true, he should be transported with the vehemency of his desire after it, and should almost forget to eat and drink, and should care for nothing else, and speak of and inquire after nothing else, but how to get this treasure. And yet people who hear of it daily, and profess to believe it as a fundamental article of their faith, do as little mind it, or labour for it, as if they had never heard of any such thing, or did not believe one word they hear.[6]

May we joyously believe it! And then may we *live* as though we believe!

NOTES

1. I am indebted to Bruce Wilkinson and his excellent "Walk Thru Eternal Rewards" seminar for a number of the insights and expressions in this chapter. I highly recommend this course to the reader. For more information, contact Walk Thru the Bible Ministries, P.O. Box 80587, Atlanta, GA, 30366.
2 John Bunyan, quoted by Bruce Wilkinson in the "Walk Thru Eternal Rewards" seminar notebook.
3. William Wilberforce, *Real Christianity* (Portland: Multnomah Press, 1982), 65.
4. C. S. Lewis, *The Weight of Glory* (New York: Macmillan, 1980), 17-18.
5. Lewis, 3-4.
6. Richard Baxter, "The Saints' Everlasting Rest," *The Practical Works of Richard Baxter* (Grand Rapids, Mich.: Baker, 1981), 39-40.

CHAPTER 10

THE STEWARD AND
THE MASTER

One more revival—only one more—is needed, the revival of Christian stewardship, the consecration of the money power to God. When that revival comes, the Kingdom of God will come in a day. Horace Bushnell

It is just as much a matter of discipline for a church member practically to deny his stewardship as to deny the divinity of Christ. Charles Finney

A distraught man furiously rode his horse up to John Wesley, shouting, "Mr. Wesley, Mr. Wesley, something terrible has happened. Your house has burned to the ground!" Weighing the news for a moment, Wesley calmly replied, "No. The *Lord's* house burned to the ground. That means one less responsibility for me."

Wesley's response was not the sanctimonious or pseudo-spiritual reply of a man who thought I would be quoting his words hundreds of years later. His reaction did not stem from a denial of reality. Rather, it was firmly rooted in life's most fundamental reality—that God is the owner of all things, and that we are simply his stewards.

Stewardship is not a subcategory of the Christian life. Stewardship *is* the Christian life. For what is stewardship but that God has entrusted to us life, time, talents, money, possessions, family, his grace, and even his Son? In each case he evaluates how we regard and what we do with that which he has entrusted to us.

The word "stewardship" has fallen on hard times. To many it is just a religious cliché used to make fund-raising sound spiritual. To some it conjures up images of large red thermometers on the church platform, measuring how far we are from paying off the mortgage.

Because of these associations, I was tempted not to use the word "stewardship" in this book. But it is such a good word, both biblically and historically, that it deserves resuscitation rather than burial.

"A steward is someone entrusted with another's wealth or property and charged with the responsibility of managing it in the owner's best interests."[1]

The steward is entrusted by the owner with sufficient resources and authority to carry out his designated responsibilities.

Scripture tells us that from the beginning God gave man, both male and female, authority over all his creation (Gen. 1:28). The psalmist praised God, saying, "You made him [man] ruler over the works of your hand; you put everything under his feet: all flocks and herds, and the beasts of the field" (Ps. 8:6-7).

God expects us to use all the resources he gives us to best carry out our responsibilities. A steward's primary goal is to be found faithful by his master in his usage of those resources to accomplish the tasks delegated to him (1 Cor. 4:2).

Our use of money and possessions is only one aspect of stewardship, and all its aspects are overlapping circles. In Exodus 36:2-7, for instance, we see the tabernacle built by people giving their time, energy, skills, *and* money and possessions. How a person views and handles his money will be affected by and in turn will affect how he views and handles his time, energy, talents, family, church, vocation, and every facet of his life. More than half of Christ's thirty-plus parables deal with the subject of stewardship, emphasizing the eternal implications of our present service for our Lord. This chapter takes a close look at one of these parables, summarizes two more, and gleans a number of key lessons that set a clear agenda for all who would serve their Master.

LESSONS FROM A SHREWD STEWARD

Christ's parable of the shrewd manager, often called the "unrighteous steward," concerns a wealthy owner who fires his business manager for supposedly wasting his assets (Luke 16:1-13). During a brief period before his termination is effective, the steward goes to his master's debtors and reduces the amount of their debt, thereby engendering their friendship. When the master learns of this he praises the steward for his resourcefulness and foresight in making friends that will be supportive to him now that his term of stewardship is over.

There are several different interpretations of this passage that attempt to explain the owner's apparent approval of what seems to be a dishonest act. One is that the steward reduced long outstanding debts so that at least his master received some payment rather than none. Another suggests the steward had grossly overcharged the debtors in the first place, planning to pocket the excess, and now lets them pay for their goods at the true, uninflated price. Regardless of the correct interpretation, however, we do know that the steward was praised for his shrewdness in using, with his own future well-being in mind, his master's money to invest in his relationships with people (Luke 16:8-9).

Jesus clearly intended to parallel the shrewd manager's position with our own. He encouraged us to emulate his wisdom in handling our Master's resources with our eternal futures in mind.

The man's termination by his master represents the fact that every steward's service will one day come to an end, and may do so at any time. We will be terminated from this life just as he was terminated from his job. As his sovereign master appointed a day for his service to end, so ours has appointed a day for ours to end, a day in which we shall give an account of our stewardship, just as he did (Rom. 14:12). We should then do exactly what this manager did—use wisely what little remaining time and influence we have before our term of stewardship (life on this earth) is done.

Eternal Friends and Houses. Jesus doesn't tell us to stay away from the mammon of unrighteousness or "worldly wealth," but to use it strategically. He says to use it "to gain friends for yourselves, so that when it is gone, you will be welcomed into eternal dwellings" (Luke 16:9). Money can be a tool of Christ. But it must be used that way now, before our period of service on earth ends. There is no second chance to use the money for Christ later. After his termination was effective, after he could work no longer, the manager would have no more leverage. But fortunately he used his final days of service to win friends who could take him into their dwellings when his work was done.

After we die, when our present assets of money, possessions, time and life are gone, Jesus told us, we may be welcomed by friends into *eternal* dwellings. Perhaps the welcoming committee of this parable will participate in the "rich welcome" some believers will receive upon entering heaven (2 Pet. 1:11). Clearly, in Luke 16, this welcoming will be contingent upon our wise use of our resources on earth to impact these "friends."

But who are these friends? The reference appears to be to believers in heaven who are there through our ministry or whose lives we have touched in a significant way through the use of our material assets. They will apparently have their own "eternal dwelling places" and will welcome us in so that we may have a place to stay as we move about the heavenly kingdom. This concept of eternal dwelling places is intriguing as well as relevant to our understanding of the eternal state. But it is not unique—the idea of believers having their own living quarters in heaven is substantiated by other texts in contexts other than the parables. The New Jerusalem is clearly a physical place, as its exact measurements are given (Rev. 21:16). And to qualify as a "city" it presumably consists of individual residences (Rev. 21:2). Jesus himself stated that he is preparing for us an eternal dwelling place on his master's estate (John 14:2-3).

174

Christ purchased with his own blood a place for us in heaven. Upon it the Carpenter from Galilee is constructing eternal residences for us. If we integrate a similar analogy, 1 Corinthians 3:10-15 suggests that in our present life we are providing the building materials for our Lord to use in this construction project, of which he himself is the foundation. If this is true, then the size and quality of our eternal dwelling is influenced by how we live our lives now. This certainly fits with the concept of reward commensurate to service taught in 2 Corinthians 5:10 and all of the stewardship parables.

If we follow through with the construction and residence imagery Scripture itself employs, then all believers are engaged in a sort of eternal building project, the results of which will vary widely. We might imagine that some of us are sending ahead sufficient materials for pup tents, some for studio apartments, some for trailer homes, some for ranch houses, and others for great mansions.

Based on Christ's words in the parable, we might further imagine that the larger our dwelling place, the more we will be able to serve as (pardon the expression) heavenly hosts—those who entertain heavenly guests. Perhaps we will even have angels as guests. Or perhaps we may be invited into angels' quarters to visit with them in exchange for the hospitality we offered them on earth when we were unaware of their true identity (Heb. 13:2)!

If this seems too fantastic, remember that we are simply trying to put together and understand Christ's own words. Obviously he meant something—if not this, then what?

The reason these concepts seem so foreign is that we tend to be so preoccupied with our life here that we never stop to think about life in heaven. And we overlook the fact that heaven is consistently described in the Bible not in ethereal, vague, or abstract means, but in very tangible and surprisingly earthly ways.

If we take these passages at face value, we must conclude that each of us will have a specific individual location in heaven, an address of our own. We will live there and will invite people in and be invited to other places. We know that we will have actual bodies in heaven (Luke 24:39; John 20:27; 1 Cor. 15:42-54), and that we will be recognizable (Matt. 17:3). We will have a place at a table to eat and drink (Matt. 8:11; Rev. 19:9). We will experience literal pleasure in heaven just as those in hell will experience literal pain (Luke 16:22-31). Given the physical nature of our resurrection bodies and all that goes with it, why then should we be surprised to find that we will also have places to live, or that having such places we will be able to welcome in others?

All this should give us cause for reflection. What kind of building materials are we sending ahead to heaven for our own dwelling place? Who have we influenced spiritually to the point that they would welcome us into their eternal dwelling places? To what needy people have we sacrificially given our resources? Apparently those whom we have influenced for Christ, directly or indirectly, will know and appreciate us and desire our fellowship in heaven. What a thought! This is encouraging both in light of saved family members, friends, and others we have impacted, *and* for many we do not even know who have been touched by our prayers, service, and financial giving.

Jesus gives us a tremendous incentive to invest our lives and our assets in his kingdom while on earth. The greater our service and sacrifice for him and for others, the larger and more enthusiastic our welcoming committee in heaven, the more eternal residences we will have opportunity to visit, and the more substantial our own place in heaven.

One day money will be useless. While it is still useful, the believer with foresight will use it for eternal good.

Trustworthy with a Little, Entrusted with a Lot. Continuing after the parable, Jesus said, "Whoever can be trusted with very little can also be trusted with much, and whoever is dishonest with very little will also be dishonest with much" (Luke 16:10). Jesus implied that all of us are being continually tested in little things. Don't we as parents, whether consciously or unconsciously, often test our own children? If a child can't be trusted to spend his father's money and return the change, neither can he be trusted to stay overnight alone at a friend's house.

This principle invalidates all of our "if only's," such as, "If only I made more money I'd help the poor," or "If only I had a million dollars, then I'd give it to missions." If I'm dishonest or selfish in my use of a few dollars, I would be dishonest or selfish in my use of a few million dollars. The issue is not what I would do with a million dollars if I had it, but what I *am* doing with the ten thousand, thousand, hundred, or ten dollars I *do* have. If we are not being faithful with what he has entrusted to us, why should he entrust us with any more? This thought raises a sobering question: What opportunities are we currently missing because we've failed to use our money and our lives wisely in light of eternity?

God pays a great deal of attention to the "little things." He numbers the hairs of our heads, cares for the lilies of the field, and is concerned with the falling of but a single sparrow (Matt. 10:29). Just as a good mechanic or a good accountant is one who pays attention to little things, so a good steward is one who pays attention to the little things, while never forgetting the big picture. What we do with a little time, a little talent, and a little money tells God a lot. It is a major factor as he considers whether to commend and promote us—or reprimand and demote us—in his kingdom corporation.

Handling True Riches. "So if you have not been trustworthy in handling worldly wealth, who will trust you with true riches?" (Luke 16:11). What are "true riches"? Clearly, they are not just more of the same worldly wealth. True riches are what are valuable to God, what will last for all eternity. What could those be but other human beings with eternal souls? Apparently God tests us in the handling of money and possessions to determine the extent of our trustworthiness in handling people in personal ministry.

How many people, including pastors and other Christian leaders, have forfeited eternally significant ministry to eternal souls because they have failed to handle their money in eternity's light?

There are also implications related to our position of authority in eternity. Having been faithful in handling our resources in this life, we are granted leadership of others in the next (Luke 19:17, 19).

"And if you have not been trustworthy with someone else's property, who will give you property of your own?" (Luke 16:12). This passage implies that while we are currently stewards, handling the property of another, we will someday be owners. Jesus confirmed this when he said, "Lay up *for yourselves* treasures in heaven." The passages we have noted concerning our eternal residences seem to verify the private ownership of property in heaven. Here Jesus made a clear contrast between handling someone else's property in the present and the possibility of owning our own in the future. The message seems to be that if we have not been good stewards with God's money while on earth, then we won't be property owners in heaven.

THE STEWARDSHIP PARABLES

The parable of the shrewd manager shows that each person should seriously and carefully invest his financial assets, gifts, and opportunities to impact people for eternity, thereby making preparations for his own eternal future.

The parable of the talents (Matt. 25:14-30), shows that each of us is entrusted by God with different financial assets, gifts, and opportunities, and each will be held accountable to God for how he has invested them in this life. We are to prepare for the master's return by enhancing the growth of his kingdom through wisely investing his assets.

The parable of the ten minas (Luke 19:11-27) shows that those with comparable financial assets, gifts, and opportunities will be judged according to their faithfulness and industriousness in investing them in God's kingdom, and consequently will receive varying degrees of eternal reward, positions of power and authority, in heaven.

Lessons Concerning the Master. Each of the stewardship parables has two major subjects, the Master and the servants. The lessons taught by each parable, beginning with the Master, may be summarized as follows:

His ownership. The Master is the true owner of all assets. The possessions, the money—even the servant himself—all belong to him. Consequently, he has the right to do with everything whatever he wishes. This chapter ends with an elaboration and application of this most critical point.

His power. The Master's will is authoritative, his decisions determinative. Behind his words there is ultimate power.

His trust. He has delegated to his servants significant financial assets and power over his money and possessions. This indicates some level of trust in their ability to manage them. It also shows a willingness to take the risks involved in handing over responsibilities to people who may fail.

His expectations. The Master has specific expectations of his stewards. They are not easy, but they are fair. He has every right to expect the stewards to do what he has told them.

His absence. The Master is gone for a season. Because he is not physically present with his servants, there is a long-distance relationship and consequent delayed accountability. It will be a test of each servant to see if he maintains the Master's standards even though he isn't there to give immediate reward or correction.

His return. The Master will come back. It may be soon, it may be later, but he could return at any time.

His generosity. Although he has the right to expect the servant to do what he commanded without promise of reward, the Master graciously gives reward and promotion to the steward who has been faithful.

His severity. The Master's instructions were reasonable and he is not one to accept excuses. The servants know of his high standards and should not presume upon his grace by being lazy and disobedient. He takes away what reward he would have given the servant who was unfaithful, and disciplines him for his poor stewardship.

Lessons Concerning the Servant. The stewardship parables give us a clear view not only of the Master, but of the servant:

His stewardship. The servant should be acutely aware that he is not the owner, not the Master, but rather the caretaker or money-manager. It is his job to take the assets entrusted, not given, to him and use them in the best way to care for and further his Master's estate. If the servant does not fully grasp the reality and implications of his Master's ownership, it renders impossible the proper exercise of his stewardship.

His accountability. Because he is not the owner of these assets, he is accountable for them to his owner. He will stand before his Master one day and must be able to adequately explain why he invested them as he did.

His faithfulness. The servant seeks to be trustworthy, to handle his

Master's estate in a way that would please him. He does this until his Master returns or until he himself dies, no matter how far in the future this may be.

His industriousness. The servant must work hard and well and not slack off in his responsibilities.

His wisdom in investing. Since he is managing his Master's assets, the servant must choose his investments carefully. He cannot afford either to take undue risks on the one hand or to let his capital erode through idleness on the other. His goal is not merely to conserve resources but to multiply them. He must be intelligent, resourceful, a seeker of wise counsel, and a strategic thinker as to what will be the best long-term investments.

His constant level of preparation for his Master's return. A man once went to visit the caretaker of a large estate, whose owner had visited the estate only twice in the past twenty-five years. Noticing that the caretaker was meticulous in his every chore, the visitor asked him, "When do you expect the estate-owner to return?" The caretaker's immediate reply was, "Why, today, of course."

Like a private ready at any moment for barracks inspection, the servant is constantly aware that this could be the day of his Master's return. If he knew the day or hour of that return he could waste time. He might even "borrow" some of his Master's money, figuring to replace it before he came back. When he ceases to expect his Master's return, embezzlement or squandering become great temptations to the steward. But he knows his Master is a man of his word, and he will keep his promise to return. The servant must live each day as if it were *the* day, for one day it will be.

In our case, our deaths are essentially equivalent to the Master's return, for they mark the day our service ends and our service record "freezes," to be evaluated as such by our Master at the judgment.

His fear of his Master. The steward knows his Master is just, but his instructions were explicit, and his expectations high. If he works well and wisely the steward knows he will fare well. Indeed, in light of his Master's past generosity, he will be handsomely rewarded. But he also knows that if he is unwise and unfaithful he will surely feel his Master's wrath. This healthy fear motivates him to good stewardship.

His individual standing before his Master. The steward knows his Master will not evaluate him as part of a group but as an individual. His Master has a keen eye. The servant's efforts will not be muddled by the incompetence of others. Neither will his failures be hidden by the successes of others. His Master may deal with other servants however he wishes, but he himself must do his job and be prepared to give his own account to one from whom nothing can be hidden (Heb. 4:13).

His single-mindedness in service. The wise steward's life revolves around his service for his Master. All side interests are brought into orbit around his one central consuming purpose in life—to serve his master well.

Overall Lessons from the Stewardship Parables. Drawing from all of these lessons concerning the Master and the servants, several overriding principles stand out from the stewardship parables:

The long-term significance of today's behavior and choices. How we handle God's assets in our present daily life has tremendous bearing on eternal realities.

The inevitability of consequences for all actions. As we do, so we will be rewarded by our Master at his return. The law of the eternal harvest is more dependable even than the laws of physics: "Do not be deceived: God cannot be mocked. A man reaps what he sows" (Gal. 6:7).

The steward's painstaking responsibility to choose wisely and live rightly. The Master's absence is both a challenge and an opportunity to prove himself faithful and be elevated to greater responsibility.

The steward's clear-cut incentives and motivations in his task. The unwise steward is lazy, but the wise steward is diligent and highly motivated. He knows his Master well enough to know that there will be potent and lasting results for his labor, whether good or bad.

The steward's preoccupation with his responsibilities, not his rights. The steward's rights are limited by his lack of ownership. If he focuses on his Master's rights he will fulfill his responsibilities. But the moment a steward begins to focus on what he thinks he deserves, on what he thinks his Master or others owe him, his perspective is lost. Inevitably the quality of his service for his Master will rapidly deteriorate.

The relative meaninglessness of everyone else's evaluation of the steward compared to the final judgment of his one and only Master. In a context that leads to his statement "each of us will give an account of himself to God," Paul asked, "Who are you to judge someone else's servant? To his own Master he stands or falls" (Rom. 14:3-4, 12).

This final principle is critical. In the day the steward stands before his Master and Maker, it will not matter how many people on earth knew his name, how many called him great, and how many considered him a fool. It will not matter whether schools and hospitals were named after him, whether his estate was large or small, whether his funeral drew ten thousand or not a one. It will not matter what the newspapers or history books said or didn't say about him. What will matter is one thing and one thing only—what his Master thinks of him.

C. S. Lewis said it brilliantly in his essay "The World's Last Night":

> We have all encountered judgments or verdicts on ourselves in this life. Every now and then we discover what our fellow creatures really think of us. I don't of course mean what they tell us to our faces: that we usually have to discount. I am thinking of what we sometimes overhear by accident or of the opinions about us which our neighbors or employees or subordinates unknowingly reveal in their actions: and of the terrible, or lovely, judgments artlessly betrayed by children or even animals. Such discoveries can be the bitterest or sweetest experiences we have. But of course both the bitter and the sweet are limited by our doubt as to the wisdom of those who judge. We always hope that those who so clearly think us cowards or bullies are ignorant and malicious; we always fear that those who trust us or admire us are misled by partiality. I suppose the experience of the Final Judgment (which may break in upon us at any moment) will be like these little experiences, but magnified to the Nth. For it will be infallible judgment. If it is favorable we shall have no fear, if unfavorable, no hope, that it is wrong. We shall not only believe, we shall know, know beyond doubt in

every fibre of our appalled or delighted being, that as the
Judge has said, so we are: neither more nor less nor other.
We shall perhaps even realize that in some dim fashion we
could have known it all along. We shall know and all
creation will know too: our ancestors, our parents, our
wives or husbands, our children. The unanswerable and
(by then) self-evident truth about each will be known to
all. . . . We can, perhaps, train ourselves to ask more and
more often how the thing which we are saying or doing (or
failing to do) at each moment will look when the
irresistible light streams in upon it; that light which is so
different from the light of this world—and yet, even now,
we know just enough of it to take it into account. Women
sometimes have the problem of trying to judge by artificial
light how a dress will look by daylight. That is very like
the problem for all of us: to dress our souls not for the
electric lights of the present world but for the daylight of
the next. The good dress is the one that will face that light.
For that light will last longer.[2]

The Full Implications of God's Ownership. From beginning to
end, Scripture repeatedly emphasizes God's ownership of all
things:

"To the Lord your God belong the heavens, even the highest
heavens, the earth and everything in it" (Deut. 10:14).

"Yours, O Lord, is the greatness and the power and the glory
and the majesty and the splendor, for everything in heaven and
earth is yours. Yours, O Lord, is the kingdom; you are exalted as
head over all. Wealth and honor come from you; you are the
ruler of all things. In your hands are strength and power to exalt
and give strength to all" (1 Chron. 29:11-12).

"Who has a claim against me that I must pay? Everything
under heaven belongs to me" (Job 41:11).

"The earth is the Lord's and everything in it, the world, and
all who live in it; for he founded it upon the seas and established
it upon the waters" (Ps. 24:1-2).

"For every animal of the forest is mine, and the cattle on a
thousand hills. I know every bird in the mountains, and the
creatures of the field are mine. If I were hungry I would not tell

you, for the world is mine, and all that is in it" (Ps. 50:10-12).

"'The silver is mine and the gold is mine,' declares the Lord Almighty" (Hag. 2:8).

God said to Israel, "The land is mine"—they were not to do with it as they pleased (Lev. 25:23). He said to the Corinthians, "You are not your own; you were bought at a price"—they too were not to do with their lives as they pleased (1 Cor. 6:19-20).

When teaching the latter passage, I sometimes ask a student in the front row to lend me his pencil for a moment. When he hands me the pencil, I immediately take it, break it in half, throw it on the ground and crush it under my foot. The reaction of the students is shock and disbelief. What right do I have to break someone else's pencil? But when I tell them it's really *my* pencil, which I planted with that person before the session, suddenly it is a different story. If it is my pencil—but *only* if it is mine—then I have the right to do with it as I please.

That is precisely Paul's point in 1 Corinthians 6. The believers in Corinth were doing what they pleased with their bodies and their lives. And why not? "It's my life." Paul said, "No, it's *not* your life. You own nothing, not even yourself. When you came to Christ you surrendered the title to your life. You belong to God, not yourself. *He* is the only one who has the right to do what he wants with your life—your body, your sexual behavior, money, possessions, everything. You owe him your full obedience."

The point is, God is not just the owner of the universe in general, but the owner of me in particular. In fact, I am twice his—first by creation, and second by redemption.

Stewardship is living in the light of this overriding truth. It is living life with the acute awareness that we are managers, not owners, that we are caretakers of God's assets, which he has entrusted to us while we are on earth. How we handle our money and possessions will be determined by whom we *really* believe to be their true owner—and ours.

Transferring the Title Deed to God. God owns all things, whether we recognize it or not. But life becomes much clearer—and in some respects much easier—when we consciously and continuously choose to recognize it.

The question is not whether we theoretically affirm God's

184

ownership. The question is whether we have deliberately transferred the ownership of ourselves and all our assets to him. Have we invited him to be what Scripture says he is—the Creator, Owner, and Controller of us, our family, our possessions, and our money? And have we extended the invitation again after we have taken things back into our hands? This self-surrender to God is the beginning of true stewardship.

When we come to grasp that we are stewards, not owners of our money, it totally changes our perspective. Suddenly I'm not asking, "How much of *my* money shall *I*, out of the goodness of *my* heart, give to God?" Rather, I'm asking, "Since all of 'my' money is really yours, Lord, how would you like me to invest your money today?"

When I truly realize that God has a claim not on a few dollars to throw in an offering plate, not on 10 percent or 50 percent but *100 percent* of "my" money, it is revolutionary. Suddenly I am God's Steward, God's Money Manager. I am not God. Money is not God. God is God. He is in his place, and I am in mine.

Not only does God own everything, God controls everything. Again, the implications are enormous. I don't have to own everything. I don't have to control everything. It is in better hands than mine. And when catastrophe strikes I can honestly adopt the posture of John Wesley, referred to at the beginning of this chapter, when he said, "No. The Lord's house burned down. That means one less responsibility for me."

As Wesley did, I must remind myself of both God's role and mine to gain perspective in the face of loss or turmoil. What a life-changing and freeing perspective is God's ownership and sovereignty when the house is robbed, the car is totaled, the bike is stolen . . . and even when the diagnosis is cancer.

To visualize and reinforce this vital concept in your mind, I suggest you sit down and actually draw up a title deed, or use this one if you wish:

Date:

> I hereby grant to the Lord my God myself and all of my money and possessions and all else I've ever thought of as mine, even my family. From this point forward I will think of them as *his* to do with as he wishes. I will do my utmost

185

to prayerfully consider how he wishes me to invest his assets to further his kingdom. In doing so I realize I will surrender certain temporary earthly treasures and gain in exchange eternal treasures, as well as increased perspective and decreased anxiety.

Signed: _____

Witness: _____

When we come to Christ, God puts all his resources at our disposal. He also expects us to put all our resources at his disposal. This is what stewardship—and life—is all about.

NOTES

1. Ben Patterson, *The Grand Essentials* (Waco, Tex.: Word, 1987), 17.
2. C. S. Lewis, *The World's Last Night* (New York: Harcourt Brace Jovanovich, 1952), 112-113.

CHAPTER 11

THE PILGRIM MENTALITY

And so it is that when a man walks along a road, the lighter he travels, the happier he is; equally, on this journey of life, a man is more blessed if he does not pant beneath a burden of riches. Tertullian

Let temporal things serve your use, but the eternal be the object of your desire. Thomas à Kempis

Once a wealthy Christian plantation owner invited John Wesley to his home. The two rode their horses all day, seeing just a small part of all the man owned. At the end of the day the plantation owner proudly asked, "Well, Mr. Wesley, what do you think?" After a moment of silence, Wesley replied, "I think you're going to have a hard time leaving all this."

The plantation owner was attached to the world he was in. Wesley was attached to the world he was going to. All of us form attachments. All of us have a place we call home. The question is, do we think and live as if this world, or the next world, were our home? Is our mind on earth or on heaven?

The old saying goes, "Those who are heavenly minded are of no earthly good." Yet Scripture *commands* us to set our minds on heaven, where Christ is (Col. 3:1). William Wilberforce, who did more than any one man to abolish slavery in England (and was thereby of obvious earthly good), said this: "It is since Christians have largely ceased to think of the other world that they have become so ineffective in this." When we are properly heavenly minded we will be of maximum heavenly and earthly good, but when we are earthly minded we will ultimately bring no good to heaven or earth. As usual, A. W. Tozer had something significant to say on the subject:

It has been cited as a flaw in Christianity that it is more concerned with the world to come than with the world that now is, and some timid souls have been fluttering about trying to defend the faith of Christ against this accusation as a mother hen defends her chicks from the hawk.

Both the attack and the defense are wasted. No one who knows what the New Testament is about will worry over the charge that Christianity is other-worldly. Of course it is, and that is precisely where its power lies. . . .

Let no one apologize for the powerful emphasis Christianity lays upon the doctrine of the world to come. Right there lies its immense superiority to everything else within the whole sphere of human thought or experience. When Christ arose from death and ascended into heaven He established forever three important facts, namely, that this world has been condemned to ultimate dissolution, that the human spirit persists beyond the grave and that there is indeed a world to come. . . .

The church is constantly being tempted to accept this world as her home, and sometimes she has listened to the blandishments of those who would woo her away and use her for their own ends. But if she is wise she will consider that she stands in the valley between the mountain peaks of eternity past and eternity to come. The past is gone forever and the present is passing as swift as the shadow on the sun dial of Ahaz. Even if the earth should continue a million years not one of us could stay to enjoy it. We do well to think of the long tomorrow.[1]

TIME AND ETERNITY

Can we of the short today really comprehend the long tomorrow? Is it possible for creatures of time to think in terms of eternity? God "has set eternity in the hearts of men; yet they cannot fathom what God has done from beginning to end" (Eccles. 3:11). Here is the paradox. We are made for eternity but we live in time. We are made for heaven but meanwhile our residence is earth.

Materialism would dupe us into believing this world is the ultimate world, the destination rather than the route to the Destination. From there it is a short step to racing off to earn, collect, accumulate, take, and consume, as if that is all there is to life. Then we wake up one day to realize how terribly unhappy we are—if, that is, we ever wake up at all.

Life's great disillusionments come as we try to force our round made-for-eternity hearts into the rectangular hole of this temporal earth. They just don't fit. *We* do not fit. No matter how far we stray from the narrow path of kingdom living, we remain children of eternity, not time. We need basic material provisions, yes, but in our inner persons we are simply ill-suited for a materially-centered existence.

Think about the special spiritual moments you have experienced. Perhaps in prayer, or at a baptism, or in communion, or in conversation with a loved one, or a simple walk on the beach or in the woods, or when you have done something that you know God is pleased with. Have you ever had a sense of moving on the edge of eternity, briefly but very really breaking into its circle, knowing in that moment that where you were was exactly where you belonged and that what you were participating in was what the entire universe must be about? Have you ever sensed that the world you were made for was not this one, but another? This was a glimpse of eternity. It was the awakening of a desire that lies deep within, where God has set eternity in our hearts.

C. S. Lewis cast light on this eternal desire:

> Creatures are not born with desires unless satisfaction for those desires exists. A baby feels hunger: well, there is such a thing as food. A duckling wants to swim: well, there is such a thing as water. Men feel sexual desire: well, there is such a thing as sex. If I find in myself a desire which no experience in this world can satisfy, the most probable explanation is that I was made for another world. If none of my earthly pleasures satisfy it, that does not prove that the universe is a fraud. Probably earthly pleasures were never meant to satisfy it, but only to arouse it, to suggest the real thing. If that is so, I must take care, on the one hand, never to despise, or be unthankful for, these early blessings, and on the other, never to mistake them for the something else of which they are only a kind of copy, or echo, or mirage. I must keep alive in myself the desire for my true country, which I shall not find till after death; I must never let it get snowed under or turned aside; I must make it the main object of life to press on to that other country and to help others to do the same.[2]

From childhood most of us learn to shut out our "true country," to stifle our thirst for the eternal, and to replace it with the pursuit of the temporal. This is how we who were created to be spiritual end up being such accomplished materialists. But when we live life with eternity in view, many things will be done differently, and those that are done the same will be done with transformed perspective—not only teaching and preaching and witnessing but washing dishes and pruning trees and repairing carburetors. Done with eternal values in view, almost any honest activity—whether building a shed, driving a bus, or caring for a patient—can be an eternal contribution to people, an investment in God's eternal plan.

TWO COVENANTS AND TWO COUNTRIES

In the Old Testament, material blessing was given for obedience (Deut. 28:2), yet in the New Testament many of the saints were poor (Matt. 8:20; 2 Cor. 11:27; James 2:5). Enjoying worldly wealth is emphasized in the Old Testament (Deut. 28:11; Josh. 1:15; Prov. 15:6), yet the New Testament talks of giving away possessions (Mark 10:17-21; 1 Tim. 6:17-18). By their obedience the Israelites would avoid persecution (Deut. 28:7), but by their obedience Christians would incur persecution (Matt. 5:11-12; 2 Tim. 3:12; 1 Pet. 1:6).

Why this disparity? Because Old Testament saints thought of this world as their primary home, while God was determined that New Testament saints see their home is in another world. No book better demonstrates the relationship of Old and New Testaments, and the two worlds they depict as home, than the Book of Hebrews. The New Covenant is said to be "founded on better promises" than the Old (8:6). The Old Testament is copy and type and shadow. Accordingly, the material blessings promised to Old Testament saints are to remind us of our future heavenly blessings—but never are they to replace them. The new covenant brings not the temporal inheritance promised Israel, but an eternal inheritance (9:15).

We no longer sacrifice animals because the Lamb of God has come. We no longer worship in a temple because we ourselves are temples of God's Holy Spirit. We no longer go to a priest because Christ is our high priest, and we ourselves are a believing priesthood. We no longer look to material riches because of the spiritual riches that are ours in Christ.

The promises of short-term material prosperity for obedience were part of a specific historical covenant with a unique historical nation. Israel lived under a theocracy, a direct rule by God. The church, God's New Testament people, is not the historical nation of Israel. The Old Covenant was not made with us. We live under human government, not a theocracy.

God demonstrated to the nations surrounding Israel his superiority to their gods by prospering the people of Israel when they obeyed him. Now he wishes to display Christ's Lordship and presence to the world around us through our superior faith, morality, integrity, and quality of life, not standard of living.

The Israelites were citizens of the Promised Land (Deut. 8:7-9; 11:8-12). Their destination was on this earth. But New Testament saints are acutely aware that they have *not* arrived at their destination, and indeed will never do so in this life. We are told our citizenship is in heaven (Phil. 3:20; 1 Pet. 2:11). The promised land was a foretaste of the glory that awaits us. We are to stake our claim and fortune and well-being in the ultimate promised land: "But you have come to Mount Zion, to the heavenly Jerusalem, the city of the living God" (Heb. 12:22). The earthly Jerusalem is not our destination but only a signpost pointing the way, just as earthly blessings are not our true rewards but are merely suggestive of the rewards to come.

The writer of Hebrews spoke of promised blessings, of a great inheritance of lasting possession (6:12; 10:34; 11:13-16). It makes clear that these promises must be patiently waited for, since they come not in this world but the next (10:35-39; 11:13, 16).

Our destination is as much superior to the Promised Land of Palestine as Christ's blood was superior to the blood of bulls and goats. The effect of prosperity theology is to promote "heaven on earth." But prior to Christ's coming there can be no heaven on earth, though heaven's peace can reign in the heart, and we have the Holy Spirit as a down payment of what is to come. The very phrases "heaven on earth" and "hell on earth" are at best illustrative, for heaven and hell are not mere states of mind but literal and eternal destinations quite distinct from our present world.

When earth becomes our heaven—when we see God's blessings as being primarily immediate and temporal—we lose sight of who we are, why we are here, and what awaits us beyond the horizons of this world.

Much disappointment comes in expecting God to do in the present what he has promised for the future. The fallacy is not in thinking God repays faithfulness. He does. The fallacy is thinking this payment takes place with the wrong means or in the wrong timing. God's primary means of payment is not with this world's currency and goods, and his primary timing is not in this world at all. Almost every time we seek a short-term payday we lose out on the long-term (Matt. 6:1-18). A person looking out for his own best interests, in the truest sense, will not seek the short-term reward.

It is therefore critically important that as Christians we take our primary cues from the New Testament, not the Old Testament, or more precisely, not from the Mosaic Covenant. The blessings of the Mosaic Covenant were largely material, while the blessings of the New Covenant are spiritual blessings in Christ. Do not misunderstand—the Old Testament is equally inspired and is full of timeless truths vital to our understanding of money and how to handle it, which explains the many Old Testament references in this book. But it was also written in a particular era of God's dealing with mankind, an era focused on an earthly kingdom, the nation Israel.

We must extract and apply Old Testament principles, but be careful to weigh and measure them in light of the New Testament description of how Christians are to view and handle our money and possessions. To arbitrarily pick and choose Old Testament passages that seem to validate modern society's standards of success, and to fail to evaluate their present application in light of clear New Testament teaching, is to irresponsibly handle the Scriptures and to take a detour from our true identity and destiny.

AT HOME IN THIS WORLD?

Scripture tells us several complementary things about our identity and role on this earth. First, our citizenship is in heaven, not earth (Phil. 3:20). Second, we are ambassadors representing Christ on this earth (2 Cor. 5:20). Third, we are aliens, strangers, and pilgrims on this earth (Heb. 11:13). These passages provide the light in which we must evaluate not only prosperity theology but the large portion of evangelical teaching, preaching, and literature that seems almost exclusively geared toward making us at home in this world.

James minced no words: "You adulterous people, don't you know that friendship with the world is hatred toward God? Anyone who chooses to become a friend of the world becomes an enemy of God" (James 4:4).

Imagine an ambassador from the United States who goes to work in another country that is generally hostile to his own. Naturally, he will want to learn about this new place, see the sights, become familiar with the people and culture. But suppose eventually he becomes so assimilated into this foreign country that he begins to regard it as his true home. His allegiance wavers, and he gradually compromises his position as an American ambassador, becoming increasingly ineffective in representing the best interests of his mother country. His loyalties are transferred, and eventually he defects. In doing so, he not only becomes useless to the cause of his own country but actually betrays it.

Peter wrote, "Since you call on a Father who judges each man's work impartially, live your lives as strangers here in reverent fear" (1 Pet. 1:17). Later he added, "I urge you, as aliens and strangers in the world, to abstain from sinful desires, which war against your soul" (1 Pet. 2:11). We are strangers and aliens here. We must never become too much at home in this world or we will become ineffective in serving the cause of the world we are here to represent. Indeed, we may actually betray it.

Our earthly bodies are called "tents," temporary dwelling places of our eternal souls (2 Pet. 1:13). Paul contrasted our brief time on earth with what he regarded as the *real* life of which this one is but a foreshadow: "For while we are in this tent, we groan and are burdened, because we do not wish to be unclothed but to be clothed with our heavenly dwelling, so that what is mortal may be swallowed up by life" (2 Cor. 5:4).

The author of Hebrews explained what it means to be a pilgrim of faith:

> By faith Abraham, when called to go to a place he would later receive as his inheritance, obeyed and went, even though he did not know where he was going. By faith he made his home in the promised land like a stranger in a foreign country; he lived in tents, as did Isaac and Jacob, who were heirs with him of the same promise. For he was looking forward to the city with foundations, whose architect and builder is God. (Heb. 11:8-10)

Abraham didn't know where he was going, but he knew with whom he was going. He was able to live in this world and not receive the things promised, knowing there was an eternity in which promises would be fulfilled, and a city awaiting him as far superior to an earthly city as its Architect and Builder is superior to men. (Note that the greatest Old Testament saints were those who ultimately saw beyond the temporal to the eternal and in doing so became the model for New Testament faith.)

194

All these people were still living by faith when they died. They did not receive the things promised; they only saw them and welcomed them from a distance. And they admitted that they were aliens and strangers on earth. People who say such things show that they are looking for a country of their own. If they had been thinking of the country they had left, they would have had opportunity to return. Instead, they were longing for a better country—a heavenly one. Therefore God is not ashamed to be called their God, for he has prepared a city for them. (Heb. 11:13-16)

Notice that faith does not mean insisting that we get what we seek now, but believing we will get it later. Once again, this is in stark contrast to the now-centered nature of prosperity theology, which sees faith as a means of claiming immediate blessing, rather than eventual blessing. Following Christ is to see and welcome from a distance our eternal reward—not to expect to get it now. The great people of faith were looking for a country "of their own," better than anything earth could offer.

If these saints had focused on their own possessions, their "real estate" on earth, they would have forfeited their Real Estate in heaven. If the great saints in Faith's Hall of Fame in Hebrews 11 would have gauged their lives by the short-term standards of the health-and-wealth gospel, today we would not know their names. They longed for "a better country—a heavenly one." Because they lived on earth in light of their fixation on heaven, God was pleased with them, so pleased that "he has prepared a city for them."

Moses also lived with this acute awareness of the eternal:

By faith Moses, when he had grown up, refused to be known as the son of Pharaoh's daughter. He chose to be mistreated along with the people of God rather than to enjoy the pleasures of sin for a short time. He regarded disgrace for the sake of Christ as of greater value than the treasures of Egypt, because he was looking ahead to his reward. By faith he left Egypt, not fearing the king's anger; he persevered because he saw him who is invisible. (Heb. 11:24-27)

195

Moses chose the path of his life based on his belief not only in God but in the eternal rewards of following God. He could endure temporal mistreatment and forfeit temporal pleasure knowing that all would be different in eternity. He could forgo pleasures and possessions that would not last because he anticipated pleasures and possessions that would not end. He turned his back on Egypt's treasures to pursue heaven's treasures. He feared God, not the king, and he persevered because he focused not on his *visible* difficult circumstances, but on his *invisible* faithful God.

THE PILGRIM, HIS MONEY AND POSSESSIONS

The pilgrim is unattached. He is a traveler—not a settler—acutely aware that the excessive accumulation of things can only distract him from what he is and does. Material things are valuable to the pilgrim, but only as they facilitate his mission. He knows they could become a god to grip him, and that if his eyes are on the visible they will be drawn from the invisible.

If you were traveling through a country on foot or on bicycle, what would your attitude be toward accumulating possessions? You would not hate possessions or think them evil—but you would choose them strategically, regarding most of them as encumbrances, unnecessary things that could slow your journey or eventually even make it impossible. Travelers do not build houses, amass furniture, and invest in the economy.

Of course, many of us are called to stay in one place and will naturally become "settlers" in the temporal sense, living in houses, building barns, owning furniture, tools, crops, and businesses. There is nothing wrong with this. But we must nonetheless maintain the pilgrim *mentality* of detachment, the traveler's utilitarian philosophy concerning things. We need to be able to live in a house without owning it, or own a house without being owned by it. If God so directs us, we need to be able to leave behind a farm or a business without having to go back.

The slaves in early America understood the pilgrim mentality. Without possessions, without rights, they lived for another world, a better one. This central theme permeated their spirituals. They sang,

"I am a poor wayfarin' stranger, a travelin' far away from home," and "Soon I will be done with the troubles of the world, I'm goin' home to live with God."

Wealth entrenches us in the present world. Financial commitments and debts can be like spikes chained to our legs and driven into the ground, making us inflexible and unresponsive to God's call to move on and serve him elsewhere. God may never call me to move on from my home or business or country. But I must be in a position to say "yes" if he does. If not, I might wonder all my life if he may have had other plans for me—plans I didn't hear or respond to because I was so tied to where I was.

DOES THE PILGRIM MENTALITY FOSTER ASCETICISM?

But how does this perspective differ from asceticism, the antimaterial philosophy objected to in an earlier chapter? Doesn't the pilgrim mentality lead to a sour or cynical view of this present world? Precisely the opposite! It is the materialist, not the Christian pilgrim, who is the cynic. The typical citizen of this world doesn't derive true satisfaction from it. Materialists can't fully appreciate the joys and wonders of creation. It is the believer who can see his Creator's handiwork everywhere, who can truly see the beauty of mountains and rivers and waterfalls. No one appreciates creation like he who knows the Creator. No one can appreciate a good meal like those who love the one who provided it. No one can enjoy marriage like the one who knows its Architect and Builder and who understands what intimacy is.

Those in love with this world do not get the best it has to offer. They expect the world to deliver them from the emptiness within, so they are forever disillusioned. The Christian pilgrim has no such illusions about the world. He appreciates it for what it is—a magnificent creation of the one who *does* fill the emptiness of the heart. "Because we love something else more than this world, we love even this world better than those who know no other."[3]

When I have opportunity to travel, I find particular joy in those places that remind me of my lifelong home in Oregon. Likewise, one of the greatest joys the Christian pilgrim finds in this world is in tnose moments it reminds him of the next, his true home. He has not seen this place, but he has read about it, and he lives with the exhilarating assurance that his beloved is making it ready for him this very moment (John 14:2-3).

In the truest sense, Christian pilgrims have the best of both worlds. We have joy whenever this world reminds us of the next, and we take solace whenever it does not. We have the promise of a new heaven and new earth, where the worst elements of this world—sorrow, pain, death, and the tears they produce—will be gone forever (Rev. 21:4). Yet we also know that the best elements of this world, the love, joy, wonder, worship, and beauty we have experienced here, will not be gone, but intensified and perfected in the remade world. "Aim at heaven and you will get earth thrown in. Aim at earth and you will get neither."[4]

In the last book of *The Chronicles of Narnia,* when the unicorn reaches Aslan's country he exclaimed, "I have come home at last! This is my real country! I belong here. This is the land I have been looking for all my life, though I never knew it till now. The reason why we loved the old Narnia is that it sometimes looked a little like this."[5]

EAGER TO POSSESS

This is the Christian attitude toward possessions, forged in the crucible of adversity: "You . . . joyfully accepted the confiscation of your property, because you knew that you yourselves had better and lasting possessions" (Heb. 10:34).

We are totally misreading this passage if we conclude that the people of God place no value on personal property. Nothing could be farther from the truth. The passage tells us they were able to joyfully surrender their earthly property precisely because they *did* value property—*real* property that is "better and lasting."

They knew that earthly goods could rust and decay and be stolen (Matt. 6:19-21). And they knew that even if by sweat and force and fretting they could manage to hold onto them, at most they would last only a short time and be destined first to the junk pile and then to total annihilation: "But the day of the Lord will come like a thief. The heavens will disappear with a roar; the elements will be destroyed by fire, and the earth and everything in it will be laid bare" (2 Pet. 3:10).

That all things in this world will be destroyed is not merely a certainty of the future of only passing interest to us today. On the contrary, Peter knew about the present-day implications of the temporal nature of possessions:

> Since everything will be destroyed in this way, what kind of people ought you to be? You ought to live holy and godly lives as you look forward to the day of God and speed its coming. That day will bring about the destruction of the heavens by fire, and the elements will melt in the heat. But in keeping with his promise we are looking forward to a new heaven and a new earth, the home of righteousness. So then, dear friends, since you are looking forward to this, make every effort to be found spotless, blameless and at peace with him. (2 Pet. 3:11-14)

Here we see the tremendous immediate life-style implications of the certain return and eternal judgment of Christ. He promises special reward to those who, uninfatuated with the present world, "have longed for his appearing" (2 Tim. 4:8).

After still more inspiring stories of hardships faced by God's people with their eyes on heaven (Heb. 11:35-40), we are challenged:

> Therefore, since we are surrounded by such a great cloud of witnesses, let us throw off everything that hinders and the sin that so easily entangles, and let us run with perseverance the race marked out for us. Let us fix our eyes on Jesus, the author and perfecter of our faith, who for the joy set before him endured the cross, scorning its shame, and sat down at the right hand of the throne of God. (Heb. 12:1-2)

The concern is not only for the sin that entangles us, but also the things not in themselves sinful that hinder us. No one runs a race carrying a television, a stereo, and a recliner. If we are to have such things, we must be able to let go of them. If we can pass them through our hands to others, or leave them at a moment's notice, only then are they safe in our possession. Otherwise we will fix our eyes on them rather than Jesus, and we will either veer off the course or stop running the race altogether.

Pilgrims of faith look to the next world, their eyes on a certain hope that will never forsake them. Eyes clear and unclouded, they see money and earthly possessions as what they are—useful for kingdom purposes, but far too flimsy to bear the weight of trust, and wholly unable to survive the coming holocaust of things.

Hebrews ends with one more reminder to believers tempted to live in the light of this world and not the next: "For here we do not have an enduring city, but we are looking for the city that is to come" (Heb. 13:14).

The hymn writer said it beautifully:

> Turn your eyes upon Jesus,
> Look full in his wonderful face,
> And the things of earth will grow strangely dim,
> In the light of his glory and grace.

GOD'S FORGETFUL PILGRIMS

All of us need to belong, to join a group of fellows and companions, comrades who inspire and encourage us. Hebrews presents the great people of God, the heroes of faith, as a group worthy of our affiliation.

Michael Griffiths has written a book called *God's Forgetful Pilgrims* in which he maintains the church has largely forgotten her wondrous identity in Christ and settled for the pathetic substitute identities the world has to offer. While combing a bookstore, I ran across the original British edition of the book, which had a different and more striking title—*Cinderella with Amnesia*. As children of God, we are prized by the Prince, chosen by him to reign at his side: "But you are a chosen people, a royal priesthood, a holy nation, a people belonging to God" (1 Pet. 2:9). Yet, beautiful and beloved as we are to the Prince, we go right on—like Cinderella with amnesia—living in drudgery as citizens of a second-class country, forfeiting heavenly possessions through clinging to earthly possessions.

200

Back in Kansas, with Oz behind her, Dorothy said, "There's no place like home." How true! But how easily we forget where our home really is. At death the Christian doesn't leave home. He goes home: "We . . . prefer to be away from the body and at home with the Lord" (2 Cor. 5:8). Home is where our Father is. While we are content to be on our Father's business here in these seventy-year motel rooms we call bodies, we are never entirely at home. How can we be? Our true home is so far superior, and the spiritual family there so vast and rich. The Great Reunion awaits us, and we long for it.

When we understand what home really is, money and things lose their glitter. We finally see them as they have been all along: pale, insipid, and cheap imitations of the true and vast wealth that is ours as children of God.

Perhaps we should say aloud, over and over, the words of the song: "This world is not my home." Once again, C. S. Lewis put it well: "Our Father refreshes us on the journey with some pleasant inns, but will not encourage us to mistake them for home."[6]

NOTES
1. A. W. Tozer, "The World to Come" in *Of God and Men* (Harrisburg, Penn.: Christian Publications, 1960), 127, 129-30.
2. C. S. Lewis, *Mere Christianity* (New York: Macmillan, 1960), 120.
3. C. S. Lewis, *God in the Dock* (Grand Rapids, Mich.: Eerdmans, 1970), 150.
4. Lewis, *Mere Christianity,* 104.
5. C. S. Lewis, *The Last Battle* (New York: Macmillan, 1956), 172.
6. C. S. Lewis, *The Problem of Pain* (New York: Macmillan, 1948), 115.

PART III

GIVING AND SHARING OUR MONEY AND POSSESSIONS

CHAPTER 12

TITHING: THE FIRST STEP
OF GIVING

The Jews were constrained to a regular payment of tithes; Christians, who have liberty, assign all their possessions to the Lord, bestowing freely not the lesser portions of their property, since they have the hope of greater things. Irenaeus

Tithes are required as a matter of debt, and he who has been unwilling to give them has been guilty of robbery. Whosoever, therefore, desires to secure a reward for himself, let him render tithes, and out of the nine parts let him seek to give alms. Augustine

On the wall of President Lyndon Johnson's White House office hung a framed letter written by General Sam Houston to Johnson's great-grandfather Baines more than a hundred years earlier. Sam Houston's signature makes the letter valuable, but the story behind it is much more significant. Baines had led Sam Houston to Christ. Houston was a changed man, no longer coarse and belligerent, but peaceful and content.

The day came for Sam Houston to be baptized—an incredible event in the eyes of those who knew his previous life-style and attitude. After his baptism Houston stated he would like to pay half the local minister's salary. When someone asked him why, his simple response was, "My pocketbook was baptized too."

Like other followers of Christ throughout the centuries, Sam Houston demonstrated the reality of God's grace in his life by reciprocating that grace in the form of financial giving.

The four chapters of this section will examine closely the biblical pattern of giving and sharing our money and possessions, ending with an examination of both the acquisition and use of funds by local churches and parachurch organizations.

THE PRINCIPLE OF TITHING

"A tithe of everything from the land, whether grain from the soil or fruit from the trees, belongs to the Lord; it is holy to the Lord" (Lev. 27:30).

It "belongs to the Lord," not to us. It applies to "everything," not some things. It is "holy," to be set apart and given to God, and used for no other purpose.

The meaning of the word *tithe* is "a tenth part." Today the term *tithing* is often erroneously used of all giving. People talk about "tithing" fifty dollars a month, when they actually make two thousand dollars a month (a tithe of which is two hundred dollars, not fifty). You can donate 2 percent or 4 percent or 6 percent of your income, but you cannot "tithe" it, any more than you can "whitewash" a wall with red paint. The Israelites were well aware of this fact, and equally aware that to present to their Creator anything less than the full 10 percent was to "rob God," because the tithe belonged to him, not to them:

> Will a man rob God? Yet you rob me. But you ask, "How do we rob you?" In tithes and offerings. You are under a curse—the whole nation of you—because you are robbing me. Bring the whole tithe into the storehouse, that there

may be food in my house. Test me in this," says the Lord Almighty, "and see if I will not throw open the floodgates of heaven and pour out so much blessing that you will not have room enough for it." (Mal. 3:8-10)

God says "Bring the *whole* tithe into the storehouse"—don't hold back any of it. The obedient Israelite didn't ask whether he could give 7 percent instead of ten, or whether he could tithe on the "net" rather than the "gross." Whatever God provided, whether in the form of material or cash or benefits of any sort, 10 percent belonged to God.

However, there was not just one standard tithe for the people of Israel, but three tithes. One of those supported the priests and Levites (Num. 18:21, 24). Another provided for a sacred festival (Deut. 12:17-18; 14:23). The third tithe was given to support the poor, orphans, and widows (Deut. 14:28-29; 26:12-13).

The first of these is often called the Levite tithe, the second the festival tithe, and the third the poor tithe. The Levite and festival tithe were ongoing tithes each year, but the poor tithe was taken only every third year. This meant that the three tithes actually amounted to an average of 23 percent per year. Since Israel was not only a spiritual community but a nation, some of these funds were parallel to taxes today. The larger portion, however, was for religious, not civic, purposes.

The practice of tithing began long before the Law of Moses. Abraham tithed to the high priest Melchizedek (Gen. 14:20). Jacob promised a tithe to the Lord (Gen. 28:22). We are not told that all others tithed, or even that these two men tithed at other times in their lives, and neither are we told otherwise. Perhaps Abel and Enoch and Noah and others practiced the tithe prior to the Law, just as they kept the Sabbath prior to the Law. Historical records indicate the Egyptians, Chaldeans, and Assyrians all tithed to their gods, as did some of the ancient Chinese, Greeks, Romans, and Arabians.

THE FIRSTFRUITS

"Honor the Lord with your wealth, with the firstfruits of all your crops" (Prov. 3:9). Three times a year the children of Israel were

207

to bring the firstfruits offering before the Lord. God said, "No one is to appear before me emptyhanded" (Exod. 23:15). The firstfruits offering included the first production of a vineyard (Lev. 19:23-25) and the first of the annual production of grain, wine, olive oil, and sheared wool (Exod. 23:16; 34:22; Deut. 18:4). The first of any coarse meal (Num. 15:20-21), of honey, and of all the produce of the land (2 Chron. 31:5) belonged to the Lord and was therefore not to be kept by the individual or family. A significant portion of the firstfruits went to the religious leaders and their ministry (Num. 18:12).

The concept and practice of firstfruits was an important statement made by the people of God. It was a way of saying, "We give of our first and best to you, our Lord, because we recognize all that is good comes from you."

The firstfruits and the tithes certainly overlapped, and it seems that generally they were the same thing. The term "tithe" stressed the exact amount, while "firstfruits" emphasized the nature and quality of the offering. In Israel's economy tangible goods were the natural way to express the tithe. Of course, the same principle extended to money as well. The first 10 percent of all income in whatever form was given to the Lord.

God is regarded as the giver of the harvest, and the offering of the firstfruits was a constant reminder to God's children of his ownership. Similarly, the rite of redemption of the firstborn of man and beast (Exod. 13:11-15) symbolized the coming redemption in Christ. Through the firstfruits and redemption symbols God was seen as the source of all life and blessing. By witnessing this regular systematic bringing forth of material before the Lord, parents hoped that their children would grow up understanding their debt to God.

The offering of the firstfruits was also a way of saying, "We trust you, God, to help us harvest and store and utilize the rest as well." To hold back any of the firstfruits, or to give anything less than the superior part of the crop in the firstfruits offering, was to incur the wrath of God. Hophni and Phinehas were two priests who determined they would take what they wanted and leave the residue for the Lord (1 Sam. 2:12-16). Scripture tells us, "Their sin was very great before the Lord." God sent fire from heaven to consume them for taking what rightfully belong to him.

The nature of "firstfruits" requires that it be taken "off the top." It is both the best and the first, meaning that as soon as it is harvested or as soon as payment is received it is to be given to the Lord. It is not to be stored up, hidden, hoarded, or distributed in any other way, but is to be given to the Lord's work.

The story is told of a farmer who owned two calves, one brown and one white. He determined that he would give one of them to the Lord, but did not say which. When one of the calves was attacked and eaten by wolves, the farmer shook his head sadly and said, "Too bad the Lord's calf died."

This mentality of keeping the best and giving God the leftovers, if even that, brought God's judgment on Israel. The spiritual community's giving back to the Lord what was rightfully his was a consistent thermometer of their faith and trust in him. When they slid spiritually, they ceased to give as they should. And when they ceased to give as they should, they slid spiritually.

THE VOLUNTARY OFFERINGS

The tithe or firstfruits was recognized as belonging to God in the first place. Hence, one was not "giving" a tithe but simply "repaying" it to the one to whom it belonged all along. This is why the Old Testament often speaks of the tithes and firstfruits as "brought" and "taken" and "presented," or even "paid," rather than "given." They were no more optional than paying taxes today. An Israelite paid them out of obedience and duty, whether he wanted to or not.

However, the Old Testament also speaks of voluntary or "freewill offerings" (Lev. 22:18-23; Num. 15:3; Deut. 12:6, 17). These were contributions beyond the tithe or firstfruits; they constituted true giving. In Ezra, when the temple needed to be rebuilt, the people were asked to provide freewill offering (Ezra 1:4, 6; 3:5; 7:16; 8:28). While the technical term "freewill offering" had some specific connotations and requirements, which is why I prefer the term "voluntary offering," it was associated with a concept of "give as you wish" or "give as you are led." As "everyone whose heart God had moved" went to build the temple in Jerusalem, so "their neighbors assisted them with articles of silver and gold, with goods and livestock, and with valuable gifts, in addition to all the freewill offerings" (Ezra 1:5-6).

No one said "I feel led to tithe" or "I think I'll give my firstfruits this month." No one asked, "Would you like me to tithe, Lord?" The answer had already been given in God's Word. So voluntary giving started *after* the tithe, after the firstfruits. The tithe was not a ceiling, it was merely a floor. It was a beginning point from which the follower of God might give much more as needs and opportunities arose.

The tithe was a test and demonstration of obedience, but the voluntary offerings were a test and demonstration of love, joy, and a heart of worship. In Exodus 35 and 36 we read of a tide of generosity among the people because they sensed the greatness of the cause of building the tabernacle. There was a contagious spirit of giving in which the people brought more than enough and literally had to be restrained from giving (Exod. 36:5-7). Keep in mind, once again, that they were not giving the tithe or the firstfruits; they were giving far beyond. This is what is really remarkable and demonstrates the moving of God's Spirit in their lives. Consider too, given the historical context of Sinai, how the grace of giving temporarily transformed this pack of gripers and whiners into joyful worshipers.

The same sort of thing happened in the days that the temple was built. David said, "I now give my personal treasures of gold and silver for the temple of my God, over and above everything I have provided" (1 Chron. 29:3). Then the family and tribal leaders "gave willingly" and generously (29:6-8). "The people rejoiced at the willing response of their leaders, for they had given freely and wholeheartedly to the Lord" (29:9).

They gave with the acute awareness that all they had was God's. David said to the Lord:

> But who am I, and who are my people, that we should be able to give as generously as this? Everything comes from you, and we have given you only what comes from your hand. . . . It comes from your hand, and all of it belongs to you. . . . All these things have I given willingly and with honest intent. And now I have seen with joy how

willingly your people who are here have given to you. O
Lord, God of our fathers . . . keep this desire in the hearts
of your people forever, and keep their hearts loyal to you.
(1 Chron. 29:14, 16-18)

Notice that David measured their loyalty to God by their
willingness to give.

Imagine a boy's father who wants his son to take out his old
friend's daughter on a date. The boy agrees to do it because his
father asks and expects it of him. But when the boy actually
meets the girl he enjoys her company so much that he asks to
take her out again—and again and again and again. At this point
the boy is no longer acting under a sense of duty, but of his own
free will. He does not have to take her out; he *wants* to.

So it is with giving. We tithe and offer the firstfruits because
God tells us to. We give above and beyond in voluntary offerings
because, having experienced the joys of giving, we want to give
all the more.

THE VALUE OF TITHING

By emphasizing the vitality of the voluntary offering, I don't
mean in anyway to demean tithing or underestimate the importance of regularly giving the firstfruits. This is where God
started his people, and therefore it is a fine beginning. Tithing is
something very significant. Its stated purpose for us is "that you
may learn to revere the Lord your God always" (Deut. 14:23).
Tithing is intended to train us to put God first in our lives.
Because the giving of the 10 percent represents the other 90
percent, tithing symbolizes the giving of our whole lives to God.

Tithing gives us perspective. It reminds us that all we are and
all we have is from another, a higher one. It is a tribute we pay to
God. Tithing is not some token or tip for good service mindlessly thrown down on a table after a meal, but a meaningful symbolic expression of our dependence upon the Lord and
our gratitude to him for all that he is and all he has given us.

Furthermore, the tithe requires calculation—adding, subtract-
ing, multiplying, dividing. In the process of specifically dealing
with the amounts God has provided, we assess God's benefits to

us. We literally count his material blessings to us, which can only be healthy.

Tithing was, and still can be, a built-in reminder at every juncture of life of our debt to God. Through the tithe, God built into the rhythm of life the unceasing reminder that he owned the land, the cattle, the jewels, the money, everything.

Parting with money wasn't any easier for the people of Israel than for us. In fact, most of them worked a great deal harder for their money than we do. Yet tithing was so built into their lives that it became "natural" to them in the best sense. Their fathers and mothers and brothers and sisters and business partners, everyone around them, practiced tithing. It became a way of life.

When they had gone their own way and stopped tithing, God told them they were robbing him. Then he invited his people to test him by tithing again and watching him provide for them (Mal. 3:8-12). The tithe is an opportunity to test God's promise to provide (Matt. 6:33).

GRACE, LAW, AND TITHING

The strongest arguments made against tithing today are on the basis of "Law versus grace." This is an unfortunate contrast in some situations, and I think this is one of them. Does being under grace mean that we stop doing all that was done under the Law?

Many people associate the command to tithe with the command to keep the Sabbath. To be sure, New Testament Christians are not obligated to keep the Sabbath with all its legislated rules under the Mosaic covenant (Col. 2:16). However, a weekly day of rest based on God's pattern of creation was instituted before the Law (Gen. 2:2-3), and it is a principle never revoked in the New Testament. The special day of observance changed to Sunday, "the Lord's day," but the principle of one special day for worship remained intact and observed.

Christ fulfilled the entire Old Testament, but he didn't render it irrelevant. Old Testament legislation demonstrated how to love my neighbor, and while the specific regulations don't all apply, the principle certainly does, and many of the guidelines are still as helpful as ever. When it comes to the Old Testament, we must be careful not to throw out the baby (ongoing principle) with the bathwater (detailed regulations).

"We don't offer sacrifices anymore, so why should we tithe?" Because there is an important difference. First, the offering of sacrifices is specifically rescinded in the New Testament. As the Book of Hebrews demonstrated, Christ has rendered inoperative the whole sacrificial system. But where in the New Testament does it indicate tithing is no longer a valid practice?

"But the New Testament speaks of voluntary offerings." Yes, and so does the Old Testament. Having a minimal standard of giving has never been incompatible with giving above and beyond that standard.

In Acts 4 we are told the disciples gave all that they had because "great grace was upon them all" (Acts 4:33). It was obvious from the beginning that being under grace didn't mean New Testament Christians would give less but more than their Old Testament brethren.

Being under grace does not mean living by lower standards than the law. On the contrary, Christ systematically addressed such issues as murder, adultery, and the taking of oaths and made it clear that his standards were much higher than those of the Pharisees (Matt. 5:17-48).

GRACE GIVING

As we have seen, the people of Israel's per capita payment of the tithes amounted to about 23 percent of their income. Yet Christianity Today reports that the per capita giving of church members in America is approximately 2.5 percent of their income.[1]

This is a revealing statistic in that it demonstrates, apparently, that the Law was ten times more effective than grace! Or to put it another way, when it comes to giving, people were ten times more responsive to the Law of Moses than they appear to be to the grace of Christ.

Obviously, something is terribly wrong. When we as New Testament believers, especially those living in a far more affluent society than ancient Israel, give at a level that is only a small fraction of that of Old Testament believers, we must take a careful look at our concept of "grace giving."

To most people the term "grace giving" simply means "give what you feel like." The problem is most Christians just don't feel like giving. And many of them never will because they are not being taught to give. As the Law was a tutor to lead us to Christ, so the tithe is a tutor that leads us on to giving. If we can learn to give without it, fine. But the giving track record of professing Christians, at least in present-day America, seems to clearly indicate we are *not* learning to give. Indeed, we are learning not to give.

Absence of Law does not mean absence of responsibility or absence of discipline. Living under grace does not mean God no longer expects anything of us. It is time to reexamine our beliefs and practices when living in the "age of grace" means that our lives are less holy and our sacrifice smaller and our giving less substantial than under Old Testament Law.

Is obedience contrary to grace? Is spontaneity equal to spirituality—or is it sometimes just carnality? The holy habits of church attendance, prayer, and Bible reading can degenerate into legalism as can tithing. But does that make them illegitimate practices or habits?

I know that some fine Bible teachers argue against tithing. But I don't think they realize the effects of their words on others. I will listen to the point of view of the Christian who says, "Tithing is not meant for us today"—provided that he gives regularly and that his giving exceeds the tithe. But the person who argues against the tithe and proceeds to give less than a tithe is effectively saying God has lowered his standards of giving and that New Testament grace means reduced commitment. Furthermore, his own substandard giving suggests ulterior motives for his theological persuasion. Where his treasure isn't shows where his heart isn't.

We must not reject a clear teaching simply because it is in the Old Testament. We must examine our hearts to discover whether when we say, "The tithe is not for today," we are really believing that New Testament grace is a license that frees us to clutch tighter to material wealth. On the contrary, the New Testament precepts, principles, and examples demonstrate that the very opposite is true. New Testament believers are called upon to be far more sacrificial and generous with their money and possessions than even their Old Testament brethren.

A friend of mine is a tangible example of what can happen when giving is viewed as a "whatever you feel like doing" affair. Early in his Christian life he believed that he was supposed to tithe, and he did so faithfully. He and his young family experienced great blessings of God as a result. They were very aware of how strongly God was using the principle of tithing to affect their whole spiritual lives through the concept of putting God first. However, when they moved to another church—a large, strong, Bible teaching church—they heard from the pulpit that tithing was a form of legalism and that New Testament "grace giving" was God's intention for us today.

Of course, there was no specific standard with grace giving. And given the financial pressures upon them, which were no greater than they had been before, this now-liberated family felt the "New Testament freedom" to drastically cut back their giving. Eventually they were giving almost nothing. Over the next several years they floundered in their commitment to the Lord and their financial problems became more serious.

Finally, in another church, they were reintroduced to the concept of tithing as a meaningful guideline rather than a legalistic ritual. When they committed themselves to tithing again, they sensed God's blessing and experienced a peace they hadn't known for years. They don't hesitate to attribute in large degree their several years of spiritual wandering to a misleading concept of "grace giving." Like many families, this one needed the tithe as a tutor in giving.

JESUS AND TITHING

There is no question that Jesus tithed. He was raised in a devout Jewish home, meaning that his parents were tithers and taught him to tithe. Tithing is clearly and repeatedly taught in the Old Testament, which was the only Bible Jesus knew. While Jesus was carefully scrutinized by his enemies and accused of every possible offense, including on a number of occasions breaking the Sabbath, never once was he accused of breaking the law of the tithe. Furthermore, the Talmud specifically forbade the strict Law-keeper from sitting at the table with anyone who did not tithe. Yet on several occasions, the Pharisees ate at the same table with Jesus. Obviously, Christ tithed. This doesn't prove tithing is still valid, but it does have some significance.

Furthermore, Jesus specifically stated that while they should have paid attention to more important things, the Pharisees were correct in being careful to tithe (Matt. 23:23; Luke 11:42). With his example of and repeated emphasis on the sacrificial giving of money and possessions, Jesus didn't ever suggest that the "floor" set by the tithe was eliminated, but simply that the ceiling of Christian giving was far above it. When Jesus told the disciples to go the second mile, he assumed they had gone the first.

THE EARLY CHURCH AND TITHING

Because tithing was so deeply embedded in the Jewish consciousness, it is safe to assume that the Jewish Christians, who dominated the formation and policies of the early church, gave their tithes to the local assembly. To be sure, they went far beyond the tithe, as we see in the early chapters of Acts. But their going beyond it did not negate it. There is no indication the early church ever retreated from the concept that the tithe was the basic minimum to be given to the Lord.

That this was still the case within the first few hundred years of the church is demonstrated in the words of the influential church father Irenaeus:

> The Jews were constrained to a regular payment of tithes; Christians, who have liberty, assign all their possessions to the Lord, bestowing freely not the lesser portions of their property, since they have the hope of greater things.[2]

Note the key phrase, "not the lessor portions." This is a direct indication that the tithe was considered a minimal standard in the early Christian community.

A few hundred years later the tithe was still a basic standard, as evidenced in the words of Augustine:

> Tithes are required as a matter of debt, and he who has been unwilling to give them has been guilty of robbery. Whosoever, therefore, desires to secure a reward for himself . . . let him render tithes, and out of the nine parts let him seek to give alms.[3]

Note the clear distinction between the mandatory tithe and the voluntary offering of giving alms. Alms were to be given—but above and beyond the basic tithe.

Another church father, Jerome, stated, "If anyone shall not do this [pay tithes] he is convicted of defrauding and supplanting God."[4]

Jerome, like Augustine, believed and taught that it is possible for New Testament Christians to "rob God" by withholding the tithe, just as it was for Old Testament believers. For its first four hundred years, at least, Christ's church considered the practice of tithing a vital minimum standard for giving.

THE BENEFITS OF TITHING

In most states, there is a mandatory seat belt law. For many years wearing a seat belt wasn't a legal requirement. But even when it wasn't required, it was still a very good idea.

Suppose the seat belt law was repealed tomorrow. Would I then stop wearing my seat belt? Would I tell my children, "Take off your seat belts, girls. They're no longer required. We're not under the law, and we're not going to be legalistic, so no more seat belts for us." Of course I wouldn't. A good idea is a good idea, whether it is the law or not.

If we believe that tithing is still a command for us, or at least a minimal obligation, then the arguments for it are obvious. I don't want to rob God and place myself under his discipline. If I believe God brings judgment on Christians today for failing to practice the minimal requirement of giving, for withholding their firstfruits from him, then I should need no arm-twisting to tithe.

But even if you don't agree with me that a Christian is obligated to tithe, there are many other strong, practical arguments for doing so. For example, the concept of tithing is clear, consistent, and transferable—that is, it can be easily taught to others. It increases the believer's sense of commitment to God's work in general and his church in particular.

Tithing can also be a significant factor in spiritual growth. I just reread ten letters written to me by church families whose spiritual lives have been revolutionized as they have discovered how to give. Though a number of them now give more than a tithe, seven of the ten specifically mention the great significance of tithing as a spiritual breakthrough in their lives.

One Christian leader said, "As I reflect on my growth as a Christian across the years, the second most important gift of grace I have received has been the discipline of tithing. The first was the surrender of my will to Jesus Christ." He went on to say of himself and his wife, "The Lord got our hearts when we began to tithe."[5]

Other arguments for tithing can be made based on need and ministry opportunity. If Western Christians all practiced tithing, the task of world evangelism and feeding the hungry would literally be within reach. Since many Christians, once they tithe, give freewill offerings beyond, the work of God could be multiplied in every corner of the world.

Many churches have demonstrated the spiritual power of tithing. The Southern Baptist denomination began in 1845. Now it has the largest missionary organization in the world, with well over 3,000 missionaries. Southern Baptists don't only emphasize missions; they emphasize *tithing* as the means to underwrite missions as well as to meet the needs of the local church. Church members understand they are expected to tithe. I am not a Southern Baptist myself, but without their strong teaching and expectations concerning tithing, it is apparent they would have a far less significant role both in their own communities and in world evangelization.

WHY NOT TITHE?

To be sure, there can be problems with tithing. We can treat the tithe as an unwanted tax or bill and be robbed of joy or thankfulness. In some churches tithing is paying membership dues. You pay to belong to a health club and you pay to belong to the church. Tithing can lead to pride that I am part of a faithful remnant that really trusts God, in contrast to all those non-tithing apostates around me.

One of the worst dangers of tithing is complacency. While arguing strongly for the practice of tithing, Don McClanen added this caution:

> The tithe can become an idol to set upon a pedestal to admire. It is often a dangerously tempting resting place rather than a

minimal starting place. Much of the Christian community thinks of tithing as a high and lofty perch that only a few fanatical radicals have reached after years of struggle, rather than seeing it at the bottom or beginning place.[6]

Someone once told me, "I wish I could win a million dollars in the lottery. Then I'd give $100,000 to the Lord, and I could do whatever I want with the rest." Tithing is not something I do to clear my conscience so that I can do whatever I want with the 90 percent. The rest also belongs to God, and I must seek his direction and permission for whatever I do with it. More often than not I'll discover he has some different ideas than I do.

There are many common arguments against tithing, including these:

"Tithing is legalistic." Any legitimate practice can be done with a legalistic attitude. The fault is with the heart, not tithing itself. What I have noticed, however, is that some people call anything "legalism" that sets a responsibility upon them or requires discipline from them. If any principle gets too close to home, starts meddling in my life, requires sacrifice or commitment on my part, then I can dismiss it simply by calling it "legalistic." Hence, legalism easily becomes a convenient label to cover up my own unwillingness to obey God.

"I must pay off my debts rather than tithe." Why am I in debt in the first place? Is God responsible for my unwise or greedy decisions that may have put me there? And even if I have come into debt legitimately, isn't my first debt to God? Is not the tithe a debt to God since he clearly states it belongs to him? If we obey God and make good our financial debt to him, he will help us as we seek to pay off our debts to others. I must not rob God to pay men.

"I can't afford to tithe." Of course I can. What if my salary was reduced by 10 percent? Wouldn't I continue to live? And if tithing is God's will and he promises to provide for those who trust and obey him, won't he allow me to get by on 90 percent rather than 100 percent? In fact, am I not a lot safer living on less inside the will of God than living on more outside it?

Some have suggested that no one ends up benefiting from a tithe he holds on to anyway. I can't keep what belongs to God. The tithe belongs to God, and if we don't give it to him, the

Devil gets it, or it just disappears in any number of ways. Whether this is true or not, many Christians testify that they live just as easily on the 90 percent as the 100 percent. Many others say their financial problems really begin when they withhold the tithe.

If tithing is God's minimal expectation, the issue is, can I afford *not* to tithe? Can I afford to be disobedient? Can I afford to rob God? There is, of course, one way to reduce my tithe, and that is to reduce my income. If my tithe seems to be a lot of money, I should praise God! Look at how abundantly he has provided.

PROFILES OF CHRISTIANS WHO ROB GOD

The Situation: Bill and Donna are in their mid-thirties. Bill has steady work as a salesman, but there always seems to be too much month left at the end of their money.

Bill and Donna sincerely intend to put in the offering box whatever is left at the end of the month. But, between house payments and bills and occasionally sticking a little something into savings, there is just never anything left. They feel bad, but what can you do when you're out of money?

The Problem: Bill and Donna don't understand "firstfruits." They should give to the Lord off the top, not out of "what's left" or not left. They don't realize that the tithe belongs to God, and that there is a word for taking money that doesn't belong to them—stealing.

The Situation: Joan is a twenty-two year old, just finishing college. Her thirty-hour-a-week job pays just over minimum wage. She earns about $500 a month. Joan's parents still provide room and board, but she has to take care of her tuition, books, and other expenses.

"I can't afford to give," says Joan. "I'm barely making it now. If I gave up a tithe that would be $50 a month, and I'd probably have to drop out of school. I'd like to give, but I just can't."

The Problem: Joan is not only robbing God, but she is robbing herself of the opportunity to grow in faith. Right now she doesn't believe God's promise in Malachi 3 (also confirmed in Matt. 6:33) that he will take care of her if she puts God first

220

by giving him what is his. If God is capable of helping her get by on $500 a month, isn't he capable of helping her get by on $450 a month? Joan's God doesn't appear to be very big.

The Situation: Bob is in his early fifties. His wife Elaine says, "For years we frittered away our income on all kinds of luxuries. Now we're twelve years from retirement and we don't have anything saved. On top of that, we've still got two kids in college that need our help."

"We'd like to give to the church," Bob explains. "But Scripture says we've got to provide for our family first. After we get our kids through school and maybe get a nest egg started, then we'll start giving."

The Problem: Bob and Elaine are keeping what belongs to God in order to compensate for their poor planning and lack of discipline in the past. Their first debt is not to their children's college education. Their first debt is to God. If it wasn't tuition costs, it would be something else. Since they have no true conviction about giving and no standard of giving to start with, they will always find a reason not to give.

The Situation: Phil and Pam enjoy giving. With their little blue Santa's helper (VISA card) they just gave each other a video recorder and a large screen television for Christmas. The kids got a computer to keep them busy while their parents enjoy the city's finer restaurants. Their three-year-old Chevy was getting a bit tacky, so they just bought a new model.

"Next year I've got a big promotion coming," says Phil. "Then we'll start giving—right now the budget's pretty tight. It's not that we don't ever give to God's work," Phil adds. "Why, when we were in Hawaii last month we attended a neat church service on the beach and I dropped a $20 bill in the offering."

The Problem: Phil and Pam are blind. They say there is no money left to give—and they do their best to make sure of it! No matter what they say to the contrary, their life-style proves without argument that toys, trips, and cars are more important to them than God, his work, and the needs of others.

They say they will give when they earn more, but they won't. If Phil and Pam have been unfaithful with a little (more than a little), they will be unfaithful with a lot. Their expenditures will always rise to meet their income. Making more money will only make them guilty of robbing God more.

Like so many of their fellow church members, Phil and Pam simply don't understand that the tithe belongs to God, not them, and that they are to return to him the "firstfruits," not "last fruits" or "no fruits."

The Situation: "There's a lot more to stewardship than money," says Gina. "We can't all give—but some of us can teach Sunday school, clean the building, and open our homes to guests. I consider that to be my giving."

The Problem: Gina rightly believes stewardship involves more than money—but she wrongly believes that stewardship ever fails to include money. Her argument is just as faulty as saying, "I can't give the church any of my time or my gifts and talents, so I'll just give my money instead." God expects all of these, not just some of them. Gina is attempting to justify robbing God by "making up for it" in other ways that she should be doing anyway.

The Situation: "I'm so far in debt I can't give a dime to the church," says Tony. "What am I supposed to do, stop my car payments? What kind of testimony would that be? And it would be bad stewardship to sell my car—I'd have to take a $2,000 loss. God doesn't want me to be stupid, does he?"

The Problem: Tony has already been stupid. In buying his new car, he put himself in a position to disobey God's command to give. He violated Scripture by spending money he didn't have. His greedy and foolish misuse of credit has put him in this fix.

Tony apparently believes that God and his church and needy people should pay for his own foolish choices. Why not take a $2,000 loss in order to get into a position to obey God? Is there any stewardship more terrible than robbing your Creator and Savior?

Here is another person who thinks the tithe is his, not God's. Nowhere in Scripture does it say "firstfruits" are to be given to those to whom they will be the best testimony, but to God. If Tony ends up having a bad testimony here it is because of his foolish choice, which is not helped but only complicated by further disobedience to God. He needs to ask forgiveness and learn from the situation so that he doesn't do it again. But does it make sense to rob God in order to have a "better testimony" to men?

The Situation: Joe is an outspoken Christian who is known as a man of faith. He stands up at church business meetings and speaks out in private conversations saying he wants to see the church build more buildings, raise the pastors' salaries, and expand into all kinds of new ministries.

Joe challenges the church to rise to the occasion, and reads passages of Scripture about walking by faith and not sight. He inspires everyone. Everyone, that is, except God and the financial secretary, who are the only ones who know the truth: if everyone gave like Joe, the pastors would have to be laid off, the missionaries would have to leave the field, the church would have to sell all of its property, and the congregation would be walking neither by faith nor sight—it would be buried three feet under.

The Problem: Joe appears to have great faith and vision when it comes to the obedience of others. It is his own obedience that he has trouble with. He fails to ask himself a crucial question: "If everyone gave like I do, where would this church be?" He is quick to commit other people's money, but clings to his own.

Joe is a hypocrite. He says one thing and does another, and in doing so he heaps up judgment for himself. He will be held accountable to God not only for his lack of giving but for his hollow words of exhortation that he himself fails to follow.

BEGINNING WHERE GOD BEGAN

To me, giving less than a tithe is simply not an option. Someday I'm going to stand before God and give an account of my life (Rom. 14:12). In that day I do not want to have to explain why, being indwelt with his Holy Spirit and having lived in the most affluent nation in human history, I failed to give at the very minimal level of those who did not have the indwelling Spirit and owned far less than I.

The concepts behind the firstfruits—the ownership and worthiness of God and the servanthood and indebtedness of man—are as true today as they were in the Old Testament. And surely the gratitude of God's people should be far greater on this side of Calvary than the other.

Without a guidepost, where do you start your giving? Why not start where God had his people start throughout the Old

223

Testament? Why not start with the tithe?

I view tithing as I view a child's first steps. His first steps are not his last, neither are they his best, but they are a fine beginning. So is the tithe. Tithing is for many the first toddler's step of stewardship. It is the training wheels on the bicycle of true giving. It may not be a home run, but it gets you on base—which is a lot further than the majority of church members ever get.

For those who still feel that the New Testament church has outgrown the need for the tithe as a guideline, let me suggest the following: figure out your pre-tax income from every source, *all* of it, including the dollar value of the benefits you receive (don't forget health insurance and retirement), then multiply by 10 percent. If you discover that you have been regularly giving to the Lord's work beyond the level of 10 percent then you are right—you don't need the tithe. Just go right on doing what you are doing and let God move you on in the grace of giving. But if your giving adds up to 7 percent or 5 percent or 3 percent, it shows you really *do* need the tithe as a teacher and guide to stewardship.

Begin with the tithe. It shows yourself, your family, and your Lord that you are serious. As you continue to tithe, you will sense God's approval. You will experience the freedom and joy there is in acknowledging his lordship of your money and possessions, and thereby your whole life.

"I can see it's right to tithe, but I can't start right now." Never put off obedience. The moment of conviction and enlightenment is the moment to act. To procrastinate obedience is to disobey. Trust him enough to begin this life-changing, eternity-impacting adventure of giving.

NOTES
1. David McKenna, "Financing the Great Commission," *Christianity Today* 15 May 1987: 27.
2. Quoted by John Davis, *Your Wealth in God's World* (Phillipsburg, N.J.: Presbyterian and Reformed, 1984), 113.
3. *Dictionary of Christian Antiquities*, Vol. 2, quoted by Fletcher Spruce, *You Can Be a Joyful Tither* (Kansas City, Mo.: Beacon Hill Press, 1966), 19.
4. *Dictionary of Christian Antiquities.*
5. Don McClanen, *The Tithe as Teacher: An Energizing Force* (Gaithersburg, Md.: Ministry of Money, 1980), 1-2.
6. McClanen, 3.

CHAPTER 13

GIVING: RECIPROCATING GOD'S GRACE

Money never stays with me. It would burn me if it did. I throw it out of my hands as soon as possible, lest it should find its way into my heart. John Wesley

Grace and gratitude belong together like heaven and earth. Grace evokes gratitude like the voice an echo. Gratitude follows grace as thunder follows lightning. Karl Barth

The single most striking characteristic of the early Christians is that they shared all that they owned and even liquidated their possessions to give to others as they had need (Acts 2:44-45; 4:32-37). In one verse we are told, "Much grace was upon them all," and in the next, "There were no needy persons among them." Why? Because they sacrificially gave to make sure all needs were cared for. Compare these Christians to the bickering

225

disciples of the Gospels, jockeying for position in the kingdom and unwilling to wash each others feet. This is the life-changing power of the indwelling Holy Spirit. There are two common errors in viewing this early church in Jerusalem. One is to see it as a specific model to be followed by Christians in every age and situation. The other is to reject it as irrelevant to us today.

First, we must recognize that these beautiful and powerful scenes in the early chapters of Acts come out of a unique historical situation. Perhaps a million Jews had made the Passover pilgrimage to Jerusalem, and the city was bursting at its seams. Many of the thousands coming to Christ would want to stay in Jerusalem to learn as much as possible before returning to their homes. More significantly, many of them probably could not return to their homes at all. As a result of their conversion to Christ, they would have become "the victims of social and economic ostracism, ecclesiastical excommunication, and national disinheritance. Their business enterprises must in most cases have collapsed in ruins and family bonds been heart-breakingly severed."[1]

The result was thousands of homeless, jobless people. Obviously this was an emergency situation calling for unusual action. It cannot serve as a strict model for all Christian communities, since not all are faced with the same extreme situations. However, it was the circumstances that were unique, not the attitude toward money and possessions. That attitude *is* a model for all Christians in every place and time.

In A.D. 140, Justin Martyr said, "We who formerly treasured money and possessions more than anything else now hand over everything we have to a treasury for all and share it with everyone who needs it."[2]

Some groups have followed this communal model and done well, while others have found it less than ideal. I do not oppose the attempt to follow closely the form of the early church. I do, however, resist the notion that those who do not adopt this specific model are thereby unscriptural or unspiritual. To hoard, be possessive, or withhold our resources or hospitality from the needy is indisputably unscriptural—but the graces of giving and sharing can legitimately take other forms than that of Acts chapters 2 and 4. That this is true is demonstrated by the fact that while sacrificial giving is an integral part of all healthy churches, never again in the New Testament do we see it manifested in exactly the same way as in the early chapters of Acts. Indeed, it appears that virtually all of the subsequent New Testament churches were different in structure than the first.

Others have taken these texts to indicate that the early church rejected the concept of the private ownership of property. On the contrary, the liquidation of possessions took place "from time to time" (Acts 4:34) and was strictly voluntary. Peter made a point of telling Ananias and Sapphira that their property was theirs till they sold it, and once they sold it the money was still theirs to use as they wished (Acts 5:3-5). Their sin was not in failing to lay everything at the apostles' feet, but in claiming they were doing so, to impress others, when they weren't.

Notice too that the state of the early church is not portrayed as one of utopian selflessness nor euphoric harmony. Not only is there the problem with Ananias and Sapphira, but also with the Greek and the Hebrew Christians who quarrelled over the inequities in the daily distribution of food to their widows (Acts 6:1).

The "bread line" of Acts 6 is likewise not a specific model for churches but a reflection of the ongoing effects of the earlier emergency. However, it does demonstrate the high priority of helping the truly needy and taking the necessary organizational steps to do so effectively (Acts 6:2-6). It would be a mistake to see Acts 2 and 4 as a socialistic or communal model for all believers to follow in every age and circumstance. However, it would be an even greater mistake to ignore their timeless model of the Christian attitude toward money and possessions, and the crying need to adopt such an attitude, with its consequent behavior, in our churches and personal lives today.

THE RELATIONSHIP OF MONEY AND POSSESSIONS

While much of this chapter will deal with the giving of money, we must always view money and possessions as virtually inseparable. As the early church in Jerusalem demonstrated, giving involves money, but much more. We can give with a meal, house, dress, shovel, bicycle, sewing machine, or any possession. I may give someone a car. Or, I may still own my car but freely loan it to others, or use it to give a ride to my elderly neighbor or to go buy groceries for a shut-in. There is a great deal of "giving" that can take place even when I retain ownership—that is, as long as I remind myself that God is the true owner, and I am but the steward.

However, two cautions are in order. First, I can easily rationalize owning unnecessary things on the grounds that I share them with others. The fact that I often invite others out on my boat does not necessarily mean that my boat is the most strategic ministry use for the money it requires. Furthermore, I must also be careful that my continued ownership of something does not involve possessiveness. If I am the kind of person others are afraid to borrow from because they know that a dent or scratch or break would bother me, I'm not having much of a ministry no matter how "willing" I envision myself to be.

One of the saddest commentaries on our independence of our brothers and sisters in Christ is a comparative inventory of our possessions. We routinely buy things for ourselves that we need very seldom, sometimes even once in a lifetime. Three friends who use chain saws twice a year will own three chain saws. People who need to use pickup trucks once a month for three hours buy pickup trucks, at incredible expense. I happen to have a reason for owning two one-hundred-foot extension cords. Why should a friend or neighbor or church member buy a hundred-foot extension cord for a once-a-year use when he can borrow mine? Or why should I rent a hedge clipper when I can borrow his?

Some churches have lists of possessions that members make freely available for the use of others. This is a good beginning. Not only does sharing our assets with others deepen our relationships, cultivate friendships, and lead to evangelism and edification, it also releases huge amounts of money that can be invested in the kingdom of God. Furthermore, it gradually frees us of our possessiveness and attachment to things.

I love books. For years I not only loved to read them, I passionately collected them. I loaned them out, but most of them just sat on my shelves. About five years ago I decided to take all my books out of my office and put them in our new church library. This saved the church lots of money and made available to others great books that were seldom used before. While some books get beat up, broken down, and lost, the point is they are being used for good in hundreds of lives. Meanwhile, I have found that though I still love books, my emotional attachment to possessing them is gone.

NEW TESTAMENT GUIDELINES FOR GIVING

Give. Christians give. There are no exceptions. "Each man should give what he has decided in his heart to give" (2 Cor. 9:7). Not all will give the same, but all will give. It is a sad commentary on the spiritual condition of Christians that half of regular attenders give nothing or next to nothing to the church.

Give Generously. When building the tabernacle, Moses was faced with a curious problem. "And the people continued to bring freewill offerings morning after morning. . . . The people were restrained from bringing more because what they already had was more than enough to do all the work" (Exod. 36:3, 7). When people catch a vision for God's work, they can hardly be held back from giving.

Out of her deep love for Jesus, Mary anointed him with a very costly ointment (Mark 14:3-9). Some criticized her because it seemed so lavish and wasteful. Generous giving to the Lord may be labeled fanatical by others. But Jesus labeled it "love." In fact, he was so moved by the woman's giving that he vowed "wherever the gospel is preached throughout the world, what she has done will also be told in memory of her."

Those who are most reasonable and calculating usually give less. But love generates lavish giving.

How much is generous? There is no one answer for everybody. When a friend was trying to figure out how much he should give each month, he decided he would give at least as much his house payment. He told me, "If I can't afford to give that much then I can't afford to live in a house this nice either."

If you have never tithed, begin there. Particularly exciting to me are the first steps beyond the tithe, where we give God his claim on the 90 percent, which also belongs to him. If 10 percent why not 12 percent? If 12 percent why not 15 percent? If 15 percent why not 20 percent or 30 percent or 50 percent or more?

There are countless people who live on a half or a third or less than many of us make, and I don't mean people who live in poverty. Why can't we live at a particular income, and simply give everything above that income to God?

Give Regularly and Systematically. The term "religiously" is sometimes used to describe a disciplined act or consistent regimen—"He exercises religiously." If anything was done religiously, you would think it would be giving, but not so. Church records demonstrate that while many people don't give at all, most of those who do give do so sporadically. They might give two months in a row, skip three months, give once, skip two more.

In fact, some people don't give when they are on vacation. They don't give if they have the flu. Obviously they don't make it to the offering plate that week—but what I mean is that they don't ever make up for the giving they missed. If I'm out of town when my house payment is due, I may pay it early or late, but I pay it. Why should my giving be haphazard and arbitrary?

It is this hit-and-miss approach to giving that Paul wished the Corinthians to avoid when he told them, "On the first day of every week, each one of you should set aside a sum of money in keeping with his income" (1 Cor. 16:2). That way when Paul arrived to get the money for the needy saints, no last minute collections would have to be made from people who had already spent what they should have given. Systematic giving is basic to biblical giving—if you give the "leftovers" to God, rather than the firstfruits, there is usually little or nothing left over to give.

For the last seven years we have had a weekend church retreat attended by half of our adults and perhaps two-thirds of our regular givers. We have elected not to take an offering on this retreat, believing that any regular givers can simply compensate for any missed giving the next week. Yet we have found that every year only a fraction of the amount missed that Sunday is ever recovered. Just because people are not physically present by the offering boxes, they end up keeping money they otherwise would have given.

We are to plan our giving in advance—not simply give if we happen to be present, or happen to feel moved by the offertory, or happen to have remembered our checkbook. Can you imagine standing before the Lord and explaining why you often disobeyed his command to give—"Lord, I could never find a pen before the plate got there." When we are gone on a day we would normally have given, we can put our check in the mail or set it aside for the next Sunday to give in addition to that Sunday's giving.

It is very rare that people give substantially unless they give systematically. They may give a few hundred dollars a few times a year and think of themselves as big givers. But the person who consistently gives fifty dollars a week every week, or two hundred dollars a month every month, is the real backbone of the church. He ends up giving far more than the "lump sum" giver, who usually comes through in late December to get his tax deduction.

People who don't give systematically invariably overestimate how much they give. When our church financial secretary was handing out giving receipts one Sunday morning, a man came up and said there must have been a mistake, because his wasn't there. The truth was that though he knew it had been a few months since he had given, he actually hadn't given the entire year.

The best way to give is to give in relation to income. If I am paid weekly, I should give weekly. If I am paid monthly, then I give monthly. If I am a farmer or nurseryman or salesman who might receive windfalls a few times a year and little or no income the rest, then I should give just as regularly as I receive income. If I receive a bonus or a royalty check or a gift, I set aside my giving to God immediately.

If I have weekly income but wait till the end of the month to give, or have monthly income but wait till the end of the year, several things happen. Most importantly, if the firstfruits belong to God and I am holding onto them, I am embezzling from or robbing God. I may have every intention of paying him back, but meanwhile I'm using money that is strictly his, not mine.

Also, the longer I wait to give, the higher the likelihood that the money will disappear. It will dissipate, be used for this emergency, or this contingency, or this indulgence. The great thing about giving immediately upon receiving is that it removes the temptation to rob God. If someone asked me to pass twenty dollars on to a friend, I wouldn't put it in my wallet and mix it with my own money. I would set it aside immediately and be

231

sure it got where it was supposed to go as soon as possible.

Also, we must realize that the needs of the church are monthly needs. A budget must be planned on the basis of regular income. The average church member should ask himself how well the church could operate if everyone gave as much or little, and as often or rarely, as he does.

Stewardship is not a once-a-year consideration, but a week-to-week, month-to-month commitment requiring discipline and consistency. When the Corinthian church expressed their desire to be financially involved in a worthy need-meeting project, Paul said, "Now finish the work, so that your eager willingness to do it may be matched by your completion of it, according to your means" (2 Cor. 8:11).

Barring an extraordinary economic turn in which the means are simply no longer available, a church should meet its budget—assuming the budget has been developed in harmony with the giving levels or expressed intentions of the church members. We should not be sending missionaries out to the field and then dropping support because of insufficient funds. By regular, systematic giving, the church should insure that it not only starts well, but finishes well in carrying out the work of God.

Give Voluntarily. When the community of saints contributed to the building of the tabernacle, the words "willing" and "freewill" were continuously emphasized (Exod. 35:21-22, 26, 29; 36:3). Everyone "whose heart moved him" gave. Likewise, for the special offering to the needy saints, Paul said, "Each man should give what he has decided in his heart to give, not reluctantly or under compulsion" (2 Cor. 9:7).

Based on these passages, I have had people tell me it is wrong to give to the Lord if you don't feel like it. Some clarifications are in order.

First, the believers in Exodus were never told that all giving was voluntary. They didn't tithe if they felt led to; they tithed no matter how they felt because it was their duty. But they did not have to give beyond this required amount. No one had to give to the tabernacle. They gave to this worthy one-time need because they wanted to, because their hearts were moved. They were caught up in a spirit of divinely inspired generosity.

When Paul said a man should give what he has decided in his

heart, without a sense of compulsion, he wasn't talking about the normal week-to-week operations and ministries of the church to which every member must contribute. He was talking about a one-time special offering for the needs of poor saints back in Jerusalem. Since this was something above and beyond the regular needs of their local church, it called for a contribution above and beyond their regular giving. They were not to rob Corinth to pay Jerusalem. They were not asked to give to the other church *rather* than their own, but *in addition* to their own.

When churches have special offerings and general giving dips dramatically, then there is no special giving involved—it demonstrates people are simply putting their giving in a different plate. Was Paul saying a believer should never feel any compulsion to give to the needs of his church, to the poor, or to world missions? Was he implying that if we are reluctant to part with our money that we shouldn't? No! We do many things because they are right, not just because we want to or don't want to.

Do we share our faith only if we feel led, read our Bibles only if we aren't reluctant to, love our wives only when we feel inspired to? Of course not. The principle is *not* "give voluntarily or don't give at all," but "as your heart is moved, give voluntarily above and beyond your regular giving."

Like many Christians in our churches today, the rich fool lived by the principle, "Only give when you feel like it." It just so happens he never felt like it. In contrast, the Macedonian believers "earnestly pleaded with us for the privilege of sharing in this service to the saints" (2 Cor. 8:4). When we catch a vision of God's grace we will give according to our duty, yes, but far more, we will give *beyond* our duty, voluntarily captivated by the grace of our ever-giving Lord.

Give Joyfully. "God loves a cheerful giver" (2 Cor. 9:7). God takes delight in the believer who takes delight in giving. Seeing the temple was in need of repair, Joash put a chest outside its gate. "All the officials and all the people brought their contributions gladly, dropping them into the chest until it was full" (2 Chron. 24:10). Whenever the chest was filled they would empty it, return it, and soon it would be full again. The key word is "gladly." The people of God, when they see a worthy cause, are to give to it gladly.

There are infinite reasons for joy in giving. One is knowing that we are investing in eternity and that one day in the heavenly kingdom we will see the tangible results of our giving, in people and in rewards. Another reason for joy is knowing that when our hearts are moved, it is often in response to the prayers of God's people. God hears their requests, then moves our hearts to respond. There is an ongoing drama of human request and divine response in which God the Director offers us the part of the giver. As the tide comes in and out, so one part of Christ's body channels its resources to a more needy part, then receives those resources back in other ways at other times—"At the present time your plenty will supply what they need, so that in turn their plenty will supply what we need" (2 Cor. 8:14).

One of the great attractions to large sporting events is not simply what goes on down on the field or court. It is the sense of identity and participation in something big that is fostered by tens of thousands of people coming together for a common purpose. Likewise, the giver senses his part in a huge community of faith, extending even beyond this dimension to the angelic hosts and saints in heaven. He finds his identity in this "great cloud of witnesses" when he prays and worships and serves and gives.

In my own experience, there is nothing more exhilarating than to participate in God's kingdom program by meeting the spiritual and physical needs of others. Nothing is so stimulating and rewarding as joining with brothers and sisters in the highest cause in the universe—bringing glory to God by extending his grace to others. From the day I came to Christ as a high school student, financial giving has been an integral part of my walk with God. For me, growing and giving have been almost inseparable. I do not consider myself a perfect model of giving. Yet many of the greatest joys of my life, and some of the closest times of intimacy with my Lord, have come in the giving of myself and my resources.

"It is more blessed to give than to receive" (Acts 20:35). Giving is the source of inexpressible joy. Do we lack joy? We may find it in giving. Giving is growing. As someone has said, "Giving is not God's way of raising money—it's his way of raising children."

Again, we must be careful not to miss the point. Someone

once told me, "God says not to give if you can't give cheerfully. I can't give cheerfully so I don't give!" God does *not* tell us not to give if we can't give cheerfully. God wants us to be cheerful, to be sure, but he also wants us to be obedient. The way to cheerfulness is not to keep from giving but to give even when we don't feel up to it. If we are not cheerful, the problem is our hearts, and the solution is redirecting our hearts, not withholding our giving. Hearts follow treasures (Matt. 6:21). Put your treasures in the eternal kingdom, and a cheerful heart will follow. God also loves an obedient giver.

Give Worshipfully. The centurion Cornelius was described as "devout and God-fearing" and one who "gave generously." When an angel of God appeared to him he said to Cornelius, "Your prayers and gifts to the poor have come up as a remembrance before God" (Acts 10:1-4). Cornelius was a worshiper, and an integral part of his worship was financial giving. Because of that, God thought of him with special fondness.

When Paul described the sacrificial giving of the Macedonian saints he said, "They did not do as we expected, but they gave themselves first to the Lord and then to us in keeping with God's will" (2 Cor. 8:5). Giving should not just be directed toward those through whom we give (such as a church, organization, or person requesting funds) or those to whom we give (such as a needy person or family). Ultimately it should be directed toward the one for whom we give—God. He is the Creator, the source, the provider, the motivator, the need-meeter. He is also the recipient, for, "He who gives to the poor lends to the Lord," and, "Inasmuch as you have done it unto one of the least of these my brethren, so you have done it to me" (Matt. 25:40). In giving, God is both the point of origin and the destination, the beginning and the end, the Alpha and Omega.

In challenging the Corinthian church to give like the saints in Macedonia, Paul pointed to the ultimate basis of all Christian giving: "For you know the grace of our Lord Jesus Christ, that though he was rich, yet for your sakes he became poor, so that you through his poverty might become rich" (2 Cor. 8:9). He climaxed two powerful chapters on giving with these words: "Thanks be to God for his indescribable gift!" (2 Cor. 9:15).

Giving is a response of the heart triggered by the grace of

235

God. Grace engenders grace. A gift inspires giving—the greater the gift, the greater the giving. We consider what he has given to us, then we give out of our unspeakable gratitude. We give because he first gave to us. He is such a great Giver that it is impossible to respond to him without giving. Karl Barth said it beautifully: "Grace and gratitude belong together like heaven and earth. Grace evokes gratitude like the voice an echo. Gratitude follows grace as thunder follows lightning."[3]

By giving, we enter into and participate in the grace of Christ. We worship. By giving in concert with our brothers and sisters in Christ's body, we jointly worship him, moved by each others' example and mutual participation. In the building of the tabernacle, building of the temple, and repair of the temple, it was the corporate involvement of the community of saints in which the spirit of God moved so dramatically to produce extravagant giving. The same was true with the New Testament saints of Jerusalem in the early chapters of Acts and those in Macedonia spoken of in 2 Corinthians 8.

Giving is most worshipful not when it is a purely individual matter, as in responding to a mailing or to a plea on television, but when giving takes place in the actual physical gathering of the saints for worship. This is why Jesus said if we are offering a gift at the altar and remember that we have wronged our brother, we are to go and be reconciled before we complete our act of worship in giving (Matt. 5:23-24). Christian giving is not just personal, but corporate. Its relational implications are both vertical *and* horizontal.

Giving does not border on worship. It *is* worship, every bit as much as praying or singing a hymn of praise. While my own church has an offering box and passes an offering plate only on special occasions, no church need apologize for making corporate giving a part of the worship service. While dispensing with passing the plate avoids some of the intrusion of money-consciousness or the danger of showiness, there is the danger of disassociating giving from corporate worship.

If giving out of worship is one of the best motives, there are many candidates for the worst. One of these is giving to get a tax deduction. I wonder how it would affect giving if churches and Christian organizations would lose their tax-exempt status. We may find out, since the United States is one of the few countries in the world that grants such a status in the first place, and even here it is being challenged. Of course, as long as we have the privilege it is only wise to take advantage of it. But both we and the Lord are the losers when we reduce giving from a heart-generated act of worship to a calculated strategy to reduce tax liabilities.

Give Proportionately. When there was an impending famine, "The disciples, each according to his ability, decided to provide help for the brothers living in Judea" (Acts 11:29). God says when it comes to giving, "Each one of you should set aside a sum of money in keeping with his income" (1 Cor. 16:2).

The Old Testament tithe was proportionate—people were not told to all give ten cattle or twenty pieces of gold. If someone had a hundred new cattle, he gave ten; if he had ten, he gave one; if one then he gave 10 percent of the value of the cow. If he earned five hundred pieces of gold, he gave fifty pieces. But if he earned only thirty pieces, he was required to give only three. The tithe was proportionate to income.

But proportionate giving is by no means equal giving. It is obviously a much greater sacrifice for a man who earns only five thousand dollars a year to give five hundred of it than it is for a man who earns fifty thousand to give five thousand of it. While it is true that the second man is giving away ten times as much, the point is he still has ten times as much to live on. Seeing the rich people throw large amounts in the temple treasury and the widow put in two tiny copper coins, Jesus called his disciples to him and said, "This poor widow has put more into the treasury than all the others. They all gave out of their wealth; but she, out of her poverty, put in everything—all she had to live on" (Mark 12:43-44).

Jesus was saying that the amount we give is important to God only in relation to the amount we keep. One person can give $25 in an act of great sacrifice, another can give $100,000 and not sacrifice at all. If someone makes $10,000,000 a year, gives away $9,000,000 and spends "only" the other million on himself, we may be deeply impressed, but God is not. This is one reason it is unfortunate and misleading to publicly laud large donors in the Christian community. Often their sacrifice is far less than those whose names will never be known.

The beauty of New Testament giving is that the believer, as he senses God's direction, can increase the proportion of his giving as God blesses him financially or as he learns to trust him more. Hence, over the years many believers give a higher and higher percentage to the Lord.

Give Sacrificially. Describing the Macedonian Christians, Paul wrote, "Out of the most severe trial, their overflowing joy and their extreme poverty welled up in rich generosity. For I testify that they gave as much as they were able, and even beyond their ability" (2 Cor. 8:3). These believers gave far out of proportion to their means.

There are three levels of giving—less than our ability, according to our ability, and beyond our ability. I think it is fair to say that 95 percent of the Christians in the Western world give less than their ability. Perhaps another 4 percent or more give according to their ability, and less than 1 percent beyond their ability.

What does it mean to give beyond our ability? It means to push our giving past the point where the figures add up. It means to give when the bottom line says we shouldn't. It means to give away not just the luxuries, but some of the necessities. It means living with the faith of the poor widow. For most of us, giving according to our means would really stretch us. Giving beyond our means would appear to break us. But it won't—because we know God is faithful.

Giving sacrificially means giving the best. If we have two blankets and someone needs one of them, sacrificial giving hands over the best of the two. Much of our giving in the Western world is not giving—it is merely discarding. Donating secondhand goods to church rummage sales and benevolence organizations and missions is certainly better than throwing them away. But giving away something we didn't want in the first place is not giving, but selective disposal. In fact, this sort of "giving" is often done because we want a newer or better version of what we are giving away. King David said, "I will not sacrifice to the Lord my God burnt offerings that cost me nothing" (2 Sam. 24:24).

Sacrificial giving is giving away what we would rather keep. It is keeping the old and giving away the new or giving away both. The giving of the early disciples was spontaneous, unguarded, and uncalculated giving.

Sacrificial giving appears to be unreasonable. In reality, though, it is perfectly reasonable, for it brings glory to God, meets the needs of others, and insures eternal rewards for ourselves—and all the while we know God will take care of our immediate needs.

One of the saddest things I have seen is a young believer who is excited about Christ and, taking the Scriptures seriously, determines to draw out his savings or sell his house or his car and give to the church, missions, or the poor. If he expresses this desire, soon he is surrounded by older and "wiser" believers who tell him he is going overboard. Perhaps in some cases his decision is rash or unwise—but in many cases may this not be the prompting of God's Holy Spirit to give lavishly as an act of love and discipleship? We must be careful not to carelessly quench such enthusiasm. Indeed, we would do well to learn from it.

We do not like risky faith. We like to have our safety net below us, a good backup plan in case God fails. Our instinct for self-preservation leads us to hedge our bets. If we give at all, we will give as much as we can without really feeling it and no more. We take away the high stakes, and we also lose the high returns. We miss the adventure of seeing God provide when we have extended ourselves, yes, *overextended* ourselves in giving.

A disciple does not ask "how much can I keep," but "how much more can I give?" Whenever we start to get comfortable with our level of giving, it is time to raise it again.

Give Quietly. Jesus said, "Be careful not to do your 'acts of righteousness' before men, to be seen by them. If you do, you will have no reward from your Father in heaven." The illustrations that follow include prayer and fasting, but he began with giving. When you give to the needy, he said, don't announce it, as do the hypocrites, who want to be honored by men. Instead, give quietly, not telling anyone, "so that your giving may be in secret" (Matt. 6:1, 4). Then God, who sees the secret things, will reward you.

Of course, sometimes our acts of righteousness *will* be seen by men. But Christ's point is one of motive and purpose—don't do it *in order to* be seen by men. What he objects to is calculated recognition and advertised piety.

239

The widespread practice among Christian organizations and churches of putting contributors' names on plaques, bricks, pews, and cornerstones, publishing donors lists, and naming schools and buildings after their patrons surely encourages the very thing Jesus was condemning. In fact, it is hard to understand how we could read this passage and still continue these practices. Ironically, Jesus said that, by granting the reward of human recognition, we deprive givers of the one reward that would count for eternity, that which is from God. (This practice will be considered in more depth in chapter 15.)

One of the greatest abuses of giving is the development of the stockholder mentality. This is sadly common in some local churches where the wealthy can wave their money and lobby and strike back by withholding their giving when they don't get their way. At a church where there was disagreement over who should serve as a new pastor, one board member informed the others, "I've poured a lot of money into this church, and I intend to get the pastor I want." God wants quiet and humble givers, not self-serving powerbrokers.

Of course, the best way to avoid exalting givers is to avoid knowing who they are in the first place. There are many good reasons for giving to be as anonymous as possible. Most churches have a financial secretary who records donations for tax purposes. At our church, and many others, this person is the only one who knows who gives what. Other times one or more pastors or elders or deacons are also aware of giving levels. In one church, the pastor personally sends his thanks for the exact amount given during the year, making a point of the fact that he knows exactly who has given how much. This is very common in Christian organizations outside the church where large donors receive personal letters, special mailings, phone calls, and other forms of reward and wooing.

There are several reasons why I believe no one in church leadership should know who is giving what. If leaders know how much people give, they will be tempted to give greater preference to big givers and less to those who don't give. This is a temptation to fall into the very trap Scripture warns against (James 2:1-5). Also, it puts them in a position of judging others with incomplete knowledge. They may conclude some people are unspiritual and others are spiritual without knowing the whole story. Other times their judgments may be accurate, but still unhealthy. Those who have served as financial secretaries carry the burden of seeing prominent and vocal church members whom everyone else admires, while they alone know that these same people give nothing to the church.

The most important reason for anonymous giving is to remove or at least minimize the temptation to give in order to impress those in the know. If I know the pastor or the board knows how much I give, I may give with the motivation, partially or completely, of pleasing or impressing them. At this point, Jesus said, I have my reward and will receive none from him. When I give at my church I am grateful there is only one person I can be tempted to impress. One fewer would be ideal.

One of the great tests for Christian leaders is whether we can trust God to provide financially without courting or favoring the big donors. And perhaps the greatest test for givers is whether we are able to give of ourselves and our resources without getting the credit.

GOD'S PROVISION FOR THE GIVER

Scripture makes clear that in many cases God blesses us financially when we generously give (Prov. 11:24-25; Luke 6:38). "Whoever sows sparingly will also reap sparingly, and whoever sows generously will also reap generously" (2 Cor. 9:6).

When God prospers us in this way it is not merely to give us new toys and more beautiful homes but to allow us to give still more: "You will be made rich in every way so that you can be generous on every occasion" (2 Cor. 9:11). God's extra provision is usually not intended to raise our standard of living, but to raise our standard of giving.

R. G. LeTourneau was an example of a man who understood God's purpose for blessing him financially. An inventor of earthmoving machines, LeTourneau reached the point of giving 90 percent of his income to the Lord. As he put it, "I shovel out the money, and God shovels it back to me—but God has a bigger shovel."

My family has personally experienced God's "bigger shovel," his abundant material provision to the giver. In some cases it is obvious—such as an unexpected check in the mail or being

241

given something just when we thought we were going to have to buy it. One time when we really needed it, it came in the form of our error in figuring the bank balance that was greatly in our favor.

In other cases God's provision is less obvious. A washing machine that should have given up the ghost a decade ago keeps on working. A car with 180,000 miles on it runs for two years without so much as a tune-up. A checking account that should have dried up long before the end of the month somehow makes it through. As God miraculously stretched the oil and bread of the widow in Elisha's day, and as he made the clothes and sandals of the children of Israel last forty years in the wilderness, I am convinced he sometimes graciously extends the life of things that otherwise would have to be replaced.

My family often thanks God for his behind-the-scenes provision, including preventing accidents and incidents that would have been very costly. God provides not only in what he gives us, but at times in what he keeps from us. Have you ever noticed that excess money just seems to dissipate in a multitude of directions? When the Israelites were building their paneled houses and God's house was in ruins, God said, "Give careful thought to your ways. You have planted much, but have harvested little . . . you earn wages, only to put them in a purse with holes in it" (Hag. 1:5-6). He goes on to explain that because they have been giving to themselves and not him, God has minimized and dissipated their profits, so they do not come out ahead (Hag. 1:9-11). We need to give careful thought to our ways, and ask ourselves if we would do better to give more to the Lord and ask him to maximize what we keep, rather than trying to hang onto more, only to have it leak out our pockets.

Two years ago, my wife and I sensed God's leading to take our daughters and spend two months visiting missionary families in Africa and Europe. My church wanted to pay my way, but when we figured how much it would cost for the rest of the family, it was absolutely prohibitive. I felt strongly my family should be with me, but there was just no way to do it. In another situation, we might have seen this as God's way of saying "no." But in this case we sensed his direction to move forward. We deliberately didn't publicly announce our intention to go, for fear the announcement itself would account for funds coming in. We wanted to watch God provide in other ways.

242

As we began to save for the trip, remarkable amounts of money began to come in. Most of the funds came from unexpected sources. But even beyond all this, every month we found we were saving far more than we should have been able to. There were no extra or emergency expenses draining our funds.

We had determined not to reduce our level of giving. While we would never touch our tithe, we were tempted to rationalize using for our trip some of our extra monthly missionary giving—after all, it was for a missionary purpose! But this just didn't seem right.

As of two weeks before the trip, an amazing amount of money had come in, but we still lacked a thousand dollars. Meanwhile there was a special missionary offering at church. Though it didn't make sense in light of the circumstances, we determined to give substantially to this offering, above and beyond our normal giving. It "didn't make sense," but we knew it was right. No one who has seen God work will be surprised to hear that within a week of the trip he gave back not only the money we had given, but more than a thousand dollars beyond it, enough to give some back to him once more before getting on the plane.

We look back at the trip and realize that, humanly speaking, we shouldn't have been able to accumulate the needed funds. But God provided abundantly.

I debated whether or not to share this example lest it appear that I see myself as an ideal giver. I most certainly do not. Furthermore, I have no desire to lose my reward from God later by calling attention to myself now. Nevertheless, Scripture does show there is encouragement in believers seeing God at work in the giving of other believers (1 Chron. 29:6-9; 2 Cor. 8:1-7). I have been encouraged and stimulated to give as I have heard the testimonies of others who are givers. I pray that my experiences would also be an encouragement to you.

As we learn to give we draw closer to God. But no matter how far we move on in the grace of giving, Jesus Christ remains the unmatchable giver. It was he who left behind him the wealth of heaven to make the supreme sacrifice to deliver us from eternal poverty and grant us eternal riches.

No matter how much we give, we can never out-give God.

NOTES
1. P. E. Hughes, as quoted by K. F. W. Prior, *God and Mammon* (Philadelphia: Westminster Press, 1965), 17.

2. Quoted by Virgil Vogt, *Treasure in Heaven* (Ann Arbor, Mich.: Servant Books, 1982), 85.
3. Karl Barth, *Church Dogmatics* (Edinburgh: T & T Clark, 1957), IV-1, 41.

CHAPTER 14

HELPING THE POOR AND REACHING THE LOST

That bread which you keep belongs to the hungry; that coat which you preserve in your wardrobe, to the naked; those shoes which are rotting in your possession, to the shoeless; that gold which you have hidden in the ground, to the needy. Wherefore, as often as you are able to help others, and refuse, so often did you do them wrong. Augustine

Obedience to the Great Commission has more consistently been poisoned by affluence than by anything else. Ralph Winter

Mother Theresa devotes her life to helping the poorest of the poor. After his firsthand observation of her arduous work among the filth, disease, and suffering of Calcutta, a television commentator told her, "I wouldn't do what you're doing for all the money in the world." Her simple reply was, "Neither would I."

What we wouldn't do for all the money in the world we are to do out of obedience to Christ, compassion for others, and anticipation of eternal reward.

GIVING HELP TO THE POOR

Who Is Responsible for the Poor? In his essay on self-reliance, Ralph Waldo Emerson wrote, "Do not tell me, as a good man did today, of my obligation to put all poor men in good situations. Are they *my* poor?"[1]

Emerson reflected our national spirit of independence. Few of us wish harm to the poor. We just don't want to be held responsible for them.

But Emerson's question is valid and still timely. Are the poor *my* poor? Am I responsible for their plight? More than one evangelical writer would have us believe that because we ourselves are not poor, because we have money and possessions beyond those of others, we are thereby causing others to be poor. We are said to be prosperous directly at the expense of the poor. We are therefore, supposedly, responsible for their poverty.

This common perspective is based on what is called the "zero sum" philosophy, the belief that wealth cannot be created but only distributed. The logic goes like this. If there are eight people at a party and a pie is cut in eight pieces, and I take two or three pieces for myself, then I have taken what belongs to the others. The fact that I had more to eat proves I took from them and am the cause of their lack.

The pie analogy is then applied to the world and its populace. The reasoning is that there is only so much wealth in the world and everyone is entitled to his share. If I have more than someone else, I must have gotten it at his expense. Essentially, I have stolen it from him. Karl Marx taught this concept, dividing all men into "the oppressors and the oppressed." Those who have much are oppressors; those who have less are oppressed.

The truth is, however, that unlike the pie that cannot be made bigger, wealth is not strictly limited, and it *can* be produced. Scripture tells us to "Remember the Lord your God, for it is he who gives you the ability to produce wealth" (Deut. 8:18). Wealth is being produced every day, as a result of ingenuity and hard work. One person's prosperity need not take place at the expense of another.

Is Capitalism to Blame? The argument of our responsibility for the condition of the poor goes further. We are told that while we may not directly exploit the poor ourselves, we are voluntarily part of an economic system which exploits them, and therefore we are culpable. This supposed enemy of the poor is "capitalism."

Every discussion of the plight of the poor involves economics, so I need to address the subject, even if briefly. Interested readers may turn to a number of fine books exploring the issues in depth.[2]

Capitalism is a free market economic system that operates without exterior control. "Control" is left to what economist Adam Smith called the "invisible hand," by which a marketplace naturally orders itself around the needs and wants of the population. The principle of supply and demand determines what sells at what price. The greater the competition, the more goods there are to chose from and the more reasonable prices will be.

It is difficult to understand how one particular system (capitalism) can be blamed for a problem (poverty) that has existed in every country with every conceivable economic structure in human history. A capitalistic society can certainly foster greed and allow the poor to be exploited. But it can also give opportunity to the poor to do what many have done in a free market economy—work themselves out of poverty.

Capitalism permits exploitation because no system can eliminate sin, but capitalism is not built on exploitation. In a free market all parties can often get what they want. You bought this book. Who came out ahead on the transaction? We would hope the bookseller, the publisher, the author, and you, as well as lumbermen, the paper company, the printer, truckers, and a lot of other people who had a part in the process. When you buy milk, who profits from it? You do—you got the milk you wanted. But others profited, including your grocer and the dairy farmer. All parties involved can profit in the buying and selling of goods. One does not have to exploit the others.

The major alternative to capitalism is socialism, and some outspoken Christians are suggesting it is a better alternative.

Socialism is an economic system controlled by the state. It supposedly spreads out the good to all, preventing the development of a rich, land-grabbing elite that oppresses the poor. In socialism, economic power is centralized in the government so that no individual can become rich at the expense of others. Unfortunately, some group has to run this system, and often they become the rich and oppressive elite. In capitalism, a large number of the rich get richer and so do some of the poor. In socialism a small number of the rich get richer and the poor stay poor.

Those who laud socialism as an alternative to capitalism ignore the fact that historically the poor usually fare better in capitalist economies than socialist ones. Furthermore, they fail to recognize that when the incentive of individual profit for labor is removed, because no one is allowed to get ahead, then someone must find a way to motivate people to work. There is just one other way—coercion. Capitalism says, "You scratch my back and I'll scratch yours." Socialism says, "You scratch my back or I'll break yours."

Can capitalism lead to exploitation of the poor? Of course. Does socialism usually lead to the oppression of the poor? Yes. The point is not that capitalism is so good, but that the alternatives are so bad. It isn't a system problem but a sin problem. Any economic system will work where there is no sin. None will work ideally when there is sin. But some may work better than others.

Not Responsible For, but Responsible To. It seems clear that neither God's Word nor an accurate understanding of economics indicates that we who are prosperous, or are living within a capitalistic system, are automatically responsible for making others poor. As we are about to see, what Scripture *does* say is that we are responsible to help the poor. I may not be responsible for the existence of world hunger. But I am responsible to do what I can to relieve it.

So, back to Emerson's question, "Are they *my* poor?" If this means, "Have I made them poor?" in most cases the answer is no. But if it means, "Am I responsible to help the poor?" then the answer is yes, they are indeed my poor. Of course, many *have* exploited the poor and need to face up to it. They should adopt the posture of Zaccheus, who determined to pay back four times over those whom he had cheated (Luke 19:8).

I am not to feel guilty that God has given me abundance. But I am to feel responsible to compassionately and wisely use that abundance to help the less fortunate.

Perhaps the best model for our attitude to the poor and afflicted is that of the Good Samaritan (Luke 10:30-37). In contrast to two religious leaders who passed by, pretending the man didn't exist, when the Samaritan found the poor man who had been stripped and beaten by the robbers, he took pity on him and stopped to help. Note that his reaction was not to feel guilt and remorse. *He* was not responsible for the condition of this man—he had not brutalized him. But he *took* responsibility to care for him.

So, at great inconvenience to himself, he immediately treated and bandaged his wounds, then "put the man on his own donkey, took him to an inn and took care of him." The next day he paid the innkeeper to watch over him until he could come back and resume care himself. Though he was not in any way responsible for having hurt him, he nevertheless took responsibility to help him however he could. Every man is our neighbor, Jesus said, and we are to show mercy and care for him in his need. "Go and do likewise" (Luke 10:37).

Caring for the Poor in Scripture. Care for the poor is a major theme throughout Scripture. The Mosaic law made many provisions for the poor, including these:

> When you reap the harvest of your land, do not reap to the very edges of your field or gather the gleanings of your harvest. Do not go over your vineyard a second time or pick up the grapes that have fallen. Leave them for the poor and the alien. I am the Lord your God. (Lev. 19:9-10)

> Give generously to him [a poor man] and do so without a grudging heart; then because of this the Lord your God will bless you in all your work and in everything you put your hand to. There will always be poor people in the land. Therefore I command you to be openhanded toward your brothers and toward the poor and needy in your land. (Deut. 15:10-11)

Along with many passages in both Testaments, the Book of

Proverbs promises specific reward for helping the poor: "He who is kind to the poor lends to the Lord, and he will reward him for what he has done" (Prov. 19:17). "A generous man will himself be blessed, for he shares his food with the poor" (22:9). "He who gives to the poor will lack nothing, but he who closes his eyes to them receives many curses" (28:27).

The Old Testament prophets boldly spoke forth God's commands to care for the poor:

> I want you to share your food with the hungry and bring right into your own homes those who are helpless, poor and destitute. Clothe those who are cold and don't hide from relatives who need your help. (Isa. 58:7, TLB)

> Feed the hungry! Help those in trouble! Then your light will shine out from the darkness, and the darkness around you shall be as bright as day. And the Lord will guide you continually, and satisfy you with all good things, and keep you healthy too; and you will be like a well-watered garden, like an ever-flowing spring. (Isa. 58:10-11, TLB)

Jesus came to preach the good news to the poor, the captives, the blind, and oppressed (Luke 4:18-19). Of course, the gospel is to the rich and the sighted as well. It is just that the poor and handicapped understand bondage enough to appreciate the concept of deliverance. Also, they are often quicker to recognize their spiritual need because it is not buried under layers of prosperity. Though he himself had little, Jesus made a regular practice of giving to the poor (John 13:29). He also repeatedly commanded care for the poor, promising eternal reward for doing so:

> Then Jesus said to his host, "When you give a luncheon or dinner, do not invite your friends, your brothers or relatives, or your rich neighbors; if you do, they may invite you back and so you will be repaid. But when you give a banquet, invite the poor, the crippled, the lame, the blind, and you will be blessed. Although they cannot repay you, you will be repaid at the resurrection of the righteous." (Luke 14:12-14)

250

Special offerings to help the poor were commonplace in the early church (Acts 11:27-30; 24:17). Church leaders adopted the deep-seated convictions of the Scriptures and their Lord when it came to the poor: "All that they asked was that we should continue to remember the poor, the very thing I was eager to do" (Gal. 2:10). "Religion that God our Father accepts as pure and faultless is this: to look after orphans and widows in their distress and to keep oneself from being polluted by the world" (James 1:27).

In another place James wrote:

> What good is it, my brothers, if a man claims to have faith but has no deeds? Can such faith save him? Suppose a brother or sister is without clothes and daily food. If one of you says to him, "Go, I wish you well; keep warm and well fed," but does nothing about his physical needs, what good is it? (James 2:14-16)

John wrote:

> This is how we know what love is: Jesus Christ laid down his life for us. And we ought to lay down our lives for our brothers. If anyone has material possessions and sees his brother in need but has no pity on him, how can the love of God be in him? Dear children, let us not love with words or tongue but with actions and in truth. This then is how we know that we belong to the truth, and how we set our hearts at rest in his presence. (1 John 3:16-19)

Giving to the poor and helpless and caring for them is so basic to the Christian faith that those who don't do it are not considered true Christians. Indeed, Christ himself says if we feed the hungry, give drink to the thirsty, invite in the stranger, give clothes to the needy, care for the sick, and visit the persecuted, we are doing those things to him: "Come, you who are blessed by my Father, take your inheritance, the kingdom prepared for you since the creation of the world. For I was hungry and you gave me something to eat" (Matt. 25:34-35). Likewise, if we do not do these things, then we are turning our backs on Christ himself. To those who did not help the poor and needy Christ says, "Depart from me, you who are cursed, into the eternal fire prepared for the devil and his angels. For I was hungry and you gave me nothing to eat" (Matt. 25:41-42).

In the full context of Matthew 24–25, those we are to help in their need seem mainly to be Christians, Christ's "brothers," who are in need as a result of persecution for their faith. Our first priority is to care for the needs of those "of the household of faith" (Gal. 6:10). While there is general application to all the world's poor, we should especially seek to find ways to help those persecuted and imprisoned for their faith throughout the world. Specific application should be made, for instance, to our brothers behind the Iron Curtain.

To Christ it appears a simple matter—those who do not care for his poor and needy brothers do not care for him, and therefore do not belong to him. We must ask, "If Christ were on the other side of the street, or the city, or the other side of the world, and he was hungry or thirsty and helpless, or imprisoned for his faith, would we go to help him?" Any professing Christian would have to say, "Yes." But the disturbing thing is, according to his own words in Matthew 25, he *is* in our neighborhood, community, city, country, and across the world, in the form of poor and needy people and especially those persecuted for their faith.

The rich man who passed by poor Lazarus is condemned not for a specific act of exploitation but for his lack of concern and assistance for a man in need (Luke 16:19-31). Christ's words suggest that the rich man should either have brought Lazarus to his table or joined him at the gate. Ignoring the poor is not an option for the godly. Likewise, in the account of the final judgment, where some are identified as righteous sheep and others unrighteous goats, the sin held against the "goats" is not that they did something wrong to those in need, but simply that they failed to do anything right for them (Matt. 25:31-46). Theirs is not a sin of commission, but omission. Yet it is a sin of grave eternal consequence.

We cannot wash our hands of responsibility to the poor by saying, "I'm not doing anything to hurt them." We must actively be doing something to help them.

But What Can We Really Do? "But I'm just one person. And

we're just a small church. How can we eliminate poverty?" The answer is, you can't. Jesus said the poor would always be with us (Mark 14:7). A relief organization produced a poster that asked, "How can you help a billion hungry people?" The answer below was right on target: "One at a time."

Just because I can't take care of all the poor in the world doesn't mean I can't begin by helping one, then two, then five, then ten, and so on. The logic that says, "I can't do everything, so I won't do anything" is straight from the pit of hell.

I must help the poor who are near, but also those who are far away. In fact, most of the truly poor and hungry and persecuted do live in another part of the world from most of us. At this point we usually hear another worn-out excuse: "Well, there's no sense giving my money to hunger relief organizations, since the people never get the food anyway." This is simply untrue. While distribution is sometimes a major challenge, some organizations are more efficient than others, and corrupt officials or soldiers may confiscate some goods, a great deal of food *does* get to hungry people. Our responsibility is to choose the best organization we can find, give our money, pray, and trust God and our fellow servants in the ministry that most or all of the food and other supplies will get to the needy. I think we should take some of our excuses for not feeding the hungry and imagine stating them at the judgment seat of Christ. In light of his uncompromising command to feed the hungry, how many of our excuses will the Lord buy?

Another common statement is this: "Feeding the hungry is just a short-term measure. They will be starving again unless they are taught how to feed themselves." Many development organizations *are* dedicated to doing that very thing—finding and implementing long-term solutions by teaching nationals the kinds of skills and getting them the kinds of equipment that can help them grow and harvest plenty of their own food. Are you giving your money, your time, or your prayers to help them do that?

The poor need not only our provisions but social justice. The law said no one should take advantage of a widow or an orphan, or God would surely punish them (Exod. 22:22). Likewise, aliens were not to be oppressed in any way (Exod. 23:9). The poor were not to be denied justice in a lawsuit. On the other

253

hand, neither were they to be favored just because they were poor (Exod. 23:3, 6). The prophets were particularly concerned about exploitation of the poor (Amos 2:6-7; 5:11-12; 8:4-6). James warns the church against courting and favoring the rich over the poor (James 2:1-13). Concern for the poor was built right into the land laws (Exod. 23:10). "I know that the Lord secures justice for the poor and upholds the cause of the needy" (Ps. 140:12).

Every church and individual Christian must ask, "What are we doing to feed the hungry and help the poor? What are we doing to secure justice for the poor? What are we doing to uphold the cause of the needy?"

Do We Deal with All Poor People the Same Way? There are a number of dangers in how we approach the poor. The worst is to ignore them. Another is to subsidize them—that is, to help them only enough to keep them alive, but not enough to develop the means by which to move out of their poverty. A third danger is to put the poor together into one group, thinking that all poor people are the same. They aren't.

This approach of lumping all poor people together as one is increasingly common in evangelical circles. The all-inclusive term "the poor" is repeatedly used, and we are told we must help "the poor" by doing this and that, as if it did not matter why they are poor. Yet neither Scripture nor experience indicate that all poor people are poor for the same reasons. And they *cannot* be truly helped by the same means.

A person may be poor for any one or combination of the following ten reasons, and no doubt others as well: insufficient natural resources, adverse climate, lack of knowledge or skill, lack of needed technology, catastrophes such as earthquakes or floods, exploitation and oppression by others, personal laziness, wasteful self-indulgence, personal choice to identify with and serve the poor, and religion or worldview. For instance, the Hindu concept of karma does not initiate improvement of circumstances and allows people to starve while one of their major God-given food sources, animals, consumes the other, grain.

So when we say, "This is what we should do to help the poor," it is like saying, "This is what we should do to cure sickness." Cures must be sought and applied not for "sickness" in general, but for cancer, heart disease, diabetes, colitis, allergies, skin rashes, and asthma in particular. It is as ludicrous to use one formula to "help the poor" as it is to give all sick people the same treatment for every disease and expect it to heal them.

If a person is poor because his home has been wiped out in a flood, the solution may be to give him the money, materials, and assistance to help him rebuild his home and reestablish his business. If he is poor because of insufficient natural resources or adverse climate, we can share the knowledge and skills and technology to help him make the best of his situation. If this is impossible, we might help him relocate to a more favorable site.

If he is poor due to exploitation or oppression or injustice in our own country, then we can do what we can to remove or mitigate the oppression. For instance, we can petition and lobby for legal, social, and economic reforms. If he is in another country, we may be able to apply the pressure of international opinion to bring about change. Such situations are difficult, but not impossible. And, of course, we can and must pray.

If he is poor due to his religion or worldview the problem is especially thorny. Certainly we can try to convince him to change his religion and worldview. Sharing the gospel is basic to that. Sadly, we must realize that without a fundamental religious or philosophical change, all the short-term aid we can give will never help solve the long-term problem. This does not mean we should withhold aid—just that we must realize its limitations.

If someone is poor because of a personal desire or conviction to give up his possessions and identify with the poor in order to minister to them, then that may be his calling from God, and certainly it is his choice. We can help him to the extent that he welcomes it, but it isn't our place to "relieve" him of what he desires to embrace.

A person may also be poor because of self-indulgence—"He who loves pleasure will become poor" (Prov. 21:17). A man may make a decent income but waste it on drugs, alcohol, cigarettes, expensive convenience foods, costly recreation, or gambling (including lotteries). Some people manage to meet their family's needs on very low incomes. Others make several times as much money but are always "poor," always in a financial crisis. This is not because their means are too little, but because they are irresponsibly living above their means.

Once we called a government agency to get the names of the needy. We drove to their homes with sacks of food only to find people living in better conditions than some who had contributed the food. I have seen people who perpetually have no money to buy groceries for their family but have a recreational vehicle worth twenty thousand dollars parked in their driveway. The government may consider this poverty, but it clearly is not. Such a person needs only to liquidate his assets to feed his family, then learn to live within his means and not squander his income. The church does not exist to subsidize the irresponsible (and neither should the government), but to supplement the needs of the responsible.

Finally, a person may be poor due to laziness. God's Word explicitly says that the result of laziness will be poverty (Prov. 24:30-34). "Lazy hands make a man poor, but diligent hands bring wealth" (Prov. 10:4). "A sluggard does not plow in season; so at harvest time he looks but finds nothing" (Prov. 20:4). "The fool folds his hands and ruins himself" (Eccles. 4:5). Ultimately, the lazy man is poor by choice.

We are not obligated to rescue a lazy person from his poverty. Indeed, we make a serious error if we try to do so. Every act of provision to the lazy person removes his incentives to be responsible for himself and makes him more dependent on others. Paul commanded the Thessalonian church to stop taking care of the lazy and reminded them of the rule he issued when present with them—"If a man will not work, he shall not eat" (2 Thess. 3:10). The point is not to let people starve—the point is that faced with starvation they will be motivated to work and support themselves as God intends. "The laborer's appetite works for him; his hunger urges him on" (Prov. 16:26).

The lazy and self-indulgent do not need financial support; they need incentives to be no longer lazy and self-indulgent. "Laziness brings on deep sleep, and the shiftless man goes hungry" (Prov. 19:15). It isn't our job to invalidate this principle of God's Word. It isn't our place to make exceptions to God's law of the harvest that says, "A man reaps what he sows" (Gal. 6:7). Any system that feeds the lazy is a corrupt system—it does them and the rest of society a grave disservice and opposes the God-ordained structure of life.

Of course, one can be unemployed without being lazy. We

need to help the unemployed with his material needs, but all the while we need to help him find work. When it isn't to be found, we need to provide it however we can. From time to time, only as a short-term measure, we help the unemployed by giving them work on our church grounds. It is important for their self-respect and their incentives to associate income with work.

If money steadily comes in to the able-bodied person who has done no work, then money eventually becomes disassociated with work. Such people then may begin to believe that society or the church owes them the basic provisions of life. The end of this is laziness and destruction of the self and family, and eventually society. A nation, state, social service, church, or individual that subsidizes the lazy spawns laziness. Rather than eliminating poverty, it breeds it.

The question then is not simply, "What shall we do for the poor," but, "Which poor?" The truly poor must be helped, but they must be helped thoughtfully and carefully, according to the fundamental causes for their poverty, and in the way that is in their long-range best interests.

Distributing Funds to the Poor. General and undiscerning distributions to the poor are catastrophic. Often the "professionally poor" receive the goods while the true poor, those who want to work but can't, or who do work but can't make enough money to provide, are hesitant to take handouts. I have seen a man choose not to work for a year and receive unemployment benefits that are twice as much as another man who works forty hours a week. Worse yet, I have seen the same man change over that one-year period and grow accustomed to not having to work to live. That was ten years ago, and he has not had a job since. He still lives off the misguided "help" of others. Meanwhile he has lost both his self-respect and his family.

There is much to learn from the Old Testament pattern of gleaning. The corners of the fields were left uncut so the poor could have food. But notice the grain was not cut, bundled, processed, ground, bagged, transported, and delivered to the poor. Provided they were able, the poor were to do the work themselves. This way they were neither robbed of their dignity nor made irresponsible by a welfare system requiring no work. The special tithe taken at the end of every third year went to the poor, including the Levite, travelers, fatherless, and widows (Deut. 14:28-29). It did not include resident able-bodied adults who simply preferred not to work for a living.

Our church is not a welfare agency, but we will help the needy. We try to help by giving not just our money or a sack of food, but our personal attention—our time, our skills, and our interest. A widow doesn't just need a check; she needs someone to take her shopping, to sit with her, and pray with her. She may need someone to mow her lawn, fix her fence, drive her to church. She needs material *and* personal support.

What many people need is not more money but personal help in handling the money they have. Good financial counseling, including how to make and stick to a reasonable budget, is a more valuable gift than five hundred dollars to bail someone out of a situation he should never have gotten into in the first place. Direction in how to find and keep a job is far more helpful than putting groceries on a shelf while someone sits home and watches television all day. And when a middle-aged man is laid off his job, he not only needs to find a new one, but he will probably need support to avoid or come out of the paralytic depression that often accompanies such situations.

A church, as well as an individual, needs to develop some sort of screening process that isn't impersonal or dehumanizing but that accurately determines whether a person is in need, and if so, why. Paul said to care for "those widows who are really in need" (1 Tim. 5:3), and went on to say that not every widow qualifies for church support. For instance, the church is not to take over responsibilities that properly belong to family members:

> Give proper recognition to those widows who are really in need. But if a widow has children or grandchildren, these should learn first of all to put their religion into practice by caring for their own family and so repaying their parents and grandparents, for this is pleasing to God. The widow who is really in need and left all alone puts her hope in God and continues night and day to pray and to ask God for help. (1 Tim. 5:3-5)

In light of this principle, our church has approached relatives to encourage them to meet the material needs of a family

258

member they may be neglecting. It is the church's role to help and encourage the family—not to take over its responsibilities.

To distribute funds to the needy a church must have accurate information and ongoing accountability to determine who is needy, why they are needy, *and* what exactly it is that they really need. Otherwise we can be guilty of the very thing our government is—trying to solve every problem at home and overseas by indiscriminately throwing money at it. In doing so, we often decrease incentives and increase dependence and hostility. Attempting to meet some needs by giving money has the same effect as trying to put out a fire by throwing gasoline on it.

Facing Up to the Poor. When asked, "What's the secret to happiness?" Tennessee Williams responded, "Insensitivity." In the short run this is the route many of us take. We become calloused to the plight of the poor, we pretend their condition isn't so bad, that they are all irresponsible, that there is really nothing we can do to help them, or we rationalize that we are already helping enough through paying taxes and occasionally giving to a charitable cause.

Jacques Ellul is right: "Each of us must face up to the poor."[3] We must either do so now, or when we stand before the Judge. Any understanding of what it will mean to postpone our dealing with the poor until we enter the eternal state should motivate us to do so now. "If a man shuts his ears to the cry of the poor, he too will cry out and not be answered" (Prov. 21:13).

It is easy to verbalize concern for the poor, but hard to actually implement it. For some it is a question of getting up the nerve to walk down the block and get to know the poor. For others it is a matter of having to drive twenty miles to find a poor person, and even then not knowing exactly where to look. That is why it is so easy in an affluent country or community to pretend the poor don't exist.

I must ask myself, where are the poor in my budget? Personally, our family gives regularly to relief ministries that bring material help and the gospel to the needy throughout the world. But this is not enough. What current efforts am I making to find a materially needy person and help him? I cannot relate meaningfully to the poor when I am isolated from the poor. Perhaps I must take regular trips away from the cozy suburbs (I live there, too). Perhaps I need also to travel overseas, not as a tourist, but to observe and to meet human need.

Our family has joined others in bringing warm clothes, space heaters, and other supplies to help local Hispanic migrant workers through the cold winter. This has led to opening our homes and church building to develop ongoing relationships. Some of us have studied Spanish to further bridge the gap, deepen friendships, and share the gospel.

Whole churches have become involved in projects of helping the poor. Our church high school group takes periodic trips to Mexico to meet and minister to the poor and to put on evangelistic Bible clubs for inner-city children. Maybe that isn't a lot, but it is a beginning. Many churches can go to the inner city, the jails, the hospitals, and rest homes—wherever there is need.

We need to examine our motives in all this. It is becoming trendy for the middle and upper classes to help the poor. It makes us feel good, soothes our consciences to make a few token gestures to the poor, then return to our lives of materialism. The challenge is not to pat ourselves on the back for giving away a sack of groceries at Christmas, but to integrate caring for the poor into our lifestyles.

We must not just open our pocketbooks, but our homes (Rom. 12:13). It is easy to be hospitable to "our own kind." But what about the poor and needy? I say these things not as an expert in ministering to the poor—on the contrary, I'm only a beginner. I have so very far to go. But if I'm to be a disciple of Jesus Christ, then go I must.

May God one day say of us as he did of King Josiah: "He defended the cause of the poor and needy, and so all went well. Is that not what it means to know me?" (Jer. 22:16).

GIVING AND THE GREAT COMMISSION

Paul once and for all told us what our top priority must be when he said, "What I received I passed on to you as of first importance: that Christ died for our sins according to the Scriptures, that he was buried, that he was raised on the third day according to the Scriptures" (1 Cor. 15:3). The gospel is of first importance. Since the gospel must be spread in order to

achieve its redemptive purpose, the spread of the gospel is likewise of first importance.

But what are our priorities in spreading the gospel? Church budgets often designate less than 10 percent of their income to missions. Even then what is called "missions" often includes ministries directed at reaching our own country or community. Hence, well more than 90 percent of an average local church budget never leaves its own community or country. No matter what our priority is, it obviously isn't foreign missions! If there are any doubts, consider what Ralph Winter wrote:

> The seven hundred million dollars per year Americans give to mission agencies is no more than they give for chewing gum. Americans pay as much for pet food every fifty-two days as they spend annually for foreign missions. A person must overeat by at least $1.50 worth of food per month to maintain one excess pound of flesh. Yet $1.50 per month is more than what 90 percent of all Christians in America give to missions. If the average mission supporter is only five pounds overweight, it means he spends (to his own hurt) at least five times as much as he gives for missions. If he were to chew simple food (as well as not overeat) he could give ten times as much as he does to missions and not modify his standard of living in any other way![4]

Ninety percent of the world's Christian workers live in countries with 10 percent of the world's population. There is a question that corresponds to this statistic: "If you saw ten people trying to lift a huge log, and wanted to help them, and nine of the people were lifting at one end and one on the other, which end would you go to?"

I've heard people say, "We have plenty of needs in our own country and our own community. People here are just as important as people off in some jungle, aren't they? A soul is a soul—God doesn't care whether it comes from our country or another." This philosophy requires several responses. First, the gravity of the needs of those who have no access to the gospel is obviously greater than that of someone living in a country with churches in every community, a Bible on the shelf, gospel programs on the radio, and Christians living next door. (Why

should some hear the gospel many times when others have never heard it at all?)

Furthermore, while it is certainly true we are surrounded by needs and should be meeting them, our country already has great resources. And almost every church and most organizations pour back into it most of their funds, resulting in still greater resources. Most importantly, however, we must realize God is interested in more than the total number of souls in heaven, and *does* in fact care where they come from.

The four living creatures will lead the hosts of heaven in singing praise to the Lamb of God: "With your blood you purchased men for God from every tribe and language and people and nation. You have made them to be a kingdom and priests to serve our God, and they will reign on the earth" (Rev. 5:9-10). The Apostle John was overwhelmed when he saw "a great multitude that no one could count, from every nation, tribe, people and language, standing before the throne and in front of the Lamb" (Rev. 9).

Christ is glorified not simply by the total number of those who worship him but by the fact that this number includes representatives from *every* tribe, language, people, and nation. Therefore, we must be making concerted efforts to see that missionaries, whether from our country or another, reach the "hidden" people who have not yet heard the gospel.

Shortly before he and his four friends were killed by the Auca Indians in their attempts to bring them the gospel, missionary Nate Saint wrote this:

> As we weigh the future and seek the will of God, does it seem right that we should hazard our lives for just a few savages? As we ask ourselves this question, we realize it is the simple intimation of the prophetic Word that there shall be some from every tribe in His presence in the last day, and in our hearts we feel that it is pleasing to Him that we should interest ourselves in making an opening into the Auca prison for Christ.
>
> As we have a high old time this Christmas, may we who know Christ hear the cry of the damned as they hurtle headlong into the Christless night without ever a chance. May we be moved with compassion as our Lord was. May

we shed tears of repentance for these we have failed to bring out of darkness. Beyond the smiling scenes of Bethlehem may we see the crushing agony of Golgotha. May God give us a new vision of His will concerning the lost and our responsibility.[5]

We are motivated first by the glory of God, but are also legitimately moved by the eternal needs of people. Many of us decry the fact that religious liberals don't believe in hell. But there is one shame even greater—that we who *do* believe in hell would make so little effort to keep people from going there.

> "Everyone who calls on the name of the Lord will be saved." How, then, can they call on the one they have not believed in? And how can they believe in the one of whom they have not heard? And how can they hear without someone preaching to them? And how can they preach unless they are sent? (Rom. 10:13-15)

Some of Christ's disciples must leave behind our money and possessions to go reach the thousands of unreached people groups of the world. Some of his disciples must stay where we are, reaching out to those around us and living life-styles that allow us not only to pray for them but to give enough to send and support the others.

Giving to mission work is a tremendous eternal investment opportunity for families and churches. The opportunities for using our financial resources to spread the gospel and strengthen the church all over the world are stronger than they have ever been. I am convinced that the central reason God has provided Christians of the Western world with such great wealth is that we may use it to help fulfill the Great Commission.

I have sometimes heard the expression, "Financing the great commission." Of course, ultimately the Great Commission of Christ to evangelize the world is something we do, not just finance. Giving our money to evangelism is no substitute for our own practice of evangelism, but it is an excellent supplement to it. There is no greater way to invest our money in eternity than in the cause of world missions. All of us should be giving regularly to our local church, which we should encourage in turn to invest an ever larger share of its budget in world missions. Beyond that most of us can invest substantially in the cause of world evangelization through any number of fine missions organizations.

CONCLUSION

One day a Nigerian brother and I were talking in our living room. After he shared what a privilege it was to be visiting our country, I said to him, "It surprises me that you seem to have such a great appreciation for America. So many countries, even those we have helped, seem to be anti-American. But wasn't it from Nigeria that many children were bought or stolen and shipped to America and sold as slaves? With all the countries that resent us without good reason, I'd think you of all people would despise us for what we did. So why don't you?"

I will never forget his measured and penetrating response, spoken slowly with his rich accent: "No matter what else you did, you brought us the gospel . . . and that is all that matters."

Two generations ago a wave of missionaries sent by the church in America had won this man's village, including his parents, to Christ. As a result he and many of his countrymen were raised in Christian homes.

David Bryant asked the question, "Who wouldn't like to end each day, putting our heads on our pillows, confidently saying, 'I know this day my life has counted strategically for Christ's global cause, especially for those currently beyond the reach of the gospel'?" [6]

The need is desperate. Isn't it time we emptied our pockets to help reach the world for Christ? Like those who pray, those who give are partners with those who go (Col. 4:2-4; Phil. 1:4). Some can go. All can pray. All can give. Will you?

As you consider your answer, imagine for a moment the warm voice of one with a different colored skin coming up to you in the eternal kingdom and saying, "Thank you—you brought us the gospel, and that is all that matters."

NOTES
1. Ralph Waldo Emerson, "Self-Reliance," in *Essays and Lectures* (New York: Library of America, 1983), 261-62.

2. See Ronald Nash, *Poverty and Wealth* (Westchester, Ill.: Crossway Books, 1986); John Jefferson Davis, *Your Wealth in God's World* (Phillipsburg, N.J.: Presbyterian and Reformed Publishing Co., 1984); Brian Griffith, *The Creation of Wealth* (Downers Grove, Ill.: Inter-Varsity Press, 1984); and R. C. Sproul Jr., *Money Matters* (Wheaton, Ill.: Tyndale House Publishers, 1985).

3. Jacques Ellul, *Money and Power* (Downers Grove, Ill.: InterVarsity Press, 1984), 151-52.

4. Ralph Winter, "Penetrating the Last Frontiers," quoted in *Christian History Magazine* (Worcester, Penn.: Christian History Institute, 1987), 7(2):30.

5. Elizabeth Elliot, *Through Gates of Splendor* (Wheaton, Ill.: Tyndale House, 1987), 176.

6. David Bryant, *In the Gap* (Ventura, Calif.: Regal Books, 1975), 13.

CHAPTER 15

FUNDING THE CHURCH AND PARACHURCH

God's work done in God's way will never lack God's supply.
Hudson Taylor

Giving is not God's way of raising money. It's his way of raising children.

A distressed woman wrote to Horace Greeley, telling him that her church was going bankrupt. She explained that they had tried fairs, festivals, suppers, mock weddings, and socials, but none had generated enough money to keep the church afloat. "Do you have any suggestions of what else we could do?" she asked. Greeley wrote back, "Why not try religion?"

That was a novel thought. Perhaps if the church did what churches are supposed to do, God and the people would come through and financial needs would be met.

This chapter will evaluate the fund-raising techniques of churches and Christian ministries, the proper use of their funds, and how to choose a worthy ministry to support.

WHY GIVING BEGINS IN THE LOCAL CHURCH

As Christians, we are to share our assets and give our money to meet a variety of spiritual and physical needs, both near and far. Many parachurch groups, such as missions, evangelistic and hunger relief organizations, schools, and campus ministries, provide excellent means through which the church can channel many of its funds. Most of these parachurch organizations, however, are supported mainly by individual donors, not churches.

In the New Testament, giving is not to the Church, the universal body of Christ, but to the church, the local Christian assembly. Even gifts that went other places were given through the church. As the Old Testament temple was a storehouse, the New Testament church is a clearing house, or rather, a conduit or means of channeling gifts to care for the needy and reach the lost.

Normally, I believe, the firstfruits, or tithe, should go directly to the local church. However, I have two major qualifications. First, I don't believe in "storehouse tithing," if that means a church hoards its funds or spends most of them on self-centered frills or monuments to ego and prosperity. Second, there is room for a great deal of giving beyond the tithe, some of which can go directly from the believer to worthy parachurch ministries and some of which should be channeled to these ministries through the church. In fact, when they understand God's principles, many believers can still tithe to their church and end up giving an even larger amount to ministries outside it. I am a local church pastor and a member of a parachurch ministry board, and I am committed to the legitimacy of both.

Giving should be done first to the local church because the giver's primary spiritual community and leadership is in the church. "Electronic churches" are a contradiction in terms. They are programs—not churches. These leaders need to be paid in order to freely devote their time to ministry. "Anyone who receives instruction in the word must share all good things with his instructor" (Gal. 6:6). Paul called this the minister's "right of support" from the church (1 Cor. 9:3-12). He said, "The Lord has commanded that those who preach the gospel should receive their living from the gospel" (1 Cor. 9:14).

Elsewhere Paul said, "The elders who direct the affairs of the church well are worthy of double honor, especially those whose work is preaching and teaching. . . . 'The worker deserves his wages'" (1 Tim. 5:17-18). Not only should the faithful church minister or missionary be paid, he should be paid well. Being paid more than he needs gives him the opportunity to live as an example to the flock, most of whom have considerable discretionary income. On hearing of his salary raise, one pastor told his elders, "This is much more than I need to live on." To this one of the elders responded, "Yes, we know. We want to watch you to see what you do with it."

Giving to the church is also a fine way to support missionaries. Like some other churches, ours has a policy of substantially supporting our missionary families. We prefer to be one of a few churches, preferably in the same area, that make up the bulk of a missionary's support. Among other things, this allows them to avoid the wearing process of spending their furloughs visiting dozens of supporting churches and individuals across the country, which often results in such fatigue that they can't wait to get back to the field so they can rest.

Just as important, by spending their furloughs with us, and perhaps a few other supporting churches in the same area, they develop close and meaningful personal relationships. This helps them not to be just a signature on the bottom of a prayer letter or a picture on a refrigerator door. For the third furlough in a row, one of our missionary families is spending a year with us. In each case the relationship has been greatly deepened, and commitment and prayer support has dramatically increased.

We also budget funds each year to allow at least one of our church leaders to visit families on their mission field. There is nothing like this firsthand exposure both to encourage the missionaries and to fire the missionary zeal of the church leader and thereby the whole church. (Of course, we have to make certain in advance that the missionaries can accommodate visitors and that the visits do not prove to be a drain on the missionaries.)

These are just a few examples of what a church can do that individual donors cannot. If a missionary is supported by a hundred individuals, he has no spiritual community or home base. Likewise, if a church supports a hundred missionaries at $40 a month, it has no missionaries to really call its own. When the local church is left out of the picture, a great deal of finances are unfocused and dissipated in the huge sea of parachurch causes.

No mission boards, youth organizations, media ministries, relief organizations, conference centers, seminaries, or Bible colleges are mentioned in the New Testament. There is only the local church, which filled the role of all of these. But history has demonstrated that there is much that local churches have been either unable or unwilling to do. Parachurch groups have filled in the gap. Many of them have done a remarkable job and have not only been servants of Christ but servants of the churches. Others, unfortunately, have competed with churches, draining their best resources, both human and financial.

As most readers are aware, most local churches and their leaders are not without their problems. But there are often even more serious problems in parachurch groups, especially when it comes to accountability to contributors. One of these difficulties stems from their physical distance from their financial supporters. How can a man whose ministry is in Chicago or Dallas or Los Angeles be accountable in any meaningful way to donors living in a small town in Idaho or upstate New York? How can supporters evaluate whether he is qualified to be an elder according to the biblical standards? One might hope that they sometimes see their pastors in real-life situations and have some feel for their character and qualifications. But all they know about this man and his ministry is what he tells them through the mail or on radio or television.

From a distance, the parachurch organization with its sharp brochures and attractive spokesmen easily outshines the comparatively drab local church where much of our giving goes to pay the utility bills and a pastor who, though a man of integrity, is plain and ordinary and maybe even a little boring. The church is small, the faucets leak, and some of the people are irritating. The custodian wears old overalls and putters about, jangling his mammoth key chain. The closer to home the situation, the less glamour it has.

The same people who would be offended if the church

restroom were unclean say, "I don't want my money to go to pay a custodian to clean the restroom, or to paint a lousy building, or pay the water bill; I want it to go 100 percent to evangelism." So they give to a parachurch group, apparently not understanding that it too has irritable people, buildings, utility bills, restrooms, leaky faucets and custodians with old overalls and key chains.

The television ministers, with their straight teeth and made-up complexions, tell great stories of thousands of conversions. And even though you don't know them personally, surely they must be men of integrity or they wouldn't have made it this far. So why fiddle with the penny-ante local church when you can send your money across the country to the big boys?

Paul didn't encourage individual believers to give to a needy cause on their own but to consolidate their funds and give to and through their local church (1 Cor. 16:2). When they sold their lands and houses, the first Christians "brought the money from the sales and put it at the apostles' feet, and it was distributed to anyone as he had need" (Acts 4:34-35). Notice again that they did not discern on their own where the funds given to God should go. These funds were given to the spiritually qualified church leaders, who distributed them according to their cumulative knowledge, collective wisdom, and leading from the Lord.

The same was true in the Old Testament. While one might give above and beyond his tithes and offerings to the needs of an individual, his basic giving to God was to a centralized location. In the Old Testament that location was the temple, for distribution by the Levites. In the New Testament it is the church—not the building, but the body of Christ—for distribution by the spiritual leaders.

Writing in A.D. 390, John Chrysostom made an interesting point about the early church's giving as part of the corporate body rather than as individuals:

> They did not dare to put their offering into the hands of the needy, nor give it with lofty condescension, but they laid it at the feet of the apostles and made them the masters and distributors of the gift. What a man needed was then taken from the treasurer of the community, not from the private property of individuals. Thereby the givers did not become arrogant.[1]

Most of the undiscerning giving among Christians today can be accounted for by the widespread sense of individuality in giving. "I give to this place and that place, as I see fit, rather than giving to the church to have it distributed as the spiritual leaders see fit. Why? Because it is my money and I will do with it what I want. Furthermore, I enjoy receiving recognition and ego-strokes from these important people I send my money to."

The proliferation of unaccountable and sometimes bogus ministries is directly attributable to this decentralization or dissipation of assets. Those to whom qualified church leaders would never channel money thrive on the sincere but naive giving of Christians who act independently of the local body of Christ. If believers entrusted the distribution of their God-given funds to qualified local church leaders (I know that's the rub—sometimes local church leaders aren't qualified either), the truly worthy parachurch ministries would receive much larger support, and the unworthy ones could be shut down.

"But how can I give to my church when I don't agree with how the money is spent?" First, I would ask myself if it may be that the church leaders are in a better position to judge this than I am. Then, I would ask if my high opinion of the organizations I support instead is based on firsthand knowledge or some media or mailing hype. If I actually saw the operation close up, wouldn't I find as much to disagree with as I do at church?

Furthermore, I would ask myself if I am trying to exercise too much control over the funds. If the Bible tells me to pay taxes (Rom. 13:1-7), knowing some of them will be wasted and even used for bad purposes, surely I can give to God even when I don't feel comfortable with every use of the funds. Of course, I must draw the line somewhere. If my money is going to liberal seminaries, groups that promote immorality, or other clearly unbiblical causes, it is time to speak to my church leaders, rather than quietly give my money elsewhere without confronting the problem.

If after prayerfully and carefully discussing this matter with church leaders, you still cannot in good conscience give regularly and substantially to your church, then perhaps (and I say this with great reservation) it is time to ask God to help you find a church where you can give obediently and wholeheartedly.

I do not encourage church shopping or church hopping. But if you are in a church where you honestly feel you cannot give generously in good conscience, then either your convictions must change or your church must change. To go on as you are, not giving of your firstfruits to your church, in my opinion, is biblically unacceptable.

FUND-RAISING IN THE CHURCH AND PARACHURCH

The very term "fund-raising" is somewhat unfortunate. Churches and parachurch organizations should be receiving funds. But should they be "raising" them? If so, should they raise them in a way that is similar to or distinctly different than their secular counterparts?

"Please be sensitive to God—send us your contribution," pleads a radio and television preacher. A commercial on one of the major Christian television network says, "$10,000 will purchase a satellite earth station, which will receive and bring twenty-four-hour-a-day Christian television to your home! Your family could be in heaven because you cared." One local church used a wedding reception to secure pledges from the guests. When some of them reneged on their commitments, the church took them to court to try to force them to pay. Another church raised funds for its building program by giving cash prizes to those bringing in the highest pledges from other church members.[2]

Though it is no doubt sincere in many cases, the promise of prayer for the giver's needs and loved ones is a classic form of manipulative fund-raising. "You pay, and we'll pray." Prayers are thus bought and sold, reminiscent of the indulgences that outraged Luther and the reformers. One common tactic is the manufactured crisis—"We must receive $300,000 by the end of the month or we'll have to close our doors." Yet $100,000 comes in and the doors stay open.

The preoccupation with lack of money is so great in some churches and organizations that you would think our basic problem—maybe our only problem—is a lack of money. This gets our eyes off God and off the reality of our spiritual revenues in Christ. We forget that our coffer of funds is secondary to our coffer of godliness. Pioneer missionary to China, Hudson Taylor,

273

said, "God's work done in God's way will never lack God's supply." If a work is constantly in want of money, always begging for donations, doesn't it seem logical that it is either not God's work or it is not being done in God's way?

Money is not an organization's greatest asset. God is its greatest asset. Godly people and the rightness of the cause are further assets. Money is simply a function of these three. If it is the right God, the right people, and the right cause, the finances will be right. If Philippians 4:19 is true, why do so many Christian organizations always speak of their financial woes? How many more desperate and exaggerated claims will we hear? How many more times will the Christian public be begged to save God from bankruptcy? David McKenna is right: "Christian fund-raising can become a sad blight on the faith and a legitimate laugh in the press when financial desperation rules a ministry and obsesses a fund-raiser."[3]

It's little wonder that a 1987 Gallup Poll indicated 40 percent of Americans feel only some or very little Christian fund-raising is honest.[4]

GIFTS AND PREMIUMS AS A FUND-RAISING TOOL

A "premium" is a book, tape, pin, plaque, memento, or any tangible object or other benefit that is offered and sent in exchange for giving to an organization. Though a premium is called a "gift," it is actually a means of compensation. If the premium offer is coupled in any way with a request for money, it is not a true gift, but an inducement to give, a means of motivating the recipient to give more or more often.

Many organizations will object to this definition, saying premiums are simply a way of saying thanks and of ministering to their audience, by getting into their hands valuable materials. Other organizations use premium giveaways as a means of studying their audience demographics—to find out who is listening and watching and from where. Granted, some such giveaways are justified, and some fine books and tapes are offered in this way. But why are they usually only promised to those who give certain amounts to the ministry? And why are they promised in advance, rather than quietly sent as a "thank-you" or ministry afterward?

The true test is this: if issuing premiums didn't result in bringing in more money, would they be issued at all? If they were actually a gift, the bottom line would be a cost to the organization, not a profit. It would then be "pointless" to give premiums, precisely because the point all along was not to dispense funds but to generate them. The idea of thanking and ministering to the donor is a true motive in most cases, but it is still a secondary one.

It is a fact that utilizing premiums greatly increases the giving revenues of an organization, and ceasing to use them significantly decreases them. The question is not whether premiums work. They do. Unless we believe the end justifies the means, though, the real question we must ask is not, "Do they work?" but, "Are they right?"

"If you give $20 or more to this ministry, we'll send you free this $15 book, along with a tax deductible receipt." "Wow," the potential giver says. "The book's worth $15 and I'll save the other $5 or more in taxes. This is great—I can give and still come out ahead!"

There are several problems here, the first of which is legal. Though this is a widespread practice, both common sense and the IRS guidelines I have seen indicate that a tax deductible receipt should only be offered for the difference between the retail value of the premium and the amount of the contribution. Actually, the true contribution *is* that difference—whatever goes for the premium is merely a purchase, not a gift.

Also, there is the ethical question of saying a book is worth $15 when it actually costs the organization $5. Wording becomes important here. It may be accurate to say, "If you bought this in a store it would cost $15." This is especially true when the organization prints its own materials and names its own prices, which are often terribly inflated. A ministry may offer a "$59 Bible" that cost it $6 to produce. Is this honest?

"Giving" in response to the offer of a premium is merely buying two things—a material object and a cash rebate, in the form of the tax deductible receipt. Of course, nothing at all is wrong with buying a book or tape or getting a tax savings. The problem is that there is an illusion that true *giving* is taking place when it is really not.

Those who seek only recognition or earthly reward for their

275

giving get that reward but lose their eternal one—Jesus said of them, "They have received their reward in full" (Matt. 6:2). Remember it is the wrong motive that is condemned by Christ—not the public knowledge of the gift. Picture in your mind the judgment seat of Christ, when rewards are dispersed for all our good works. One believer says, "But Lord, didn't you forget something—remember that five hundred dollars I gave to the building fund?" Christ responds, "Remember that brick with your name on it? That was your reward. I hope you enjoyed it."

God looks on the heart, and he knows the real motives for our giving. Everyone's motives are sometimes mixed, so to say that a giver receives no eternal reward simply because others somehow learned about his gift would go beyond what the Scriptures teach. Numbers chapter 7 lists by name the donors to the tabernacle; the centurion who built the synagogue in Capernaum was recognized; and Barnabas, who sold his field and brought the proceeds to the apostles, was recognized for his gift (Acts 4:36-37). But it is doubtful that these donors gave just for the recognition they were given.

I'm thankful that some ministries have been curtailing their use of premiums and public recognition to motivate giving. Perhaps it is time for individual Christians to contact those ministries we believe in and express our discomfort with the premium concept if, in fact, we sense the premiums are given away only for fund-raising. We may also, if the organization's goals are worthy, indicate our commitment to ongoing financial support without receiving anything in return. (Make certain before you criticize that they are specifically making the premium contingent only on a dollar amount sent in. Certain giveaway ministries that send out free books on request have been harshly criticized, even when no appeal for money was actually made in the presentation.) Tell them you believe in their ministry so much you don't need any extra payoff for giving to it. Tell them you would prefer God's reward later to man's reward now.

SHOULD NEEDS BE MADE KNOWN?

Fund-raising attempts can be manipulative, playing not only on guilt but fears and anger. Some organizations come up with a new enemy each month that demands huge amounts of money to combat. Manipulation comes in many subtle forms, right down to the practice of not putting the organization's name on the return address, knowing the recipient might not open it if he knew what it really was.

Some people resent being presented with pictures of starving children and stories of great crises, feeling they are being manipulated into responding. Sometimes this is the case. But I don't agree that showing such pictures or relating true needs is necessarily wrong. If the honest presentation of a real situation results in a sense of conviction, this is not the fault of the presenter. It may well involve the working of the Holy Spirit in the person's life. But to the degree that the presenter of the need twists the knife to get the money to his organization, to that degree he becomes manipulative.

The question of when information becomes manipulation is one of the most difficult and relevant questions any ministry must ask. Richard Foster wrote:

> Christian fund-raising has reached the end of its tether after it has adequately informed us of the need. Convincement is the proper terrain of the Holy Spirit, and we dare not abrogate his work. To be quite honest, I will no longer read appeal letters that have the appropriate sentences underlined in red, and promise to give me a special trinket if I give, and enclose a hand-written (though printed) final note of appeal just in case I have decided to say no. It is with sadness that I refuse to read them, because I am certain that they are often for very good causes; but the approach has moved from information to psychological manipulation.[5]

Some "faith missions" and other organizations do not believe that specific needs or opportunities should be made known but that God should be trusted to move hearts to respond in giving. I certainly respect this position, and God has tremendously blessed it in many lives and ministries. Yet I feel that in many cases conveying specific needs is biblical. Somehow the Philippians were made aware of Paul's material needs and they responded. Paul made the Corinthians aware of the needs of the

Jerusalem poor and went one step further to encourage them to take an offering for that specific need, to be distributed by his "organization" (1 Cor. 16:1-4). In that sense, he moved from information to persuasion, but never to manipulation.

Paul said to the church, "We do not want you to be uninformed, brothers, about the hardships we suffered" (2 Cor. 1:8). He saw other believers as participating in his ministry through their prayers (2 Cor. 1:11). It is difficult to pray effectively when the facts are not known. The same is true of giving. Most often, I give in response to a known need, though admittedly I am sometimes most comfortable when that need has been told me by another, rather than the person with the need.

The abundance of ministries produces a competition for donor's funds. This results in a sense of urgency—we must get these funds before someone else does. This in turn leads to a variety of sales techniques, some of which may be appropriate for sales but inappropriate for ministry, some of which are inappropriate for either.

It also results in the courting of large donors, which seems very close to the favoritism of the rich that James warns against (James 2:1-5). I know of one situation where two wealthy women in their early twenties were placed on the board of a Christian organization. While both are committed Christians with a strong heart for ministry, the motives of the organization were questionable. What more effective but thoroughly unbiblical way to keep, cultivate, or reward a large donor than put him on the board?

Support-raising for missionaries is a challenging and, for many, a very humbling experience. Nevertheless, God can teach some strong lessons and build some strong relationships through it. But the best approach to "support raising" involves the presentation of the ministry, the sharing of the basic facts, and the opportunity to form an ongoing partnership. When it goes beyond that into persuasion—especially in the touting of credentials, the attempt to impress, "the selling of self," and the repeated follow-up contacts pressing for a commitment—it has gone from biblical opportunity-sharing to unbiblical high-pressure fund-raising.

Speaking from a pastor's perspective, it is my opinion that the raising of personal support has gotten out of hand. Support is one thing, but the "support mentality" is another. There are those who come to believe financial support is owed them, no matter what they do, as long as it is generally associated with ministry. For instance, we have had men going to seminary who have asked and, in several cases, clearly expected the church to pay their way. Their assumption was that if they were doing anything for God, the people of God should pick up the tab.

This is an interesting assumption, since no one is expected to pay an engineer or a physical therapist or a nurse to get their training. They take a job, work extra hours, and make sacrifices. If God provides another way, they gladly accept it, but they don't assume someone owes them a free ride. Why should the seminary student be less willing to sacrifice for his sense of calling than those going into other professions?

Now, in fact, our church *does* provide substantial financial assistance to some Bible college and seminary students—as we see their faithful ministries, observe their sacrifices, and are moved by God to help and encourage them. But the initiative comes from us, based on our observation of their lives. It does not and should not come from them, based on their own subjective perception of their value to the body of Christ.

George Müller was a nineteenth-century Englishman who founded orphanages that cared for thousands of homeless children. He was well known for his great faith in God to provide for every need of the ministry. For reasons they could not explain, the hearts of people were often strongly moved at particular times—the exact times they were needed—to provide funds or materials for the orphanages. The following were George Müller's fund-raising guidelines. While I don't believe the first is universally valid, I certainly respect it. The others I think should be practiced by virtually every parachurch organization and church:

1. No funds should ever be solicited. No facts or figures concerning needs are to be revealed by the workers in the orphanage to anyone, except to God in prayer.
2. No debt should ever be incurred.
3. Money contributed for a specific purpose should never be used for any other purpose.

279

4. All accounts should be audited annually by professional auditors.
5. No ego-pandering by publication of donors' names with the amount of their gifts; each donor should be thanked privately.
6. No "names" of prominent or titled persons should be sought for the board or to advertise the institution.
7. The success of the institution should be measured not by the numbers served or by the amounts of money taken in, but by God's blessing on the work, which is expected to be in proportion to the time spent in prayer.[6]

Fund-raising will never rise above the spiritual quality and perspective of the people who lead the church and the Christian organization. In addition to many other qualities, the Christian leader is not to be a lover of money, nor one who will bend the truth for financial gain (1 Tim. 3:3, 8). He must not be "greedy for money" (1 Pet. 5:2). Kenneth Kantzer was right when he wrote:

Christian fund-raising will cease to embarrass us when we have godly leaders whose desire is to give rather than get. Such leadership must be supported by followers who seek nourishment rather than entertainment, and whose giving is motivated by obedience rather than promises or premiums. Those who ask for money and those who respond serve the kingdom best when their primary concern is the careful use of God's resources for taking His Good News to the lost.[7]

FUND-RAISING THROUGH PLEDGES AND FAITH PROMISES

A wide variety of fund-raising gimmicks are used by churches, including raffles, bingo, and other forms of gambling. Whenever one person wins money or prizes that are underwritten by others' having put up money and lost it, no matter what it is called, it is still gambling.

Not all attempts at fund-raising are gimmicks, of course.

Pledges and faith promises are fund-raising devices commonly used both by churches and parachurch ministries. An individual is asked to designate a specific amount of money that he will give by a certain date as it comes in, or in regular monthly installments. Some pledges are merely statements of intention, and the follow-through is left to God and the individual. Others are serious commitments that bring a phone call of reminder from the church when not followed through on. Too many misses and the phone call may turn into a personal visit from the pastor or fund-raiser. Still others are legally binding documents, producing a monthly payment plan little different than buying a house, and resulting in legal liability if defaulted on.

When a pledge is simply an expression of desire or intent, or an agreement with God that is left for his Holy Spirit to enforce, it is not necessarily unscriptural. But when it becomes a legal contract, or anything close to that, left for other men to enforce, it seems to have strayed far from the principles of giving we examined in chapter 13.

It is common in some denominations to bring in a professional fund-raiser or "canvassing director" from outside the membership. No matter how well-intentioned, his presence communicates a sad message. Apparently, the local church lacks the know-how and technique to get money out of pockets and into the plate, so a "pro" who has studied the most effective ways to get money from reluctant people is now going to take a whack at it.

It is difficult to see how hiring a professional fund-raiser fits with the concept of the local church as a giving family, moved by a faith and vision that comes from Christ and is encouraged by her own leaders. The scriptural principles of giving should be taught without apology, and needs can be communicated, but any real pressure toward giving should be left to the Lord of the church as he speaks to the individual heart.

A pledge is usually a commitment made in light of known or anticipated income. A "faith promise" is making a commitment to give a certain amount of money when I don't know where it will come from, but I am trusting God to provide. Its strength is that it can prompt not only trust but discipline and ingenuity to consciously earn and save up money in order to give it to God. The tangible nature of a certain amount, say $500, makes a clear goal, and most of us work well with such goals. This approach also encourages prayers of dependence and provision, since the giver does not know where the full amount is going to come from and must look to God for it.

On the other hand, there is a highly subjective element to the faith promise approach because it assumes God has determined an exact amount of money that is to be provided and given. This amount can be discerned only though the person's "feeling." Since Scripture never says God has determined or will reveal such an amount, to "trust God" for it is to obligate him to something he really hasn't promised in the first place.[8]

When the Macedonians gave "beyond their ability," they were certainly exercising risk-taking faith, which is a more important point than whether or not it corresponded to a particular amount they had promised. Whether one uses the faith promise approach or not, God does honor prayer and faith and dependence. He also always honors sacrificial giving, and the earnest desire to give more substantially in the future.

The faith promise approach has certainly been effective and has produced good results in many churches and individual lives. Another practice is to adopt the positive elements of prayer and dependence, in concert with sacrifice, self-discipline, and ingenuity in generating funds, determining to give to God *whatever amount he chooses to provide* above and beyond our normal income and needs.

Two crucial issues relevant to the subject matter of this chapter have been placed at the back of the book. Appendix B is entitled "Financial Integrity and Accountability in the Church and Parachurch." Appendix C is "The Use of Ministry Funds for Buildings." You may wish to read them separately or in conjunction with the present subject matter.

WHAT TO LOOK FOR WHEN GIVING TO A MINISTRY

As stewards, we are to invest wisely in eternity. This means we must give intelligently, based on an accurate appraisal of those to whom we entrust God's money that he has entrusted to us. In other words, we need to do our homework before we give. Either we must give all funds to our church and trust our leaders to make their decisions carefully, or if we give directly to other ministries, we need to do the homework ourselves. This might include carefully examining the organization's own publications (including financial statements), personally meeting with a ministry representative, visiting an office and observing the actual work as it happens, or consulting with others who are in a position to know more intimately what this ministry is really like.

An organization's literature is often not enough by which to evaluate it. Usually it will present itself in the most positive light. For instance, there will be stories of great revivals and changed lives—but these may be exceptions, exaggerations, and even fabrications. You will almost never hear a report of failure, infighting, immorality, or misappropriation of funds, except in the form of a defense when alleged abuses reach the media.

Some organizations are much more distinctively Christian than others. Some once-Christian schools and benevolence organizations are faithfully supported by the giving and estates of believers who would be heartsick if they really understood that their beneficiaries long ago abandoned their Christian beliefs and are now Christian in name only.

Normally, it is important to give to distinctively Christian organizations. While there are many secular groups that use their funds for benevolent purposes, many other fine Christian groups are doing the same, making it hard to justify missing the opportunity to clearly give in the name of Christ. Why not give, knowing that those extending the gift on your behalf will do so in Christian love, with an awareness of eternal realities, and a sensitivity to spiritual needs as well as physical?

Secular organizations such as the United Way do many good things. But there is a basic philosophical difference. They focus on the short-term needs of people, without a view to their eternal welfare. Most of the organization's workers will not believe in Christ as God's Son, or in redemption, justification by faith, eternal life, or heaven and hell. Given the choice between giving to a secular organization and a distinctively Christian one doing similar work, why not give to the Christian organization?

Every organization has legitimate overhead and "home office" expenses. But some are unnecessarily high. Others have been known to spend well more than half of incoming gifts for further fund-raising efforts. Some devote their greatest energies and resources not to meeting needs, but to selling themselves to the public, cultivating donors, and competing for available funds. Others are very sincere but are culturally insensitive, have poor contacts or distribution methods in foreign countries, and are sometimes attempting short-term solutions that contribute to long-term problems.[9]

Certain characteristics should be looked for in any ministry. They appear below in checklist form to emphasize the fact that we must carefully evaluate any ministry before entrusting our God-given funds to it. You may wish to copy this list and evaluate various ministries in light of it:

❐ A definite and personal sense of commitment to Christ

❐ An unclouded commitment to the authority of Scripture

❐ A strong sense of God's calling to a worthy mission

❐ A prayerful dependence on God more than current strategies or techniques

❐ A clear understanding of the full human dilemma (sin as well as poverty and hunger)

❐ An obvious love and concern for those ministered to

❐ Evidence of maturity, Christ-likeness, and integrity

❐ A spirit of servanthood and humility rather than presumption or arrogance

❐ A God-centered rather than man-centered operation (without constant pictures of or references to particular men.

❐ Furnishings and life-styles that are modest and unpretentious

❐ A responsible use of funds for the purposes they are given

❐ Nonmanipulative fund-raising tactics (no continuous crises or inducements to give that will result in lost reward from God)

❏ A dependable structure of personal and financial accountability

❏ A track record of spiritual fruit

❏ Good personal relationships among ministry staff

❏ A responsibility for the local church

❏ A cooperative rather than competitive relationship with other
ministries, demonstrated in avoiding duplication of efforts

❏ A clear understanding of cross-cultural ministry factors

❏ A view toward long-term accomplishments

❏ A pronounced eternal perspective on life, ministry, and
resources

NOTES
1. John Chrysostom, quoted in *Christian History Magazine* (Worcester,
Penn.: Christian History Institute, 1987), 7(2): 23.
2. Mel Rees, "Church Fund-raising," *Ministry* July 1985: 4.
3. David McKenna, "Financing the Great Commission," *Christianity Today*
15 May 1987: 27.
4. McKenna, 25.
5. Richard Foster, *Freedom of Simplicity* (San Francisco: Harper & Row,
1981), 151.
6. Eugene Habecker, "Biblical Guidelines for Asking and Giving," *Christianity Today* 15 May 1987: 34.
7. Kenneth S. Kantzer, "Reclaiming Our Honor," *Christianity Today* 15
May 1987: 40.
8. Garry Friesen deals with these and other possible weaknesses of the
faith promise approach in his book *Decision Making and the Will of
God* (Portland, Oreg.: Multnomah Press, 1980), 361-67.
9. For example, there have been cases where local farmers in the Third
World have been put out of business by deliveries of free food from
relief organizations. The farmers have worked all year to grow their
crops only to see their food go to waste and their efforts go
unrewarded because no one will buy them when they can get free
food. Consequently, the farmers lose their incentive and no longer
choose to grow food, insuring the crisis will get worse and creating an
endless dependence on the outside world. A sensitive relief organization (and there are some excellent ones) will work toward encouraging
rather than discouraging local workers and the local economy, with a
goal not only of immediate famine relief, but ongoing famine pre-
vention.

PART IV

HANDLING OUR MONEY AND POSSESSIONS

CHAPTER 16

MAKING MONEY, OWNING POSSESSIONS, AND CHOOSING A LIFE-STYLE

Can a man be poor if he is free from want, if he does not covet the belongings of others, if he is rich in the possession of God? Rather, he is poor who possesses much but still craves for more. Tertullian

How different our standard is from Christ's. We ask how much a man gives. Christ asks how much he keeps. Andrew Murray

A critical question for all who would follow Christ is the question of life-style. Do we have the right to earn or to keep large amounts of money? Does Scripture call all disciples to surrender their possessions and "live by faith?" Do we have the right to own private property, and if so, how much? Is it acceptable to God to live comfortable life-styles? Wealthy

289

life-styles? Should we seek to live "simple" life-styles, and if so, how simple? These and related questions are the focus of this chapter.

GOD'S WAY TO EARN MONEY: WORK

Only governments and counterfeiters make money. The rest of us have to inherit it, win it, steal it, or work to earn it. Work is the God-ordained means both of contributing to society and providing for our material needs.

In God's ideal plan, every person is a worker. Regardless of age or handicaps, almost everyone can make a meaningful contribution to family and society through his work, even if it is very simple work or doesn't receive pay. Provided he is able-bodied, at least one family member will normally work for pay. The income he receives from his diligent employment is his God-given means to provide for his family (Prov. 20:4; 1 Tim. 5:8).

Scripture puts great value and emphasis on work as the primary means of making money to meet material needs:

> He who works his land will have abundant food, but he who chases fantasies lacks judgment. (Prov. 12:11)

> The sluggard craves and gets nothing, but the desires of the diligent are fully satisfied. (Prov. 13:4)

> All hard work brings a profit, but mere talk leads only to poverty. (Prov. 14:23)

> Whatever your hand finds to do, do it with all your might. (Eccles. 9:10)

> Make it your ambition to lead a quiet life, to mind your own business and to work with your hands, just as we told you, so that your daily life may win the respect of outsiders and so that you will not be dependent on anybody. (1 Thess. 4:11-12)

> For even when we were with you we gave you this rule: "If a man will not work, he shall not eat." (2 Thess. 3:10)

> Our people must learn to devote themselves to doing what

is good, in order that they may provide for daily necessities and not live unproductive lives. (Titus 3:14)

God gives us the skill to work, and we are to develop our skills to do our work well (Exod. 35:10, 30–36:1). The Christian is to perform his work with this distinct perspective: "Whatever you do, work at it with all your heart, as working for the Lord, not for men, since you know that you will receive an inheritance from the Lord as a reward. It is the Lord Christ you are serving" (Col. 3:23-24).

Employees are expected to do their work diligently and well, knowing that even if their employers don't reward them, God will (Eph. 6:5-8). Employers are to be careful to pay fair wages (Deut. 24:14-15; Jer. 22:13; James 5:4-5). Fair prices and honest scales are to characterize a Christian's business tactics (Deut. 25:13-16; Prov. 16:8; Prov. 20:10). A believer will tell the truth, and the whole truth, when he sells a car, a house, a product, or a service.

PRIVATE OWNERSHIP OF PROPERTY

Clearly, it is right and pleasing to God to earn money by working. But what is to be done with this money? Does a Christian have the right to buy and maintain his own private possessions and land?

The right to private ownership of property was so ingrained in ancient Israel that not even the king had the right to take land that belonged to someone else (1 Kings 21:1-3, 16, 19). The very command, "Thou shalt not steal," is based on the assumption that property can legitimately belong to one person or family and not to others (Exod. 20:15). Even more explicit is the command not to covet your neighbor's house, wife, servant, ox, donkey "or anything that belongs to your neighbor" (Exod. 20:17). The law lays out strict rules for the protection of private property, requiring restitution for all violations of another's property (Exod. 21-22).

At the same time, God told the people, "The land is mine" (Lev. 25:23). As a reminder of whose it was, the land couldn't be used every seventh year (Exod. 23:11). And while land could be bought from others, every fiftieth year was the Jubilee, and the land would be given back to the family it came from (Lev. 25:8-17). Hence, when land was sold the transaction price was to be determined by how many years remained before Jubilee. In a sense, then, the land was not sold at all—"what he is really selling you is the number of crops" (Lev. 25:16).

Every seventh year was the year of release, when all debts were canceled (Deut. 15:1-3). This prevented permanent indebtedness and the servitude it involved. Even in the sixth year the people were to lend generously to those in need, knowing the loan would probably end up being a gift because of the upcoming year of release. To deny a loan for that reason was to "harbor a wicked thought." By giving generously they would assure themselves of reward from God (Deut. 15:9-11).

Both the year of release and the Jubilee were designed to avoid permanent and hopeless poverty. Effectively, they also put a limit on a person's wealth, or at least on his ability to make wealth at the long-term expense of others by accumulating their land. The Jubilee signaled a fresh start for both the poor and the rich—neither would spend a lifetime in extreme wealth or extreme poverty.

We have already seen that the New Testament norm was the sacrificial sharing of one's own property. Yet this in no way negates the private ownership of property—it is what one privately owns that he voluntarily shares with others.

LIFE-STYLES IN THE GOSPELS AND EPISTLES

Some teachers and movements in the church have considered Christ's apostles' life-styles as the norm for all his followers. But a reading of the New Testament demonstrates a striking difference between the itinerant nature of the ministry of Jesus and the apostles and the more settled communities of Christians reflected in the Epistles.

In the Gospels Jesus calls certain people to the radical choice of leaving all to follow him. In Acts 2 and 4 we see radicalism in a temporary community, in light of the great needs created by the Diaspora attending Passover in Jerusalem. But in the Epistles we see settled and established communities much like ours today. These Christians are to have a radical attitude toward money and possessions (2 Cor. 2:8-9) as they live with their families in their homes and carry on their businesses. They are told to "lead a quiet life," "work with your hands," and "not be dependent on anybody" (1 Thess. 4:11-12).

The believer's raising a family and his need for steady employment to provide for that family assume a local existence, with established roots and ties in family, church, and community. Paul said the believers were not to be idle wanderers or parasites, but should "settle down and earn the bread they eat" (2 Thess. 3:12). The challenge to such disciples is to maintain the pilgrim mentality. They are to use their roots and ties to glorify God, not to become complacent or immobilized. They are to be content where they are, yet open to God's direction should he lead them elsewhere.

Life-Styles in the Gospels. Certain Christians today regularly speak out in their magazines, books, and messages against the lukewarmness and materialism of today's Christians. Much of what they have to say is accurate, but they commonly make two critical mistakes. First, they camp in the Gospels and ignore or brush off the Epistles. Yet the Epistles demonstrate the form that churches took after Christ's death, resurrection, and ascension, and after the Holy Spirit was sent to indwell his people. Since the church was not born until after the Gospels, we must look not only to the Gospels but to the Epistles to draw conclusions about the life-styles of Christians.

The second mistake is failing to deal with the larger context of the Gospels themselves, quoting only isolated texts that tell people to give away everything. Readers and listeners get the impressions that Christians who retain any possessions are not true disciples. But a more careful and thorough reading of the Gospels demonstrates exactly what is later borne out in the Epistles—that by God's calling there are *two* kinds of disciples when it comes to the matter of owning money and possessions. An overview of the Gospel of Mark will demonstrate this.[1]

In Mark 1:16-20 Jesus called his first four disciples to leave their fishing business to follow him. Notice that this abandonment of possessions was neither inherently virtuous nor aimless. It was done with a clear purpose in mind, in order to practically facilitate the goal of the call. Christ's ministry was an itinerant one, requiring a great deal of traveling, most of it on foot. To follow him the disciples simply *had* to leave their boats and nets. The real point is not that they left their boats, but that they followed Jesus. That they left behind their major possessions is merely the inevitable result of their response to his call to physically follow him. Furthermore, it appears that even these four apostles did not irreversibly divest themselves of all possessions. Just ten verses after they are said to have left their nets, we are told the apostles went to "the home of Simon and Andrew," where Simon's mother-in-law lived, and presumably his wife and children as well. Also, the Gospels make repeated reference to traveling by boat on the Sea of Galilee. It seems fair to assume that the boat belonged to one or more of the fishermen-turned-apostles. This is substantiated by the fact that Peter and several of the others were back in a boat fishing again within days of Christ's death (John 21:1-3).

Peter later said to his Lord, "We have left everything to follow you" (Mark 10:28-30). He did not say, "We have sold everything," though they may well have liquidated nearly all of their major possessions (Luke 12:32-33). The point is, they "left" their possessions to physically follow Christ.

The apostles were a distinct historical group that have no direct equivalent today. Nonetheless, I believe we can look at them as representatives of a particular calling of God to traveling missionary work. Such work necessitates leaving behind major possessions that would tie one to a specific location and prohibit his ability to go where Jesus calls him.

A Second Kind of Disciple. Mark said that Jesus "saw Levi son of Alphaeus sitting at the tax collector's booth. 'Follow me,' Jesus told him, and Levi got up and followed him" (Mark 2:14). We are not told that Jesus commanded him to sell his possessions and give to the poor. On the contrary, in the very next verse Jesus and the disciples are having a dinner party in Levi's house, along with many other tax collectors and "sinners" (2:15). Levi's house is used to introduce many people to Jesus. Given his profession and the number of people at the party, it was no doubt nicer and larger than the average house.

This is not merely an acceptable use of possessions but an explicitly God-ordained one. Levi, at this point in the narrative, represented a second type of missionary activity that does not involve divesting oneself of all one's possessions but utilizing them for the same ultimate cause.

Not long thereafter, while large crowds were following Jesus, he went up into the hills and chose twelve of his followers to be his apostles (Mark 3:13-19). This unique group would join him in his itinerant ministry, traveling, preaching, and casting out demons. But only twelve were chosen to travel with them. Others of the large crowds were not chosen as apostles but still remained his disciples.

Where did these "disciples but not apostles" go? Where else but back to their families and homes and livestock and jobs? Just as Jesus had for many years served God working as a carpenter and living in a house on a piece of land, so they were to serve God, raising their families, retaining their basic possessions, living and working in their own communities. Clearly, the majority of Christ's followers did not rid themselves of all their possessions, nor were they expected to do so.

On the day Jesus chose the twelve, no doubt there were others who would have been delighted to be chosen also. They may well have been disappointed to have to return to their houses and jobs to serve Christ out of a context of a "normal" life. But notice it was Christ's choice, not theirs. We must not regard their calling as a second-class one, for it was Christ who did the calling.

After Jesus had healed the Gerasene demoniac, "The man who had been demon-possessed begged to go with him" (Mark 5:18). Here we have a man not only willing but eager, indeed almost desperate, to leave all else behind and follow Christ. The next verse is extremely significant: "Jesus did not let him, but said, 'Go home to your family and tell them how much the Lord has done for you, and how he has had mercy on you'" (Mark 5:19). While Christ called the apostles to leave their homes, he called this man to go to his. Indeed "he did not let him" adopt the life-style of the apostles. Christ insisted, in this man's case, that God's kingdom could be better served if his home was his base of operation.

Was this an unproductive calling? Judge by the results: "So the man went away and began to tell in the Decapolis how much Jesus had done for him. And all the people were amazed" (5:20).

This is a clear instance of a man called not to leave all and travel the countryside, but to "settle into" his community, with all that requires in terms of basic shelter, possessions, and vocation, and to *use* his place and possessions to further the kingdom.

Notice again that the central point is not the preference of the individual but the call of Christ. There were two callings of Christ—one to leave family and possessions behind, and one to go back to them. But both callings served the same ultimate purpose—the glory of God and the furtherance of his kingdom.

In the following chapter, Jesus sent the twelve out by twos and told them they were to take no food or money and were to stay in houses with and be fed by those receptive to their message (Mark 6:8-11). Once again we see the two types of disciples. One type is the traveling missionary who takes no possessions except those which facilitate his travels (staff, sandals, and the clothes on his back). The other type is the "settled" disciple who provides the shelter and food and other supplies for the traveling missionary. Note that in order for there to be the first type of disciple, there simply *must* be the second type. In order for some not to have possessions and not have a permanent home and not generate income, others *must* have possessions and a home and generate income to care for themselves *and* the traveling missionaries.

We must also be careful to note that a particular life-style calling of God may change or manifest itself in different ways. Later Jesus told the apostles that his previous orders about what possessions not to carry no longer applied—they were now to take with them a purse, a bag, and even a sword (Luke 22: 35-36).

The Disciple's Eternal Values. In a probing call to discipleship, Jesus said:

> If anyone would come after me, he must deny himself and take up his cross and follow me. For whoever wants to save his life will lose it, but whoever loses his life for me and for the gospel will save it. What good is it for a man to gain the whole world, yet forfeit his soul? Or what can a man give in exchange for his soul? (Mark 8:34-37)

The number of economic terms in these few verses is

striking—save, lose, gain, forfeit, give, and exchange. Every disciple of Jesus is given a radical call as to how he views and handles his money and possessions and every other facet of his life. Whether one has been called to leave his possessions behind for kingdom purposes or to retain ownership for generous and sacrificial kingdom purposes, he must keep in mind that a wrong view of material gain in this world will lure him away from the next. The money and possessions of the present will be of no use on the day his soul is laid bare before his Creator. On that day, money and possessions will be seen as either having facilitated the mission or having blurred or hindered it.

In Mark 10 we meet the rich young man, who is told to leave everything and follow Christ (Mark 10:17-31). This is a critical passage regarding the believer's life-style, for some have claimed that Christ's command to the rich young ruler is a universal call, and that those who do not follow it are not true disciples.

The rich young man asks what he can do to inherit eternal life (10:17). After telling Jesus he has kept the commandments, we are told "Jesus looked at him and loved him" (10:21). This is an important statement, for it reflects Christ's disposition toward this rich man, and also suggests that when he "looked at him" Christ saw and discerned the particular interworkings of the man. Based on his appraisal of the individual man, Jesus issued a particular call to him. This call had more sweeping and immediate financial implications than any he had given, far more than to the Gerasene man or anyone else outside the twelve, perhaps even more than to some of the twelve themselves.

Christ actually gave the man five commands: go, sell, give, come, and follow. "One thing you lack," he said. "Go, sell everything you have and give to the poor, and you will have treasure in heaven. Then come, follow me" (10:21).

This is a particular call given on a particular occasion to a particular man whose particular interworkings were known to the Lord Jesus. Having evaluated the state of his heart, Christ issued the specific command he knew was necessary and best for this specific man. That this is the case is suggested in the passage itself, but in the greater context of both the Gospels and the Epistles, it is the only possible conclusion.

There are two common errors in interpreting this passage.

One is to conclude that Christ always called his disciples to sell their possessions, give to the poor, and go out as missionaries of faith, supported by the rest of the Christian community. Indeed, given this approach, there would be no "rest of the Christian community." We would all own nothing, and be out wandering with no place to stay, no means to travel, to be supported by begging or going on welfare.

The other error, which is equally serious and no doubt more common, is to conclude God *never* calls his disciples to sell all, give to the poor, and follow his call to be a traveling missionary or evangelist. As there were then, so today there are two kinds of disciples—one who gives up his income and all his possessions to further the cause in full-time traveling ministry, and one who maintains an income and retains some of his possessions to generously support the same cause.

There may be some overlap between these two kinds of disciples, such as the many foreign missionaries who settle down locally on the field and retain some possessions, but usually considerably less than their brethren at home. Paul, for instance, was mainly a traveling missionary, yet he settled in Corinth for eighteen months and Ephesus for three years, supporting himself by making tents.

But it is important to note that there is not a third calling of Christ, nor a third kind of disciple who does whatever he feels like with his money and possessions and fails to use them for the ultimate cause. Such people are common today in the Christian community, to be sure, but by the standards of the New Testament they are clearly *not* disciples.

A Summary and Application of the Scriptural Teaching. The command to exercise hospitality is frequent in the New Testament (Rom. 12:13; 1 Tim. 5:10; 1 Pet. 4:9). Obedience to this command not only assumes but virtually demands that one has a house, bed, chair, food, drink, medicine, and other provisions—which might include books, extra clothing, tools, and any number of things—to share with the traveling and needy.

The Apostle John commended Gaius for his hospitality to "the brothers, even though they are strangers to you," and added, "You will do well to send them on their way in a manner worthy of God. It was for the sake of the Name that they went out, receiving no help from the pagans. We ought therefore to show hospitality to such men so that we may work together for the truth" (3 John 5-8). Notice how by making available to him his material resources one type of disciple "work(s) together" with the other.

One of these two kinds of disciples is no more spiritual than the other just because he lives a different life-style. Indeed, Mary of Bethany, perhaps the most devoted of all Christ's disciples, lived in a large house, with considerable possessions, which she and her family made regularly available to the twelve, while Judas Iscariot "left all" to follow Christ. Paul and his traveling ministry team were extremely grateful for the hospitality that so greatly facilitated their ministry (Acts 28:7; Rom. 16:23). Without the support and provision of those disciples called by Jesus to have and share their possessions, those called to leave them simply could not carry out their mission.

But in light of all this, what do we do with Luke 14:33, which reads: "In the same way, any of you who does not give up everything he has cannot be my disciple." Does "give up" mean give away? If it does, then how does this fit with Christ's injunction for even the twelve to have sandals, staffs, and cloaks, and for other disciples to go back to their homes and to provide food and housing for the twelve? How does it fit with the indication that some of his disciples were relatively well-off people who owned land and financially supported him and retained ownership of their property (Luke 8:1-3)?

Given the clear context of both the Gospels and Epistles, "giving up everything" must mean giving up everything to kingdom purposes, surrendering everything to further the one central cause. For some of us, this may involve ridding ourselves of most possessions, but for all of us it must involve dedicating everything we retain to further the kingdom. For those who claim to be disciples, however, it cannot mean hoarding or using kingdom assets for self-indulgence.

DETERMINING A GOD-HONORING LIFE-STYLE

When it comes to our attitude toward wealth, Jesus gave commands. When it comes to our specific possessions and life-style he gave us principles. Jesus did not hand us a precise checklist of what we can and cannot own, and how we can or cannot spend money. Jesus did not say just one thing about money and possessions. He said many things. They were not random clashing noises, but carefully composed melody and harmony to which we must carefully listen as we develop our life-styles. If he gave us a checklist we would not have to depend prayerfully and thoughtfully on him to guide us into the kind of life-style that pleases him.

On the one hand Christ said, "Do not lay up for yourselves treasures on earth" (Matt. 6:19). On the other hand Paul gave these instructions to a pastor:

> Command those who are rich in this present world not to be arrogant nor to put their hope in wealth, which is so uncertain, but to put their hope in God, who richly provides us with everything for our enjoyment. Command them to do good, to be rich in good deeds, and to be generous and willing to share. In this way they will lay up treasure for themselves as a firm foundation for the coming age, so that they may take hold of the life that is truly life. (1 Tim. 6:17-19)

Note that Paul did not say, "Command those who are rich to stop being rich." The implication is that there is a legitimate diversity in the amount of money and possessions owned by Christians. Of course, there is no room for opulence and waste. There is no room for making wealth a source of security, nor for lack of generosity or hospitality, nor for unwillingness to share. Paul left a door open for a Christian to be "rich in this present world"—but *only* if he carefully follows the accompanying guidelines related to his attitude toward and his use of that wealth. The rich are not told they must take a vow of poverty. But they are told, essentially, to take a vow of generosity. They are to be rich in good deeds, quick to share, quick to part with their assets for kingdom causes—and in doing so they will lay up treasures in heaven.

But who are these "rich," and how rich are they? The answer is that almost everyone who reads this book will be rich, both by first-century standards and by global standards today.

300

Statistically, if you have sufficient food, decent clothes, live in a house that keeps the weather out, and own a reasonably reliable means of transportation, you are among the top 15 percent of the world's wealthy.

If you have any money saved, a hobby that requires some equipment or supplies (fishing, hunting, skiing, astronomy, coin collecting, painting), a variety of clothes in your closet, two cars (in any condition), and live in your own home, you are in the top 5 percent of the world's wealthy.

Hence, when we speak of the rich we are not talking about "them" but "us." Those we think of as rich today are really the super-rich, the mega-wealthy. But it is we, the rich, to whom Paul is speaking. The allowance of "rich Christians" by 1 Timothy 6:17 immediately follows a sobering warning of what awaits those who desire to get rich (1 Tim. 6:11). If we are rich, and we are, we need not conclude we are necessarily living in sin. But we must carefully adhere to Paul's instructions of what our attitudes and actions are to be.

We say, "There's nothing wrong with wanting to be rich." God says, "People who want to get rich fall into temptation and a trap and into many foolish and harmful desires that plunge men into ruin and destruction" (1 Tim. 6:9). We say, "There's nothing wrong with being eager to get rich." God says, "One eager to get rich will not go unpunished" (Prov. 28:20). We say, "The rich have it made." Jesus said it is terribly hard for a rich man to enter the kingdom of heaven (Matt. 19:23).

Jesus spoke of the "deceitfulness of wealth" (Mark 4:19). The psalmist warned, "Though your riches increase, do not set your heart on them" (Ps. 62:10). As we saw in chapters 3 and 4, the implications and dangers of materialism are far-reaching. None of us should think himself immune to the value-changing nature of wealth: "To suppose, as we all suppose, that we could be rich and not behave the way the rich behave, is like saying we could drink all day and stay sober."[2]

Nevertheless, the door remains open to legitimate differences in the amount of wealth we own. When Peter pressed Jesus concerning the Lord's plans for John, Christ responded, "What is that to you? You follow me" (John 21:22). Each of us has a call of God. We should not be preoccupied with God's dealing with others, nor should we make unhealthy comparisons with our own situation. There are some things that no Christian should do, such as hoard, live in opulence, or fail to give generously. But there are other things some Christians can rightly do that others cannot or choose not to, such as own land, a home, a car, a business, go on a certain vacation, or spend money on this particular thing or that.

How much money and possessions can we safely keep? Enough to care for our basic needs and some basic wants, but not so much that we are distracted from our basic purpose or that large amounts of money are kept from higher kingdom causes. Not so much that we become proud and independent of the Lord (Deut. 8:13-14) or are distracted from our purpose or insulated from our sense of need to depend on God to provide (Matt. 6:26-29).

Those who want to get rich set themselves up for spiritual disaster. Those who happen to be rich, simply as a result of circumstances, hard work, or wisdom, have done nothing wrong. They need not feel guilty unless they do not make their riches available to the work of God, or their life-styles are self-centered and excessive. John Piper wrote:

> The issue is not how much a person makes. Big industry and big salaries are a fact of our times, and they are not necessarily evil. The evil is in being deceived into thinking a $100,000 salary must be accompanied by a $100,000 life-style. God has made us to be conduits of his grace. The danger is in thinking the conduit should be lined with gold. It shouldn't. Copper will do.[3]

WHY LIVE MORE SIMPLY?

There are a thousand ways to live more simply. We can buy used cars rather than new, and modest houses rather than expensive ones. We don't have to replace old furniture just for appearances. We can mend and wear old clothes, shop at thrift stores, give up recreational shopping, use fewer disposables, cut down on expensive convenience foods, and choose less expensive exercise and recreation. Some of us can carpool, use public transportation, or a bike instead of owning a car or a second car.

But these are things few of us will do unless we have clear and compelling reasons.

One good reason to live more economically is to loosen the grip of materialism on our own lives. Giving away what we don't need is the greatest cure for materialism. How can we expect to embrace the Christian experience of Paul, Luther, Wesley, Müller, Taylor, and a host of others without also embracing their attitude toward possessions and the simple life-style it fostered?

Another good reason for simpler living is the reward God promises us if we lay up treasures in heaven rather than earth. As we saw in earlier chapters, eternal rewards are to be a major motivation in my life. If I choose a smaller house now, investing the difference in cost in God's kingdom, God will give me a bigger house in heaven. Why settle for an expensive necklace now when by selling it and giving the money to meet needs it could contribute toward an imperishable crown in eternity?

Perhaps the clearest reason for a simpler life-style is the dire spiritual need of the world. John Piper wrote:

> We should be content with the simple necessities of life because we could invest the extra we make for what really counts. Three billion people today are outside Jesus Christ. Two-thirds of them have no viable Christian witness in their culture. If they are to hear—and Christ commands that they hear—then cross-cultural missionaries will have to be sent and paid for. All the wealth needed to send this new army of good news ambassadors is already in the church. If we, like Paul, are content with the simple necessities of life, hundreds of millions of dollars in the church would be released to take the gospel to the frontiers. The revolution of joy and freedom it would cause at home would be the best local witness imaginable.[4]

There is also the cause of feeding the hungry and helping the unfortunate. Someone has said, "Live simply that others may simply live." Of course, there is no necessary relationship between my simple living and someone else's being rescued from starvation or reached with the gospel. There is only a relationship if I, in fact, use the resources I have freed up to feed the hungry and reach the lost. This itself assumes I will continue to make a decent wage. For if I go off and pursue simple living for simple living's sake, spending what little I earn on myself, it does no good for anyone else.

In fact, it is a violation of Scripture to try to make only enough money for my family's immediate physical needs. Scripture says, "He who has been stealing must steal no longer, but must work, doing something useful with his own hands, that he may . . ." That he may what? Have just enough to live on? No, ". . . that he may have something to share with those in need" (Eph. 4:28). We should work not only because it is healthy for us, and to care for our families, but to take our excess income and use it to help the needy. Even though it may appear to be nonmaterialistic, earning only enough to meet the needs of myself and family and no more, when I could earn enough to care for others as well, can be a selfish and unchristian philosophy. The point is not merely saying "no" to money and things, but using money and things to say "yes" to God.

Certainly, our life-style must not be characterized by waste. After miraculously feeding the five thousand Jesus told the disciples, "Gather the pieces that are left over. Let nothing be wasted" (John 6:12). If ever waste wasn't an issue, you would think it would be when the provision wasn't worked for in the first place! We should remember Christ's words, "Let nothing be wasted," when we look in our refrigerators and garbage cans.

What keeps us from living on less? One is our love for things. But another is our fear of loneliness and isolation in a life-style change. If simple living was the norm in our contemporary Christian communities, it would be much easier to live that way. But we don't want to be left out or looked at as weird. We need examples to follow, models of a simpler life-style that we cannot just read about but observe firsthand to convince us it is really possible. We need to see people we can respect, people like us who have changed the way they live. We need to make changes together with partners who understand and support our commit-ment to change. This is one reason I highly recommend that you discuss the issues of this book with others.

Once when I preached a message on money, some friends in our church took some radical steps to increase their giving. My wife and I realized that in some areas they were applying my message with more trust and abandon than we were. As a result we were encouraged to further increase our own giving. "Spur one another on toward love and good deeds" (Heb. 10:24). How often, instead, do we lull each other into complacency and materialism?

SIMPLE LIVING OR STRATEGIC LIVING?

During World War II, when fuel was precious, billboards routinely asked the motorist, "Is this trip necessary?" Every resource used for individual convenience was one less resource for the country's central concern, winning the war. As Christians, we are engaged in a great battle that also requires great resources (Eph. 6:12). We too must realize that spending resources on our own private concerns leaves less resources for our kingdom's central concern. We should ask, "Is this thing necessary? Does this thing really contribute to my purpose in being here on this earth? Is this thing an asset to me as a soldier of Christ, or is it a liability?"

Ralph Winter uses the term "wartime life-style," which is generally a more helpful concept than "simple life-style."[5]

If I am devoted to "simple living," I might reject owning a computer because it is modern and nonessential. But if I live a wartime life-style, then the computer may serve as a strategic tool for kingdom purposes. My computer is serving that purpose as I'm writing this book. Likewise, a microwave oven might be a luxury in one case but a useful tool in another, facilitating and freeing time to engage in the cause for which we are fighting. Simple living may be self-centered. Strategic living is kingdom-centered.

The church in America, taking its cue from America, has adopted a peacetime mentality and consequently lives a peacetime life-style. But Scripture says we are at war, not at peace. We must therefore make sacrifices commensurate to the crisis, that the war, our war, may be won. Here is Ralph Winter's practical proposal:

The essential tactic to adopt a wartime life-style is to build on pioneer mission perspective and do so by a very simple and dramatic method. Those who are awakened from the

305

grogginess and stupor of our times can, of course, go as missionaries. But they can also *stay home and deliberately and decisively adopt a missionary support level as their standard of living and their basis of life-style, regardless of their income.* This will free up an unbelievable amount of money—so much in fact that if a million average Presbyterian households were to live within the average Presbyterian minister's salary, it would create at least two billion dollars a year. Yet that happens to be only one-seventh of the amount Americans spend on tobacco. But what a mighty gift to the nations if carefully spent on developmental missions![6]

Of course, the wartime mentality can be taken to such an extreme that we feel it is unfaithful to enjoy any possessions, pleasures, or special activities. This is not my perspective. Even in wartime, it is important to have a break from battle. Soldiers need their rest and recreation. Life is not just utilitarian. There is nothing necessarily wrong with spending some money for modest pleasures that renew and revive us, especially since our battle is a lifetime in duration.

I am thankful that I own "for fun" possessions, such as a bicycle, tennis racket, and running shoes. They aren't necessary; yet they contribute to my physical and mental health. Our family spends money on vacations that aren't necessary, yet they bring personal renewal and valuable relationship-building opportunities with one another and other families as well. My wife and I sometimes go out to dinner, enriching our relationship and renewing our vigor to return to life's battles. The previous quote is not proposing we live at a poverty level, but as if our income was more modest, yet still adequate to allow breathing room for some legitimate recreational spending.

If I have a wartime mentality, then I don't look at an increase in income as an opportunity to spend more but an opportunity to invest more in the cause. I might determine that I will live on a certain amount of money each year, an amount that allows some room for discretionary or recreational spending. All income beyond that I will give to God's kingdom purposes. If he provides twice that basic amount of money I have designated for my living expenses, then I will be giving away 50 percent of my

income. If he provides four times that much I will be giving away 75 percent of it. If my situation radically changed, however, I might need more for my family needs.

Suppose a wife wishes to go to work when the children are grown. Suddenly the family has a second income. Ninety percent of the time this second salary simply ushers in a higher standard of living. Expenditures rise to meet income. But why? The one income has been more than sufficient till this point—for needs, that is, maybe not wants. If the cause of Christ is so worthy, why not devote the entire second income to the cause?

Do such proposals seem strange? If so, why? Have we forgotten that all Christ's disciples are committed to using their money and possessions to further the kingdom cause? Have we distanced ourselves so far from the battlefield that our peacetime life-styles have left us comfortable and complacent, unfit for battle and oblivious to the battle's eternal stakes?

CONCLUSION

"A biblical life-style will necessarily recognize itself as being in opposition to the prevailing values and life-style of its culture. *It is informed by a different view of reality.*"[7]

This view of reality is not a harsh or austere view. It need not lead to ascetic or bare-bones living, or to condemnation of those Christians who have greater opportunity or feel greater liberty to possess more than I do. Rather, it is a view toward the riches of the eternal kingdom. Those who hold such a view are sincerely grateful for the refreshing pleasures and helpful possessions of this life.

But regardless of what material things surround it, this view of reality remains focused on the ultimate pleasure of possessing Christ. Our Lord is pleased when we live in a way that reminds ourselves of and introduces others to what is truly the greatest pleasure and possession of life, both here and hereafter.

NOTES
1. I am indebted here to Gregory L. Waybright's unpublished doctoral thesis, *Discipleship and Possessions in the Gospel of Mark* (Marquette University, 1984).
2. L. P. Smith, quoted by David E. Neff, "Drunk on Money," *Christianity Today* 8 April 1988: 15.

3. John Piper, *Desiring God* (Portland, Oreg.: Multnomah Press, 1986), 166-67.
4. Piper, 157.
5. Ralph Winter, "Reconsecration to a Wartime, Not a Peacetime, Life-Style," *Perspectives on the World Christian Movement,* edited by Ralph Winter and Steven Hawthorne (Pasadena: William Carey Library, 1981), 814.
6. Ralph Winter, "Penetrating the Last Frontiers," quoted in *Christian History Magazine* (Worcester, Penn.: Christian History Institute, 1987), 7(2):30.
7. Peter H. Davids, "New Testament Foundations for Living More Simply," in *Living More Simply,* edited by Ronald J. Sider (Downers Grove, Ill.: InterVarsity Press, 1980), 51.

CHAPTER 17

DEBT: BORROWING
AND LENDING

Their property held them in chains . . . chains which shackled their courage and choked their faith and hampered their judgment and throttled their souls. They think of themselves as owners, whereas it is they rather who are owned: enslaved as they are to their own property, they are not the masters of their money but its slaves. Cyprian

God opposes usury and greed, yet no one realizes this because it is not simple murder and robbery. Rather, usury is a more diverse, insatiable murder and robbery. Martin Luther

I heard the story of a man who jumped off a ten-story building. While onlookers were terrified, the man seemed perfectly calm. As he plummeted by the window of a fifth-story apartment, he

309

looked at the wide-eyed occupant and assured him, "Everything's all right so far."

This apocryphal story reminds me of the attitude many people take toward debt in its early stages—"Everything's all right so far." But what happens to most debtors later on is as predictable and catastrophic as what happened to the man when he finally reached the ground.

The average American family devotes a full one-fourth of its spendable income to outstanding debts.[1] Since 1945, consumer debt in the United States has multiplied thirty-one times. The IRS calculates that the average filer spends more than ten times as much money paying off interest on debts as he gives to charitable causes.

If all evangelical Christians were out of debt, countless millions of dollars could be freed up for the kingdom of God. Our families would also be stronger, since surveys indicate that financial pressures caused by indebtedness are a major factor in more than half of all divorces.

We speak with disdain of the national debt and politicians who cannot limit their spending to available revenues. But the truth is, our national debt is simply an extension of the same irresponsible mentality that many of us consistently demonstrate in our own financial dealings.

Home mortgages, auto loans, credit cards—all are normal to us, but debt evokes severe warnings from God's Word. We must take a closer look at the phenomenon of debt to understand the underlying problem it presents to the Christian.

THE NATURE OF DEBT

Credit is a grant to pay later for what is received now. Interest is the fee the creditor receives and the debtor pays for this grant. Whenever a person goes into debt, he obtains money he has not earned. He is mortgaging his future time, energies, and assets for the money or possessions he receives in the present.

In contrast to a hundred years ago, debt is no longer regarded as an earned privilege for the few but an inalienable right for all. Borrowing has become an integral part of our way of life.

Why are people so anxious to lend me money? Why do banks and credit companies repeatedly badger and beg me to borrow money from them, listing thirty different ways I could use the money? Why do I receive mailings almost every week telling me that $2,000 or $5,000 has already been approved for me, and to receive it I need only sign and send in the attached agreement? The answer is simple—they want me to borrow because they will profit tremendously from my debt.

Why does a credit card statement showing that someone owes $500 say he needs to pay only $35 of it this month? Because the creditors do not want the debt repaid in full. If most people paid the full amount at the end of the month, the lenders would go out of business. To stay in business, they must get me to borrow in the first place, then to pay back less than I owe for a long enough period of time that the extra money I pay them in interest is enough to make their profits and keep them in business.

Our self-centered, debt-centered economy is reminiscent of those electronic "bug-zappers." They emit a light attractive to insects, which blissfully fly right into the trap, only to be mercilessly killed by the electric field. The VISA tags say, "Want me? Buy me!" Zap!

WHAT DOES SCRIPTURE SAY ABOUT DEBT?

Scripture speaks of debt with the utmost sobriety. Debt is warned against throughout Proverbs, God's book of practical wisdom to live skillfully in this life (Prov. 1:13-15; 17:18; 22:26-27; 27:13). Those who are in debt are warned to get out of debt as soon as possible (Prov. 6:1-5). Debt is described as bondage: "The rich rule over the poor, and the borrower is servant to the lender" (Prov. 22:7).

There is some debate over the proper translation of Paul's statement about debt in Romans 13:8. The *New American Standard Bible,* for instance, renders the first part of the verse, "Owe nothing to anyone." This would appear absolutely to prohibit going into debt. On the other hand, the *New International Version* reads, "Let no debt remain outstanding." This might allow debt, but insists that it be paid off as soon as possible.

Hudson Taylor, Charles Spurgeon, and equally credible people held to the interpretation that Romans 13:8 prohibits debt altogether. However, if going into debt is categorically sin, it is difficult to understand why Scripture gives guidelines about lending and even encourages lending under certain circumstances. (See Appendix D, "Lending Money, Charging Interest, and Being Cosignatory to a Loan.") If debt is always sinful, then lending is aiding and abetting sin, and God would therefore never encourage it.

In Scripture, being in a position to lend money to others is considered a blessing, while being in the position of a borrower is considered a curse (Deut. 28:44-45). It seems clear that unless there is an overwhelming need to do so, it is extremely unwise for the children of God to put themselves under the curse of indebtedness.

At the very least, Romans 13:8 clearly indicates that borrowing should not normally be done and no debt should remain outstanding—it should be paid off as soon as possible. The common practice of incurring debt upon debt is a violation of this principle.

When Scripture says, "The borrower is servant to the lender," it does not absolutely forbid debt, but it certainly issues a strong warning against it. God says we are to not be servants of men (1 Cor. 7:23). How can we be fully free to serve God when we are indentured to human creditors?

The Mosaic Law reflects a strong connection between debtors and slaves. Both debts and slavery were canceled in the year of Jubilee and, more often than not, the person was a slave precisely because he was a debtor (Deut. 15:2, 12). The slave was simply a debtor who was unable to pay back his debts, and therefore was sold into slavery. Few sights were (and are) more pathetic than the well-meaning person who thought it necessary to go further and further into debt, one day waking up to realize that he was a slave for life.

The ultimate act of desperation in a time of great famine was to mortgage fields, vineyards, and homes (Neh. 5:2-4). The implication is that such things should never be done under normal circumstances.

Scripture, then, definitely discourages debt. It condemns the misuse of debt and the failure to repay debts (Ps. 37:21; Prov.

3:27-28). We should avoid debt, and in those rare cases where we may end up in debt, we should make every effort to get out of it as soon as possible (2 Kings 4:1; Matt. 5:25-26; 18:23-24).

SOME INITIAL QUESTIONS
BEFORE GOING INTO DEBT

Ultimately, the best credit risks are people who will not borrow in the first place. The worst credit risks are those who always feel they need to borrow. Those who do not have any convictions against credit and borrowing will inevitably find the "need" to do so, while those with the convictions against it will always find other ways to get around it, which boils down to choosing to spend less money. In other words, the less hesitancy you have to go into debt the more probable it is you should not do so.

What questions should I ask when considering whether to go into debt? The basic question is whether the additional money for which I become obligated and the bondage it will create is worth the value that I will receive by getting the money or possessions now.

Is this simply a pattern of debt that will eventually catch up with me? When it comes time for me to repay my debt, what new legitimate needs will I have that my debt will keep me from meeting? Or what new illegitimate wants will I have that will tempt me to go further into debt?

After warning against the dangers of indebtedness, Christian books on finances often proceed to give innumerable cases when borrowing is appropriate, exceptions that include houses, business, education, and even items such as cars and furniture. Others make exceptions for so-called secured loans, those backed by collateral, such as a house or car that can be returned if the debtor cannot pay. While I too feel we cannot absolutely close the door on debt, I am acutely aware that everyone's tendency is to rationalize that his particular situation is one of these exceptional cases. Most of us, I think, should consider debt as theoretically permissible—so we, at least, won't condemn others for it. But debt should be a course we ourselves would never take unless there are clear reasons to do so. Furthermore, we should seek out several wise counselors first to see if they agree that a particular situation does indeed present such a clear and overriding reason.

SOME DEEPER QUESTIONS ABOUT DEBT

Other more basic spiritual questions should be asked before going into debt. Is my not having enough resources for what I want God's way of telling me that it is not his will for me to buy it? Or is it possible that this thing may have been God's will but I don't have the resources to buy it because of past unwise decisions? And if lack of wisdom in the past has put me in a position where I cannot now afford it, wouldn't I do better to learn the lesson by foregoing it until, by his provision and my diligence, I save enough money for it?

I should also ask myself whether I believe that God knows best what my needs are. Since debt is spending money that I don't have, is my choice to go into debt proof that I believe I need more than God has given me the means to have? Since I don't have the resources to buy this particular thing, and since I feel the need for this thing to the point that I'm going to borrow to get it, am I saying God has failed to meet my needs?

If God knows best, and if he knows this thing is one of my needs, then why hasn't he provided the funds? Is he perhaps encouraging me to pray for provision rather than to take things into my own hands by securing a loan? In this age where we seem unwilling to wait for almost anything, does he want me to learn what it means to "wait on the Lord" (Ps. 27:14; Isa. 30:18)? Some people take this approach: "I'll fill out a loan application and if it goes through then I'll take that as God's indication he wants me to borrow the money." The lender's approval of a loan doesn't show God's approval of my decision to go into debt anymore than winning the lottery would demonstrate that God approves of gambling, or stealing ten thousand dollars and getting away with it would indicate he approves of stealing.

Does God provide for those things he wants for us? If so, doesn't that mean that if I can't afford it now, it isn't God's will now? Is securing a loan a means of bypassing or compensating for the insufficient power and provision of God? Borrowing may be a strong statement of my doubts about his power, his goodness, or his love for me, as well as his promises to provide.

Furthermore, even if all is well in answering these questions, by taking out a loan that commits me to certain payments over the next number of months or years, am I presuming upon God? Obviously, if I will require larger amounts of income to make these payments, I am presuming. Oh, I may "know" that I will receive a promotion and pay raise in September, but God has not guaranteed me that. Plans change, companies go out of business, and employees fail to get promotions they knew they were going to get.

But even if my indebtedness doesn't require me to make more income, it will almost invariably require that I continue to make at least as much as I do now. While my income today might be enough to make debt payments over the next twenty years, is it right to assume that I will continue to generate the same level of income for this next twenty years that I do now? While many people's income increases over the years, many others' decreases. Still others incur increased financial commitments that are unanticipated and beyond their control, such as health-related expenses or the need to care for an elderly relative.

We are not sovereign, omniscient, or omnipotent. One of the strongest arguments for not going into debt is that I am not God. Since I don't know and cannot control all that the future holds, how can I be sure that I can pay off debts incurred today? I can be sure God will provide for my basic material needs if I seek first his kingdom, for his Word promises me this (Matt. 6:25-34). But where does it promise me he will provide for all the debts incurred by my own greed, impatience, or presumption? Indeed, if I was seeking first his kingdom, would I be putting myself in bondage to debt in the first place?

Some financial counselors place a home mortgage in a different category from other kinds of indebtedness. One reason it is different is that the loan is secured by the equity of the house. If financial crises arise and the payments can't be made, the home can always be sold and the equity (which is the current sale value of the house minus the amount still owned on the mortgage) can be regained.

Some would even consider buying a reasonably priced house an economy over renting. While rental rates on houses may increase as much as 3 to 6 percent annually, the payments on a straight thirty-year mortgage remain constant throughout the thirty years. Unless the economy is in a bad slump, or the house is located in an area with a depressed economy, the value of the house, if kept in good repair, could increase also at the rate of 3 to 6 percent annually.

The financial problem arising most often for homeowners is caused by their attempting to buy the kind of house they can't really afford. Good financial counseling can help home buyers stay within their economic range. A formula commonly used suggests that the purchase price of a home should not be more than two and one-half times a family's gross annual income. In the same way, the monthly payment for a home mortgage, which includes tax and insurance, should not be much more than a person is presently paying to rent a home. While it is true that most of the monthly mortgage payment during the first years goes for interest, a certain amount is tax deductible. Money paid out for rent is neither tax deductible, nor is any equity being built.

I am mainly addressing the problem of discretionary, unnecessary, and impulsive debt. Not all debt is in the same category. I'm sympathetic, for instance, to the plight of the farmer, the accident victim, the unemployed, the abandoned spouse, and others who find themselves in situations where, after prayer and evaluation, debt seems the best or the only alternative. In such cases we need to trust God to provide the funds to help us get back out of debt as soon as possible.

Trust is a matter of believing that God will take care of my basic needs. When we go into debt, however, we are often not doing so in order to meet basic needs but to fulfill our wants. I need shelter, but do I need this particular two-thousand-square-foot house in this particular neighborhood? I need food, but do I need to eat out at high caliber restaurants? I need clothes, but do I need ones bought at this particular store and bearing this particular label? Of course, none of these things are necessarily wrong. But going into debt to get them may very well be.

Often we define our wants as needs; then through debt we effectively try to maneuver God into a position where he is obligated to "provide" them in the form of our future payments. In reality we have set up the rules of the game and are now expecting him to play by them. A major role reversal has occurred. We have assumed the role of Master and demoted him to the obedient genie who exists to underwrite our causes and fulfill our agendas.

Before going into debt, I must ask myself not only, "Am I mortgaging my future to pay for the whims of my present," but, "Am I mortgaging God by supposing to commit him to a program he may not even approve of?"

Is debt my way of getting around dependence on God? Is debt my way of circumventing the avenue of prayer and patience and waiting on God to provide? What statement do I make to God when I go into debt rather than live on what he has provided? What am I really saying when I take out this loan? How does it reflect on my view of God and on my own spiritual life?

If I "must" go into debt to provide for my "needs," is it because my needs are really wants in disguise? Is it because I have spent so much money on my wants that nothing is left for my needs? Is it because I have robbed God and forfeited his financial blessing by failing to give back to him the firstfruits of my income?

Have I really exhausted all other avenues to avoid going into debt? Have I, for instance, given up expensive activities and liquidated valuable possessions?

Unless we can answer these questions to our satisfaction and God's, we would be wise to stay out of debt.

WHEN DEBT IS ESPECIALLY DANGEROUS

God doesn't promise to bail us out of unwise financial decisions. Many Christians have learned valuable but extremely painful lessons through losing their houses, businesses, and other valued assets for not knowing the difference between presuming upon God and trusting in him. God disciplines his children, and one way he does that is in making us face the consequences of unnecessary debt—and I believe most of our debts *are* unnecessary. When we go into debt for illegitimate reasons, we go on our own. God is not party to our decision and is, therefore, not obligated to fulfill our financial commitment.

Our family's only debt is on our house. We bought the house

with a large down payment, and though we signed a thirty-year contract eleven years ago, we have voluntarily increased monthly payments to the point that we will be out of debt in a few years. By taking measures to get out of debt as soon as possible, we have minimized the amount and duration of our indebtedness.

Though time appears to have justified our original decision, it is our hope and intention to never go into debt again. If we do, it will only be after carefully calculating the cost. Though we don't believe debt is always wrong, having witnessed in count-less lives the effects of debt unwisely incurred, we have become acutely aware of its dangers. Here are some of the most serious ones:

Debt is especially dangerous when a possession's resale value is less than what we owe. This is precisely the case with most items, including cars, clothes, and furniture. Usually the moment I buy such things, I cannot turn around and sell them without a significant loss. If I have bought an asset that can definitely, not just theoretically, be resold at or above its original cost, I can at least get out of the debt by surrendering the asset. The higher the depreciation the greater the risk I am taking, and consequently the greater my presumption in going into debt. But who can know for certain which assets will appreciate? People in our part of the country thought for years houses always appre-ciate—since then many have sold them for $10,000 less than they paid. God is certain. The economy is not.

Debt is especially dangerous when it tempts us to violate our convictions. A Christian couple assumed a large home mortgage based on both their incomes. But when the wife became preg-nant, they realized that in order to keep the house they would have to violate their convictions against leaving their child in a day-care center while the mother worked.

Whenever we make life-style decisions that force us or even tempt us to go against our convictions, the consequences are severe. This couple should never have put themselves in that situation in the first place. Now that they have, it would be far better to realize their error, confess, ask God's forgiveness, and take whatever losses they might need to take in order to get out of their house and into one appropriate for a single income. If they don't do this, they will provide a beautiful house for their children to grow up in while robbing them of what is infinitely

318

more important—the presence of their mother. Like so many of us, in seeking a higher standard of living, this couple is in danger of sacrificing a higher standard of life.

Debt is especially dangerous when we are tempted to rob our primary Creditor (God) to pay our secondary creditors (men). I know Christians who give nothing to God or cut back on their giving in order to make their monthly payments on this item and that. Furthermore, I have talked to believers who say it would be a "poor witness" not to make their car payments and furniture payments and clothing payments and therefore feel that God would have them pay their creditors rather than him. One Christian financial counselor routinely advises people not to give anything to the kingdom of God unless they are completely out of debt, regardless of what got them into debt in the first place.

Why do we expect God to pay for our irresponsibility? Is disobedience to God a better alternative than a "poor witness"? I believe our position should always be to pay God first and others second. If I am faithful in giving to him, only then can I look to him for help in finding the resources to pay others.

But I must also be aware that God will not simply eliminate the consequences of my unwise decisions. If by giving to God I can no longer afford to make payments, then I need to liquidate my assets, take losses where I must, and cut all spending to a minimum to eliminate the payments once and for all. But *never* should I rob God—especially not to pay for my indulgences and unwise decisions!

Debt is especially dangerous when our monthly payments strap us to the point that we have little freedom to respond to the Holy Spirit's promptings to give generously to meet others' needs. Here I am talking not just about the tithe but the freewill giving, that which is above and beyond the minimum as well as the generous sharing of my material assets that should be part of my daily routine. Life presents numerous encounters and opportunities in which I have the privilege of contributing to meet the needs of others. This may involve not only the giving of cash but buying someone groceries or perhaps just taking someone out to lunch or doing a little something special for him. If my indebtedness leaves me unable to respond to God in this way, I have robbed myself and others of incalculable blessings.

Debt is especially dangerous when it restricts our freedom to respond to the Holy Spirit's call to make a move or change. God might desire to move me out of my current neighborhood or job. How rooted am I in my present situation? How dependent am I on the level of income my current job provides? How irreversibly committed am I to the possessions I have amassed and the ongoing financial obligations they entail? Am I so deeply committed to maintaining my present debt-oriented life-style that I cannot escape from it? Let me ask you this—if God called you today to go to the mission field, how long would it take you to free yourself from your financial responsibilities in order to follow him? If God called you today to go to Asia to minister the gospel, to work as a carpenter, to serve as a nurse, how would you respond? Would you simply dismiss the thought because your debts demand a level of ongoing income that effectively immobilizes you?

Is it impossible for you to pull up stakes in response to God's leading because the stakes have been driven so deep by your debt on your tent? Have your debts robbed you of the pilgrim mentality all disciples are to have? In fact, has your indebtedness so deafened you to God's voice that you would not hear or recognize his call to pull up stakes in the first place?

THE CONSEQUENCES OF DEBT

Debt lingers. The new boat is fun for a while, but two years later, when it is sitting in the garage, the motor needs repair, and the kids don't want to ski anymore, you are still paying for it.

Debt causes worry and stress. Stress experts say the bigger a person's mortgage (or any debt), the bigger the stress he experiences. Debt is an enemy of mental health.

Debt causes denial of reality. We drive our bank-financed cars running on credit card gas to open a department store charge account so we can fill our savings and loan funded homes with installment purchased furniture. We are living a lie and hocking our futures to finance it. When the creditors call and write, some people start ignoring them completely, believing that somehow they can go right on spending money they don't have.

Debt leads to dishonesty. I know of Christians who have borrowed money, usually from other Christians, and who repeatedly lie to avoid repayment. "The check's in the mail" is not a funny expression when it has been told you repeatedly by a brother in Christ, enslaved first to debt and now to dishonesty. Some people lie on credit applications, not revealing their true level of debt for fear they would be disqualified for further loans. Others resort to stealing and other criminal acts in desperation stemming from debt.

Debt is addictive. There are striking comparisons between the person deeply in debt and the drug addict. Indeed, the drug addict may be able, with help, to escape his addiction with less future consequences than the debt addict. Those who are in debt with one income will almost always go into debt with two incomes, just as they will if the one income is doubled. Debt is an internal problem. It isn't simply a matter of insufficient funds but insufficient perspective and self-control.

Debt is presumptuous. Scripture says the just shall live by faith. The borrower, however, lives by presumption. Undertaking any significant debt is a gamble that your income will continue to be sufficient to make payments. Scripture states we don't know what a day may bring forth and we must be careful not to presume upon it (Proverbs 27:1).

Debt deprives God of the chance to say no or to provide through a better means. God can give us direction either by providing funds or withholding them. When we borrow, we eliminate one of his options. If we really need something, there are alternatives to debt. One of them, as we will see in the following chapter, is accumulated savings that allows us a margin on which to draw when needed. But if the money for a need isn't there, our first course is to seek provision from God, not the banker (John 14:13-14).

Debt is a major loss of opportunity. If instead of paying 10 percent interest, what if you were receiving 10 percent interest on the same money? Your loss is not simply the amount of interest you are paying. Your true loss is the difference between the money you are losing and the money you could have earned. Much more serious, however, debt is a loss of opportunity to invest in eternity for the kingdom of God. Seen in this light, one of the greatest tragedies of debt is that it will result in loss of eternal rewards.

Debt ties up resources and makes them unavailable for the

kingdom of God. Whenever we teach at our church on the subject of giving, invariably many people respond sincerely in this way: "Now that I understand God's principles of giving, I'd love to double or triple our giving, or even more. But we're so strapped with debt that it is just impossible." The unwise decisions we have made in the past inhibit our present and future generosity. The solution is not to shrug our shoulders helplessly, but to give as much as we can now and commit ourselves to systematically get out of bondage so we can give more in the future.

ILLUSIONS ABOUT DEBT

People go into debt for many reasons, most of which are faulty. Our desire to have certain objects and opportunities clouds our thinking and leads us to rationalize when making the decision to go into debt. Here are some of our primary illusions:

"The money I borrow is mine." In actual fact, borrowed money belongs to us no more than our neighbor's lawnmower belongs to us when we borrow it. We must return borrowed money as surely as we must return his lawnmower. It simply isn't ours.

"The amount I borrow is the amount I'll end up paying back." Wrong again. I will actually end up paying back far more than I borrowed. If I buy a $70,000 house with a $7,000 down payment, borrowing $63,000 at 10 percent on a thirty-year contract, my $70,000 house will actually cost me $200,000. So why call it a $70,000 house when I'm actually paying three times that much?

"Borrowing actually saves me money because of the tax benefits." If I am in the 20 percent tax bracket, whenever I spend $100 on interest that is deductible (not all interest is), then that means I have saved twenty dollars, right? Wrong. In actual fact I haven't saved $20. I have spent $80.

When we were first buying our home eleven years ago, we were advised to take out the longest term loan possible because of the great tax savings generated by deductible interest. I was not particularly astute in financial matters, but when I sat down and looked it over, I kept coming to the conclusion that desiring to pay more interest in order to get tax savings was like giving someone $100 in exchange for $20, then bragging that I had come out $20 ahead. Of course, those in higher tax brackets receive a larger "rebate" on their interest. But this doesn't change the deficit nature of debt. When I am in debt, I am coming out behind, not ahead. My object should be to pay less interest over time, not more.

"It is foolish to pay back a loan that has lower interest than your money can make somewhere else." While this may appear to be true on paper, in actual fact, it overlooks the psychological element. Debt is a burden. Removing debt is removing a burden. As long as I owe money I am a servant. Someone else has a hold on my assets. There is a great mental and spiritual release when we get out of debt. Scripture says we are to let no debt remain outstanding (Rom. 13:8), and doesn't add "unless we can get higher interest on our money somewhere else."

THE LURE OF HOUSES AND CARS

Owning a home is not a God-given right, nor is it even best for many people. It is not always correct to say, "Renting a house is pouring money down the drain." When you rent, you get what you pay for—a home to live in. It is also an incorrect assumption that living in a house always pays off financially. In our area in the last six years, those who rented rather than bought have come out far ahead.

Even when a home is appreciating in value it may have hidden costs, which renters don't have to pick up. A monthly house payment doesn't include the cost of replacing the door, fixing the plumbing, hiring someone to clean the sewer line or fix the broken garage door or rebuild the sagging deck. Nor does it include having to repair or replace the washer, dryer, refrigerator, or anything else that goes bad.

On the other hand, rental property repair expenses have to be paid for some way, and since the landlord is not in business to lose money, he passes on these costs to the renter in higher rental rates. So, if the decision is made to buy instead of rent, make certain that the house is in reasonably good condition and see that a certain amount of the household budget is set aside for repair and replacement. Unless the house is in an economically depressed area, most homeowners find that the growing equity in a house, through debt retirement and property value appreciation, compensates for repair and replacement costs many times over.

Fantastic as they sometimes are, rationalizations about houses often pale in comparison to those about cars. Studies, including those published in the *Wall Street Journal,* prove that it is far less expensive to maintain a used car than to buy a new one. "The cheapest car anyone can ever own is always the car they presently own," and "the longer a car is driven, the cheaper it becomes to operate."[2]

Yet, when we get the "car bug," we deceive ourselves into irrational decisions. A man who was supposed to be on a tight budget tried to explain to me why he had made a wise decision in buying an $8,000 car which got forty miles per gallon to replace his old paid-for car (still running fine) that got only twenty-five miles per gallon. Essentially, this man had committed himself to paying $180 per month in order to "save" $20 per month. In short, he was coming out $160 per month behind. Given the high depreciation on his new car, by the time he was done with his payments it would be worth little more than his old, fully depreciated car. Yet his desire for the new car was so strong it overrode all rational thinking, convincing him that he'd made a wise "investment."

CREDIT CARDS

Seventy-five thousand people each day in the United States receive approval for VISA and MasterCard credit cards. For many of them, it is one of the worst things that could happen. Finance companies that issue credit cards trip over themselves in their attempts to persuade the consumer to take advantage of the "privilege" of having a charge card. They will give clothes, clocks, videos, and cases of soda pop to people willing even to fill out an application form. How easy is it to get credit in America? One pharmacist with an income of $27,000 owns more than 800 credit cards. His line of credit for a single month is $9 million.

Considering that only a century ago it was generally considered a sin for a Christian to be in debt, it is amazing that credit cards have been so widely accepted in the Christian community. In fact, many Christian organizations and even some churches are now accepting credit cards for their donations. I know of at least one Christian college that has sponsored its own credit card for alumni, encouraging them to use it regularly since a small amount of money from each purchase is "given" to the college by the credit card company.

Handed the controls of a deadly weapon with a hair-trigger, many people (*consumers* is the technical term) are being propelled by their credit cards further into irresponsible debt that entails exorbitant interest, often in the neighborhood of 15 to 20 percent annually, and sometimes even more. The person with a $2,000 balance is told he can pay just $75. But he doesn't realize the first $32.50 of that $75 is interest. He goes right on charging "sale" items and digging an ever-deeper hole.

Some people use credit cards simply for the convenience, paying off the full amount owed on every statement, so they don't ever pay interest costs. This is certainly a far wiser use of credit cards than the norm, but it also has its drawbacks. Citibank calculates that a consumer using a credit card will buy 26 percent more than he would if he was carrying cash, even if he pays it all off without interest charges. The convenience of having a credit card is also a liability—its very convenience constitutes temptation.

If you use a credit card and do not pay the full amount when your bill is due, meaning that you leave a balance on which you pay interest, then you should not own a credit card. Furthermore, even if you do pay the full amount when due and therefore avoid interest charges, if it is easier for you to lay down a credit card than to part with cash, then you also should not own a credit card. If you determine to carry a credit card and say, "I won't use it except for emergencies and when I would have used cash anyway," all right. My wife and I do this, and though we rarely use the credit card, we still watch carefully to make sure we don't abuse it. If we ever do, we have vowed to perform plastic surgery—cutting the card in half.

CHURCHES AND DEBT
It is tragic that many churches and denominations spend more on interest payments than they do on world missions. How different

than the people of Israel who "gave more than enough" for the tasks at hand! (Exod. 36:6-7) Debt ties the hands of a church. It allows no movement, no freedom, no flexibility to redistribute funds. If attendance drops, if the economy suffers, if giving dips for whatever reason, then the pastors or missionaries or someone must go unpaid while the building the people moved into ten years ago, which already needs major maintenance, is still being paid for.

Three major Old Testament building programs were mentioned in the Bible, and all of them were financed directly by up-front giving. There was no borrowing, no "temple bonds," not even pledges—just straightforward giving. Did God's Spirit empower Israel to do things that the church he indwells cannot? When churches "have to" borrow money for their budgets or projects, it is time to take a closer look. Normally, lack of money in churches is rooted in lack of conviction in church members. To borrow money without addressing the fundamental issue of conviction in the long run solves no problems and creates a great many.

Countless churches that have gone deeply into debt know the horror stories of buildings never finished and buildings finally finished with auditoriums mostly empty because the church was split or dissipated by money pressures. On the other hand, churches that function debt-free almost invariably have great success stories to tell.

Our church operates on a debt-free basis. We find that if people aren't inclined to give toward a project, even after they have been properly educated concerning it, it is an indication that their heart isn't in it. And if people's hearts aren't in the project, it shouldn't be undertaken. It is healthy to stretch our faith, but no church's endeavors should exceed its convictions.

When you pay as you go, you can take an offering and use it to gauge the hearts of the people. When you borrow, you often find out too late—and the hard way—that people are not in the project. Soon you find they are no longer in the church either.

In the twelve years we have been a church we have continually thanked God for our commitment from the beginning that we would never borrow money. We have been tempted to make an exception or two, but we haven't. If we are to encourage our people to live as much as possible without going into debt, it seems only reasonable that we would operate that way as a church. What is right for church families is right for the church family.

It is interesting how many people emphatically state, "But unless you are already rich you can't build a house or a church building or go into business without borrowing money." This is simply false. There are many debt-free churches and families of every income level. There are also many businessmen, Christian and otherwise, who have saved up money for years in order to go into business debt-free. These are the ones who are able to ride out ups and downs in the economy because they are not saddled by debt. They also don't grow and expand too fast by using other people's money only to find they have overextended themselves.

With discipline, purpose, and patience, a business can be started and maintained without debt, just as a church building project can be. Likewise, the average individual who buys a house for $50,000 with a down payment of $5,000 could have most of his house paid for by diligently saving for six or seven years, and all of it paid for by saving for eleven or twelve—with interest working for him instead of against him. The problem is simply a lack of discipline and patience. Either we cannot make ourselves save substantially, or we are too impatient to wait that long.

GETTING OUT OF DEBT

Scripture makes it clear that if we have borrowed money, whether for good reasons or for bad, it is our responsibility to pay it back as soon as possible (Prov. 3:27-28; Matt. 5:25-26). Not to pay back a debt is to join ranks with the wicked (Ps. 37:21). No matter how legal, the alternative of bankruptcy is normally not a moral option for the Christian.

If you are in debt, two questions are relevant: First, how did you get into debt, and second, how can you get out? The reason the first question is important is to help you in making future decisions. If you have gotten into debt unwisely, you must do

327

more than get out of debt, you must recognize that you made wrong choices and commit yourself to not making them in the future. For you, debt is not the main problem but a symptom of a more basic problem—either greed, impulsiveness, or lack of discipline—that must be dealt with.

How can you get out of debt? First, you must incur no new debts. You must stop borrowing. But in order to stick with this, you must learn to control your spending. Because so many people have ongoing struggles in this area, I have included Appendix E, "Practical Guidelines to Control Spending." You may wish to read it immediately after finishing this chapter.

Systematically list all your debts, and establish a schedule to repay them that is workable within your budget. By comparing the different interest rates on your debts, you may prioritize your debt reduction. All other things being equal, pay off most rapidly those debts at the highest interest.

If your debt is beyond your ability to pay at the prescribed levels, contact your creditor and explain your plan of repayment. Normally creditors will welcome this, since they are often faced with bankruptcies in which they end up receiving little or nothing.

If it is possible for you to do so, eliminate smaller debts and consolidate remaining debts in order to pay as few bills as possible.

In this process, it is usually important to get wise counsel. You may get this from a friend, a counselor, or church leader. In some areas you can contact the Consumer Credit Service, which offers debt counseling at no cost. Liquidate unnecessary assets and use the funds to reduce debts. You may be able to move into less expensive housing, get a cheaper car, sell that boat, and convert other unused or unneeded items to cash.

If you have done everything else and it still seems insufficient, then consider ways to increase your income in order to eliminate your debts. However, if you are already working at a full-time job, more work is not the solution, though it may sometimes be temporarily necessary in order to reverse the consequences of past decisions.

Be patient. It may have taken you five, ten, twenty, or thirty years to get into the financial situation you are in, and it cannot be reversed overnight. However, by following these guidelines, in concert with the other principles of this book, you will be well on your way out of bondage and into the freedom of being able to respond generously to needs and eternal investment opportunities.

CONCLUSION

Good friends of ours went deeply into debt to get into a nice house. They were making house payments of $880 per month in addition to the never-ending hidden costs of homeowning. For several years they experienced real financial bondage, despairing because they wanted to give freely in response to needs God had laid on their hearts, but the house left them no money. Finally they made the difficult and courageous decision to get out of their house, take their losses, and find housing they could afford.

"All I have needed Thy hand hath provided—'Great is thy faithfulness,' Lord, unto me!" We sing it, but do we mean it? Does our life-style of debt allow us to pursue what he has not provided and does not intend for us? Will we take the hard but liberating steps to get ourselves out of the hands of debt and place ourselves in the only hands in which the child of God belongs?

After all is said and done, there remains one debt that all our money and possessions must be unreservedly committed to, yet which we can never retire: "Let no debt remain outstanding, *except* the continuing debt to love one another" (Rom. 13:8). The church father Origen put it this way: "The debt of love is permanent, so we must pay it daily and yet always owe it."

NOTES
1. Larry Burkett, *How to Use Your Money Wisely* (Chicago: Moody Press, 1986), 76.
2. Ron Blue, *Master Your Money* (Nashville: Thomas Nelson), 116, 118.

CHAPTER 18

SAVING, RETIRING, AND INSURING

Make as much as you can, save as much as you can, and give as much as you can. John Wesley

Earthly goods are given to be used, not to be collected. Hoarding is idolatry. Dietrich Bonhoeffer

We live in a society where billions of dollars each year are put into savings accounts, retirement funds, and insurance policies.

Are these wise ways for Christians to steward our God-entrusted funds? Is it unspiritual to have these things? Is it irresponsible not to have them? Are they morally neutral investments that can be used well or poorly depending on our attitude? Do savings and insurance pose significant dangers to us that we have failed to consider? Are there principles of

331

Scripture that we can use to evaluate whether or not they have a legitimate place in our lives?

These are some of the difficult questions we will seek to address in this chapter.

SAVING

Saving in the Scriptures. The purpose of saving is to set money aside for future purposes. By foregoing an expenditure now we make resources available later.

Scripture tells us that the wise man anticipates future needs while the foolish man spends and consumes all his resources with no thought for the future. "In the house of the wise are stores of choice food and oil, but a foolish man devours all he has" (Prov. 21:20).

The believer is to learn from the foresight of God's creatures: "Go to the ant, you sluggard; consider its ways and be wise! It has no commander, no overseer or ruler, yet it stores its provisions in summer and gathers its food at harvest" (Prov. 6:6-8).

To make no provision for predictable times of need is to be foolish. Winters follow summers, and even the ants know there will be no food in the winter unless it is stored up in the summer. It is a short-sighted person who fails to store up provisions (money, food, or materials) for upcoming times of predictable need.

Joseph devised a careful savings plan in light of the famine coming upon Egypt (Gen. 41:25-57). Every year for seven years a large portion of the harvest was stored. Then, when the seven years of famine came, the stores of grain were drawn on.

Saving Today. Often our future needs aren't as predictable as in these biblical examples; ants know winter follows summer, and Joseph was told of the coming famine in a dream. Still, a nurseryman or carpenter and any number of workers may have seasonal incomes, and therefore must discipline themselves to save for the lean months so they don't have to go into debt. Even for those of us with more steady and dependable incomes, it seems wise to set aside enough funds to allow for unanticipated expenses as well as for those opportunities to give and to share that are sure to come our way. Although we live in the most affluent society in human history, eighty-five out of one hundred Americans have less than $250 in savings when they reach age sixty-five.[1]

This means that if they have worked from age twenty, they have managed to save less than six dollars per year. If the reason for this lack of savings was a radical faith in God and a conviction that we should not hang on to resources but give them to meet others' needs, then Americans would be joining ranks with the poor widow of Mark 12 and the Macedonian Christians of 2 Corinthians 8, and this statistic would be no cause for shame. But clearly the reason is not trust in God but self-indulgence, presumption, lack of foresight, and little discipline. God does not bless a lack of savings for such reasons.

In the event of a loss of income or unexpected major expense, the average American family is three to six weeks away from bankruptcy. Yet in other countries with far lower incomes, people have learned to save enough funds to provide for future needs, both expected and unexpected. To be shortsighted is to invite ruin and poverty. To feast in the present without regard to possible or probable famine in the future is to steward our resources poorly and to presume upon God and others to bail us out.

We must learn not only to weigh our expenditures in light of their immediate value but in light of their ultimate cost. Money that is needlessly spent is a double loss. Not only is it gone, but its potential is also gone—had we set it aside it *could* have been multiplying on earth through savings or in heaven as an eternal investment through giving.

For this reason, it is wise not only to give but to save before we spend or we will spend everything and have nothing to save. We will also set ourselves up for falling into debt when a true need arises. Another value of savings is that it is a discipline that both demonstrates and develops authority over our money. Instead of letting our money take us wherever our whims are inclined, by saving we assert our control over it.

Reasons for Saving. After I give the firstfruits to the Lord, I can take money off the top of my paycheck to save for future purposes. For instance, I may be saving for a family vacation.

My plan is not to save money for its own sake but in order to spend it at a later date for a specific purpose.

Long-term savings is a way of using the years of plenty to prepare for the years of less, as Joseph did. Anticipating retirement, I might set aside some money to supplement a reduction of income. Or I might systematically save for my children's college education, which could be ten years away.

Of course, there are also many poor reasons for saving. Some people are money-lovers, who save out of greed. Some save because they are materialists and only want more to spend on themselves later. Others save because they are misers, unwilling to part with their precious money. Still others save out of fear. They are afraid of what the future holds and feel they must accumulate whatever they can in order to ward off the uncertainties ahead. By stockpiling money, they insulate themselves from God and no longer depend on his provision and protection.

It is not accurate either to say, "Saving money is biblical" or "Saving money is unbiblical." It may be either, depending on the reasons.

The Dangers of Hoarding. Hoarding is savings taken to an extreme. It is the accumulating of assets for no particular purpose other than to ward off future disaster or to provide wealth for many years in the future. The classic example of hoarding is the rich fool, who said:

> I will tear down my barns and build bigger ones, and there I will store all my grain and my goods. And I'll say to myself, "You have plenty of good things laid up for many years. Take life easy; eat, drink and be merry." (Luke 12:18-19)

God then called him a fool, told him his life was over, and asked, "Who will get what you have prepared for yourself?" Jesus promised, "This is how it will be with anyone who stores up things for himself but is not rich toward God" (Luke 12:21).

Hoarding goes beyond the level of basic responsibility all of us should take for our lives. It is an attempt to so completely cover our material bases that God is simply unnecessary. Rather than responsibly taking steps for future provision while trusting in God's sovereignty, hoarding is an attempt to exercise our own sovereignty.

One of our nation's ideals is to reach "financial independence." But from whom do we wish to be independent? Are we seeking to be independent of God? Independent of our family? Independent of Christian brothers and sisters? I certainly favor seeking to be independent of the government or my parents in the sense of earning my own living. There is obviously a kind of dependence that is terribly unhealthy. But is there not also a kind of independence that is equally unhealthy?

"Whoever trusts in his riches will fall, but the righteous will thrive like a green leaf" (Prov. 11:28). When we stockpile riches for every conceivable scenario, are we not trusting in our riches rather than God?

The clear teaching of the New Testament is that we are to be the *channels* of money and possessions rather than *storehouses*. Whatever role saving has in our lives, and Scripture seems to allow some latitude, it must always be secondary to giving, and it must never be a substitute for trusting God.

Should We Save for the Coming Disaster? I have read Christian books and heard Christian speakers take the position that all of us should store up years of water and food and even ammunition for our families. One author says believers should secure passports now in order to be prepared to flee the country during a nuclear holocaust. Certain Christian financial counselors encourage us to invest in gold, diamonds, art, and antiques to hedge against various economic catastrophes that may be ahead. One Christian resource suggests the placing of assets in off-shore tax havens and Swiss bank accounts. Numerous such advisers put a great deal of emphasis upon gold, claiming that gold is the ultimate answer to the future security of our families.

It seems to me there is a definite difference between legitimate investing and conscientious planning for the future on the one hand, and a mentality of hoarding and survivalism on the other. Does the same Christ who said we should look to the birds and the lilies and trust our heavenly father to provide for our futures, and that we are to lay up treasures in heaven and not on earth, really want us to stockpile gold bullion and store up two years of freeze-dried food in a bomb shelter?

I can hear a voice saying, "One day you will be sorry when catastrophe strikes, the economy collapses, and you don't have any gold to barter with." But somehow the more closely I read Scripture, then listen to this voice, the more certain I am it is not God's.

When we amass wealth to protect ourselves against imminent doom, where is our faith? Yes, very difficult times may well be ahead. Realism and good planning should characterize the children of God. But panic and hoarding should not.

I remember the reactions of people during past shortages of gasoline, sugar, and other supplies. One man, storing drums of gasoline in his garage, said he was bound and determined to get as much gas as he could before the hoarders got it! If great economic catastrophe awaits us, will it be a time that draws Christians together to share every resource we have, or will it drive us apart to hide in our own basements or mountain retreats, guarding our private stores from others? If we faithfully use our assets for his kingdom now, rather than hoarding them, can we not trust our faithful God to provide for us then?

James had this to say to the wealthy stockpilers found even in the church of his day:

> Now listen, you rich people, weep and wail because of the misery that is coming upon you. Your wealth has rotted . . . your gold and silver are corroded. Their corrosion will testify against you and eat your flesh like fire. You have hoarded wealth in the last days. . . . You have lived on earth in luxury and self-indulgence. (James 5:1-5)

James didn't suggest that these people can avoid future tribulation by hoarding up wealth. On the contrary, it was their hoarding and self-indulgent use of wealth that *assured* them of God's coming judgment in the first place. Far from the solution, hoarding is part of the problem!

The Book of Exodus contains a graphic lesson against hoarding. When God provided manna from heaven to meet the needs of his people, he told them they would have just enough for each day and were not to try to store it up. But Israel had its hoarders, who could not trust God for his promised daily bread.

They determined to save up for the future in case God didn't come through. The result was that God made the stored manna foul, filling it with worms (Exod. 16:16-20). Their "savings" may appear to have simply reflected good planning. But the truth is they were stockpiling, and God would have no part of it.

God will provide for his obedient and responsible children. Any savings or retirement or insurance or survival plan that draws my attention from this fact is undermining my relationship with God.

Distinguishing Saving from Hoarding. There is a definite difference between responsible saving and greedy hoarding. Saving is a means of not presuming upon God. Hoarding is a means of replacing God. Saving can be a means of not presuming upon others to assume responsibility for my own irresponsible lack of foresight. Hoarding is a means of replacing others who would have helped me in a time of need.

Ants only store what they need. The more hostile the climate, the larger the anthill because more storage space is needed. But the milder the climate, the smaller the anthill, because ants only store for the coming winter, not for a decade of winters.

When I save, I lay something aside for future need. If I sense God has called on me to do so, I will give it away to meet a greater need for others. When I hoard, I am unwilling to part with it to meet the needs of others.

The fundamental difference between saving and hoarding is not simply the amount but the attitude. Nonetheless, there is a vast difference between savings of five hundred or even a few thousand dollars for a "rainy day" and savings of a quarter of a million dollars that could last a rainy decade. Some, in fact, lay up more than enough to survive a stormy century! In seeking to lay up for our future needs, we must not neglect God's needy. "God pours out his choicest blessings on those who are anxious that nothing shall stick to their hands. Individuals who value the rainy day above the present agony of the world will get no blessing from God."[2]

Saving for Retirement. Most people pay Social Security taxes and have no choice in the matter. Many people have pensions and retirement plans through their work and may have little control over them either. However, people are usually advised to

337

maintain their own retirement programs in addition to Social Security and those provided through their work. Financial counselors speak of the three-legged stool of retirement—Social Security, employee retirement programs, and individual savings (often through Individual Retirement Accounts and other investments).

We must ask the basic question of retirement savings that we asked of savings in general. Is this hedging our bets? Is this a backup in case God doesn't come through? How is this different from the rich fool, storing up for his later years to live out his life in comfort and security?

How much is reasonable and responsible to save for retirement? At what point does reasonable saving cross the line and become greedy hoarding? I must also ask what would happen if I took part of the funds I would otherwise put into retirement and invested them in the kingdom of God. Financial counselors would tell me I would be "jeopardizing my retirement years." Is it possible that God might suggest I would be "enhancing my eternal years?" If I waste the money or am just a poor planner, that is one thing. But will God really fail me if I invest these funds in his kingdom in an honest effort to obey his words in Matthew 6:19-21 and many other passages?

I emphatically agree with financial counselor Larry Burkett's assessment of the saving-for-retirement obsession currently at work not only in our culture but the church:

> Retirement planning so dominates the thinking of Christians who have sizable incomes that they overkill in this area enormously. The fear of doing without in the future causes many Christians to rob God's work of the very funds He has provided. These monies are tucked away in retirement accounts for twenty to forty years. God's Word does *not* prohibit but rather encourages saving for the future, including retirement (Prov. 6:6-11; 21:20), but the example of the rich fool, given by the Lord in Luke 12:16-20, should be a clear direction that God's balance is "when in doubt—give; don't hoard."[3]

The rich fool never had the opportunity to use the money and possessions he had stockpiled for himself. Will our own excess funds hoarded for the future one day become as filled with worms as Israel's hoarded manna?

Can Any Resources Remain "Untouchable"? The goal of much retirement planning is to provide a regular monthly interest income sufficient to meet all needs, without ever touching the principal that generates the interest. This way it is impossible to outlive our money.

Should this be the Christian's goal? I met with a man who had inherited a million dollars and wanted to invest it in God's kingdom. A Christian financial counselor told him, "Whatever you do, just give away the interest earnings, not the principal. Remember, the principal is always untouchable."

When the man asked my opinion, I shared with him that, no matter what he ended up deciding, he could not tell God the principal was untouchable. Who are we to declare any resource off-limits to the one who provided it and the one to whom it really belongs? The principal is his as much as the interest. And, contrary to what many seem to think, he knows how to invest the principal as well as the interest. And he also knows how to take care of our needs without a million dollars in the bank!

If you have a large amount of money, God may desire you to give it all away at once. Or perhaps he will lead you to give more gradually from the principal, so that the amount steadily decreases over the years. You may still choose to save a reasonable amount of money to provide for your own basic needs. But beyond those basics? This is a question we must prayerfully consider in light of the Scriptures, not just the financial columns and talk shows.

Like many pastors, I have elected not to participate in the Social Security system (that option isn't open to most people). Furthermore, until five years ago my church did not provide a retirement program. Because two of the "three legs of the retirement stool" were missing, it seemed wise for me put money in IRAs and have some small investments in mutual funds. When our church initiated a better-than-average retirement program, I began to cut back on the investments and just kept the IRAs without adding to them.

All things considered, I now have one and a half of the three retirement legs. "But a stool with one or two legs can't hold up."

That is where God comes in—I want to be sure the stool doesn't hold up on its own. I want to be sure God is holding it up. I don't feel right asking him to hold up a stool when I haven't taken reasonable steps to put on a leg or two. Yet, I also don't feel right having taken everything into my hands and left no material needs for him to provide or me to trust or pray for in the future.

A financial counselor would tell me I am not laying up nearly enough for retirement. On the other hand, when I read the Scriptures, I sometimes wonder if I am laying up too much. I live in this tension, and I suppose it will never be resolved. But I also know that whatever posture I take with savings, I must leave room, a great deal of room, for God. For it is God, not a retirement fund, in whom I must trust.

The rich fool was a fool because he took matters into his own hands, planned for his own retirement, but did not make sure his heart and life were right with God. He never consulted with the Creator of the Universe as to what he should do with his money or the rest of his life. I do not want to be a fool by not planning for the future. But I also don't want to be a fool by overplanning for it. Most of all, I want to make plans for the *right* future, the eternal one.

Many of us have accumulated not just financial reserves, but possessions of considerable value. At any time not just our savings but our other material assets must be considered fair game for divine distribution. This applies to everything we have, but it seems to me we should be especially quick to evaluate luxury items and other things that are unnecessary yet financially valuable. Antiques, art, coins, and other collections may be of great financial worth and could be used for strategic purpose in the kingdom of God—but not when they are lying in a safe.

Is God calling us to liquidate some of these and invest them in his kingdom? Are we willing to seek his will in this matter through diligent prayer and biblical meditation? If anything we have is off-limits to God, if it is not fair game for prayerful dialogue, then let us be honest about it—we aren't stewards, we're embezzlers. We aren't serving God, we are playing God.

Retirement from What and for What? Our strong tendency is to see financial planning through cultural rather than biblical eyes.

For instance, where did we get our concepts about retirement in the first place? What do we read in Scripture about retirement and saving up for retirement? Try doing a biblical study on the subject—I can guarantee you, it won't take you long! And how many people in other places and times in history have been able to even consider the option of retirement or of saving up money to last twenty-plus years?

When it comes to the "retirement dream," we must ask, "Whose dream is it?" It is the American dream, not necessarily God's dream. For some people, retirement has replaced the promised return of Christ as the new "blessed hope," the major future event of which we live in anticipation.

When a man retires at sixty-five, studies show his chances of a fatal heart attack immediately double. Perhaps this is because our minds and bodies were not made for an arbitrary day of shutdown. Nowhere in Scripture do we see God calling healthy people to stop working. Of course, it is perfectly legitimate to work without pay. It is your option to give labor to ministry and volunteer work rather than to your present job. But as long as God has us in this world, he has work for us to do. The hours may be shorter, the work different, the pay lower or nonexistent, but he has no desire for us to take still-productive minds and bodies and permanently lay them on a beach, lose them on a golf course, or lock them in a dark living room watching game shows.

If you have saved for retirement and no longer have need to work for pay, then work for God, for the church, for the poor, for underprivileged children. And don't forget the great opportunity that is yours to go as a financially self-supported missionary, for two or five or ten years or whatever God has for you. If you are here, God isn't done with you. In fact, your most fruitful years of ministry may be ahead. That is true whether you are in a retirement home or anywhere else—God has a unique ministry for you.

Now, if your purpose in laying up funds for retirement is to become a self-supported missionary at home or overseas, that sheds a different light on the subject. The rich fool was not rich toward God. If you are motivated by a desire to be freed to serve him more effectively, then he will view your retirement savings differently than those of one who is concerned only for his

341

comfort and pleasures and not for God's kingdom.

How Much Is Enough? Is saving large amounts of money for retirement as absolutely essential as we are constantly told in this affluent society? Reading 2 Corinthians 8:3-15, can you pick up even a hint about the need or the wisdom of saving up money for retirement? If the Macedonian Christians, surrounded by virtually no material things, and giving beyond their means to the point of leaving themselves impoverished, did not need to think of tomorrow, why do we, surrounded with all our material wealth, need to be so concerned about thirty years from now?

We may use retirement programs for good purpose, but they are just one more tool the Provider can use. He, not they, is the heart and soul of our future well-being. The truth is that we really do not *need* retirement programs. I am not saying that we cannot use them and should not have them—only that, as children of God, we do not *need* them. Our brothers and sisters in other ages, as well as most of those today in other places, did not and do not have retirement programs. Yet they found and find God absolutely sufficient to meet their needs.

Since most of us have some sort of retirement savings, perhaps the burning question is, how much is really enough? Once again, we must look at it in terms of the available alternatives to invest in eternity. It is not an overstatement to say that if even half the funds tied up in the retirement programs of all Christians were made available to Christian ministries today, the cause of world missions would be propelled forward as never before. This is *not* simply because of the value of the money itself, though its value is great, but because with the giving of such treasure would be the giving of hearts and the corresponding prayer and commitment that God would use to reach the world.

How much is too much? I cannot answer the question for you. I have a hard enough time trying to figure it out for myself. But I do know that each of us must ask the question. And we must also shut out the distracting noises of the world, put our ear to God's Word, and quietly listen for his answer.

INSURANCE
The Nature and Implications of Insurance. Insurance is a

guarantee against loss. By purchasing an insurance contract or policy at a comparatively small rate, the purchaser is assured of recovering from a large loss should it occur. Both possessions and people can be insured. Possessions most often insured are a person's house and car, and most of the things therein. Buildings, boats, collections, weapons, books, businesses, and almost anything else can be insured—even the hands of professional musicians. Common forms of insurance on people are medical and disability insurance and life insurance.

There are obvious benefits to insurance of all varieties. For an affordable amount of money a person can avoid or be compensated for considerable losses. If theft, fire, accident, disease, or death occurs, people are very happy they have insurance. If, on the other hand, these things don't occur, they are happier still and glad to have parted with their money just for the peace of mind insurance has brought them in the meantime.

There are laws that relate to minimal liability insurance for automobiles, and there are regulations for deeds, permits, and loans related to having fire insurance on houses. In such cases, insurance is not even an issue for the Christian. He simply obeys the law (Rom. 13:1-7).

Are there any biblical principles that suggest insurance may have any disadvantages or dangers to the believer? Perhaps one is a loss of the perceived need to trust in God's sovereign hand. Scripture teaches that God desires to develop our character through trial and losses. When everything—except perhaps certain things of sentimental value—is restored when a house burns down or catastrophe strikes, we are saved of much heartache, but are we also saved of the need to trust a sovereign God?

If my car gets hit, its replacement is guaranteed. If I get sick, the doctor and hospital will be paid for. If I stay sick, my family will receive a full income. If I die, my family will be taken care of for many years. Of course, the mental and emotional loss may be substantial, but thanks to my insurance policies, there is no such thing as significant material loss. The situation is airtight. So airtight, in fact, that in a person's mind there may be no need or place for God's material provision.

The Corporation vs. the Community. There was a time when people had to trust God for the medical bills if they got sick. If they stayed sick, they and their family had to depend on God and the Christian community for support in various material and personal ways. If someone died, others had to be involved in the ongoing care for the material needs of the family. With insurance, all that has changed. But is the change for the better?

A hundred years ago, before insurance was widely available, if a house burned down, neighbors and fellow church members invariably rallied and sacrificially gave of their assets of time and money and helped to rebuild. Now the insurance company takes care of that. The friends and neighbors and church members feel bad and offer brief emotional support, of course, but then they return to their own lives, barely affected and minimally involved in what has happened.

Likewise, in the past, the man who was injured and could no longer work was helped by his family, his church, his neighbors, his community. His "insurance" was his own participation in the community. People cared, people helped, people prayed, and God worked through these personal relationships to meet not only material but emotional and spiritual needs. Today, the injured man is compensated by his unemployment insurance, workman's compensation insurance, or disability insurance. Because he is "taken care of," people do not so readily get involved in his life.

For purposes of discussion, let us call the formal contractual insurance issued by an insurance company "corporation insurance." The spontaneous and informal provision issued by a community, whether geographical or spiritual, we will call "community insurance." History has demonstrated that the more prevalent corporation insurance becomes, the more community insurance is minimized and sometimes virtually eliminated. If there is the one, there is little or no perceived need for the other.

Of course, this is not only a problem with corporation insurance but with the endless number of government programs that dole out money, devoid of the sort of holistic care that happens in a network of established relationships. And the fault is not just with corporation insurance itself but with the community, which fails to realize it is still needed in many ways. In fact, it may not be so much that insurance has pushed away people from supporting relationships as that insurance has stepped into the void created from people having stepped out of such relationships.

But regardless of who is at fault, a tragic erosion of community, church relationships, and commitment has occurred. The natural events of life that once drew people together do so no longer. Because "everything's taken care of," people seldom get meaningfully involved in each others lives.

"But can't God work through an insurance company just as he can work through a church or community?" God can work through anything. But he desires to work through people in personal ways, not simply through a huge and impersonal pool of assets that issues computer-printed checks from another part of the country. An insurance agent may be exceptionally kind, compassionate, and helpful. I know several such people. He may go beyond the call of his job. But he may not be a church member, and often is not even a neighbor. Even if he is, the money he distributes isn't his; it is the corporation's, paid (not contributed) by a million people who don't know or care to know who each other are.

Health Insurance. We can look at health insurance in one of several ways. First, when we consider the exorbitant medical costs of our society, it seems dangerous and irresponsible to not have health insurance. After all, if the rest of us are paying to have health insurance, why should the extended family or the church or the society be expected to pick up the tab for someone who could have bought health insurance but chose not to buy it?

My church provides health insurance for all of our staff members, and I am grateful for it. Even if it was not provided, I would probably choose to have it. However, while the stark realities of the situation—specifically the increasing number of cases resulting in hundreds of thousands of dollars in medical bills—compel me to this decision, I believe quite honestly that it is not ideal.

What *is* ideal? A Christian community that is spontaneously self-insured. I don't mean a situation where everyone signs contracts and pays premiums to the church, nor where the church acts as an insurance company in any formal way. I refer to a situation in which the church takes responsibility to care for its members who are ill or disabled, just as it did in the first century and has always done until recent history.

Whether a large benevolence fund is maintained or special

345

offerings are taken as the needs arise, the church should be there to meet needs. It is the church, not the insurance company, that is the body of Christ. It is the church, not the insurance company, against which the gates of hell will not prevail. God can provide however he wishes, but his ideal plan is to provide through his church.

Consider for a moment what would happen if all the massive amounts paid out in insurance premiums of every variety were given instead to the church. Much of this could be passed on immediately to the cause of reaching the world for Christ. The rest could be accumulated, if this seemed the best way, and saved at a significant rate of interest. As needs arose, the money could be drawn upon. Perhaps the same could be accomplished through special offerings. If a church is too small for this, several churches could join together. But totally apart from the potential financial advantages of this arrangement, God's people would be acting as God's people, personally involved in the lives of the needy, and God would be seen to work through them, just as he did in the early church.

I am told that the Amish communities function in this way. And I have heard of a few churches that operate on this basis, though I have never seen one firsthand. I know that there are a thousand hitches and red flags and dangers and impracticalities that come to mind. It would take a large church to make it work, and one massive hospital bill—a premature baby or a long-time comatose patient who required several months of hospital care—could wipe out a small church financially. But I also know that if proper thought and prayer were given to it, and those involved were true disciples of Christ, God could be greatly honored by such a caring community.

Life Insurance. Life insurance is really death insurance, since it is payable upon a person's death. The purpose of life insurance is to provide the difference between what the family of the insured will have and what they will need after the provider has died. Generally, the intent is to replace the provider's income that will have been lost.

The same concerns about the other forms of insurance apply equally to life insurance. A life insurance salesman explains to me that I must have so much insurance in order for my wife and children to be taken care of as they are presently for another five, ten, or fifteen years after my death, factoring in inflation. The result is a computer readout with lots of zeros, indicating a huge amount of money that will naturally require a large insurance premium.

But where does God fit in all this? If I die tomorrow, it seems reasonable in this economy to have a moderate amount of funds designated, either through savings or through life insurance, to care for many of my family's basic needs. On the other hand, to supply them with a huge chunk of money to be appropriated over the next ten years till my children are grown, and another forty years till my wife dies seems too much. *If* life insurance is appropriate, its purpose must be to provide for my family for a season, not to protect them against any and every eventuality, and certainly not to profit them by my departure.

Something is terribly wrong when a man's most effective avenue of material provision for his family is his own death. I have had unemployed and otherwise distraught men tell me that due to their large life insurance policies they are worth more to their family dead than alive. Sadly, I saw one of these seriously contemplate suicide on this very basis.

When I die, I do not want the church to say, "Randy was a good provider—all his family's needs are taken care of." I want them to realize my family *does* have needs and will continue to have them. Yes, I may have seen to some of their material needs through accumulated assets, some savings, and a modest life insurance policy. But they need the ongoing help and support and wisdom and counsel and encouragement of the church. In fact, at some point they may need material help as well. Would that be so terrible? Isn't it OK to sometimes need help from others?

Time and time again, I have seen Christians stay at a distance from other hurting Christians because they believe the insurance company, the government, hospice, or some benevolence organization is taking care of them. When it comes to caring for their needy, even some of the pseudo-Christian cults put the evangelical church to shame. What a tragedy!

What the life insurance salesman does not address is that there are many things that could and probably will happen over the next five or ten or fifteen years, not the least of which would hopefully be my wife's remarriage. Of course, this process is not certain, and it might take several years. (I hope she hasn't already picked someone out!) I believe it is sometimes unhealthy for a woman to bring large amounts of money into her second marriage. Furthermore, I want my children to know that it is God who will meet their every need, not Daddy who died ten years ago.

Is Insurance God's Tool or God's Substitute? The greatest danger of insurance is that it so easily undermines our sense of dependence on God. I must carefully evaluate my own perceptions and motivations when it comes to buying insurance. Is insurance a God-given means of provision, or is it in reality a theological end-run that makes trust obsolete and God unnecessary? The more prone I am to trust in insurance, the more likely it seems I should have as little as possible.

The kings of Israel paid tribute to foreign powers, specifically the kings of Egypt and Syria. Isaiah condemned them for trusting in worldly powers rather than trusting in God (Isa. 30:1-2). Is there a principle here that applies to insurance? Is dependence upon the worldly power of the insurance corporations an act of independence of the God who has promised to provide for those who trust him? Is collective insurance a financial equivalent to the tower of Babel? Is it a secularistic, socialistic substitute for God?

Since no absolutely clear parallels to the kinds of insurance policies we might buy today are mentioned in Scripture, it would be hard to prove that buying insurance was either right or wrong. Some may look on insurance as a legitimate way of providing for their families. Others see it as a lack of dependency. The sin of presumption might be committed in either case.

If one had been available, would Jesus have bought an insurance policy? Would the apostles? If not, why not? If so, what kind and how much?

Is insurance and savings and retirement a horizontal means to gain my family's future financial security without me or them having to look vertically to God? Is it a way for me to hedge my bets in case God doesn't come through? Is insurance for me a means by which faith becomes obsolete and God unnecessary? Do I really have to depend on God once all my bases are covered?

The bottom line question we must all answer is this—in my own life, is insurance a legitimate tool of God or an illegitimate substitute for him?

Our own choice has been to use insurance sparingly. Of course, we buy insurance when it is legally required—we insure our home and have liability insurance on our cars. We do not have specific insurance on valuable items, and we do not carry collision insurance (it costs more than the car is worth). When we had the choice, before it became part of our compensation package, we chose high-deductible, low-cost health insurance. We don't have disability insurance or mortgage insurance and have only the small life insurance policy provided by our church (given a choice we would buy the cheapest term insurance available, rather than whole life).

In short, we do have insurance, more than some, less than others. We want to be responsible, yet leave plenty of room for God. We also want to be able to use the money for God's kingdom that would otherwise go to additional insurance.

Once again, I am not trying to set our choices up as the ideal. They aren't. Everyone must measure his own situation and convictions. For instance, we have only one debt, on our house, and it is comparatively small. Royalties from my writing, though not large, would be of some help to my family after my death. There are many other factors that will apply to one situation and not to another. In this area, as in others, sometimes I find myself thinking we should have a little more insurance; other times I wonder if we should have less. Again, this tension is healthy. As we continue to grow in Christ, we continue to evaluate and are determined to follow his lead as God molds our convictions.

Why Worry? While the Bible does not teach the "prosperity doctrine," it does clearly teach what we might call the "provision doctrine." God promises to provide materially for the one who follows Christ wholeheartedly. "But seek first his kingdom and his righteousness, and all these things [what you eat, drink, and wear] will be given to you as well" (Matt. 6:33). Unlike the pagans who "run after all these things" and "worry about tomorrow," the believer is to follow Christ, live the radical life of faith, and trust God to provide (Matt. 6:25-34).

In this same passage, Jesus said God cares for the birds. Yet birds are not created in the image of God. Christ did not die for birds. The Holy Spirit does not indwell birds. Birds will not reign with Christ in eternity. But we will! So Christ asked his disciples, "Are you not much more valuable than they?" (Matt. 6:26). If he takes care of the less valuable, will he not take care of us, who are much more valuable?

The birds work and provide for their immediate future by building nests and obtaining food for their young. On the other hand, they do not simultaneously maintain a nest in the mountains and one at the beach. Neither do they fill their cellars with freeze-dried worms just in case their Creator does not provide for the future. In short, the birds do the work God created them to do; they sing when they work, they don't hoard for the future, and they instinctively trust their Creator to take care of them. Should we who know the grace of God do any less?

Contrast this philosophy with that of a pitch for life insurance that preys upon the very anxieties Jesus told us we are not to have (not all insurance salesmen take this approach—many are honest and sensitive, not manipulative). Jesus said, "Accept my sovereignty and goodness, and you won't have to worry about tomorrow. Trust me." The salesman says, "Buy our policy and you won't have to worry about tomorrow. Trust me." The question we must ask is, "Does God offer adequate coverage?" and "Does he have the resources to back up the offer?"

All of us trust in something. The more trustworthy the object of our trust, the less we need worry. The stock market is not trustworthy. It may do us well for a day, a month, a year, or even a few decades. But because the stock market is uncertain, it can only produce anxiety when it is the object of our trust. God is the only totally trustworthy object and, therefore, the only one who will not—who *cannot*—betray a trust.

Why is this so hard for us to accept? If we believe God can create us, redeem us, and bring us through death to spend a glorious eternity with him, why can't we take him at his word when he says he will take care of our material needs?

If God calls on you today to share your resources with another, you must not say, "I can't, Lord, because I don't know where my own provisions are coming from." Yes, you *do* know where they are coming from. They are coming from God. You may not know the form that it will take nor the way it will get to you, but you do know the Source of your provision. Like the poor widow, you know that God is going to take care of you, even if there are no visible resources.

A question: If God has control of everything, and God takes care of his children, and God gives everything necessary to those who walk with him, and you are his child, and you are walking with him, and worrying never helped anything anyway, but has hurt plenty . . . then why worry?

CONCLUSION

In each of the matters dealt with in this chapter—saving, retirement, and insurance—the issues are really the same. Does our long-term savings or retirement plan or insurance policy reduce our sense of dependence on God? Does it reduce or increase our level of flexibility and openness to God's direction? Considering what the monies spent on these things would do if directly invested in the kingdom of God now, do we feel this money is being well used?

If, on the other hand, we do not have substantial savings or retirement funds or insurance, is it because we are consciously trusting God and giving substantially to meet others' needs, *or* is it simply because we are lazy, undisciplined, and irresponsible? God honors the sacrificial pilgrim of faith, not the lazy fool. God would have been no more pleased with the rich fool had he squandered his money rather than hoarding it. Either way he would have failed to invest his assets in God's kingdom. There is sometimes a fine line between faith and foolishness.

We know a godly missionary family who took their retirement savings and poured everything back into the mission. I suggest God looks very differently at these people than at the Christian who spends his money on short-term indulgences with no thought of saving for upcoming needs or providing for his family's future. Both may "have nothing" at a given stage in life, but God's voluntary obligation to the one is much different than to the other. To those who seek first his kingdom and to those who sacrificially give of their assets to his kingdom, his promise is one of material provision (Matt. 6:32-33; Phil. 4:19).

No matter how much it clashes with the prevailing opinion, we cannot afford to dismiss the thoughtful exhortation of William MacDonald:

> Reserves are crutches and props which become a substitute for trust in the Lord. We can't trust when we can see. Once we decide to provide for our future, we run into these problems. How much will be enough? How long will we live? Will there be a depression? Will there be inflation? Will we have heavy medical bills?
>
> It is impossible to know how much will be enough. Therefore we spend our lives amassing wealth to provide for a few short years of retirement. In the meantime, God has been robbed and our own life has been spent in seeking security where it cannot be found.
>
> How much better it is to work diligently for our current necessities, serve the Lord to the maximum extent, put everything above present needs into the work of the Lord, and trust Him for the future.[4]

If we do choose to have savings accounts and set aside retirement funds and buy insurance, let us be careful to do so only enough to avoid presuming on God, but never enough to avoid trusting him.

NOTES
1. Ron Blue, *Master Your Money* (Nashville: Thomas Nelson, 1986), 13.
2. William MacDonald, *True Discipleship* (Kansas City, Kan.: Walterick Publishers, 1975), 97.
3. Larry Burkett, *Using Your Money Wisely* (Chicago: Moody Press, 1986), 26.
4. MacDonald, 96-97.

CHAPTER 19

INVESTING AND LEAVING
MONEY

Avoid sin rather than loss. Richard Mather

If you wish to leave much wealth to your children, leave them in God's care. Do not leave them riches, but virtue and skill. For if they have the confidence of riches, they will not mind anything besides, for they shall have the means of screening the wickedness of their ways in their abundant riches. John Chrysostom

My friend, a Christian financial counselor, once told me the sobering story of a land investment that he and his brother took on together. First he described the difficulties of making the payments. Then he told of the extra time and energy it took to develop the land, which he found himself constantly thinking about. The venture put tremendous stress on his family, to the point that his wife became ill. Finally the tensions of the

353

partnership literally destroyed his relationship with his brother, which had been very close prior to the purchase but remains distant to this day. When he summarized the story, these were my friend's exact words: "It looked like a great investment, but the price I ended up paying for it was enormous." Some investments seem to work like a dream. Others, like this one, turn out to be nightmares.

This chapter addresses the question of whether or not to invest our money. Next it looks at the matter of leaving our money and possessions—how our estates should be distributed when we die.

INVESTMENTS AND BIBLICAL PRINCIPLES

While Scripture doesn't directly teach that we should get involved in investments, it does provide illustrations of investing, including real estate ventures (Prov. 31:16). Jesus also spoke illustratively of investing in such a way as to gain financial returns (Matt. 25:14-29; Luke 19:12-19). We cannot conclude from this that Jesus formally advocates investments—only that he does not forbid them. His injunctions to invest in eternity by laying up treasure in heaven rather than on earth, should certainly serve as a caution to us both to limit and put in perspective our earthly investments.

Investing does not simply profit the investor (sometimes it does not even do that), but it profits the business in which we are investing. A Christian should avoid investing in any business or enterprise that makes its profits based on people doing what they should not do. For instance, in most cases I am convinced that people should not take out a second mortgage on their home. Therefore, for me to invest in high-yield second mortgages may appear to be financially wise, but it is actually putting up funds for and making profit by the unwise decisions of others.

Mutual fund investments, the single most common investment vehicle today, involve just this kind of risk. They distribute their investors' money in a wide range of companies, some of which will be doing things with the money a Christian would not condone. Can we in good conscience invest money when even a small portion of it is going to underwrite the abortion business or support the tobacco and alcohol industries? To the Christian there are more basic questions than whether or not an investment makes a profit.

How Much Risk Is Appropriate? Continuing with the example of mutual funds, some funds are quite conservative and strive after steady consistent growth. Others tend to be more volatile, having potential for great gain but also the potential for great loss. What level of risk can I, in good conscience, participate in with God's money?

Scripture clearly teaches the investment principle of steady plodding as opposed to hasty speculation. "The plans of the diligent lead to profit as surely as haste leads to poverty" (Prov. 21:5). The man eager to get rich with a high-yield, high-risk investment is setting himself up for loss and disillusionment. The Living Bible translates Ecclesiastes 5:13-17:

> There is another serious problem I have seen everywhere— savings are put into risky investments that turn sour, and soon there is nothing left to pass on to one's son. The man who speculates is soon back to where he began—with nothing. This, as I said, is a very serious problem, for all his hard work has been for nothing; he has been working for the wind. It is all swept away. All the rest of his life he is under a cloud— gloomy, discouraged, frustrated, and angry.

"He who gathers money little by little makes it grow" (Prov. 13:11). Many Christians have not been content to gather money little by little. Consequently, they have lost a great deal of money—not to mention sleep—on investments that were "certain" to make them wealthy.

The higher the potential return of any investment, the higher its risk. I saw a prospectus that virtually promised investors their money would be multiplied ten times in a one year period—a 1,000 percent return! Now, why would this company pay a 1,000 percent interest for investors' money when at the time bank loans were costing less than 15 percent interest? The answer is obvious. The proposition was so risky or illegitimate that no bank would get involved. (Keep in mind that banks thrive on loaning money—when they refuse to there is a good reason for it.)

Every investment involves a certain level of risk, and the Christian must determine how much risk he is comfortable with. Even a farmer takes a risk when he plants the seed. He is uncertain of what weather is ahead, and he doesn't have any guarantee his crops won't be lost in a tornado or insect plague, or that his barn won't burn down once the crop has been harvested. Life involves risks. However, some risks, such as the farmer's, are necessary, reasonable, and well worth taking.

When Risk Becomes Gambling. There is a difference between reasonable or necessary risks and gambling. When we gamble, we step out of the realm of reality. Gambling is irresponsible. It is a shortcut to God's created pattern of working to get money. In gambling, wealth is not distributed on the basis of work or service or of personal need, but purely on the grounds of chance. Gambling preys upon the weakness of undisciplined and unrealistic people. It ruins families, and it is associated with alcoholism, drug use, organized crime, and vice of every variety. Because of this, it is inconceivable that churches would use gambling, such as bingo and raffles, as a means of fund-raising.

The gambler's ambition is of course to win—but if he wins, he can do so only at the expense of others. It is their loss from which his winnings come. Gambling thrives on the gullible, undisciplined, and lazy. The state lotteries are an example of this. Coffers are filled with revenues from people who should have used their money for constructive purposes. Ironically, the state ends up doling out support funds to many of the same people who buy lottery tickets.

Even if we end up winning, which of course most people do not, our winnings are tainted by the fact that we violated God's means of provision. It is hard and wise labor that brings financial profit (Proverbs 14:23). Shortcuts to profit are usually shortcuts around the Creator's design for living.

Not all risk-taking is gambling. But if risk becomes great enough, it can turn investments into gambling. The stock market certainly involves a level of risk. Yet for some people it may be a reasonable place to invest, especially if they make their choices carefully. Of course, no matter how careful one is, it is possible to lose a great deal of money, perhaps all of it. Anyone

356

who invests in the stock market must be patient enough and detached enough so that his investments don't become the focus of his life and distract him from his single-minded purpose as a follower of Christ. Any Christian whose heart and happiness go up and down with the stock market has no business being in the stock market.

Occasionally I have invested small amounts of money. Several years ago, I put six hundred dollars in a computer company, and three months later it had tripled in value. I decided to sell it one morning and take the profits, but just as I was about to make the call, the phone rang. Someone was in the hospital and I needed to get there right away. I left immediately and ended up spending the whole day in the hospital. The next morning I called to sell the stock. I discovered that in that one day the value of the shares had dropped dramatically. As it turned out, my visit to the hospital had cost eight hundred dollars.

Fortunately, I was also able to realize God was in the hospital call and I didn't need to worry about the "loss." I was still four hundred dollars ahead, though the same principle would apply if I had lost the entire investment. If we are to put our money into investments we must understand and be comfortable with the element of risk. And when we evaluate whether or not to invest, we need to look at not only the money, but the amount of time, energy, and emotional attachment it involves for us.

Why Am I Investing? Nothing is an investment unless it is likely to bring you profit that exceeds what you have put into it, and at some point you intend to exchange it for that profit. Otherwise it is just a purchase. This means that apart from rare exceptions we do not "invest in a gold ring," or "invest in a new car" or "invest in a mountain cabin." If we intend to keep them, these things are purchases, not investments.

The fundamental question to ask about investing is "Why?" Larry Burkett cited four bad reasons for investing: greed (1 Tim. 6:9); envy (Ps. 73:3); pride (1 Tim. 6:17); and ignorance (Prov. 14:7).[1]

Reasonable foresight and planning are one thing, but it is important that investments not be motivated by fear and personal insecurity since God promises to provide for the believer's material needs. If you are investing to enhance your personal kingdom rather than God's, your reason for investing is not biblically sound.

If you are investing to multiply assets that can eventually provide for your family, the needy, and ministry purposes, then that is a good motivation. Many Christian foundations and individual believers invest a certain amount of principal and give the earnings to kingdom causes. However, once again we must ask ourselves whether God is a qualified investor. If I gave him not only the interest but the principal, could he not multiply it in the lives of others better than I or a mutual fund manager? Once wisely and prayerfully given away, money is safely in God's hands. But as long as it is kept, even with the highest intentions, there is the possibility either that it will leave us or we will leave it before giving ever takes place. Many Christians found this out the hard way through the stock market crash of October 1987.

Guidelines for Investing. There are some fundamental principles of investing. Never risk money you can't afford to lose. Never make uninformed or hasty decisions to invest. Never make any investments or other major financial decisions without counting the possible financial, mental, emotional, and spiritual costs. And remember that a person with a million dollars in investments may be in greater financial bondage than one who has no investments at all.

Also, if we are poor stewards, we need to stay out of investments. We need to first learn basic financial responsibility, including how to give to God and how to get out of debt.

Ironically, some of the very people most heavily into investments are most deeply in debt, including credit card debt. For these people, there is a surefire proposal that will earn them a guaranteed 18 percent return at no risk. All they have to do is take the money they might put in investments and, instead, pay off all their credit card debts and not incur any more. Does it make sense to be seeking potentially profitable investments while taking actual substantial losses due to debt?

Avoiding the Disastrous Investment. How do we avoid disastrous investments? First, we need to recognize the signs (they are not always as apparent as prime beachfront property in South

Dakota). The typical get-rich-quick scheme offers a tremendous profit at what is supposedly a minimal risk. Usually it involves an unprecedented opportunity or great breakthrough in an area you know little or nothing about, such as real estate in another part of the country, a new microchip that will revolutionize the computer industry, or a discovery that will cure cancer.

Typically, these investments are brought to your attention by a friend, who heard about them from a friend, whose brother-in-law is a financial wizard and says this is the best thing since chewing gum. He is usually sincere and genuinely feels he is doing you a favor. The person who is selling the deal also makes you feel like he is doing you a favor by allowing you this incredible opportunity. He emphasizes that you must make your decision within the next few days. You are impressed when this knowledgeable and believable person assures you, "This is a great investment opportunity." (Have you ever heard anyone trying to sell something by calling it "a lousy investment opportunity?")

In our area, a Christian investment firm held a seminar at a Christian college. They presented a sure-thing investment opportunity too good to pass up. A couple in our church got on the bandwagon, as did many of those who attended the seminar, and took out their entire savings of $10,000. Not long afterward, the Christian investor and his Christian company disappeared with everyone's Christian money. The most tragic thing about this story is that it is not at all unique. I have heard the same story, with different names and places, over and over again.

When we were in a small group with five other couples, our discussion one evening centered on money. When I opened up the discussion, one couple shared in tears that they had lost their entire retirement savings on a bad investment. Then another couple related that they had invested in condominiums that never materialized and lost almost all their money. Still another couple told of their huge losses from another investment. A fourth couple then shared they were co-signatories for a loan to a respected Christian businessman in the community, whom they were sure would make good on it. He did not make good on it, and they became responsible for the debt. Years later, this man was generating a tremendous salary and living in affluence, yet hadn't even begun to pay them back, and probably never would.

Here were four Christian couples in a group of six who had independently become involved in investments and other financial commitments that had resulted in tremendous losses. And it was not the financial loss itself that was most striking but the heavy toll it had taken on their hearts and minds, as well as their relationships with others, including their spouses. As we studied the Scriptures that night, we were struck by the huge loss of money and time and energy that potentially could have been invested in God's kingdom. How easily lost are treasures entrusted to men, and how eternally secure are those entrusted to God! (Matt. 6:19-21).

Losses from unwise investments seem to be even more common in the Christian community than outside it. The main reason for this is the spiritual credibility that someone can project simply by calling himself a Christian. Who would believe that a Christian man who leads in prayer, quotes the Scriptures, and shares his investment under the roof of a fine Christian college would possibly lie, cheat, and steal from Christian people? Because such things are more expected in the secular world, secular people are naturally more suspicious, more cautious, and not as gullible. Of course, many are still taken advantage of anyway.

Particularly tragic is the fact that pastors and other Christian leaders sometimes become involved in these get-rich-quick investments. In their sincerity, perhaps even thinking of the potential assets for the kingdom of God, they influence others to become involved. One pastor took a second mortgage on his house and invested in a project that a member of his congregation was heading. Following the pastor's example, other families became involved as well. Within a year, all the money had been lost. Another pastor spoke openly of the opportunity to invest in a particular invention of a local Christian that was sure to make tremendous profits. Many people followed, thinking that if the pastor was involved, it must be all right. Once again, all the money was lost.

Of course, not every investment in which the money is lost is a dishonest investment. An investment can be completely honest but still a bad investment. Likewise, it is possible for an unwise investment to get lucky and make money, or a wise investment to end up losing it. Every investment involves risk.

Some professing Christians who raise money for investments are dishonest all the way. Others are as honest as they can be but are simply unwise. There is an unfortunate myth that if our hearts are right, God will automatically bless us, even if our heads are empty when it comes to sound business and investment practice. We must be careful not to presume upon God's favor and expect him to bail us out of unwise decisions. P. T. Barnum said, "There's a sucker born every minute." Often, it seems, he can be found in a pew.

Some people wrongly assume that laws protect them against bad investments. Since many bad investments are entirely honest, and since even some dishonest ones are legal, this is simply not true. Furthermore, even those schemes which are illegal at best may end in the prosecution of the people responsible. Rarely do investors get their money back.

Wise Financial Counsel. David said, "I will praise the Lord, who counsels me" (Ps. 16:7). "Your statutes are my delight; they are my counselors" (Ps. 119:24). Ultimately, we can get the best financial counsel from God's Word. If we do, we will often find it gives us perspectives dramatically different from those of human counselors, both secular and Christian. The many scriptural principles dealt with in this book are far more important than independent counsel from myself or any others, no matter how much experience they have had in the realm of finances.

However, there is also a great deal to be gained from seeking out wise human counselors. Every Christian, whether considering investments or not, should seek God's wisdom through the input of the wise:

> Wisdom is more precious than rubies, and nothing you desire can compare with her. (Prov. 8:11)

> The way of a fool seems right to him, but a wise man listens to advice. (Prov. 12:15)

> Plans fail for lack of counsel, but with many advisers they succeed. (Prov. 15:22)

> Listen to advice and accept instruction, and in the end you will be wise. (Prov. 19:20)

> The quiet words of the wise are more to be heeded than the shouts of a ruler of fools. (Eccles. 9:17)

These passages make clear that in important decisions, financial and otherwise, we should seek a number of counselors, not just one. And the point is not just quantity, but quality—they must be truly wise. Since wisdom begins with the fear of God (Prov. 9:10), it stands to reason that usually these counselors should be Christians who are walking with God and living by his principles in their own lives. The counsel of the ungodly must not be our standard (Ps. 1:1). Having weighed the Scriptures and our counsel from others, we need to ask for wisdom from God, who generously gives it to those who diligently seek it (James 1:5).

There are a great many investment counselors around, some of whom are Christians. Unfortunately, it is much easier to find a Christian financial counselor than a biblical financial counselor. Any financial counselor should be evaluated not just on the basis of his professed faith but his knowledge of Scripture, his knowledge of finances, his investment and counseling track record, and how others whom you trust appraise his character and skills.

Unless you know for certain this is an exceptional person, it is usually best to receive your initial investment advice from pure financial counselors, to whom you pay a direct fee, rather than salesmen of financial products whose fee is paid by their commission on what they sell you. It is almost impossible for a financial counselor to give you objective advice when he has products to sell you. For him to recommend alternatives that would be better for you but earn him no money is the mark of a man of integrity, and while such people certainly exist, it is more than you can reasonably expect. Usually he will not try to cheat you, but he will naturally limit his horizons to those alternatives that will earn him money. This is, after all, what he does for a living.

For instance, many studies have demonstrated that a number of "no load" mutual funds (those with no sales commission cost) perform as well as "load" funds, which charge an initial fee of 8 percent or so that goes to the salesman. Hence, your investment must increase by 8 percent in order for you just to break even.

Only after that can you begin to earn money. With a no-load fund, you can start making money right away. That is great for you, but not for your counselor, since he receives no commission. He has vested interests in persuading you to make a decision that is to his advantage, but not necessarily to yours. This is another reason why wise counsel should be sought from a variety of sources, not just one (Prov. 11:14; 24:6).

It is important not just to receive "earthly" investment counseling, but to actively seek counsel from those oriented toward and knowledgeable about heavenly or eternal investments. By this I mean people who can advise you as to where to put your money to work in God's kingdom. Once again, however, you must beware of vested interests.

Some time ago, I was approached by two wealthy women who asked me to adopt the role of periodically advising them about which Christian ministries to invest their funds in. They shared some bad experiences where those from particular ministries had gotten their names as "wealthy donor prospects" and pressured them to give. I decided then that the only way I could really advise these women with integrity was to make sure I had nothing to gain from them myself. I laid out this ground rule—I would be available to advise them, but they were never to do anything for my material benefit, not even so much as buy lunch for me. Only when we eliminated the possibility of vested interests on my part did I feel they could fully trust me—and I could fully trust myself—to counsel them objectively.

Of course, once you receive counsel, the decision is yours to make. You should only make a decision with which you are perfectly comfortable. If you doubt the wisdom or rightness of investing in general or a certain investment in particular, then you shouldn't proceed with it—"everything that does not come from faith is sin" (Rom. 14:23).

Consulting with Your Marriage Partner. I also encourage you to discuss carefully and come to complete agreement with your spouse before making an investment or other major financial commitment. "A prudent wife is from the Lord" (Prov. 19:14). Many unwise decisions have been made by one partner, usually the husband, when the other's reservations should have been interpreted as a message from God to slow down and think more carefully. The long-term consequences to both finances and marital harmony are severe when a couple is divided on major financial decisions. Neither a hasty nor a split decision is honoring to God.

Four out of five married women will one day be widows. Since wives survive their husbands 80 percent of the time, it is very important that husbands include their wives in major financial decisions. If the husband dies today, does the wife know what to do? Does she have access to and understand such things as the bank accounts, investments, will, and insurance policies? Financial ignorance is one more pressure she doesn't need.

Couples should communicate all along about these things. One of the best gifts a husband can leave his wife is to tell her both verbally and in writing exactly what she would need to know and do in case of his death.

LEAVING MONEY:
THE QUESTION OF INHERITANCE

The highest calling of parents is not to leave their children a good inheritance, but to leave them a godly heritage. Many of the world's multimillionaires have left massive inheritances but have also left a heritage of greed, self-indulgence, betrayal, adultery, arrogance, snobbery, and self-centeredness. On the other hand, countless Christians have left no material inheritance to their families, but a godly heritage that serves as a point of reference for spiritual and moral values their entire lives.

It is often good to leave some inheritance to children (Prov. 13:22; 19:14). However, in a society with as much affluence and opportunity as our own, I believe Christian parents should seriously consider leaving the bulk of their estate to churches, parachurch ministries, missions, and other kingdom purposes, and only a smaller portion to their children.

New Testament principles and examples clearly suggest we should not strive to leave a huge estate in the first place. If we do, it is evidence that we have hoarded God's provision rather than substantially shared it. John Wesley made a great deal of money on his many books, as well as some of his hymns—about

50,000 pounds sterling in all. Yet at his death his estate was worth only twenty-eight pounds.

Wesley was left with so little, not because of poor planning but good planning; not because he had squandered it but had generously given it to the cause of Christ. Wesley's stated goal had been to have as little left as possible when he died. At the end of his life he wrote in his journal, "I left no money to anyone in my will, because I had none."[2] What a contrast to many Christians who die with huge bank accounts and vast estates that could have been invested in the kingdom all along as God provided the assets!

I don't view leaving an estate to the church or Christian ministry as "giving" in the fullest sense. When we die, we have no choice but to leave our money somewhere. We are thus not making a sacrificial gift, nor are we depending on the Lord to provide for our needs. I believe our treasures in heaven will be in proportion to what we do and give before we die, not what we tell others to do with what is left after we are gone. Nevertheless, all of us will leave an estate, whether large or small, that can be invested for great good in the cause of Christ. Such a decision may not be sacrificial or generous, but it is still wise and can bring great glory to God.

Qualified to Inherit? Throughout the Western world, in Christian families as well as non-Christian, an enormous amount of wealth is being passed on to people totally unequipped to manage it. Anyone can spend money—but precious few can handle it responsibly and biblically.

It is an irresponsible act and the poorest sort of stewardship to pass on money and assets to anyone—children or otherwise— who has demonstrated he is incapable of handling it with a view to eternity.

I realize this is controversial. But I believe we should entrust money to our children after our death only if we would trust them with it now. If we do not follow this policy, two disastrous things can happen. First, we lose our assets and the opportunity they represent to the kingdom of God. Second, we may do irreparable damage to our children or other heirs.

The person who is not qualified to handle large amounts of money can be ruined for life as a result of receiving it, regardless of his age, but especially if he is under thirty. Given a large amount of money, he can quit work or slack off and become accustomed to having whatever he wants and doing whatever he wishes. When the money runs out, if he wasn't irresponsible before, he probably will be now. And even if the money never runs out, he is likely to be an unproductive and lazy human being, lacking in character, judgment, and initiative.

The parent who would leave money to his children under these circumstances is not rewarding them but taking revenge on them. We should not give huge amounts of money to those not mature enough to handle it any more than we would give an unlimited supply of candy to a five-year-old.

Millionaire Andrew Carnegie said:

> The almighty dollar bequeathed to a child is an almighty curse. No man has the right to handicap his son with such a burden as great wealth. He must face this question squarely: will my fortune be safe with my boy and will my boy be safe with my fortune?[3]

"An inheritance quickly gained in the beginning will not be blessed in the end" (Prov. 20:21). Before leaving our estates to our children "because that's what everyone does," we must think of the long-term results of large financial windfalls gained without diligent labor.

I believe we Christian parents should consider entrusting at least a small amount of our estates to our adult children while we are still alive. Based on what we see our children do with these funds, we may develop our convictions as to how much money, if any, we choose to leave to which children.

What Is Fair or What Is Right? "But to be fair we have to leave the same amount of money to each child." Our understanding of "fairness" is a recent invention that is largely inaccurate in many situations, including this one. If parents have grown children who are equally spiritual and equally good stewards and in roughly equal circumstances with equal responsibilities, then, yes, equal inheritance seems most appropriate. But if there are significant variables in our children's stewardship abilities or circumstances and needs, I believe it is entirely appropriate to leave them differing portions of our estate.

To leave deliberately large amounts of money to a child whom you know to be wasteful is simply to underwrite and participate in the sin and sorrow that will surely result from his wasteful and immoral life-style. How different is it to pay drug dealers and prostitutes and lose all your money gambling or give it to anti-Christian cults than it is to leave money to someone whom you have reason to believe may use it for such purposes himself? Isn't it immoral to leave money to people who have demonstrated they are morally incapable of handling it well?

A young man, preoccupied with fairness, came to Jesus and said, "Teacher, tell my brother to divide the inheritance with me" (Luke 12:13). Jesus was unmoved by his plea, refused to get involved in the dispute, and went right into this warning: "Watch out! Be on your guard against all kinds of greed; a man's life does not consist in the abundance of his possessions" (Luke 12:15). He went from there into the parable of the rich fool who hoarded up his assets, was about to die and was asked by God, "Then who will get what you have prepared for yourself?" (Luke 12:20). Jesus was noticeably unsympathetic to the fairness doctrine when it comes to funds that should be invested in his kingdom!

The question is not what is fair, but what is right. The real questions are, will your children need your money and will they use it wisely? If the answer to the first question is no, then you should not feel compelled to leave it to them. If the answer to the second question is no, you should feel compelled not to leave it to them. If the answers markedly differ from child to child, you should deal differently with them according to those real differences.

But much of this evaluation process concerning our children or other heirs can be avoided in the first place by leaving most of what God has given us to him and his work. My observations of families that have fought terribly over inheritances confirms this conviction. There are siblings whose relationships are ruined for life because "It isn't fair—he got cash and I got stuck with a house I can't sell," or "She took that antique chair I wanted," or "It isn't fair that he got as much as I did when he doesn't even have a family to care for." This kind of bickering over what didn't belong to them in the first place is not only disgusting and tragic, it is largely avoidable.

It would be far better for parents to choose certain objects of personal meaning to leave to each family member, then give the rest to the kingdom of God. The less left to the children, the less there is for them to fight about. Of course, the kind of people who will fight over what belonged to their deceased parents are the kind of people who will not use these assets to the glory of God anyway.

If parents decide to give most or all of their estate to God's kingdom, they should explain their plans to their children as they get older. This will prevent false expectations and free them from the common mixed feelings (including guilt feelings) that stem from what they have to gain by their parents' deaths. Even good children can find themselves thinking about and looking forward to all the money and possessions that will be theirs when their parents die.

Family members who respond negatively to your decision to leave money to the cause of Christ instead of them demonstrate the kind of character and attitude that proves they are unqualified to receive the money in the first place. But committed Christians who understand money, possessions, and eternity will be the first to say, "That's great, Dad and Mom—it's your money and God's, not ours, and we're delighted to see you leave it to kingdom causes. You're a great example to all of us." This is the response we hope for and anticipate in our own daughters. No one loves their children more than we do. But our love has been demonstrated in ways that make insignificant what we do or do not leave them in our will.

By carefully thinking through this issue that is normally not thought through at all, you can be a model of stewardship for others. You can encourage the body of Christ to think in terms of eternity rather than unthinkingly follow the world's pattern of inheritances.

There is nothing so tragic as seeing parents who have made much money for their children but never taught them to handle it. Is there a way to avoid the dilemma and heartache of such a situation? Are there things we can do to help our children be more biblical and responsible stewards? The answer is "yes," and that is the subject of the next two chapters.

The Will. You are responsible for the distribution of your assets after death. The execution of your will according to your instructions is the final outworking of your stewardship in this world. The will is the only instrument by which you can confidently know your stewardship will be completed as you desire.

More than three out of ten Americans die before retirement. Ten out of ten die eventually. Yet seven out of ten Americans die without a will, largely due to procrastination. Many fear that preparing for death will somehow bring it sooner. The Christian should not submit to this kind of superstition. Furthermore, our view of death is fundamentally different anyway. Death is the door we must enter to go to our true home.

When no will is left, the courts make many important decisions that any responsible person will want to have made himself—including who the children's guardians should be, and where the material assets should go. Some people write their own wills to avoid the expense, and run the risk of an error that will invalidate the entire will. Attorney-drawn wills are actually quite inexpensive considering the vital purpose they serve. Certainly, the most costly alternative is no will at all.

Once written, wills should be periodically updated. For instance, our current will leaves one-third of our estate to be divided between our children, held in trust by their designated guardians, with whom we have, of course, discussed this and who are mentioned by name in the will. The bulk of this money would probably go to a college education, if that is the course they choose. Another third is left directly to these guardians to be used as they see fit in caring for the entire family, including their own children. The final third is designated to go to our church, to be distributed for the cause of world missions at the discretion of our church elders.

As our children get older, the long-term cost for their care will be less. Hence, by the time they are eighteen the will can be revised to reduce their share, taking into consideration both their proven characters and circumstances. Of course, the share designated to the guardians can be eliminated by that time, since they would no longer need to serve that role with our grown children. In the future, then, the percentage given to our church and to world missions will substantially increase, presumably becoming the majority of the estate.

CONCLUSION

David said, "I have never seen the righteous forsaken or their children begging bread" (Ps. 37:25). Why is this? Because their parents have left them so much money? No, because "They are always generous and lend freely; their children will be blessed" (Ps. 37:26).

In A.D. 390 John Chrysostom gave these words to Christian parents, and they are as timely today as they have ever been: "If you wish to leave much wealth to your children, leave them in God's care. Do not leave them riches, but virtue and skill."

NOTES
1. Larry Burkett, *Using Your Money Wisely* (Chicago: Moody Press, 1986), 66.
2. Richard Foster, *Freedom of Simplicity* (San Francisco: Harper and Row, 1981), 66.
3. Quoted by Howard Dayton, *Your Money: Frustration or Freedom?* (Wheaton, Ill.: Tyndale House, 1979), 65.

CHAPTER 20

BATTLING MATERIALISM
IN THE CHRISTIAN FAMILY

There are only three ways to teach a child. The first is by example, the second is by example, the third is by example. Albert Schweitzer

"If it had grown up," she said to herself, *"it would have made a dreadfully ugly child: but it makes a rather handsome pig, I think."* And she began thinking over other children she knew, who might do very well as pigs.* Lewis Carroll, *Alice's Adventures in Wonderland*

In Zambia a man buys a new suit and a motorcycle. Meanwhile his wife and children suffer from malnutrition. His youngest child starves to death before his eyes. If he hadn't bought the suit, or if he sold the motorcycle, he could feed his family for a year.

Across the Atlantic, in the United States, another man chooses to work twenty hours of overtime a week while his wife takes on a job to increase their already large income. They eat in the best restaurants, belong to an elite club, and supply their children with all the latest fashions. They gave their girl a prize horse for her twelfth birthday and their boy a new car for his sixteenth. Their children have everything from private telephones to color televisions to expensive ski equipment. They plan to send them to the most prestigious colleges in the country. Dad doesn't have the time or interest for personal talks, family devotions, or church. In fact, the children rarely see their father for more than a few minutes . . . but they know his checkbook is always there.

Two countries, two men—two materialists more similar than we think. The first man will stand before God and give an account for the precious wife and children he allowed to suffer and die rather than surrender the prestige and pleasure of his things. The second man will give account for another deadly form of abuse—his emotional and spiritual neglect of his family, whose deepest needs he sacrificed on the altar of his own lust for money and possessions and the status they afford. He must answer for rearing his children in an indulgent and irresponsible "easy come and easy go" environment that will so warp their values and inhibit their characters that they will probably never recover.

On the day of judgment, no thinking person would want to stand in either man's shoes.

MATERIALISM IN THE CHRISTIAN HOME

Scripture states that it is the responsibility of parents to make basic material provision for their children. For a Christian willfully to choose not to provide for his children or for other needy relatives is to deny his very faith and to be judged worse than an unbeliever (1 Tim. 5:8). Likewise, it is the responsibility of grown children, not the state or insurance company, to take care of their parents and other relatives in their old age or illness (Mark 7:10-12; 1 Tim. 5:8, 16).

Jesus rejected any "spiritual" attempts to excuse failure to provide materially for one's family (Mark 7:9-13). When there are loved ones who need our help, God calls us to give to him *and* to them, not to him instead of them. Even Christ was not too busy dying for the sins of the world to take the time and concern to entrust his mother's welfare to one of his own apostles—who from that point forward would make sure her needs, including material ones, were cared for (John 19:25-27).

Parents are to plan wisely and save for their children's future (2 Cor. 12:14). Given the poverty levels of some parts of the world, of course, these injunctions can apply only where there are sufficient resources.

AFFLUENZA

It is one thing to provide for our children, but quite another to smother them in things until they turn into self-indulgent materialists. An alarming number of children from Christian homes develop a basic identity as consumers rather than disciples. They grow up endlessly grasping for dolls, robots, plastic ponies, and everything else a production-oriented society can offer. Children raised in such an atmosphere—and that now includes most children in the United States—are often afflicted with the disease David McKenna calls *affluenza:*

> Affluenza is a strange malady that affects the children of well-to-do parents. Though having everything money can buy, the children show all of the symptoms of abject poverty—depression, anxiety, loss of meaning, and despair for the future. Affluenza accounts for an escape into alcohol, drugs, shoplifting, and suicide among children of the wealthy. It is most often found where parents are absent from the home and try to buy their children's love.[1]

Perhaps the clearest picture of affluenza is the typical American Christmas. When the annual obstacle course through crowded malls culminates in Christmas, what is its fruit in our children? More often than not, the trail of shredded wrapping paper in our living rooms is highlighted by broken, abandoned, and unappreciated toys. Far from being filled with the spirit of thankfulness for all that Christmas means, the children are grabby, crabby, picky, sullen, and ungrateful for what they have received—precisely because they have received so much.

We love our children. So do their grandfathers and grand-mothers, aunts and uncles, cousins and friends. And all of us seem to think love is measured by the giving of things. We *say* this isn't so, but go right on acting as if it were. But our children are not battery operated. Their deepest needs are spiritual, mental, and emotional, and these needs are not and *cannot* be met by flashing lights and doll houses. This sometimes dawns on us, but we soon forget. Another Christmas, another birthday, and again we immerse our children in things. In doing so, we educate them in a perspective on life directly at odds with the very Scripture we seek to teach them at home and in Sunday school.

Things we would have deeply appreciated in small or mod-erate amounts become unappealing or even revolting in exces-sive amounts. As a man who has gorged himself at a banquet finds the thought of food repulsive, so the one glutted with material things loses his regard and respect for them. Eventually he doesn't care what happens to them. The prevalent disrespect of children for their own possessions, and those of others, is a direct result of their overindulgence.

When we mistake the giving of material things for the sharing of grace, we do a great disservice to our children. A child who grows up getting most of what he wants has a predictable future. Unless he learns to overcome his upbringing, he will misuse credit, default on his debts, and be a poor worker. He will function as an irresponsible member of his family, church, and society. He will be quick to blame others, to pout about his misfortunes, and to believe that his family, church, country, and employer—if he has one—owe him. Having counseled numer-ous such adults, I believe many of them are this way because their parents, sincere but misguided, led them down that very path.

Parents who indulge their children out of "love" should realize that, far from loving them in the true sense, they are performing child abuse of the spirit and character. Though there are no laws against it—no laws of man anyway—such mistreat-ment will often result in more long-term personal and social damage than physical abuse.

One Christian counselor advised some parents that if they

374

don't give their children as many material possessions as their friends have, then it will turn them against the Christian faith. Where do we come up with perspectives like this? Certainly not from God's Word.

Many Christian families today are held back from following God's call to a more simple or strategic life-style because they don't want to deprive their children of material advantages. Meanwhile, they deprive their children of countless spiritual and eternal advantages.

If you decided to move to a remote mission field, your children might not have organized athletics, school dances, a nice bicycle, or a car, but the spiritual benefits could be enormous. As Christian parents, we must learn to choose what is best for ourselves and our children on earth in light of heaven's value system. Our concern should be an eternal standard of living. This kind of perspective is contagious within a family. It is the greatest heritage we can give our children.

THE PARENTAL MODEL

Everything learned in life, from ways of coping to table manners, is learned in families. Families are the heart and soul of society. The home, not the school, is the primary place of learning. In the home character is built, habits are developed, and destinies are forged.

Every good financial perspective and habit encouraged in this book is developed best by parental model. Children learn most effectively not just from what we say but from what we do. Our actions speak louder than our words—sometimes so loudly that our children can't hear a word we are saying. The training of our children in regard to money and possessions begins at birth. For better or for worse, *we* are their tutors, every hour of every day. Consciously or unconsciously, we continually train them, engraving our values in them as if drawing with a stick in wet cement. Albert Schweitzer put it this way: "There are only three ways to teach a child. The first is by example, the second is by example, the third is by example."[2]

Years ago, when my daughters were just two and four, I took them out for breakfast at a restaurant. On our way back to the car, I was surprised to see both of them had toothpicks in their mouths. Then I reached to my own mouth and found I too had a toothpick. Unconsciously, as a matter of habit, I had picked up that toothpick on the way out of the restaurant. My little girls, who at the time didn't even know what a toothpick was for, had climbed up the side of the counter and imitated my action.

As I thought about it afterwards, I realized that when I was a child my father often had a toothpick in his mouth. To this day, even when I have no need of one at all, I put a toothpick in my mouth whenever I leave a restaurant, and now my own children do the same. This small and insignificant illustration captures the essence of parenthood. Children imitate everything we do, whether important or unimportant, healthy or unhealthy. Sometimes our children will fail to listen to us. Rarely will they fail to imitate us.

Though I was not raised in a religious home, I thank God for a father who never bought what he could not afford, who didn't waste money, who chose his investments carefully, and who did not, though he was generous, let me have everything I wanted. Though he may not have always set out to teach me these things directly, his example made an indelible impression on my life.

NO SUBSTITUTE FOR YOU

Unfortunately, the giving of things is often a substitute for the giving of personal attention. Many children receive first a playhouse, then a train set, then skis, then a motorcycle, then a car, all to compensate for the fact that their parents—most often their father—are not available to spend time with them. Any *thing* is a poor substitute for a person, and anything you can give your child is an especially poor substitute for you.

I spoke recently with a Christian man who loves his wife and five children and wants the best for them. He works hard so that they can have a beautiful house, lots of material things, and enough money for the children to go to college. In fact, he works so hard that the last three years he hasn't had time to go on vacation with his family. This man's children are growing up with lots of material things. They are also growing up without a father.

It is time spent with our children, not money given to them, that will leave the lasting impressions. Our children will not remember what we did *for* them nearly as much as they will remember what we did *with* them.

Nearly 40 percent of American children will be raised by single parents. Some of the best parents I know are single parents, but one of their greatest temptations—often subconscious—is trying to compensate for their children's loss of attention by giving them more and more material things. When there is a divorce involved and visitations by a Disneyland Daddy (or Magic Mountain Mommy), there is a tendency for parents to outdo one another in giving material things. The real loser in this process is the child, who grows up glutted with things but starving for love and discipline.

Can we change the pattern of materialism in our homes? Certainly. Let us take Christmas as an example. Deep inside, most of us know that without a return to simplicity in our Christmas, the incarnation of the Christ child will be forever lost in the din and clatter of materialism and possessiveness. But what can we *do* to change?

We can make a commitment to buy far less. There can be fewer presents and more of those handmade. What few presents we do buy can be bought far in advance to avoid the unnerving jostling through stores that has, tragically, become the essence of Christmas to so many. We can focus on Christ rather than ourselves.

My wife has often staged a "Happy Birthday Jesus" party for our children and their friends. Each child brings one gift he has personally made for Jesus. (After all, whose birthday is it?) We can visit shut-ins, take food to the needy—focus on giving rather than receiving. This year, a few nights before Christmas, our family sat around a candlelit table holding hands. Then each of us shared what we most deeply appreciated about the Lord. After praying together and singing Christmas carols, we went around and shared what each of us appreciated about each other. It was an unforgettable evening.

If a child receives four presents they can be spread out on each of four days before Christmas. On Christmas night, after reading Scripture and singing carols, each giver can present his gift in turn to the recipient. In the quietness and simplicity of the celebration, we can pray and express our gratefulness to God for his greatest of all gifts, the Lord Jesus. By taking our focus off the receiver and putting it on the giver, Christmas can become a symbol of God's giving heart rather than man's grabbing hands.

This is only a beginning. You may wish to make more radical changes in your Christmas. But the point is, you *can* make Christmas different. Don't be victimized by the world's materialism. Worship Christ in simplicity.

TEACHING YOUR CHILDREN ABOUT MONEY

"Train a child in the way he should go, and when he is old he will not turn from it" (Prov. 22:6).

Deuteronomy 6 describes this training process as being both formal and informal. We are to both "teach" our children, and "talk" of the principles of Scripture as occasions arise throughout the day. Often, the informal discussions open a door for the formal, and vice versa.

Every experience your child has with money is a teaching opportunity. Some lessons he will learn the hard way. A child who puts his tongue on a light bulb will probably never do it again. Likewise, a child who loses or ruins his favorite possession through carelessness learns an invaluable lesson. So does the one who sees the joy in another's eyes because he has shared with him. Parents can often help by verbalizing the lesson, but there is no substitute for the child's own experiences and the impressions, both pleasant and painful, they leave.

When we are alert to life, all kinds of teaching opportunities emerge. For instance, when our children were very small, they often went with us to our bank's "money machine" located in the local supermarket. They saw us put in the card, and out came money. It all looked so easy. One time I explained we were not going to do something because we didn't have enough money. One of the girls said, "Well, just go to the money machine and get some more." It provided an opportunity to discuss exactly what money is, how we must work to earn it, and that there is not an infinite amount of it available to us. This is easy enough to do but we must take the time and effort to do it—especially in that teachable moment when their interest is piqued.

Often we have no idea how deeply we affect our children by even our casual and offhand comments. One night, when one of my daughters was seven years old, she prayed, "Dear Lord, I thank you so much that we are not too rich or too poor." This pleased me but also surprised me—where did it come from? As I thought about it, I remembered that probably six months earlier I briefly shared with her a verse in Proverbs: "Give me neither poverty nor riches" (Prov. 30:8-9) and applied it to a situation we saw while driving somewhere. I had long since forgotten that conversation. But obviously my daughter hadn't.

OUR CHILDREN'S OTHER TEACHERS

Our society is much more aggressive in teaching our children about money than we are. As an educational experience, spend just one Saturday morning watching cartoons and children's programs. Take special note of the commercials. Advertising goes straight to the kids, inundating them with a materialistic perspective and subtly encouraging them to manipulate their parents into buying worthless products.

While some parents, including myself, are rightly concerned about the wrong sexual values taught by television, equally dangerous are the wrong material values. More Christian parents are now teaching their children what God says about sex, and I applaud this development. But we need to give equal attention to teaching them what God says about money and possessions.

You can develop your children's critical skills by asking them on the spot what this advertisement is saying and what its purpose really is. Ask them, "How important do you think these things are to God" and "How would they improve your character or spiritual life if you owned them?" Don't dismiss these ads as silly—discuss them with your children. Only with such dialogue and training can they learn to discern the faulty underpinnings of society's incessant appeals to spend money and accumulate things.

One night, my daughters asked me to play the game of LIFE. LIFE is a popular board game that I had seen and heard about but never played. Someone had loaned the game to the girls and they had been playing it off and on for a few days when they decided to teach Dad how to play. As the game progressed and I started to catch on, I was amazed at how accurately it reflected our society's materialistic mind-set. For instance, one of my girls was disappointed when she landed on a space that made her a teacher rather than a doctor or lawyer—despite the fact that in real life she wants to be a teacher! Then why her disappointment? Because that meant she would receive a lower salary for the rest of the game. And money, after all, is what LIFE (and, for many people, *life*) is all about.

LIFE, like life, presents the choice of whether to have children. But since there is a minimum amount of money but no minimum amount of children required to win the game, my girls were consistently choosing money over children. When I chose children instead of money, they thought it was a bad move—never considering the personal implications if their mother and I hadn't made that same "bad move" in life! Choosing children might mean losing the game, and who plays a game with the intention of losing? Clearly, this little board game was not just reflecting values—it was instilling them!

The whole event turned out to be an excellent teaching opportunity. Nanci and I shared with our daughters Scripture's infinitely higher regard for children than money, and how "winning" and "success" are very different in God's eyes than the world's. But I couldn't help but think of all the Christian parents who wouldn't dream of letting their children play with Ouija boards or listen to rock music, but probably wouldn't think twice about letting them play LIFE (or its equivalent) without addressing the blatant materialistic values it reflects and fosters.

Surrounded by so much unbiblical instruction about money, even in the most subtle and unlikely forms, we parents need some strong allies. Certainly there is much that churches can do to lead the way in teaching basic biblical principles of stewardship to children, youth, and adults. Sermons, classes, special seminars, small-group discussions, parent support groups, family-oriented radio programs, books and tapes—all these are potential avenues to challenge and equip parents to teach their own children in this vital area.

Since the Master Teacher spent so much time on the subject of money, the Christian school seems a natural place to devote a unit to handling money. What better context in which to explain and demonstrate what money is, what it does, what God says about it, and how to earn, give, save, and spend it! Older children could be taught subjects ranging from how to balance a checkbook to how the economy works. The class could create its own product, sell it at a school carnival, and give the profits to a missionary. This would point out both the positive ways that wealth can be generated and the importance of using wealth generously and wisely. The possibilities are endless—but we must begin with a conviction of how important the subject really is.

The following chapter offers practical suggestions that parents can implement to teach their children the principles and practices of biblical Christian stewardship. If you are "on board" with the idea that we must teach our children tangible alternatives to materialism, and want to know *how* to do that, then the next chapter is for you.

CONCLUSION

How can we teach our children the emptiness of materialism in a direct and memorable way? Try taking them to visit a junkyard. Show them all the piles of "treasures" that were formerly Christmas and birthday presents. Point out things that hundreds of dollars were paid for, that children quarreled about, friendships were lost over, honesty was sacrificed for, and marriages broke up over. Show them the miscellaneous arms and legs and remnants of battered dolls, rusted robots, and crashed cars. Let them look at the expensive furniture and electronic gadgets that now lie useless after their brief life span. Point out to them that most of what your family owns will one day be in a junkyard like this.

Finally, ask them this telling question: "When all that you owned lies abandoned, broken, and useless, what will you have done that will last for eternity?"

NOTES
1. David L. McKenna, "Financing the Great Commission," *Christianity Today* 15 May 1987: 28.
2. Quoted by Malcolm MacGregor, *Training Your Children to Handle Money* (Minneapolis: Bethany Fellowship, 1980), 111.

CHAPTER 21

TEACHING OUR CHILDREN TO DEAL WITH MONEY AND POSSESSIONS

Sharper than a serpent's tooth it is to have a thankless child. William Shakespeare

The less I spent on myself and the more I gave to others, the fuller of happiness and blessing did my soul become. Hudson Taylor

This chapter is a practical follow-up to the last. It assumes the reader is committed to teaching his or her children to be good financial stewards and suggests a number of specific ways to do this.

LEARNING THE HARD WAY

Children learn by experience, both good and bad. Consequently, from time to time, my wife and I allow our children to make a poor financial decision, such as spending impulsively. This is hard for me to do. Invariably I used to explain to my kids why they should hang on to their money instead of wasting it on this little bauble or that sixty-second horsey ride. But I found that though they were reluctantly practicing obedience, they were not learning wisdom. I could talk all day, but still my convictions were mine, not theirs.

When I occasionally began letting them buy some of these things, they started learning for themselves the hard way. When something of true value came along, they couldn't afford to buy it. Meanwhile, the little trinket they bought last month was broken or lost or of no interest. Now they wanted to buy a book they could keep and read and share, but they couldn't because the money spent on the fleeting pleasures of plastic rings and colored stickers was gone forever.

We must be careful not to bail out our children at this point by saying, "Well, I guess you learned your lesson, so I'll give you the money to get what you want." On the contrary, the only way children *will* learn their lesson is by being allowed to face the consequences of their own unwise spending. If we can keep ourselves from interfering with the natural laws of life, mistakes can be our child's finest teachers.

When a child loses or breaks a toy, a parent who feels sorry for him will often replace the toy with a new one. Meanwhile, the child is deprived of learning the way life functions. You must care for things, being careful not to lose or break them, because there are consequences to having them lost or broken. If the consequences are removed, the wrong lesson is learned—"It's OK to be careless, because you still get what you want anyway." The wrong perspective and behavior is reinforced rather than challenged and replaced.

If a twelve-year-old squanders his lunch money, what should his parents do? Nothing. He must either earn some more money, use money he has saved, or go without lunch. The lessons of life are really very simple and effective—if we will just stay out of it!

"But what if it wasn't the child's fault—what if someone else broke his toy or stole his lunch money?" Aren't there many losses and misfortunes in life that aren't the fault of the person, yet must be accepted and dealt with? A child whose toys are replaced and whose money is replenished by parents simply does not learn the way life operates. He is therefore not being prepared for the real world of stewardship.

Since debt is a reality in this society, better that our children learn about it firsthand now in small choices rather than later in big ones. Suppose your child wants a bicycle. You could get him a good used bike for twenty dollars or maybe even for free if you checked around. But perhaps this isn't good enough for him. He wants a brand-new bicycle like his friends have. One way to teach him the cost of having nice things is to tell him if he really wants it, you will loan him the money at the going rate of interest, either bank loan interest or the higher credit card interest, maybe 18 percent. Work out a payment schedule with him, showing him how much this $80 bicycle will *really* cost him and how long it will take to pay it off.

At this point, he may back out of the deal. If so, good for him. But if he doesn't, let him go ahead. By the time he pays off the debt from miscellaneous chores—perhaps as much as six months down the road—he will never forget the cost of borrowing. By then a used bicycle, which is what his briefly beautiful bicycle is by now anyway, will be much more appealing than it ever was before. The lesson he learns from the bicycle can give him wisdom later on when it comes to buying a car or a house or any number of things.

CHILDREN, WORK, AND MONEY

As parents, we must help our children learn to associate money with labor. Money and possessions simply do not fall out of the sky. They are earned through work—good, hard, and well-done work. We can encourage our children to work at tasks, to make things, to sell things. We can also teach them that work can be meaningful and fun as well as financially profitable.

A common mistake we make as parents is to dole out money to our children arbitrarily as life goes by. This teaches them to think money has no cost, that it comes easily or automatically. As a result, they will disassociate money from work. They will begin to feel that it is their right to have money available even when they haven't worked for it. It is this faulty way of thinking that later puts able-bodied people on welfare rolls. While the government fosters this kind of handout mentality, it is usually learned first not out in society but in the home.

Children will always appreciate bicycles, athletic equipment, and extra clothes much more when they have had some role in working for them. The child who receives a new car as a gift on his eighteenth birthday is going to have a very different value system than the one who works hard, saves up his money, and makes his own decision to buy a $800 car rather than an $8,000 car.

While money should be associated with work, not all work should be associated with money. It is important that children not always be paid for their chores. There needs to be not just the motive of profit but the motive of responsibility and the joy or goodness of the work itself. However, there are a multitude of "extras" beyond the basics, which every parent can define, that can be legitimately rewarded on a financial basis. There are also jobs outside the home that children can take on as they grow older—including paper routes, washing cars, mowing lawns, and baby-sitting.

However we do it, it is important that we teach our children a basic work ethic. On the other hand, it is equally important that children learn to put work and other commitments in their proper place. When I was a youth pastor, I saw many teenagers suffer spiritually because they regularly missed church and youth group and special retreats due to jobs, athletics, music, school activities, and other involvements. While all these can be good, something is wrong when they consistently result in young people missing vital opportunities to cultivate their spiritual lives. Any young person who is encouraged or allowed by his parents to put other pursuits above ministry, fellowship, prayer, mutual discipleship, and the teaching of God's Word, will live out those same priorities as an adult church member—if he isn't too busy to go to church at all.

SAVING

Children learn the value of money and the discipline of self-control through saving. While some banks are reluctant to deal with small accounts, it is possible to put your child's money in your account and keep deposit and withdrawal ledgers between yourself and him. You can pay him whatever interest rate you are earning. He will be impressed to learn firsthand that saving money produces even more money.

Children need reasons and incentives to save. If your child wants a major item, say a telescope, develop with him a plan of saving up for it over a period of six months or a year. Perhaps he will be able to save ten or twenty dollars a month. Help him think of jobs to accomplish this goal. If he sticks with his plan to save this money over a long period of time, buying that telescope will not be an impulsive decision. And once he gets it, he is likely to take good care of it.

Children should be shown how to save both for short-term and long-term purposes. For instance, they might be saving up enough to go see a movie next week. Or they might be saving to buy a sleeping bag three months from now or to have spending money on a major family vacation a year from now.

Many parents know what it is like to have teenagers who go to annual school events that are extremely costly. Not only seniors going to a prom but freshmen attending a Christmas dance may want to buy expensive dresses and rent tuxedos. Afterward the "thing to do" is go to a fancy restaurant. Frustrated parents have told me that between the clothes and the dinner, it is common for such an evening to cost two hundred dollars per couple!

Any parent who just picks up the tab for such events is doing his children no favor. If a teenager feels these events warrant that kind of money, he needs to work for it himself, months in advance if necessary. Then and only then will he truly understand the cost. When this is the only alternative, it is amazing how many creative options young people can come up with and still have a great time, including borrowing clothes, using one's "old" clothes, and choosing a "cheap" place for dinner. Of course, once more the parents' example is crucial. If you think nothing of spending huge amounts of money for a single evening out, they will learn to do the same.

I don't believe it is a universal truth that parents should pay for their children's college education, at least not all of it. For one thing, sometimes they cannot. But even when they can, it might be better if they didn't. A year spent working right after high school for the purpose of earning money for college has some great potential advantages for developing character and financial responsibility. Both of these will make someone a far better college student, if that is the route he chooses.

One family in our church promised to pay exactly half their children's college education. This kind of shared responsibility seems to me a good balance. After their son went off to school and "had a great time" but failed three classes, they modified their arrangement. He would have to pay *all* the tuition up front, then present his report card at the end of the term. At that time they would pay him half the cost of all courses in which he achieved a "C" or better. These are wise parents who see the importance of incentive and responsibility. They understand what many parents do not—that the quality of one's college education often improves dramatically when he has a substantial part in paying for it.

I suggest a separate college savings account for the children into which both parents and children regularly contribute from the time the children are young. In some cases it is possible to do this under the "Uniform Gifts to Minors" arrangement, so that the interest generated by this account is taxable not on the parents' income but on the children's. Usually this means that the taxes will be much lower or nonexistent, depending on the child's overall earnings.

Since some savings can be channeled into investments, children can also be taught about such things as the stock market. When I was a grade-schooler picking berries and harvesting cauliflower, my father encouraged me to take some of the money and invest in companies through the stock market. This was a very interesting and rewarding experience. While I made a fair amount of money on the transactions, even if I hadn't it would have been well worthwhile. I came to understand at an early age how the stock market and our whole economy works, and that knowledge has been very helpful ever since.

GIVING

The most fundamental lesson any child can learn about finances—even more important than saving—is the lesson of giving. As parents, we should direct and encourage our children to give. But this needs to be more than simply taking our own dollar and giving it to our child to put in the offering. In such cases the child is not giving—he is simply functioning as the middleman in a transfer of money from parents to the Lord. In order for giving to *really* be giving, it must come from the child's own assets.

In our case, we taught our children to tithe from the very earliest age. No matter where their income came from, even as a gift, 10 percent belonged to the Lord and it was absolutely untouchable. If Grandpa gave them ten dollars for Christmas, the question was not, "What can I do with ten dollars?" but, "What can I do with nine dollars?"

I have read several sources that say emphatically, "Don't require your children to tithe." I disagree. It makes no more sense to me than to say, "Don't make your children wash their hands before they eat or wear coats on a cold windy day or put away their toys." As we do not give our children the option of choosing whether they go to church or clean their rooms, so we have not presented tithing as an option.

For those who say, "But giving must be from the heart, not forced by someone else," we would respond, "But giving is also a habit, and like all good habits it can and should be cultivated." There is no better way for a parent to cultivate it than to simply make it one of the many standard practices of the family.

I know people who were raised on the tithe who would no sooner stop tithing than they would stop brushing their teeth. Tithing is so ingrained in their thinking that their children have never once expressed a desire to forgo it. It would be as unthinkable not to tithe as not to close the refrigerator door, not to turn off the faucet, or not to pray before a meal. Of course, keeping to a routine is no guarantee of spirituality. But the holy habit of giving is like the holy habits of Bible study, prayer, witnessing, and hospitality. These things need to become part of our life-style and, if we are not raised with them, we are at a great disadvantage to try to change our habits as adults.

We first started giving our children a salary of fifty cents per week when they were ages three and five. We called it a "salary" because they had to do certain tasks to receive it—"allowance" too often means a regular doling out of funds with no commensurate work responsibility. One nickel of that fifty cents was sacred, designated to the Lord. They would often choose to give more than this, and we encouraged them to do so, reminding them that true giving starts after the tithe.

But when our children did choose to give more, they did it fully aware that they had worked for this money, and that giving it away would leave them with less money to spend. We did not intervene and reward them for their giving by compensating for what it cost them. To do so would be to violate the very essence of giving. We must let God reward as he wishes and not interfere with the process.

Whenever one of the girls says, "This week I want to give all my allowance to God," we have been careful to avoid stifling her spirit by teaching her to be "reasonable" when it comes to giving. We want our children to give as their hearts are led. If this means giving "unreasonably" as the widow of Mark 12 and the Macedonian believers of 2 Corinthians 8, so be it! They will be in good company.

When the girls were seven and five, I gave each of them three jars that I had carefully labeled with their names and the designations "Giving," "Saving," and "Spending." I told them that every time they earned their salary (which was by then one dollar per week) they were to first put at least 10 percent into the giving jar, then distribute the rest between the other two jars as they wished. But once they put money in the giving jar, even beyond the tithe, it was dedicated to the Lord and they could not take it out again. Every Sunday morning they would empty their giving jar and bring it to the offering box at church.

Also, once they put money in saving, they were not to take it out and spend it on anything on the spur of the moment, but were to reserve it for some upcoming special expenditure. However, they were free to transfer money from saving and spending to giving, or from spending to saving. As the jars were lined up, it went this way—they could transfer money to any jar on the left, but never to a jar to the right.

I will never forget the night I explained this new system to my daughters. They were so excited they immediately took the money they already had and distributed it between the jars. They arranged the jars just right on their dressers, and spent hours figuring things with pad and pencil while their dinner grew cold.

In light of the occasion we allowed this. My seven-year-old asked me to show her how to figure percentages on our calculator. Soon she was writing on labels, completely on her own, "Giving $.20 a week," "Saving $.30 a week," and "Spending $.50 a week." To this day we have conversations about their money management stimulated by the use of these three jars. This simple system has resulted in more financial education than anything else we have done.

It is important to realize that a child cannot learn money management unless he has money to manage, and unless that money was somehow earned by his own efforts. Parents who shovel out money according to the dictates of the moment are not teaching their children stewardship. There must be a regular and earned income, as opposed to a parent's pocketbook that appears infinitely deep, for real stewardship decisions to be made.

THE GIVING FAMILY

There is no substitute for emphasizing in the home the cultivation of the spiritual life. Family devotions, parents' and children's quiet times, Scripture memory, special prayer for missionaries, and living below our means are some of the countless things that provide the proper context for all the ideas we are suggesting. Like everything else in the home, good stewardship of money is caught as much as taught.

I highly recommend that families become involved in a special missions project. Family members can work together to financially support, pray for, and correspond with a missionary, a needy family, or an orphan in a foreign land. Supporting missionaries also reminds children of the incredible abundance in America.

If you are planning a major family vacation, why not plan to visit a mission field? Combine the fun with the education and encouragement to missionary families, provided, of course, it works well and is not an inconvenience to them. The four of us were able to spend two months visiting five of our church's missionary families in England, Austria, Greece, Egypt, and Kenya—all for less money than many Americans spend on a car. None of us will ever outlive the impact of either the trip itself *or* the planning, working, praying, and saving for it. We had the thrill of seeing God provide for our trip and seeing his exciting work in these different countries.

TEACHING OUR CHILDREN SELF-CONTROL

Few things we can teach our children will prove as important as the discipline of saying "No." We must model delayed gratification and teach the discipline of avoiding an expenditure when the money could accomplish a higher purpose by being given away, or saved, or used in some better way. Self-control is repeatedly commanded and commended as one of the highest Christian virtues (Gal. 5:22-23; Tit. 2:1-12).

Our children need our help to develop sales resistance. They are by nature impulsive spenders. Self-discipline does not come naturally. Every time we say no to our child about ice cream, candy, a new doll, or squirt gun, we can teach him something. We can teach him that in order for things to be special, they must be the exception, not the rule. We can teach him that there are higher values than immediate gratification, and better ways to use our money than to follow our impulses. A child raised this way will usually follow the same pattern of decision making when he is on his own.

Self-control learned by children in one area often carries over into others. A child who learns to say no to unnecessary purchases is much more prone to say no to the lures of sexual immorality or drugs.

Children whose parents won't give them all or even most of what they want are invariably much more content than their spoiled counterparts. They ask for things far less often than other children, and when they do ask for something they are much more selective. When their parents say no, they can accept a no, aware that no amount of begging, nagging, or badgering will get them their way, but will only result in discipline. The child used to getting whatever he wants continually spends his time learning how to sharpen his skills in manipulating his parents.

Of course, parents should sometimes say yes to their children's requests. Given an overall context of good stewardship, this can teach the lesson of generosity rather than indulgence. A model of tightfisted stinginess is as negative as a model of greed and indulgence. Balance is the key. Our goal is not to be penny-pinchers obsessed with money and fretting over every expenditure, but joyful, responsible, and generous stewards of God's abundance. The point of being careful with our money is simply to free up more resources to be used for kingdom purposes.

SPENDING

Children can learn to shop intelligently, to look around and not buy the first thing that strikes their fancy. We can teach them how to compare values and discover the best places to buy. To avoid impulsive spending, our family has a general rule of not making any major purchase until we have thought about it for at least several months. If we still want it four months later, it is no longer an impulsive expenditure.

I also suggest less shopping for entertainment. Aimless wandering through malls and shopping centers usually produces unnecessary spending. It also breeds discontent to look at all the latest models of things we don't need and can't afford anyway.

However, I do recommend a family "field trip" to a shopping center for a specific purpose—but not to buy something. Look at all the things, then ask yourself and your children if they are really worth the price in light of what else could be done with the money, especially to help others and invest in the kingdom of God.

I walked through a nearby shopping center one day, expressly to identify the products in the store that could be described as things I needed as opposed simply to things I might want. The result was more amazing than I anticipated. Other than a few items of food and the most basic clothing, the other 99.9 percent of the store was nothing but nonnecessities. When I took our girls on the same sort of tour, their job, which they thoroughly enjoyed, was to identify needs as opposed to wants. It was a memorable experience as they realized how few needs and how many wants we really have.

An effective way to teach children how to properly spend their money is to show them how you spend it. By the time children are ten years old or so, they are old enough to be let in on the family budget.

One technique is to bring home an entire paycheck in one dollar bills. Or you could use play money to illustrate the same thing. Put the money in piles to show exactly how much goes to what expenses each month. This way children can actually visualize where the family's money goes. It helps them to compare what is expensive and what is not, and what is priority to the family and what is not.

Some things will surprise the children, and they will ask you questions that can be mutually enlightening. You will probably end up reevaluating and making some healthy changes yourself. Comparing the amount you give away to the amount you spend on yourself may be particularly convicting. Your children may see things from a responsible perspective for the first time. A child who is told to turn off the lights when he leaves the room or to shut the front door behind him suddenly understands *why* when he sees the stack of money that goes to pay the electric bill.

PROGRESSIVE RESPONSIBILITY

As parents, our ultimate purpose is not simply to give our children food and shelter the first twenty years of their lives. Our purpose is to present to the Lord, the church, and the world a reasonably mature adult who is capable of being a good servant, a good steward, and a good citizen.

It is important that as our children grow up they undergo a process of being weaned away from their parents. This means that as a child gets older he should be progressively earning more money and accepting more responsibility for his finances. By the time he is ten, he might have his own savings account. At twelve he might have a part-time summer job. By sixteen, he could have his own checking account. At seventeen he might be paying for his transportation, his recreation, and some of his clothing. Of course, this will vary a great deal according to family needs, preferences, location, work opportunities, and the child's stage of development. The principle, not the exact timetable, is the important part.

As long as a son or daughter is a teenager or in his early twenties, I think it is reasonable to provide his food and lodging. But we must discern when this is in fact healthy and when it is developing bad habits of dependence that will be hard to break when he finally has to function in the "real world." We must also realize that what is good for one child is bad for another and be careful to discern what is best for each.

Of course, the goal is our children's increasing independence of us. This should entail increasing dependence on the Lord so that dependence is transferred rather than eliminated. As we entrust them with more and more financial responsibility, we should find them becoming more and more financially trustworthy. As they prove themselves trustworthy, in turn we will trust them with more—and so will God.

REWARDS

In chapter 9 we saw that God uses a system of positive reinforcement, both through granting short-term rewards and promising long-term rewards. Though God has built into each of us the need for incentives and motivation by reward, some parents don't follow his pattern with their children. Dr. James Dobson wrote:

> Adults are reluctant to utilize rewards because they view them as a source of bribery. Our most workable teaching device is ignored because of a philosophical misunderstanding. Our entire society is established on a system of reinforcement, yet we don't want to apply it where it is needed most: with young children.[1]

The great success of AWANA, Boy Scouts, Girl Scouts, and similar programs for children is largely due to their emphasis on achievement, recognized in the form of patches, badges, ranks, and other tangible rewards. Of course, like every good thing, this can be taken to an extreme. But we must realize that since all children are created to mature through proper motivation, we must gear our training toward motivating them in the most effective ways toward the most healthy ends.

God rewards us both for what we do *and* how and why we do it (1 Cor. 4:2, 5). Because having a good attitude sometimes requires a great deal of work itself, we periodically reward our children in small material ways simply for their attitudes. But while attitude is always important, we usually reward them for specific actions related to a job or responsibility.

Of course, not all rewards are material. As God promises a "well done" to his faithful servants, so a parent's praise is a child's finest reward. Our children's biggest smiles come out when we commend them for their actions and attitudes. And when we *do* give a material reward, we often tie it to a relationship-building experience, such as a breakfast out with Dad, or ice cream with the whole family. Our children know they are not earning our love. But they also know it is possible to gain approval and other rewards through their honest and faithful efforts. Without this training, they will not know how to responsibly function in their vocations *or* in their service for Christ, who is the ultimate Judge and Rewarder (Heb. 11:6).

CHILDREN WHO SHARE

"We really wish Jimmy knew how to share." Most parents identify with this wish. We are appalled and embarrassed at our children's displays of greed and possessiveness. We sincerely want them to learn to share—yet too often we ourselves do not provide them a model for sharing.

When we need to use a certain tool or kitchen gadget, perhaps that we will use only once or at most a few times a year, many of us buy it ourselves rather than borrow from our neighbor. This does two things—it results in unnecessary expense *and* it circumvents the development of a relationship with our neighbor that would be naturally cultivated by the sharing of resources. It also does a third thing—it trains our children to think and live independently rather than interdependently.

And what do our children learn when they hear us—and they do hear—complaining about the fact that we loaned someone our car and he returned it dirty or dented? They may have even heard it said, "That's the last time we loan our tent to the youth group." If we view our assets as really belonging to God, we are glad to lend out a book, realizing it may come back with a torn jacket or dog-eared pages, or—a common experience—it will never come back at all. But this is simply part of sharing. To learn true sharing, children must *see* it. We must not just talk about sharing. We must share.

Hospitality is one of the strongest ways we can teach our children to share. By opening our homes to others and being gracious hosts and hostesses, we teach our children both to share and to enjoy the fruits of sharing. They see firsthand the value of encouraging other people and drawing close to them through the unselfish use of possessions. You might even look back with your children at some of the people you have opened your home to and wonder if, without knowing it, you have entertained an angel in disguise (Heb. 13:2).

CHILDREN WHO ARE THANKFUL

"Sharper than a serpent's tooth it is to have a thankless child." Any parent who has one knows exactly what Shakespeare meant. In the midst of the abundance they have always known, and with the sin nature they have always had, our children will not naturally be thankful. We must teach them to be thankful.

"Praise the Lord, O my soul, and forget not all his benefits" (Ps. 103:2). As parents we can lead the way by counting our blessings and expressing in front of the children our own thankfulness to God for all he has done for us. Then we must be careful not to nullify this by demonstrating a complaining and ungrateful spirit for things that don't go our way. All too often they hear such remarks from us as, "What a shame it had to rain today," or "This stupid car is always breaking down," or "That's the second year in a row without a raise."

Often we ask our children at night to identify a number of things they are thankful for that God did for them that very day. At first this may be difficult, but in time it develops a sensitive eye to the ways God has cared for them. At the top of the list of things to be thankful for is God himself, our loving Redeemer. Next are the family and friends and church he has given us.

Children can also give thanks for material things, but for more than just toys—for a body that works, a bed to sleep in, a house to live in, for the air, sunshine, rain, the beauty of the flowers and the trees. They can pray in thankfulness for a country in which they are free to worship and share their faith.

Giving thanks for all these things draws their hearts not to the things themselves but to the One who graciously provides them. The focus is not on the gifts but the Giver. Then even when the body hurts, the bed is hard, and the house is cold and creaky, there remains the constant assurance that God is still there and still faithful.

As children develop thankfulness for their food and other provisions, they can learn to see them not as "easy come, easy go" commodities, but as precious and personal provisions of a heavenly Father who loves them. Otherwise, in a throwaway society of paper plates, paper towels, plastic spoons, and disposables of every variety, it is hard to develop a proper appreciation for things.

The obstacles to thankfulness are many, but they must be overcome in the Christian home, where we are to give thanks in all circumstances (2 Thess. 5:18). And let us not apologize for insisting that our children develop still another old-fashioned habit—saying "Please" and "Thank you."

CONCLUSION

Nothing will so interfere with a child's relationship with God—or even prevent him from having such a relationship—as a life centered on things. Our greatest legacy to our children is to help them develop their inner lives, their spiritual selves, their hearts for God. We must intertwine this with the building of strong character, moral fiber, and rugged biblical values that can endure the beatings of a godless, materialistic society.

While many parents will leave their children only a big inheritance, we can leave them what really matters—a rich heritage. They can then pass on this legacy to their own children. Godly generations and eternal impact can result from our simple acts of faithfulness to our Lord's life-changing instructions about money and possessions.

NOTES
1. James Dobson, *Dare to Discipline* (Wheaton, Ill.: Tyndale House Publishers, 1970), 56.

CONCLUSION

WHERE DO WE GO FROM HERE?

I continually find it necessary to guard against that natural love of wealth and grandeur which prompts us always, when we come to apply our general doctrine to our own case, to claim an exception. William Wilberforce

The antagonism between life and conscience may be removed in two ways: by a change of life or by a change of conscience. Leo Tolstoy

Someone in our church sent the following anonymous letter in response to a sermon on giving preached the previous Sunday:

> I was never so disappointed in a service as I was Sunday. I have an unbelieving friend that I got to come with me, and what were you preaching about? *Money!* I can assure you

she was not impressed! And why money, when there are so many beautiful things to say? You'd better reconsider such messages in the future. Leave money to God, and he will handle everything, believe me. I love this church and usually like the sermons, but that was terrible.

The writer signed off with the knife-turning flair so typical of anonymous letters: "A Christian who loves to go to church to hear the Word."

It was one of our other pastors who preached that particular message on giving, and I can objectively say it was an excellent exposition of Scripture, involving no overstatement or manipulation. Many people were deeply appreciative of the message, but this person's negative reaction is not unique.

Talking about something as sensitive as money among Christians today is often difficult—unless, of course, we choose simply to rephrase or baptize the world's position on the subject. If we do so, we will be quite popular. The letter illustrates that many who think of themselves as those who "love to hear the Word" are offended when they hear what the Word actually says, especially when it threatens their comfortable beliefs and life-styles.

Is the solution to avoid sensitivities and defensive reactions by avoiding the subject of money? No! If we are to proclaim "the whole will of God" (Acts 20:27), then we simply *must* give attention to this subject that is such an integral part of the Scriptures.

When churches and parachurch organizations address the subject of giving, perhaps a fundamental mistake we often make is tying it to a specific need or request. We preach on giving because giving is down or to kick off a building fund drive. Or we send a pamphlet on giving along with a letter that says our ministry or school will shut down if we don't get $50,000 in the next four weeks. The result is that people view the instruction on giving merely as a fund-raising tool, a means to the end of accomplishing our personal or institutional goals, and indeed it may be just that. This is unfortunate, because this matter of money and possessions is an issue of discipleship at the very heart and soul of our walk with Christ, with profound effects for both time and eternity.

In a society so preoccupied and consumed with money and possessions, Christians will inevitably be continually exposed to wrong thinking and wrong living. Certainly we cannot expect the Christian community to respond to what Scripture says about money, possessions, and eternity unless we raise the issues and teach and apply the principles. Otherwise the world's view, as opposed to the Word's view, is sure to prevail in our midst.

I encourage readers to ask their pastors to address these subjects from the pulpit. Most pastors would welcome such an invitation. Perhaps this book could serve as a resource for them. But that is just a beginning. Small groups and Sunday school classes need to discuss these issues, either on their own or, better yet, as a follow-up to Sunday messages. Body members need to disciple each other in financial stewardship. Young believers need to see biblical life-style principles embodied in their brothers and sisters. Those who have learned about the bondage of debt the hard way need to warn others. Young couples need to hear older couples tell of their joy in giving over the years and how God has used it in their family. Husbands and wives need to be encouraged to discuss and practically apply these far-reaching truths. One small step that we have taken in our church is to assemble and distribute a booklet comprised of the financial testimonies and lessons learned by ten of our families.

Financial stewardship is a subject that is not dealt with best in isolation. People respond most completely in giving and living when they have a tangible example they can follow in their leaders and their peers (Num. 7:3; 1 Chron. 29:9; 2 Chron. 24:10). One Christian told me, "When I look at the Bible, I get really convicted to change my life-style—but then I look around at all the other Christians who live like I do and I end up saying, 'It's OK—everybody else lives this way too.'" To turn the tide of materialism in the Christian community, we desperately need bold models of kingdom-centered living.

Whole churches can stimulate each other by example. Paul exhorted the Corinthians to follow the example of the Macedonians: "Excel in this grace of giving" (2 Cor. 8:1-7). Then he told the Corinthians others would be encouraged to follow *their* example in giving (2 Cor. 9:12-14). Individuals, families, and churches here and there can establish beachheads of strategic life-style, disciplined spending, and generous globally-minded giving. By infectious example, we can in time claim more territory for Christ than we ever dreamed possible.

A revival of lavish giving and strategic living is a revival of grace that will be accompanied by the power of God. As the body of Christ gets serious about learning and living God's instructions concerning money and possessions, the cause of Christ will be furthered and the person of Christ exalted in us and through us as never before.

DEPOSITING THIS LIFE IN ETERNITY'S ACCOUNT

When Hudson Taylor opened a bank account for the China Inland Mission, the application form asked for a list of all his assets. Taylor wrote: "Ten pounds and all the promises of God." We must not forget our greatest resources are spiritual—not material. They come from another world—not this one.

One morning I was having breakfast at a restaurant when a frazzled, agitated woman blew through the door and loudly complained to her friend, "The wipers aren't working again on my Porsche, and the Audi is in for repairs. I've had it!"

I had to smile, but at the same time I was saddened for this poor woman. What a contrast to the believer with eternal perspective who can say:

> I have learned to be content whatever the circumstances. I know what it is to be in need, and I know what it is to have plenty. I have learned the secret of being content in any and every situation, whether well fed or hungry, whether living in plenty or in want. I can do everything through him who gives me strength. (Phil. 4:11-13)

In the third century, Cyprian, bishop of Carthage, wrote this description of the affluent:

> Their property held them in chains . . . chains which shackled their courage and choked their faith and hampered their judgment and throttled their souls. . . . If they stored up their treasure in heaven, they would not now have an enemy and a thief within their household. . . . They think of themselves as owners, whereas it is they rather

who are owned: enslaved as they are to their own property, they are not the masters of their money but its slaves.[1]

It was out of this same conviction that John Wesley said, "Money never stays with me. It would burn me if it did. I throw it out of my hands as soon as possible, lest it should find its way into my heart."

The Philippians were told that their faithful gifts to Paul's missionary ministry were "credited to your account" (Phil. 4:17). The accountant is God. It is he who is keeping accounts of what we do with our money and our life. At the moment we meet Christ—at our death or his return—all accounts are frozen, all assets and expenditures opened for the Final Audit. And then it is God himself, the owner, manager, and head teller of the bank of eternity, who will make eternal dispersals based on how our account reads after the last deposit is made and the account closed.

C. T. Studd was a rich and famous English athlete who sold his entire estate, gave the money away, and went to the mission field to serve Christ. He summed up the perspective that motivated him in these words:

Only one life,
 'twill soon be past.
Only what's done
 for Christ will last.

FROM WHOM ARE WE TAKING OUR CUES?

After Jesus completed some characteristically radical statements about money, we are told, "The Pharisees, who loved money, heard all this and were sneering at Jesus" (Luke 16:14). The frightening thing about the Pharisees' response is that they were the religious conservatives of their day. The lesson for us is that we may believe the Scriptures, defend them, be willing to die for them, and still be materialists who reject and even mock the radical teachings of Christ about money and possessions.

We must examine our values and consider whether we are taking our cues from our God or our society. It isn't enough to say we believe the Scriptures. We must open our hearts, our minds, and, yes, our life-styles to all God has to say to us.

Our hymnbooks say a lot about following Jesus. But our pocketbooks say even more. A study of thirty-plus denominations points out that although income after taxes and inflation increased 31 percent in the previous seventeen years, member giving as a percentage of disposable income decreased by 8.5 percent in the same period. The study's director concluded, "People are objectively richer, but the wealth is not expanding the ministry of the church."[2]

What can we say to such statistics? What does it mean when God has entrusted millions of professing Christians with greater wealth than there has ever been in human history, and yet many are actually giving less of it to kingdom purposes than ever before? Surely it means that we are taking our cues from the wrong place.

The great British preacher G. Campbell Morgan said:

> The measure of failure on the part of the Church is the measure in which she has allowed herself to be influenced by the spirit of the age, because she has been untrue to the facts of her own life. We are sometimes told today that what the Church supremely needs is that she should catch the spirit of the age. A thousand times no. What the Church supremely needs is to correct the spirit of the age. The church in Corinth catching the spirit of Corinth became anemic, weak, and failed to deliver the message of God to Corinth. The church of God in London, invaded by the spirit of London, the materialism, militarism, sordidness, and selfishness of London, is too weak to save London. . . .
>
> If the Church's failure is due to the fact that the spirit of the city has invaded the church, the Church's success is due to the fact that the Spirit of the church invades the city. . . .
>
> The Church of God always fails when she becomes conformed to the methods, maxims, and manners of the city. The Church of God always succeeds when, true to the supernatural nature of her life, she stands in perfect separation from the city. Only thus is she able to touch and help the city.[3]

As Christians of the Western world, our senses have become

dulled by the glut of our affluence. While God's Word and God's world scream for our attention, we go right on, mindlessly living out of sync with eternity's musical score. We go right on ad-libbing our own rendition of the concert, while an audience of angels and saints shudders at our apparent indifference to the direction of the Composer and Conductor.

Each Christian, each family, and each church must understand that, with or without us, God is moving. He is accomplishing his kingdom program. He is using the time, energy, skills, and material resources of his disciples all over this globe to touch and change lives for all eternity.

The question is not whether God is going somewhere. The question is whether we are choosing to get on board.

A HARD LOOK AT OURSELVES

> God's will is that our lives should be "a perpetual crisis of dependence on him." We defeat his will in our lives when we lay up treasures on earth.
>
> The life of faith does not follow automatically when a person becomes a Christian. It requires deliberate action on his part. This is especially true in an affluent society. The believer must put himself in a position where he is compelled to trust God. . . . It is only as he gets rid of his reserves and other false supports that he can truly launch out into the deep.[4]

What are we to make of such words? Are they spoken out of naivete and irresponsibility? Or out of biblical faith and discipleship? Or could they be either, depending upon the person speaking them and the condition of his heart and life, as well as the source of his convictions?

> How utterly in keeping with this age of grace it is for us to sell our prized possessions—our diamonds and other jewelry, our original paintings, our antique furniture, our sterling silver, our stamp collections—and put the proceeds to work in the salvation of souls throughout the world.[5]

It isn't surprising that unbelievers would scoff at such a proposal. But isn't it revealing when professing disciples of Jesus Christ resent and resist and rationalize and defensively pontificate on why such a perspective is too naive and too foolish and too restrictive and too demanding and too legalistic and too . . . *anything?* Is the truth simply that we are far more familiar and comfortable with the world's teaching about money and possessions than with Christ's? Are we perhaps so far removed from the realm of New Testament discipleship that what was once obvious and elementary to any true Christian is now radical, foreign, offensive, and even repulsive to us?

Why do we take such consolation in the words and life-styles of those celebrity Christians who judge success by the standards of the world? Why do we take our cues from people so conspicuously different than Jesus? Why do we listen to men who, had they lived in the first century, would have sold tickets to the feeding of the five thousand and charged a fee to watch the raising of Lazarus?

Is there a time to stop kidding ourselves? Is there a time to say the obvious—that the New Testament call to discipleship and compassion and giving simply leaves no room for the way many of us are currently thinking and living? Is it time to get beyond the theoretical expression, "I'd be willing to give up anything if God asked me to," and to actually start giving up things in order to do what he has commanded us to?

There are amazingly few prophetic voices in the church decrying our self-centered affluence and indifference to global need. One such voice maintains that we have turned away from the biblical Jesus, the true Jesus, and created in our own image a cultural Jesus who is agreeable to our own materialistic life-styles:

> The Jesus of the Bible differs from the cultural Jesus in what he asks of you. To follow the biblical Jesus is to do exactly what he would do in your circumstances. . . . Am I suggesting that if you follow Jesus you won't be able to go out and buy a BMW? You got it!
>
> You might say, "But I know a lot of godly people who own BMWs." Well, when they really get godly they will repent of their BMWs, because BMWs are luxury cars that

symbolize conspicuous consumption instead of passionate concern for the suffering of the world. Let me put it quite simply: If Jesus had $40,000 and knew about the kids who are suffering and dying in Haiti, what kind of car would he buy?

There's no room for conspicuous consumption. . . . It's time to repent of our affluence.

Am I suggesting that you can't be rich and follow the biblical Jesus at the same time? Hey, I'm not the guy who dreamed up the line that it's harder for rich people to enter the kingdom of heaven than for a camel to go through the eye of a needle. That's somebody else's line.

Please, if this offends you, be offended. Reject Jesus if you must, *but don't take the biblical Jesus and turn him into something that he is not.* . . .

Sometimes I worry about us evangelicals. We work overtime proving that the Bible is inerrant. Then we refuse to accept what it says. . . .

The cultural Jesus asks you only to believe the right stuff. The biblical Jesus asks you to live the right stuff.[6]

Once again, such words are liable to offend us. We may angrily pass them off as unfair and judgmental. But on what biblical or even humanitarian basis do we refute them? If we step aside from our obvious vested interests in disbelieving these conclusions, and really look at the matter objectively in light of scriptural principle and Christ's example, is the author's viewpoint really so controversial?

Is it really unfair to ask whether Jesus would spend $40,000 on a luxury car, given the staggering human needs and the eternal investment alternatives? And if the answer is "obviously, Jesus would not take such a step," then why is it so strange to conclude that we who are called to "follow in his steps" (1 Pet. 2:21) should also not take such a step?

Tolstoy said that the antagonism between life and conscience may be removed either by a change of life or by a change of conscience. Many of us have elected to change our consciences rather than our lives. Our powers of rationalization are unlimited. They allow us to live in luxury and indifference while others, whom we could help if we chose to, starve and go to hell.

We have a silent agreement with each other not to talk about such things, I know. "Laying guilt trips" on each other is the modern unpardonable sin. But we would do better to violate that agreement and come to terms with the conditions of discipleship now, rather than to postpone the discussion till the judgment seat of Christ, where we will find ourselves woefully ill-equipped to argue with the Judge.

But we need not wait for God's judgment and correction later. We may avoid later judgment by judging and correcting ourselves now: "But if we judged ourselves we would not come under judgment" (1 Cor. 11:31).

If we fear appearing to be foolish to others by taking seriously the New Testament view of money and possessions, we must remind ourselves of what the Bible says about being fools for Christ (1 Cor. 1:18-31; 4:8-13). The question is not whether we will be seen as fools, but when and to whom we will be seen as fools. Better to be seen as a fool now in the eyes of men—even Christians—than to be seen as a fool forever in the eyes of the only One whose judgment will ultimately matter.

OUR ACCOUNTABILITY
AS GOD'S MONEY MANAGERS

In ancient times only the eunuchs were entrusted with the king's harem. Other men could be captivated by strong passions for these beautiful women, but the eunuch could work with them without violating them or the king's trust. In a sense, the Christian is to be a eunuch in regard to money and possessions. He is not to be infatuated or preoccupied with them, led astray by them, or entangled in an affair with them. They are part of his daily life, he handles them, and he appreciates them for what they are, but they hold no captivating sway on him.

Money and possessions are assets when they meet our basic needs, serve our God-given purposes, and allow us to focus on Christ and his kingdom as the objects of our desire. They are liabilities when they themselves become the objects of our desire.

For better or for worse, we are God's money managers. The only question is, how well will we do our jobs? And whether we realize it or not, we spend every day of our lives answering this question.

In the context of financial stewardship, Jesus said, "From everyone that has been given much, much will be demanded; and from the one who has been entrusted with much, much more will be asked" (Luke 12:48).

In all of human history, has there ever been a community of believers who has been given more than we? That has been entrusted with more than we? Has there, then, ever been a community of believers of whom God will ask or demand more than we? God has entrusted a fortune to us. And we must make no mistake about it—we will be required to answer to him for what we have done with it (Rom. 14:12).

Church father John Chrysostom warned his fellow believers, "You have taken possession of the resources that belong to Christ and you consume them aimlessly. Don't you realize that you are going to be held accountable?"

We must stop saying Scripture is unclear on this subject. While it does leave some room for differences in individual life-styles, it leaves no room whatsoever for materialism, greed, envy, pride, selfishness, hoarding, irresponsible spending, un-justifiable debt, or indifference to the needs of the poor or lost. When any of these is justified on the basis of "legitimate life-style differences," we may be fooling ourselves and each other, but we are not fooling our Lord.

God has given us in Christ all the resources we need to obey him. If we are disobedient, it is not because we can't obey but because we won't. We have willfully chosen not to. If we fail to live according to his words about money and possessions, it is not because we are unable. We must stop kidding ourselves and start repenting. No one repents of inability. We can only repent of what we first admit to be sin.

For some of us, it is time to drop to our knees and ask God's forgiveness for our self-indulgent life-styles and indifference to human need. For others, it is time to joyfully move on in our process of enlightenment, applying more and more of the biblical principles we have examined. For each of us, it is time to commit or recommit ourselves to a life of obedience and exhilarating discipleship, with all that implies in the handling of our money and possessions. It is time to turn our backs on the

American dream of unlimited material prosperity. It is time to trade in our own material dreams for the kingdom dreams of the risen Christ.

In any case, we must not procrastinate obedience. Nothing is more fleeting than the moment of conviction. If we turn our backs on that moment, the next may not come until we stand before our Lord—when it will be too late to reclaim a lifetime of squandered assets and opportunities.

COMING TO GRIPS WITH ETERNITY

The meager flame of this life will appear to be snuffed out by death, but on the other side it will rage to sudden and eternal intensity. In light of this knowledge we must learn to "fix our eyes not on what is seen, but on what is unseen" (2 Cor. 4:18) and live each day in the light of the long tomorrow.

A. W. Tozer lived in that light. He said, "Any temporal possession can be turned into everlasting wealth. Whatever is given to Christ is immediately touched with immortality."[7]

Martin Luther lived in the same light, saying, "I have held many things in my hands and I have lost them all. But whatever I have placed in God's hands, that I still possess."

God tells us to prepare for the long tomorrow by using our short todays to exchange earthly treasures for heavenly ones.

Jim Elliot was right when he weighed the cost-to-benefits ratio of serving Christ and came to this conclusion: "He is no fool who gives what he cannot keep to gain what he cannot lose." The corollary might be stated, "He is a great fool who tries to hold on to what he cannot keep, and loses what he could have gained."

Five minutes after we die, we will understand what is most important. We will see with the clarity of eternity. The blinders will be gone. We can choose either to take off the blinders now while we still have our earthly lives to live, or to wait for them to be taken off after death when it will be too late to change anything we've done on earth.

May what will be most important to us five minutes after we die become most important to us now.

NOTES

1. Quoted by Art Beals, *Beyond Hunger* (Portland, Oreg.: Multnomah Press, 1985), 166-67.
2. Sylvia Ronsvalle, quoted in "Earning More, Giving Less," *Christianity Today* 2 Sept 1988: 47.
3. G. Campbell Morgan, *Living Messages of the Books of the Bible* (Old Tappan, N.J.: Revell, n.d.), 120, 123.
4. William MacDonald, *True Discipleship* (Kansas City: Walterick Publishers, 1975), 92-93.
5. MacDonald, 108.
6. Anthony Campolo, "Will the Real Jesus Please Stand Up?" *World Vision* Oct.-Nov. 1988: 4-6.
7. A. W. Tozer, "The Transmutation of Wealth," *Born after Midnight* (Harrisburg, Penn.: Christian Publications, 1959), 107.

APPENDIX A

MATERIALISM, MAN, AND MORALITY

Materialism treats the temporal as if it were eternal and the eternal as if it were nonexistent. It is the inevitable consequence of atheism or agnosticism and invariably leads to the elevation of things on the one hand and the depreciation of people on the other. If people are created by a purposeful God, only then do they have purpose and value. If they are merely the product of time, blind chance, and impersonal evolutionary forces, there is no fundamental defense for the intrinsic value of a human being.

The materialist may say people are more important than things, but on what basis can he support such a contention? What makes a person more valuable than a dog, a tree, or even a rock? He is different from them only in degree, not in kind. On the other hand, if man is God's special creation, made in his own image, created to rule over the world, then he is different not merely in degree, but in kind, distinct from and superior to the

413

material realm. This, in fact, is precisely what Scripture teaches about man (Gen. 1:27-30; Ps. 8:3-8).

But if we accept the prevailing belief, taught almost universally in the Western world, that man is simply one more rung on the endless evolutionary ladder, who is to say one rung is more valuable than the previous? On what basis is a man's life worth more than an animal's? Because he is more powerful or has a superior intellect? How does this differ from saying smart and strong people are worth more than retarded and weak people? Or that an intelligent chimpanzee is more valuable than a severely retarded child? Today, the same car is likely to have one bumper sticker saying, "Save the Whales," and another, "Abortion: A Woman's Right." Save the whales; kill the children!

In evolutionary terms, it is a very short step from believing the fit will survive over the unfit, to believing that they deserve to survive. The world has seen numerous examples of the outworking of this philosophy in our own century, most notably Hitler's Third Reich.

If there is no eternal, there is no soul. Our minds are not really minds, but the illusory product of the brain, that pulsating piece of matter that is nothing more than a sophisticated thing. When our brains cease to function, it is not simply our body that dies; *we* die. In this framework, man's fate is no different than the animal's or the tree's or the rock's—so why should he be treated differently?

Materialism is an attempt to find meaning in a universe that has been stripped of meaning through the denial of its Creator. This is the heart and soul of materialism—it is not a random form of behavior but the logical conclusion of an incorrect theology. Materialism does not begin with a wrong view of things; it ends there. It begins with a wrong view of God, which produces a wrong view of man and a wrong view of things.

Only man is arrogant enough to suppose he can put God out of business by denying him. Once God is "dethroned," there is no line of defense for the value of every human being, and therefore no line of defense for any values at all. If we think about it, it is totally predictable that a materialist culture will sanction abortion, infanticide, euthanasia, and every other form of God-playing imaginable. We should never be shocked at what a materialist does. He will do whatever he *can* do to serve his twisted philosophy of life. This is why technology is so dangerous in the hands of the materialist.

Increasingly we hear the issue of money raised in moral discussions. "Consider the expense to the taxpayer of unwanted children." "Do you realize what it does to everyone's health insurance premiums to provide care for hopelessly deformed infants and human vegetables?" "The Social Security system simply cannot sustain the numbers of elderly and infirm there will be by the end of the century."

No matter how they are phrased, such statements pave the way for the elimination of human life for financial reasons. This is already widely true of abortion, somewhat true of infanticide, and will increasingly be true of euthanasia of the elderly and helpless, the so-called noncontributors to the economy, the leeches of society. Many Americans were shocked some years ago when a congressman was quoted as saying the elderly and infirm had an obligation to unburden society by means of their voluntary euthanasia. Yet, given the premises of materialism, his comment was but a natural conclusion.

The most blatant forms of immorality, the most hideous violations of human dignity will inevitably become commonplace in a materialistic society, provided only that they are cost-effective. After you cut through all the noble-sounding rhetoric, money, not God and not human worth, is the only bottom line consideration of materialism.

Materialism will inevitably produce the kind of society increasingly evident in America—a society of individualism, where people live parallel lives, not meaningfully intersecting with others. A society where independence is the only absolute, where self-interest is the only creed, where convenience and expediency and profitability are the only values. A society where people know the price of everything, but the value of nothing—where people have a great deal to live on, but very little to live for.

LOVING THINGS, USING PEOPLE

All this may sound like philosophy and sociology and ethics, but it is also extremely practical. The problem of materialism boils down to this: While God created us to love people and use things, the materialist loves things and uses people. He may deny this, but his philosophy of life insures that it will be true. Note the tendency to treat and target people as objects rather than subjects. For instance, the prevalent term "consumer" speaks not of a person, but an economic unit, of value to a company only as an object that can potentially contribute to its profits.

We have every reason to be alarmed about our country's materialism, but no reason whatsoever to be surprised by it. For our outer materialism is nothing more nor less than the logical and inescapable extension of our inner capitulation to the philosophy of materialism.

The twenty-five-year-olds of the 1980 *Fortune* study cited in chapter 3 are not the "bad apples" of society, not the abandoned street kids or reform school grads. They are "the best," the product of the best homes and best schools in this country. They have believed and are living out what the educational system of our homes, schools, media, and peers—sometimes, sadly, even our churches—has taught them. They are the product of a worldview without God and therefore without spiritual values. Since every person must value something, what other values could we expect from a generation of materialists than materialistic values? As a society, we are reaping exactly what we have sown.

Materialism can never be corrected by high-sounding courses in ethics or the campaign speeches of politicians calling on us to restore the moral fiber of our nation. Moral fiber must come from somewhere. It must be cultivated in our educational institutions, beginning with the home. Moral fiber cannot simply be grabbed out of the sky in the midst of a moral vacuum. Materialism can only be corrected by a different view of God. This in turn can only come from a belief in and study of the Scriptures, which tell us about God, and which alone give us the context to truly understand the critical God-related subjects of man, money, and possessions.

APPENDIX B

FINANCIAL INTEGRITY AND ACCOUNTABILITY IN CHURCH AND PARACHURCH MINISTRIES

Largely in response to financial improprieties, several national organizations have been established to provide financial accountability for Christian ministries.[1] Accountability should certainly include periodic audits and reviews by external organizations. But it must begin internally with more wise and careful choices of those in leadership positions. It must also begin with a commitment to *plural* leadership that does not leave one person, or one commanding individual surrounded by passive ones, in a position to embezzle, squander, or otherwise misuse funds.

The spending patterns of some Christian organizations are exemplary. They are continuously conscious of God's ownership

417

of their assets and the fact that financial gifts have been given them by other stewards who may have sacrificed to further God's kingdom through their giving. They spend this money carefully and thoughtfully, with a view toward the purpose for which it is given and the eternal kingdom in which it is to be invested.

Other Christian organizations think nothing of providing luxury cars for executives, booking first-class flights around the world, putting up personnel in luxury hotels, wooing donors over hundred-dollar dinners, and making costly, frequent, and unnecessary phone calls all over the world. Of course, a good deal of travel and international communication is sometimes vital to a ministry. It isn't these expenditures I'm objecting to, but the excessive and unnecessary use of funds given to the ministry in good faith by people who assume it is being used carefully. This problem is largely attributable to lack of accountability to others who could point to the misappropriations and insist that they either be eliminated or made public.

The situation described in 2 Corinthians 8 specifically involves the handling and distribution of church funds, and the need to do this in an aboveboard and accountable fashion. A substantial offering was being collected in Corinth, to be distributed to the poor in distant Jerusalem. Paul assured the Corinthians that not only Titus, whom they knew to be a man of integrity, but another unnamed man highly thought of in the Christian community had been "chosen by the churches to accompany us as we carry the offering" (8:19).

Paul mentioned still another nameless brother, with equally impeccable credentials, who would also watch over the carrying of the funds (v. 22). Titus and these two men, who would join Paul and his group, formed a company to be trusted to the utmost in handling and distributing the offerings (v. 23).

Paul assured the Corinthians that his group would administer the funds "in order to honor the Lord himself and to show our eagerness to help" (v. 19). But Paul did not resent the direct involvement of the other two character-approved men in this process of watching over the funds. On the contrary, he welcomed it and probably initiated it himself.

Any Christian leader who resists the principle of financial accountability stands on unbiblical ground. An independent, as opposed to interdependent, spirit has no place in leading the body of Christ. A man who puts too much trust in himself is not to be trusted.

I spoke with a Christian leader who had been caught embezzling funds. His downfall came when he was in a personal financial crisis. Because of his position and its lack of checks and balances, the money could be easily "borrowed" from an account that didn't belong to him. He rationalized that he could and would pay it back later. All men are faced with temptations, but many financial temptations and sins could be avoided by more careful structures in which improprieties cannot easily occur.

I know of a large church where all contributors' checks are stamped, "Pay to the order of Grace Church, *or* John Smith, pastor" (not real names, of course). What is accomplished by such an unwise procedure? At very best it will generate unnecessary questions and suspicion. At worst it will bring temptation to the pastor, and someday it may well result in his downfall and great hurt to the church and the reputation of Christ.

Paul said, "We want to avoid any criticism of the way we administer this liberal gift" (v. 20). He went out of his way to include other character-approved men both from inside and outside his own group to assure the money was handled in an aboveboard manner and to avoid any doubts or criticisms that could bring discredit to them, their ministry, or their Lord.

Paul said, "For we are taking pains to do what is right, not only in the eyes of the Lord but also in the eyes of men" (v. 21). Here are two important points. First, we need to *take pains* to do what is right—a system of financial accountability may seem awkward, cumbersome, time-consuming, or a nuisance. At times it may seem unnecessary. But it is *right,* and we must therefore take pains to do it.

Second, it is not enough for leaders to say, "Our conscience is clear before the Lord." Our actions must be as above reproach as possible, "not only in the eyes of the Lord but the eyes of men." Whatever system of collection and distribution of funds we chose, it *must* involve awareness and accountability with a plurality of character-approved men or women, preferably not only chosen by each other but by a church or constituency. While two character-approved family members might appropriately sit together on a board, there is no place for the sort of nepotism that makes organizations top-heavy with underqualified relatives and childhood friends who look the other way rather than foster personal and financial accountability.

If all this seems unnecessarily picky, we must realize the particular sensitivity of financial matters—especially in view of the current milieu of corruption that has surfaced in religious organizations. This has produced among believers and un-believers alike a deep skepticism related to the use of funds by religious leaders. The financial and sexual scandals of recent years have reduced giving not only to the organizations involved but to many faithful and reputable ministries as well. Worse yet, they have eroded people's confidence in Christian leaders on both the national and local scenes.

In light of the serious consequences of past carelessness, every church and Christian organization needs to ask itself what steps can be taken—even if they are unprecedented and incon-venient steps—to *be* and to *appear* financially above reproach in the eyes of both God and men.

NOTES
1. One of these is the ECFA, Evangelical Council for Financial Account-ability, with over three hundred Christian organizations in membership as of 1988. The ECFA monitors members, investigates alleged abuses, and issues public reports.

APPENDIX C

THE USE OF MINISTRY FUNDS FOR BUILDINGS

Are buildings a legitimate use of contributions? If so what kinds of buildings, and how many? These are difficult questions, but Christians, churches, and parachurch organizations must face them. Buildings come in every variety. Some churches have buildings worth no more than a typical private home of one of its members. Others have over a hundred million dollars worth of land and buildings—and some parachurch ministries more still. Can this extensive accumulation of material wealth be justified in light of world need? And how can we tell when it is and when it isn't?

John White tells a story that reflects my own view about buildings and God's kingdom cause:

> Many years ago I stood one night in the rain, looking wonderingly at the walls of what was then the China

421

Inland Mission headquarters in London. I had read many CIM books . . . and had been thrilled and quickened by the way God had supplied the mission's needs "through prayer to God alone." That night as I looked at the dirty but solid brick wall I reached out my hand to touch it. It seemed like a holy thing. Not that the CIM was anything other than a human organization blessed and used by God. But to me the walls were an awesome and tangible monument to the reality of God's response to faith. It was as through God himself had put them there. "This is what God did," I said, glowing warmly, feeling the solidity of the wet bricks as awe stole over my whole body. "A solid monument to God's response to faith." There are many so-called monuments to faith around the world today. People would like us to believe that God raised them in answer to believing prayer. I don't think so. Many are monuments to human ingenuity, to public-relations know-how and clever advertising, to skill in milking Christian suckers. And since we would not need to depend on public-relations know-how and clever advertising if we truly believed in God, I suppose it is correct to say that the buildings of which I speak are monuments to unbelief rather than monuments to faith. We view them with understandable (but culpable) pride. We have made it. We need nothing. May God have mercy on us![1]

The point is that buildings for ministries are inherently neither right nor wrong. In some cases God is glorified through the proper financing, construction, and use of a building. In other cases, through massive indebtedness, internal disunity, extravagance, pride of accomplishment, and misuse of a facility, God is not glorified. Indeed, he may well be offended or outraged.

I hear people criticize local churches for their buildings. "If that money was given to the poor, or used for missions, far greater things could be accomplished." This is often true. On the other hand, by providing for a growing congregation's basic needs, a building can serve edifying and evangelistic purposes, broadening and deepening the home base so that much more money, prayer, and personal involvement is ultimately given to missions and to the poor than otherwise would have been.

I have been on both sides of the building quandary. As a young believer, sitting in a congregation, I was unenthused by building projects. I thought my money could be better placed directly into missions, so I gave almost all of it to parachurch groups. I made much of the fact that the first church had no buildings. I now see this to be a much less relevant argument, since God has put us in a different place and time than the first church, with our own distinct needs and opportunities.

For the past fourteen years I have been a pastor, and my perspective has changed somewhat. While I am still not a building fanatic, I do see how in some places and in some times buildings can be valuable tools that can effectively contribute to the Christian ministry. For a church to build facilities for ministry use makes as much sense as a growing family finding a house adequate for its needs.

Our own church buildings are constantly in use. Our main building is a facility that is used for worship on Sundays, and for everything from weddings and funerals to basketball and school recess throughout the week. We stick Sunday school classes everywhere we can, including staff offices and storage rooms. Classrooms built for twenty sometimes house fifty, so we are building more. Our youth groups meet three different nights of the week because there is insufficient room for any of them. Every classroom and even our kitchen has been used for our grade school. Without a doubt, this practical facility has greatly enhanced our church ministries.

We also have a church office that doubles as a ministry center. Since moving out of our rented trailers and into this office, we find our staff communication and efficiency is greatly enhanced, and we can meet the needs of our people much more effectively.

Yes, we could function without our buildings—just as a family could get by without their house, by using tents or living at the neighbor's. We used rented facilities for the first five years of our church and found they prevented us from many significant ministries that our own buildings have allowed. And, yes, we have considered planting daughter churches, and we probably eventually will. But this is not the answer for every church in every stage of its development. The daughter churches usually end up building anyway. The point is we believe after weighing all the factors that these practical and nice but nonextravagant buildings are a wise use of funds and a true investment in eternity.

On the other hand, we must continually be careful to be sure the construction of a building doesn't detract from our giving to meet needs and evangelize our community and the world, but ultimately contributes to it. We must consciously battle the rationalizations that turn churches and organizations away from building Christ's kingdom to building their own. Certainly, something is desperately wrong when a church (as some do) spends more money paying the interest on its building loan than it does on world missions.

To the extent that a church facility can be attractive and still functional and economical, I am in favor of attractive buildings. I also appreciate the desire to create a worshipful atmosphere. But worship does not require extravagance. Whether in the church or a parachurch ministry, I believe buildings should be built only as necessary, soundly but economically, and in such a way that they allow maximum ministry use, which means more than one day a week.

Opulent edifices are often monuments to the ego of one man or organization or congregation. Considering the opportunities to invest in eternity, to reach the lost, and care for the poor—thereby bringing glory to the only one who deserves it—in my opinion such buildings have no place among the people of God.

NOTES
1. John White, *The Golden Cow* (Downers Grove, Ill.: InterVarsity Press, 1979), 65-66.

APPENDIX D

Lending Money, Charging Interest, and Being Cosignatory to a Loan

There are many possible motives with which we might lend money. One motive is to meet another person's need; another is to profit from the loan through receiving interest. Nothing is inherently wrong with lending, and it is a mark of God's blessing to be in the position to make a loan (Deut. 28:12). The righteous is one who gives and lends (Ps. 37:21, 26). God approves of the generous person who lends freely (Ps. 112:5).

In certain cases, lenders graciously forgave the debt that was owed them (Matt. 18:32-33). In Israel, every fifty years was the year of Jubilee, in which all debts were forgiven (Deut. 15:1-2; Neh. 10:31).

In the New Testament, Jesus specifically stated that when we lend to people we are not to expect repayment (Luke 6:34-35). The person borrowing is morally obligated to make the payment (Ps. 37:21). It is just that we, in the spirit of giving, are to lend just as we might give, expecting nothing in return. Built into the disciples' prayer is the well-known but seldom practiced phrase, "Forgive us our debts, as we also have forgiven our debtors" (Matt. 6:12).

It seems clear that the lender must generally know or evaluate the character of the borrower. To distribute money into the hands of a drug addict or compulsive gambler or a cultist is irresponsible. Furthermore, we must weigh whether a loan is what this person really needs. Given the many dangers of debt, are we really helping him by making him indebted him to us? Loaning money to bail out someone without financial discipline is like trying to put out a fire with gasoline.

We must also evaluate the effects of the loan on our relationship. While we may think lending money to people will endear us to them, experience often proves the very opposite. One of the best definitions of a distant friend is "a close friend who owes you money." If someone irritates you and you wish never to see him again one of the most effective means to ensure this is to loan him money!

Perhaps it is to release this level of tension that Jesus tells us to lend expecting nothing in return. While the borrower's responsibility remains the same, and the conscientious borrower will in fact repay, the lender's posture is to be one of grace. If our inclination is to force repayment, we should not loan in the first place.

CHARGING INTEREST

In the Old Testament, specific stipulations were made about borrowing and lending. For instance, while collateral could be held, it was wrong to hold an essential security, such as a garment needed for warmth on cold nights (Exod. 22:26-27; Deut. 24:10-17).

Charging interest is the means by which a lender profits from a borrower. The charging of interest was common practice in Babylon, Rome, and many other ancient cultures. In Israel, interest could be charged to foreigners, but not as a means of exploitation (Deut. 23:19-20). Loans to brothers, to fellow Jews, were to be made interest free (Exod. 22:25; Lev. 25:35-37; Deut. 23:20). In such cases, charging interest was strictly forbidden.

Whether interest is charged or not, there is to be a spirit of graciousness in lending (Deut. 15:8, 10). Certainly, it is important not to take advantage of a person's misfortune. We must loan primarily to help him, not to help ourselves. Indeed, by New Testament command, we are not even to take our brother to court to recoup our losses, for it is better to experience loss ourselves than to live in conflict with a believer or bring this conflict before unbelievers (1 Cor. 6:1-7).

On the other hand, it could also be pointed out that Israel had a largely noninflationary economy, and a lender's money was worth the same to him when it was returned as when he loaned it. Perhaps in an inflationary economy an interest rate might be charged to match the inflation rate. But even if this isn't done, the gracious heart won't quibble about minor losses when his whole purpose in lending is to extend grace and not to demand repayment anyway.

Throughout church history, Christian teachers have taken a strong position against exacting usury on a loan in order to make personal profit. Whereas usury is often thought of today as charging excess interest, the word actually meant charging *any* interest at all. Ambrose said, "If anyone commits usury, he commits robbery and no longer has life." Calvin declared that the professional money lender should be banned from the church. Luther commented, "After the devil there is no greater human enemy on earth than a miser and usurer, for he desires to be above everyone."[1]

Still, Jesus spoke without condemnation of gaining interest by deposit to a moneylender (Luke 19:23). While this was merely a reference in a parable and does not necessarily imply his approval, it seems unlikely that he would use as a positive illustration what he believed was fundamentally wrong.

It would seem that the charging of interest is not wrong per se. It might be appropriate for lending institutions, but not for individuals if they are loaning to fellow believers to help meet their basic needs. If interest is charged, perhaps it should not be more than the current rate of inflation. If the borrower's purpose is to invest what we loan him for profit, that is a different matter, and it would probably be better not to become involved in the first place. Someone who doesn't have the money to invest can't afford to borrow to invest.

In other words, there is a time to lend, a time to give, and a time to do neither. If the need isn't real or legitimate, I should neither give nor lend. If the need is legitimate, not the result of an unwise choice in which there is a lesson to be learned, I might give. If, on the other hand, the need is real but a gift would contribute to the person's irresponsibility or his loss of dignity, then lending may be the best option.

Certainly, I must be careful not to encourage my brother to take the course of debt unless it is absolutely necessary. The last thing the person badly in debt needs is to incur still another debt. When the needs are legitimate, a Christian policy ought to be to give freely and lovingly. When the situation merits it, I may make a loan, but only in the same helpful spirit as the gift.

SIGNING FOR ANOTHER PERSON'S LOANS

Being a cosignatory is assuming responsibility for the debts of another in order to assure a creditor that the borrower will not default on payment. If the person for whom I sign does not come through, I am legally assuming his entire liability.

Scripture is very clear on this matter of being security for another's debts—we are simply told not to do it (Prov. 11:15). "Do not be a man who strikes hands in pledge or puts up security for debts; if you lack the means to pay, your very bed will be snatched from under you" (Prov. 22:26-27). In fact, we are told if we have already put up security for our neighbor, we should go and humble ourselves and plead and allow ourselves no sleep until, like a gazelle, we are freed from the snare we have put ourselves in! (Prov. 6:1-5). To assume responsibility for the debt of another is to demonstrate poor judgment (Prov. 17:18). If you doubt this teaching of Scripture, consider that no less than 50 percent of all cosigners end up paying back part or all of the other person's debt![2]

When I sign for someone else, I am saying, "I will answer for all of this person's financial decisions, wise or unwise. I am now legally and financially accountable for whatever he chooses to do."

If your desire is to help someone, give him or loan him the money outright, or find another way to help, perhaps through sound advice. More often than not, he shouldn't be going into debt in the first place, so the best favor you can do him when he asks you to sign with him is to just say no.

NOTES
1. *Christian History Magazine* (Worcester, Penn.: Christian History Institute, 1987), 7(2):18.
2. Howard Dayton, *Your Money: Frustration or Freedom?* (Wheaton, Ill.: Tyndale House, 1979), 50.

APPENDIX E

PRACTICAL GUIDELINES TO CONTROL SPENDING

For many people, spending money becomes an addictive behavior similar to alcoholism or gambling. With compulsive spending, the true enemy is within. We need to replace our preoccupation with short-term gratification and make our spending decisions from the long-term perspective. We must replace our self-indulgence with self-control, which is a fruit of the Holy Spirit's work in our lives. "Like a city whose walls are broken down is a man who lacks self-control" (Prov. 25:28). Without self-control on the inside, our lives are made vulnerable to an infinite variety of assaults from the outside.

The following guidelines are designed to help you exercise self-control in your spending, that you may become a better steward of God's resources and free more funds to use for kingdom purposes:

431

Realize that nothing is a good deal if you can't afford it. Sixty thousand dollars sounds like an excellent price on a house worth seventy-five thousand. Eighty dollars seems like a great deal on barely used skis that cost $250 new. But if you can't afford them, it simply doesn't matter. No thing is worth going into financial bondage.

Recognize that God isn't behind every good deal. But suppose you *can* afford to buy this terrific item. What if the money is there? Does that mean you should buy it? Not necessarily. Self-control often means turning down good deals on things we really want because God may have other and better plans for his money.

Understand the difference between spending money and saving money. Saving money is setting aside money for a future purpose. Money that is saved stays in your wallet or the bank and can be used for other purposes, including your needs or the needs of others that arise. On the other hand, money that is spent leaves your hands and is no longer at your disposal. Hence, when you buy a fifty-five dollar sweater for thirty-five dollars, you do *not* save twenty dollars—you spend thirty-five dollars. Whether the sweater was worth thirty-five, fifty-five, or two hundred dollars is irrelevant. The point is, the thirty-five dollars is gone, and you have saved nothing. The next time you hear of a great sale on something you don't need, remember—if you keep "saving" like this you will soon be broke!

Look at the long-term cost, not just the short-term. When you buy a nice stereo, you will end up buying lots of tapes. When something breaks you will get it repaired. When you have an old car you don't care about a dent. When you buy a new car you will pay for insurance or pay to have a dent fixed. When you are given a "free" puppy immediately you are spending $12 a month on dog food, and the next thing you know you are putting $600 into a fence and paying $250 to the veterinarian to stitch up his wounds from a dog fight. Within a year or two, you may end up spending a thousand dollars on your free puppy. Count the cost in advance—almost everything ends up much more expensive than it appears.

Pray before you spend. When something is a legitimate need, God will provide it. How often do we take matters into our own hands and spend money impulsively before asking God to furnish it for us in some other way?

Waiting eliminates most impulsive buying. It is interesting how many things that were are so attractive at one time hold no interest two months later. Take a look at garage sales and you get the picture. Furthermore, the waiting period gives God the opportunity either to provide what we want, to provide something different or better, or to show us that we don't need it and would better use the money another way.

Examine every purchase in light of its ministry potential. Every time I spend money, I gain something and lose something. What I lose is not merely money but what could have been done with the money if used in another way. Hence, money spent always represents lost opportunity. When I spend twenty dollars on this object, a hundred on this one, and a thousand on still another, I must weigh the value of these things against what the same amount of money could have done if used in another way—for instance, to feed the hungry or evangelize the lost.

I don't say this to induce guilt trips but to indicate the obvious—whenever money is used one way it prevents it from being used in another. I must weigh and measure against each other various alternatives as to how to use my money. I sometimes choose to spend money on unnecessary things that still seem good and helpful and contributory to myself and my family. Sometimes I feel entirely good about this; sometimes it seems more borderline or questionable.

Often, however, there is a clear line we feel would be wrong for us to cross. For instance, we cannot justify spending hundreds of dollars on a piece of jewelry when that same money could keep people alive or reach them with the gospel. We are not saying it is wrong for everyone to have jewelry. We are simply saying that jewelry, like everything else, must be subject to the scrutiny of conscience, the Holy Spirit, and the Word of God. It must be evaluated in light of not only what is gained but what is lost. And while you cannot impose your specific convictions on other Christians, in the evaluation process you will often find God speaks specifically to you.

Understand and resist the manipulative nature of advertising. Responsible spending says yes to real needs and no to most "created needs." We have far fewer needs than we believe. The temptation to overspending is immense. Advertising thrives on instilling discontent. Its goal is to create a sense of need, to stimulate desire, to make you dissatisfied with what God has provided for you, to make you think you need and deserve more. People have master's degrees in persuading us to buy things we don't need. Advertising enlarges our wants by telling us, "You need this car," "You won't be loved unless you wear these kinds of clothes," "You won't have fun unless you use this product." Advertising is seductive and manipulative. It programs us. We must consciously reject its claims and counter them with the Word of God, which tells us what we really do and do not need. Furthermore, to the degree possible, we need to withdraw ourselves from advertising that fosters greed or discontent. That may mean less television, less flipping through sales catalogs, and less aimless wandering in shopping malls.

Learn to walk away from things you want but don't need. Once I received a large, unexpected check, the largest I ever remember. After deciding to give a certain amount to the Lord, I still had $2,000 left. Before long I was out looking at something I had wanted but had never been able to justify. The price tag said $1,995. I looked it over, comparison shopped, came back the next day, and was seriously considering buying it. But in my heart there just wasn't peace when I thought about what that money could do for God's kingdom. Finally, I determined I shouldn't make the purchase. The moment I turned and walked away a completely unexpected thing happened. I was suddenly filled with a sense of deep relief and joy. I hadn't realized how this item was possessing me. It was wonderful to be free of it.

Realize the little things add up. Like water from a leaky faucet, money trickles through our hands. The little drips don't seem like much, but they add up to gallons. The dollar here and ten dollars over there may seem inconsequential, but they add up to hundreds of dollars per month that could be used for kingdom purposes. If a swimming pool is full of leaks, you can pump in more water, but it will never be enough until the leaks are fixed. We can take in more and more income, but until we fix the little leaks in our spending habits, we will never be able to divert the flow of money for higher purposes.

Set up and live by a budget. Imagine that you entrusted a large sum to a money manager, telling him to take out only what he needed to live on, then wisely invest the bulk of it. A month later, you call him to see how the investments are coming. Embarrassed by your call, he finally admits, "There are no investments. None of your money is left." In shock and disbelief you ask, "Well, where did it all go?" Sheepishly, your money manager responds, "Well, I can think of a few things, but for the most part I honestly don't know. Lots of little items came up and the next thing I knew it had all been spent."

If this sounds ridiculous to us, how does God feel when at the end of the month nothing is left from the money he entrusted to us, and yet we don't even know where it went? If some of us ran a corporation and handled its money like we do our own we would be put in prison for misuse of funds!

"Be sure you know the condition of your flocks, give careful attention to your herds; for riches do not endure forever" (Prov. 27:23-24). Flocks and herds are the rancher's basic units of wealth. God is saying, know what your assets are and know where they go. The Living Bible renders Proverbs 24:3-4: "Any enterprise is built by wise planning, becomes strong through common sense, and profits wonderfully by keeping abreast of the facts."

We must get a grip on our assets. If you don't have thought-out plans for what to do with your money as it comes in, rest assured that thousands of other people do have plans for it. If you don't harness it yourself, they will end up with it.

Two practical steps can be of immense help in getting a grip on your spending. The first is *recording expenditures*. The second is *making a budget*. Together these steps will help you detect problem areas by bringing out realities you were not aware of, fostering healthy family discussion about what you do with your money, and creating a structure that will help you develop careful and self-disciplined spending habits. This will also improve your mental and marital health, since financial disorder is one of the leading causes of personal and familial stress.

I recommend you pick up one of the good, practical books on finances that deals specifically with budgeting.[1] Such books show how to make a careful record of expenditures so you can find out where your money is going. Meanwhile, you can be determining where you think it *should be* going. This will be the basis for your budget, which will include how much you have determined to give and to save, and how much is available for spending.

Living on a budget will free up large amounts of money. I have counseled with families that follow a budget and do fine on incomes of $10,000 a year. I have counseled with others who make $10,000 a month and are always in financial crisis. It is not how much money we have, but how we handle it that really matters. A good budget is a tool to help us handle it wisely.

NOTES

1. I recommend Ron Blue's *Master Your Money* (Nashville: Thomas Nelson, 1986); Larry Burkett's *Your Finances in Changing Times* (San Bernadino, Calif.: Campus Crusade for Christ, 1975); Howard Dayton's *Your Money: Frustration or Freedom* (Wheaton, Ill.: Tyndale House, 1979); and Malcolm MacGregor's *Your Money Matters* (Minneapolis: Bethany House, 1980).

STUDY GUIDE FOR

MONEY, POSSESSIONS, AND ETERNITY
BY RANDY ALCORN

LESSON ONE:
WHY IS MONEY SO IMPORTANT TO GOD?
Class Assignment: Preface, Chapter 1

What exactly does the Bible say to us about our money? And why does it devote what the author suggests is "a disproportionate amount of space" to passages concerning our money and possessions?

In this lesson we will look at some key Scripture passages that will help us unlock the dilemma of God's view of what our financial understanding and economic goals should be.

(One student can read aloud each passage before discussion. Or you can break up the class into groups of three or more, assigning each a passage to study for about ten to twelve minutes and report their answers back to the class. The reports should be confined to five minutes each.)

1. Luke 3:7-14. In this passage John the Baptist forcefully exhorts a crowd of questioners on how to live—and how to give.

Verse 11. To whom do our wealth and possessions really belong, based on this verse? How does any wealth imply a responsibility along with our own enjoyment?

Verses 12-14. What are the special responsibilities of those who work with money in their professions? And of all those who receive money for hire?

What can we conclude here about the goodness of the money and things we have been given, as well as the dangers when they are wrongly used?

2. Luke 19:1-10. What principles about the proper use of money can be drawn from the story of Jesus' dealings with Zacchaeus?

3. Matthew 19:16-30. In this passage Jesus tells a rich man to take quite a radical step in regard to his wealth. What can we conclude here about the relative importance Jesus put on wealth, as set in the context of his full biblical teaching on possessions?

4. Acts 19:18-20. Here is another radical response to ill-gained wealth. In what ways might new (or mature) Christians today be prompted to take such steps?

5. Acts 2:22-55. This is a historic example of true communal living, in the context of Christian fellowship. What principles can be drawn from this passage to help us discover what God intends wealth and possessions to mean to us?

6. Acts 4:32-35. How should our gratefulness to God for our salvation prompt unusual generosity, beyond the letter of the law?

In the coming weeks we will be seeking to form a balanced view of God's plan for our use of our money and possessions for his kingdom.

As the author states, "In a sense, how we relate to money and possessions is the story of our lives." What we need on this journey is a road map to help us both understand God's perspective and learn to make more intelligent decisions—as well as learn the discipline to keep them in the future.

"The key to a right use of money and possessions is a right perspective—an eternal perspective," says Alcorn in his Preface.

PRAYER: Lord, grant us a glimpse of your perspective and your plan for us and for all that we possess. Amen.

LESSON TWO:
ASCETICISM AND MATERIALISM: TWO WRONG WAYS
Class Assignment: Chapters 2 and 3

This week we will look at two opposing viewpoints on the importance of money: asceticism and materialism.

Alcorn writes: "There are two equally incorrect beliefs about money. First, that it is automatically and always evil. Second, that it is automatically and always good." We need to examine these two views carefully in order to come to a biblical understanding of what is the truth about our wealth and possessions. Each of the following passages sheds special light on the concept of "extreme, false, or dualistic" asceticism, the idea that what is spiritual is good, and what is physical is automatically evil of itself. This is rooted in a dualism that is neither biblical nor practicable. (See Alcorn's historical background on this issue.)

1. Proverbs 30:8-9. What does Scripture say about denial of material good and the spiritual harm it can bring?

2. Luke 7:36-50. What arguments does Christ give here for the enjoyment and appreciation of good material gifts? How are love and forgiveness, true spiritual values, inseparably connected with a physical gesture of kindness in this story?

3. First Timothy 4:3-5. What are the keys to proper use of the gifts we have been given, as listed here?

(Use other examples of misguided asceticism from the book or other sources to illustrate the wisdom of Scripture.) If asceticism, then, is not the simple answer to how we should treat material things, what about the opposite extreme, materialism?

Christ clearly warned against the excesses in the other direction in these words: "Watch out! Be on your guard against all kinds of greed: a man's life does not consist in the abundance of his possessions" (Luke 12:15).

Read together the parable of the Rich Fool in Luke 12:13-21. Alcorn writes: "Greed is not a harmless pastime but a serious offense against God. Just as the lustful man is an adulterer (Matt. 5:28) and the hateful man a murderer (1 John 3:15), so the greedy man is an idolater (Col. 3:5)." What is it about greed that makes it a sometimes subtle but clearly dangerous form of idolatry?

(Read the above verses and use anecdotes from the book or other sources to illustrate.)

Read together the parable of the Rich Man and Lazarus in Luke 16:19-31. Alcorn here brings out the "doctrine of reversal," the fact that in eternity many people will find themselves in the opposite conditions from their situation on earth. Have two creative students conduct an extemporaneous dialogue of a modern-day rich man (a stockbroker, for instance) and a "Lazarus" (a homeless person). How is the doctrine of reversal at work in our society today?

PRAYER: Lord, all things come of thee, and of thine own do we give back to thee. Amen.

LESSON THREE:

THE PIT OF MATERIALISM
Class Assignment: Chapter 4

In chapter 4, The Dangers of Materialism, Alcorn proposes that materialism is "the two things God hates most—idolatry and adultery" (p. 65).

1. The Old Testament prophets were quick to point out Israel's unfaithfulness, as indicated by their turning to idols (see Isa. 57:3-9; Jer. 3:1-10; Ezek. 16:1-48). In what ways have possessions become idols, even "mistresses" to the greedy today?

2. Read aloud Ecclesiastes 2:1-11. This is the fruit of unbridled materialism: emptiness and meaninglessness. What are some signs of this emptiness as brought about by excessive greed in our society? (If possible, bring pictures from magazines that emphasize this decadence and loss of meaning. The more "sophisticated" the magazines, the more ads for empty luxuries, shown by models with jaded expressions.)

3. Turn now to 1 Timothy 6:9-10. "For the love of money is a root of all kinds of evil" (v. 10). What does this passage say about a life devoted to money and possessions? What does it say about the effect of such a life on one's faith in God?

Read aloud the quotes on page 69—testimonies by five wealthy men as to the lack of satisfaction that wealth brings.

440

4. Why is the righteous rich man such a rare phenomenon? See Isaiah 10:1-3; Jeremiah 5:27-28; 15:13; Hosea 12:8; Amos 5:11; and Micah 6:12.

Use a chalkboard to list adjectives or phrases that describe materialism in our society:

MATERIALISM IS . . .

Let each class member come forward to add one word or phrase to the board.

PRAYER: Lord, grant us the eyes to see the lure of money and possessions for what it really is—and to desire you more. Amen.

LESSON FOUR:

MATERIALISM, THE CHURCH, AND THE GOSPEL
Class Assignment: Chapters 5 and 6

"The Lord decried the fact that priests and prophets alike were corrupted by money" (read aloud Micah 3:11), says Alcorn (p. 87). "Peter reminded church leaders that they were to be characterized by an eagerness to serve, not a greed for money" (read 1 Pet. 5:2). "Paul insisted that no lover of money was qualified to be a church leader" (read 1 Tim. 3:3).

Then how did materialism creep into the church to do the damage it is currently doing?

Preachers of the gospel of materialism may think that they are justified in connecting this kind of prosperity with the Christian life—but what is the true picture?

1. In the following passages there is a link between material wealth and God's blessing. Have various class members read aloud. Choose one key word in each passage.

Abraham—Genesis 13:1-7; Isaac—Genesis 26:12-14; Jacob—Genesis 30:43; Joseph—Genesis 39:2-6; Solomon—1 Kings 3:13; Job—Job 42:10-17.

2. What are the implications here? Is not God able to bless as he sees fit in our lives?

3. In particular, what blessings are promised to those who give faithfully of their finances (Deut. 15:10; Prov. 3:9-10; ll:25; Mal. 3:8-12)?

4. Yet the Old Testament also warns against the dangers of wealth (Deut. 28:1-13). These thirteen verses are followed by what curses to those who don't obey God?

5. And clearly it is not only Christians who experience prosperity—perhaps they are a minority. See Psalm 37:35 (read aloud) and Ecclesiastes 7:15. Consider the Pharisees of Jesus' day (Luke 15:1-2; John 9:34). How did their lives show that prosperity does not necessarily imply spirituality?

6. What wisdom did Jesus teach on the doctrine of prosperity (Matt. 5:45; 19:23-24)?

7. What was the apostle Paul's view? (Phil. 1:29; 2:5-11; 3:7-8).

8. What should be our perspective on our own obedience, regardless of whether we become wealthy in this life?

PRAYER: Father, grant us your peace in our giving and in our receiving, that it may all be to your glory. Amen.

LESSON FIVE:
THE TWO WAYS OF WEALTH
Class Assignment: Chapter 7

"Jesus always had two kingdoms in mind," writes Alcorn, ". . . two treasuries, two perspectives, and two masters" (p. 124). We can't lay up treasures both on earth and in heaven. What we value most—the temporal or the eternal—will determine which kingdom is ours.

1. Whichever kingdom we choose, we will want to "invest" in it. On the chalkboard, have students list various ways in which people invest in this world. Then on the opposite end of the board write answers of ways to invest in God's kingdom.

2. Read aloud Matthew 13:44, or have a student read it to the class. "The kingdom of heaven is like treasure hidden in a field . . . ." What can it mean to Christians today to "sell all we have" to seek that treasure? Which ideas on the right side of the board qualify as this spirit of investing? Discuss.

3. What did Paul have to say about the treasure of this world? (See Phil. 3:7-11.) In what ways is Christ himself the Christian's treasure?

4. What are some implications of this view that can affect how we handle our money day to day?

We will look at these issues in more detail later.

Read together the section "Momentary Sacrifice, Eternal Gain," pages 132-133. Discuss 2 Corinthians 4:17.

PRAYER: Lord, help us to truly learn how to lay up treasures in heaven. Amen.

LESSON SIX:
THE STEWARD'S TASK
Class Assignment: Chapters 8 and 9

What is a steward? Webster says that it is one who is employed to manage domestic concerns; a fiscal agent; one who supervises the provision and distribution of funds.

We are called to be stewards of a most crucial estate, agents of the spiritual welfare of ourselves and others—people with eternal destinies. Read "A Lost Sense of the Eternal" (pp. 138-141). Pray together David's prayer in Psalm 39 (p. 140).

1. What are some of the characteristics of God, our Master and Judge? (See Prov. 24:12; Jer. 17:10; Acts 17:31; Rom. 2:12-16;1 Pet. 4:5.) What should be the implications for our daily conduct?

2. After reading the following verses that describe one place of eternal destiny—hell—draw symbols on a chalkboard that represent its horrors (Matt. 10:28; 13:40-42; 25:41-46; Mark 9:43-44; Luke 16:22-31).

3. Now read these verses about what awaits the believer after death at that other destination—heaven (Rev. 5:11-13; 7:15; 19:9; 21:19-21; 22:5; Luke 22:29-30). Choose and draw symbols representing this eternal choice.

Which set of symbols inspires us, suggests life and purpose, and can be the goal for all of our choices, including stewardship of all that we own?

4. Are there degrees of reward in heaven? Copy the two charts on page 158 onto the chalkboard to discuss the exact relationship between

regeneration and rewards. This will help to summarize many of the points of chapter 9.

5. The three disciplines of fasting, giving, and prayer, developed by Christ in Matthew 6:1-18, are suggested as ways to forgo our own possessions, power, and pleasure in this life and to accomplish higher purposes for God's kingdom, in which we are also stewards.

Yet we are reminded too that possessions, power, and pleasure can also be used for good. Make a chart of "Possessions—Power—Pleasure," listing those things in these categories available to us that have both their "down" side as well as a side that is usable for the kingdom.

After listing as many as possible, close in conversational prayer around the room, asking for wise stewardship of all these things.

LESSON SEVEN:
STEWARDS AND PILGRIMS
Class Assignment: Chapters 10 and 11

"Stewardship is not a subcategory of the Christian life," says Alcorn. "Stewardship *is* the Christian life" (p. 172). What is stewardship? It is the right use of all that God has entrusted to us: life, time, talents, money, possessions, family, his grace, and most of all his Son.

1. Read together the parable of the shrewd manager, often called the "unrighteous steward," in Luke 16:1-13. See page 173 for several different interpretations of the parable. What is true wisdom here? What does it mean for our lives?

2. Jesus said, "Whoever can be trusted with very little can also be trusted with much, and whoever is dishonest with very little will also be dishonest with much" (Luke 16:10). This is the principle of stewardship that carries over into eternity. Have three people in the class read the following verses and pick out the key word in each:

Luke 16:11-12, 17, 19.

3. Turn next to the parable of the talents (Matt. 25:14-30). How does this parable support the key ideas above?

4. Now look at the parable of the ten minas in Luke 19:11-27. What further support for good stewardship in all things do we find here?

On one side of the chalkboard write "The Master" and on the other side, "The Servant" (steward). Under "The Master," list the italicized headings under "Lessons Concerning the Master," found on page 178-179. Then list the lessons concerning the servant under "The Servant" (pp. 179-180).

Read together the overall lessons from the stewardship parables on pages 181-182.

Besides the existence of two kingdoms, Scripture teaches us there are two covenants and two "countries"—this world and our heavenly home. (See pp. 190-193.) Because we have not yet reached our true home, we are "pilgrims" along the way.

"The pilgrim is unattached. He is a traveler—not a settler," writes Alcorn. "Material things are valuable to the pilgrim, but only as they facilitate his mission" (p. 196).

Make a chart showing how the pilgrim relates to "Asceticism," and then to "Material Needs." Under the first heading, list the kinds of things one can do without (there can and should be honest disagreement here).

Under the second, list the things he must have to survive. Is there ambiguity? Where does Christian discernment come in?

Alcorn writes, "In the truest sense, Christian pilgrims have the best of both worlds. We have joy whenever this world reminds us of the next, and we take solace whenever it does not" (p. 198).

PRAYER: Lord, help us to be faithful stewards and true pilgrims in this life you have given us. Amen.

LESSON EIGHT:
TITHING AND GIVING
Class Assignment: Chapters 12 and 13

What is a tithe? It is a tenth "of everything from the land, whether grain from the soil or fruit from the trees" (Lev. 27:30). As Alcorn puts it: "It 'belongs to the Lord,' not to us. It applies to 'everything,' not some things. It is 'holy,' to be set apart and given to God, and used for no other purpose" (p. 206).

1. Malachi 3:8-10. Is it possible to rob God of what is rightfully his? How can tithing prevent that?

2. See how this practice of tithing began with Abraham (Gen. 14:20) and Jacob (Gen. 28:22). How can we expect to do less? See Deuteronomy 14:23 for the stated purpose of tithing.

3. Jesus supported tithing, as shown in his dialogue with the Pharisees; but he expected more than outward obedience from them, and in that they failed (Luke 11:42). Does that in any way excuse a lack of tithing?

4. We have seen that the early Christians often went far beyond tithing to share all that they had (Acts 2:44-45; 4:32-37). See pages 224-226 for the historical background of this situation. How many of our social problems would be solved if it could be said of us as well, "Much grace was upon them all" (4:33)?

5. How are we to give? In each case have one student look up a reference and explain the specific context or intent of the admonition:

Generously (Mark 14:3-9); regularly and systematically (1 Cor. 16:2; 2 Cor. 8:11); voluntarily (2 Cor. 9:7); joyfully (2 Chron. 24:10; 2 Cor. 9:7); worshipfully (2 Cor. 8:5); proportionately (Mark 12:43-44; Acts 11:29; 1 Cor. 16:2); sacrificially (2 Sam. 24:24; 2 Cor. 8:3); quietly (Matt. 6:1, 4; James 2:1-5).

PRAYER: God, grant us your grace to learn the practice and the joy of giving back to you. Amen.

LESSON NINE:
GIVING—REACHING OUT
Class Assignment: Chapters 14 and 15

Care for the poor is a major theme of Scripture, Alcorn reminds us.

1. Have a student read these admonitions from the Mosaic Law concerning provisions for the poor: Leviticus 19:9-10; Deuteronomy 15:10-11. Why are we to give to the poor? What does this say about God? About our situation on earth?

2. If every person is our neighbor, as Jesus taught, what are the specific lessons of Luke 19:8 and 10:36-37? (Compare Prov. 19:17; 22:9; 28:27.)

3. Jesus came to preach the gospel—the good news—to the poor, the blind, and the oppressed (Luke 4:18-19) as well as the privileged. Read aloud the parable of the banquet, Luke 14:12-23. How does this parallel our situation today in which the needy seem more open to a gospel of help and hope?

4. How does this understanding affect our own personal responsibility of giving? How do we evaluate the many good causes that constantly ask for donations, in the light of Christ's priorities? How can we use our understanding to help influence our church's giving to such funds?

5. Turn together to pages 279-280 to discuss some wise guidelines for the church's raising and using funds for giving. Then examine Alcorn's list of qualities by which to judge any ministry or parachurch organization (pp. 284-285). Why is each of these important in relation to biblical teaching and standards?

6. As individuals, and as a church, what is our eternal perspective on life, ministry, and resources?

PRAYER: Lord, grant us clarity of purpose, wisdom of action, and faithfulness in our giving. Amen.

LESSON TEN:
A FAITHFUL LIFE-STYLE
Class Assignment: Chapter 16

Do we as Christians have a right to earn and/ or keep large amounts of money ourselves? Are we called to give up all wealth and "live by faith"? Or need we find a "happy medium" way to live?

Concerning these questions, Scripture gives us wonderful guidelines for the making, using, and giving of what we possess.

1. What advice do each of these verse have for us today? Have one student read each and give a perspective on its wisdom.

Proverbs 12:11; 13:4; 14:23; Ecclesiastes 9:10; 1 Thessalonians 4:11-12; 2 Thessalonians 3:10; Titus 3:14.

God's way to earn money: We must work! But then what is to be done with this money? See Alcorn's section on private ownership of property (pp. 291-292).

Various life-styles in relation to money are represented in the Bible. We have seen the restrictions of the Old Testament, the free and communal sharing of the church in Acts, and much in between.

2. Mark 1:16-20. What Christian life-style is implied here?

3. Mark 2:14-15. Here is another approach. How does it differ in style of discipleship?

4. Mark 8:34-37. Read these verses for a principle that applies to anyone's "cross," once he determines what it is. Must following Christ in this radical way always involve our money and possessions?

5. See also Mark 10:17-31. Then discuss the two common errors in interpreting this passage (pp. 297-298).

6. Must all the rich give up being rich? See 1 Timothy 6:17-19. How is this "way" a reliable guideline for disciples today?

Alcorn quotes Peter H. Davids: "A biblical life-style will necessarily recognize itself as being in opposition to the prevailing values and life-style of its culture. It is informed by a different view of reality."

PRAYER: Thank you, Lord, for your view of reality and the power to give and to serve you within that reality. Amen.

Next week the lesson will cover the issues of borrowing, saving, and investing money. If possible, arrange to have a Christian who is an expert in these areas come to speak to the class. If you have arranged this ahead of time, ask for students to write out their questions on pieces of paper at the end of this session. Give them to the financial expert to answer and discuss next week.

LESSON ELEVEN:
Guest Speaker

If you are not able to get a financial expert to come, ask three students to each take one of the chapters assigned (17-19), read it, and report to the class the main findings Alcorn presents about these important topics of financial accountability and the Christian.

LESSON ELEVEN (Alternative):
BORROWING, SAVING, INVESTING
Class Assignment: Chapters 17, 18, and 19

Lesson 17: What does Scripture really say about debt? What are the most likely pitfalls for Christians facing a question of borrowing or lending? How could getting out of debt become a spiritual issue?

Lesson 18: Why is saving an instance of good stewardship? What are the dangers of hoarding as they relate to greed? What should be our view of retirement—our use of time and money in that period of life? Does a Christian really need insurance? Why or why not?

Lesson 19: What does Scripture teach about investments? Should high-risk living be part of a Christian's life? In the light of eternity, to whom does wealth belong—us, our heirs, God and his work?

PRAYER: Lord, teach us day by day to value your gifts of money and possessions, to be good stewards of what "seems" to be ours, and to be able to let go of it as we are called to. Amen.

LESSON TWELVE:
MATERIALISM IN THE CHRISTIAN FAMILY
Class Assignment: Chapter 20

"Scripture states that it is the responsibility of parents to make basic material provision for their children," writes Alcorn. To neglect to provide for our families is to deny our faith and be judged worse than an unbeliever (1 Tim. 5:8).

Jesus rejected any "spiritual" explanations of not caring materially for one's family (Mark 7:9-13). Parents are to plan wisely and save for their children's future needs (2 Cor. 12:14).

Yet, as we saw with an earlier chart of what a "pilgrim" needs on this earth and what he or she does not—there can be much disagreement in decision making about material things.

In class time today use the background provided in the book to draw

449

up profiles of three imaginary Christian families, their income, their living conditions, their buying habits, saving habits, and what their life-style says to their children about materialism.

Call them the "Simplelifes," the "Mediums," and the "Affluents." Have a creative student at the chalkboard both writing and drawing symbols of their life-style as the class makes various points about their imaginary life.

What five Christian principles can you and the class draw from each developed situation to offer to each of these three families?

Example: The "Mediums" may find that they are inconsistent even as they try to find a middle-of-the-road stance on every financial issue. They should look out for unexpected materialism in the areas that are dearest to their family's well-being (such as vacations or prestige colleges).

Principle One for the Mediums:

Test every choice by a spiritual view of what will most glorify God in this situation; what is financially possible or attainable through sacrifice; and which will come through a concensus of family members (those old enough to be involved in decision making).

Students will, of course, offer ideas based on their own questions, needs, and experiences. But make sure that none of the family "profiles" is actually based on anyone in particular. This will keep the exercise more objective, and the principles drawn from these "families" will be clearer.

Albert Schweitzer points out (as quoted by Alcorn) that "there are only three ways to teach a child. The first is by example, the second is by example, the third is by example" (p. 375).

The side of town we must live on, the school we attend, the car we drive, all speak a message to our children.

What are our life-styles saying to our children about the importance we place on material things in relation to God's work and God's kingdom?

PRAYER: Lord, open our eyes to that which we find difficult to see—anything that could become an idol and turn us from your will. We ask this for our children's sake as well as our own. Amen.

LESSON THIRTEEN:
THE BOTTOM LINE
Class Assignment: Chapter 21 and Conclusion

For this class session, bring pens or pencils and plain white paper for your students.

They will each be writing a letter to their child (or other dependent person over whom they have responsibility or influence) to summarize the teachings about the Christian and financial responsibility that have been discussed to this point.

Students should have read chapter 21 and the Conclusion to Alcorn's book. Let them review the points given on these pages as they prepare to write, if necessary.

Stress that none of the students will be required to read their letters aloud, so they are free to be as candid as possible with their advice and admonitions.

But do allow time at the end—about fifteen minutes—for volunteers who might want to share some of the conclusions they reached and how they were able to share them in specific situations with their child.

At the beginning of the chapter are two quotes. The first, from Shakespeare, is one which you hope does not fit into the context of any of these letters!

The second, from Hudson Taylor, is the epitome of the example a Christian parent can give and how it can affect a child's life for eternity.

Where do we go from here?

Now ask students to read their own letters to themselves silently. Pretend that they were written to them by a parent or mentor twenty or thirty years ago and supported by the example of a life of spiritual and financial accountability.

How would our lives be different if we had known these things? What can we still do about putting some of them into practice?

Read aloud the final section of the book, "Coming to Grips with Eternity," on page 410. Substitute this adapted prayer for the last two lines:

PRAYER: Lord, "may what will be most important to us five minutes after we die become most important to us now." Amen.